AN

ANCIENT GEOGRAPHY,

Classical and Sacred.

BY S. AUGUSTUS MITCHELL,

AUTHOR OF A SERIES OF GEOGRAPHICAL WORKS.

AN ENTIRELY NEW EDITION, DRAWN FROM THE BEST AUTHORITIES, ANCIENT AND MODERN.

DESIGNED FOR THE USE OF

SCHOOLS AND COLLEGES.

Illustrated with Numerous Engravings.

PHILADELPHIA:

PUBLISHED BY E. H. BUTLER & CO.

1860.

ADVERTISEMENT.

THE following work was undertaken with a view to furnish a manual, omitting the minute details of complete treatises on the subject, but embracing all the information commonly required, and at the same time by simplicity and distinctness of arrangement well adapted to the use of teacher and learner. Much has been introduced relating to politics, antiquities, and literature, but only what was conceived to be appropriate, noteworthy, and interesting. The discussion of the etymology of the principal proper names has been allowed a special place; the authorities that have been mostly relied on in this matter, being Passow, Gesenius, and the writers of the articles in Dr. Smith's Dictionary of Greek and Roman Geography, whose views are partly original and partly drawn from sources of the highest character. It is hoped that no apology will be thought necessary for introducing into this little work the opinions of scholars on the origin and connection of these geographical terms, as these opinions are not simply curious, but often have an important historical bearing. The accentuation of the Latin forms of the proper names has received careful attention. The place of the accent has been marked in nearly all cases not determined at sight by the three simple rules relating to the position of the vowel of the penultima, and also in a few other instances which it was thought would be likely to receive a false accent.

The sign of the accent should invariably have been put over the vowel or diphthong of the accented syllable, but in some words it has been left over the consonant following such vowel or diphthong. Many passages and expressions illustrative of the text have been adduced from those Greek and Latin writers whose works are most generally read by young persons, and still more might have been added, had space allowed.

The authorities and the editions of the Greek and Latin writers chiefly consulted for the present work, are the following:—

CLUVERIUS, Introductio in Universam Geographicam. Leyden, 1670.

FORBIGER, Handbuch der alten Geographie. 3 vols. 8vo. Leipsic, 1842–47.

FREUND, Latin Lexicon.

GESENIUS, Hebrew Lexicon.

GROTE, History of Greece. New York, 1854–56.

HORATIUS; ed. Stallbaum, Leipsic, 1854.

HUMBOLDT, Aspects of Nature. 1849

——— Cosmos. 1845–58.

LEAKE, Tour in Asia Minor. 8vo. London, 1824.

LIDDELL AND SCOTT, Greek Lexicon. New York, 1846.

MELA, De Situ Orbis. Leipsic, K. Tauchnitz, 1831.

MÜLLER, Lexicon Geographicam Antiquam Illustrans. 8vo. Leipsic, 1831.

NIEBUHR, Vorträge über alte Länder- und Völkerkunde. Berlin, 1851.

OVIDIUS; ed. Merkel. 12mo. Leipsic, Teubner, 1852.

PASSOW, Greek Lexicon. 5th ed. 1841–52.

PLINIUS, Naturalis Historia; ed. Janus. 12mo. Leipsic, Teubner, 1854.

RITTER, Die Erdkunde, u. s. w. Berlin, 1834.

SCHMITZ, Manual of Ancient Geography. 12mo. Philadelphia, 1857.

SCHWEGLER, Römische Geschichte. Tübingen, 1856.

SMITH, Dictionary of Greek and Roman Geography. 2 vols. 8vo. London, 1853–57.

STRABO, Geographica; ed. Meineke. 12mo. Leipsic. 1852.

THIRLWALL, History of Greece.

VIRGILIUS; ed. Wagner. 8vo. Leipsic, 1848.

WORDSWORTH, Greece: Pictorial, Descriptive, Historical. Roy. 8vo. London.

PHILADELPHIA, December, 1859.

CONTENTS.

INTRODUCTION.

ANCIENT GEOGRAPHY is a description of that portion of the earth known to the inhabitants of the ancient world, from the remotest times to the final overthrow of the Western Empire.

There is a striking uniformity in the earliest notions entertained by the nations of antiquity in reference to the form of the earth. The general opinion held by each nation was that its inhabitants occupied the exact centre of an immense plane surrounded by water, and that the earth itself was the centre of the visible universe. An examination of the views of Hebrew, Hindoo, Chinese, Persian, and Grecian authorities, proves conclusively the general recognition of this predominant idea.

The history of ancient geography may be divided into four periods:

I. The *mythical period*, extending from the remotest ages to the time of HERO'DOTUS, about 450 B. C.

In regard to this period but little is known definitely, the principal source of information on the subject being tradition and fabulous tales.

According to HOMER, who flourished probably about 1000 B. C.,

---

QUESTIONS.—What is Ancient Geography?—What is said of the notions held by ancient nations in reference to the earth's surface?—Into how many periods may ancient geography be divided?—What is the first period?—Why so called?—Over what time does it extend?

the supposed flattened disk of the earth was surrounded by the river Oce'anus. Hesiod (c. 700 B.C.) places the source of Oce'anus in the Cimmerian rock Leucas in the West. The shores on the further side of this supposed river, Oce'anus, are conceived as supporting the heavens, which are supposed to form a metallic dome above the earth. Homer, without drawing any distinct boundary line, divides the whole surface into two halves, one of which contained Euro'pa, and the other, Asia with Libya. These ideas received gradual correction with the progress of Grecian colonization and Grecian civilization. HECATÆUS of Mile'tus, one of the earliest and most distinguished of the Greek geographers, who flourished 525 B.C., by the exercise of a cultivated and independent judgment, did much to separate fable from fact, and to give definite form to the geographical knowledge of the period:

II. The *historical period*, extending from the time of HERO'DOTUS to that of ERATO'STHENES, that is, from 450 B.C. to 275 B.C.

During this period geography may be said to have first derived its materials from the actual observation and inquiries of travellers and men of science.

HERO'DOTUS, of Halicarnassus in Caria (born about 484 B.C.), ranks as the first of Grecian historians who devoted himself, with the spirit of a true inquirer, to the improvement and arrangement of the geographical knowledge of his countrymen. He was a thorough enthusiast in travel, and made personal explorations of Egypt and the northern coast of Africa. He also visited Phœnicia, Palestine, and Babylon, and explored with considerable care the Propontis and the Euxine. His knowledge of Europe is, on the whole, very correct, and of the

---

QUESTIONS.—What was Homer's idea of the earth?—How did he divide it?—What distinguished geographer flourished about 525 B.C.?—What was the second period?—Over what time does it extend?—On what was geography based during this period?—What historian devoted himself to improving geographical knowledge?—When and where was he born?—What countries did he visit?—What seas did he measure?

south-eastern portion, Greece, Macedonia and Thrace, are described with a familiarity which could only be employed by one thoroughly acquainted with their geographical features. His description of Asia, though not equally precise, contains an interesting account of Persia, Assyria, and Arabia. Egypt and Libya, which he had personally visited, are described very fully.

Subsequent to the time of Hero'dotus, THUCY'DIDES of Athens (born 471 B.C.), the author of the history of the Peloponnesian War, and XE'NOPHON (born at Athens about 444 B.C.), in the *Ana'basis* and *Cyropedi'a*, added much valuable and accurate information to the sum of geographical knowledge. NEARCHUS, who accompanied the Asiatic expedition of Alexander the Great (325 B.C.), sailed down the Indus, and from its mouth round the southern coast of Asia as far as the mouth of the Euphra'tes. The results of his observations during the voyage, which lasted five months, were taken down and preserved. The expedition, of which he formed the directing chief, furnished a vast amount of information in regard to India, its extent and its resources.

During this period, the erroneous opinions, which had prevailed in regard to the earth's form, were successfully dissipated by the various schools of philosophy, and the idea of the earth having the form of a globe was gradually adopted by persons of education :

III. The *period of systematic geography*, extending from the time of ERATO'STHENES to the era of CLAUDIUS PTOLEMÆUS, that is, from 275 B.C. to A.D. 161.

The extension of the Roman Empire at this epoch over almost the entire known surface of the globe, was a great spur to geographical inquiry. The progress of scientific study in the

---

QUESTIONS.—What countries particularly does he describe fully?—What historians after him contributed much to geography?—When and where were they born?—Who accompanied Alexander on his expedition to India?—What did he write, and what information did he furnish?—What progress was made in geographical science?——What was the third period?—Why so called?—Over what time does it extend?—What led to the increase of geographical knowledge?

various philosophic schools led to the commencement of the application of mathematics to geographic data, and to the formation of a definite and rational theory in regard to the earth's surface. The advance in geographical knowledge was far more rapid and more marked than at any previous period.

ERATO'STHENES of Cyre'ne, born 276 B.C., composed a great geographical work, which contained a summary of all that had been written on the subject up to that time. He first brought astronomy and geometry to his aid in calculating the measurements of the earth, and thus enjoys the honor of being the first to make geography a science. He determined approximately the circumference of the earth. He recognised the division of the globe into two hemispheres by the *æquator*, and this equator he divided into three hundred and sixty degrees, reckoning each degree at seven hundred stadia. He calculated the length of the inhabited earth at seventy-eight thousand stadia, and its breadth at thirty-eight thousand stadia. A line parallel to the equator, and passing through the island of Rhodos, Caria, Lycaonia, Cataonia, Media, and the Caspian gates as far as the Indian Cau'casus, divided, according to him, the inhabited earth into two equal parts, the Northern half being Europa, and the Southern, Asia.

Geography is much indebted to POLYBIUS, the historian (born about 204 B.C.), who collected a great deal of information during his extensive travels. He, like his predecessors, regarded the earth as a globe, and recognised the three grand divisions of Asia, Libya, and Europa. He divided the surface of the earth into six zones.

The most important, however, of all the ancient geographers was STRABO, born at Amasei'a in Pontus, who flourished about the

---

QUESTIONS.—Who was the most distinguished geographer of this period?—When and where born?—What peculiar honor belongs to Eratosthenes?—State what results he arrived at.—What did he give as the measurement of the inhabited portion of the earth?—What line did he suppose divided Europe and Asia into halves?—What historian of eminence flourished subsequently?—When and where was he born?—How did he divide the earth?—Who was the most important of ancient geographers?—Where born?—When did he flourish?

beginning of the Christian era. He adopted the system of Era-to'sthenes as his basis, but availed himself of the corrections of later authors and of his own observations.

POMPONIUS MELA (who probably flourished about A. D. 40), a Spaniard, published the first formal manual of geography in the Latin tongue, entitled *De Situ Orbis*, in which he describes with considerable accuracy the most important countries, mountains, lakes, and towns. He furnishes more information in regard to ancient Britain than any of his predecessors.

The elder PLINY, born, it is supposed, at Vero'na, in A. D. 23, in his great work, *Naturalis Historia*, devotes five, out of thirty-seven, books to the subject of geography. This work is a vast storehouse of learning, though many of its statements are not trustworthy, on account of the credulity of the author, and his carelessness in the compilation of his materials:

IV. The *period of mathematical geography*, extending from the time of CLAUDIUS PTOLEMÆUS to STE'PHANUS of Byzantium, that is, from A. D. 161 to A. D. 500.

Although Erato'sthenes and Strabo had reduced geography to a regular and natural system, yet CLAUDIUS PTOLEMÆUS (born at Pelusium in Egypt) was the first to regard geography from a geometrical point of view. He was the first to calculate and employ the terms *latitude* and *longitude*, the degrees of which he carefully marked for each country and town he described. He not only assumed, but proved, the spherical form of the earth. He calculated, by the most accurate measurement, the earth's circumference at a hundred and eighty thousand stadia. In the amount of his geographical knowledge he was in advance of any

---

QUESTIONS.—Who wrote the work *De Situ Orbis?*—Of what country does he speak most fully?—What writer on Natural History added much information to the stock of geographical knowledge?—What character for trustworthiness does he bear?——What was the fourth period?—Why so named?—Who first applied geometry to geography?—Where was he born?—For what is he distinguished?—What did he prove in regard to the shape of the earth?—What did he estimate its circumference?

previous writers, and his work remained the standard book on geography until the revival of letters in the fifteenth century.

After the time of Ptolemy, no geographer of importance is known in antiquity. Pausanias, who flourished about A. D. 174, wrote a description of Greece, in ten books. Ste'phanus of Byzantium, about A. D 470, was the author of a large geographical encyclopedia, the materials of which were compiled from earlier authors. Of this work only a portion of an abridgment remains. With the decay of the Roman Empire, all the sciences declined, and geography ceased to be cultivated to any extent until the gradual awakening of the world from the lethargy of the dark ages.

QUESTIONS.—What writers after the time of Ptolemy contributed to geographical knowledge?

ASIA. (ἡ Ἀσία, *Asia.*)

§ **1.** ASIA, the largest division of the earth, is situated in three distinct zones, and is superior to the other divisions in wealth, magnificence, and variety of productions in the animal, and still more in the vegetable kingdom. Barley and wheat here grow spontaneously; and animals domesticated with us, such as the horse, the ox, and the dog, roam wild. Asia is the cradle of the human race, and from the Orient the first rays of true religion and of civilization appeared.

Name.—The term Asia has been thought to have anciently designated Lydia only, but the statements of Greek writers point to a wider use of the name in the west of Asia Minor, and indicate that it was employed by the Asiatics themselves. In Trojan, and other Asiatic names, as *Ass*a′racus, *As*cania, *As*canius, among various nations whose origin may be traced to Asia, the root AS often appears, in such connections as make it probable that the primary reference is to the *Sun*, especially as an object of worship, and that the *Asians* (Ἀσιανοί) are *the people of the Sun*, or *of the East*. *Asia* and *Euro′pa* (*Ereb, evening*; see pp. 138 and 89) would thus be correlative designations, and by this view we are brought back to Homer's division of the old world into two parts: πρὸς ἠῶ τ' ἠέλιόν τε, and πρὸς ζόφον, *the Land of Sunrise*, and *the Evening Land*.

Boundaries.—After the time of Strabo (c. A. D. 25), the boundaries recognised were as follows:—

I. On the side toward Europe:—TANAIS (*Don*); PALUS MÆO′TIS (*Sea of Azov*); BO′SPORUS CIMMERIUS (*Strait of Kaffa*); PONTUS *or* EUXI′NUS (*Black Sea*); BO′SPORUS THRACIUS (*Channel of Constantinople*); PROPONTIS (*Sea of Mar-*

QUESTIONS.—§ 1. For what is Asia distinguished?—What is probably the signification of the name *Asia?*—What would be the correlative term?—How was Asia bounded on the west?

mora); HELLESPONTUS (*Dardanelles*); MARE ÆGÆUM (*Archipelago*); and the *Mediterranean*.

II. On the side toward Libya:—SINUS ARA'BICUS (*Red Sea*); and the Isthmus of ARSI'NOË (*Suez*).

III. The eastern and northern portions were supposed to be surrounded by an ocean. According to some of the old poets, the south-eastern parts of ASIA and of LIBYA were united by continuous land, enclosing the Indian Ocean on the East and South. According to the authority of Hero'dotus, the Greeks recognised the Nile as the dividing line between Asia and Libya.

§ 2. **Divisions.**—The Asiatic continent was subdivided into two grand divisions, varying in extent of territory at different historical epochs, and known in history under different distinct names. The earliest division of the *Greek* writers was into UPPER ASIA, and LOWER ASIA: the former title being applied to the region east of the river HALYS. At a later period, the river EUPHRA'TES was regarded by Greek authorities as the boundary between the two divisions.

The *Roman* writers divided Asia into (1.) ASIA INTRA TAURUM (Asia this side of the Taurus), or the western portion north and north-west of the Taurus: (2.) ASIA EXTRA TAURUM (Asia beyond the Taurus), which embraced the remaining portion of the continent.

Subsequent to the fourth century of the Christian era, the divisions recognised were (1.) ASIA MINOR, or, simply, ASIA; and (2.) ASIA MAJOR, or, ORIENTA'LIS. The former was bounded on the east by mountain-ranges; the latter on the west by the northernmost branch of the Euphra'tes.

QUESTIONS.—How was Asia separated from Libya?—What was known to the Ancients about the Eastern and Northern boundaries?—What wrong notion concerning the Indian Ocean was entertained by the ancient poets?—What river formed the boundary between Asia and Libya?—Who makes this statement?——§ 2. Into how many parts was Asia divided?—How many different divisions of Asia do we know?—Where did the ancient Greeks mark the boundary between the two parts?—What boundary did they afterward adopt?—What was the Roman boundary?—How long since the term "Asia Minor" came into use?—What was the boundary of Asia Minor on the east?—Of Asia Major on the west?

Seas. *North:* OCE'ANUS SEPTENTRIONA'LIS, or HYPERBOREUS.

East: OCE'ANUS ORIENTA'LIS, or EO'US.

South: OCE'ANUS I'NDICUS; MARE RUBRUM, or ERYTHRÆUM, with its two gulfs, the SINUS PE'RSICUS, and the SINUS ARA'BICUS (*Red Sea*).

West: MARE INTERNUM or INTESTI'NUM (*Mediterranean*), subdivided into (1.) MARE PHŒNICIUM, the portion washing the Syrian and Phœnician coast; (2.) MARE CILICIUM (*the Gulf of Scanderoon*); (3.) MARE PAMPHYLIUM (*the Bay of Adalia*); MARE ÆGÆUM (*the Archipelago*); HELLESPONTUS (*Dardanelles*); PROPONTIS (*Sea of Marmora*); BO'SPORUS THRACIUS (*Channel of Constantinople*); PONTUS *or* EUXI'NUS (*Black Sea*); BO'SPORUS CIMMERIUS (*Strait of Kaffa*); PALUS MÆO'TIS (*Sea of Azov*).

Lakes.—MARE CASPIUM *or* HYRCANIUM. Much confusion existed among the ancients with regard to this sea, and it is not a little remarkable that the earliest account of it, which is to be found in Hero'dotus, is by far the most accurate: OXIA PALUS (*Lake of Karakoul*), which has been supposed to be the Sea of Aral.

Mountains.—TAURUS, and ANTI-TAURUS; IMA'US (*Western Himalaya*); MONTES EMO'DI (*Eastern Himalaya*); PAROPAMI'SUS or CAU'CASUS I'NDICUS (*Hindu-Kusch*); CAU'CASUS; MONTES HYPERBOREI (*the Ural Mountains*).

Rivers.—PAROPAMI'SUS (*Obi?*); BAUTI'SUS (*Hoang-Ho*); GANGES; INDUS; TIGRIS; EUPHRA'TES; HALYS (*Kisil Irmak*); TANAIS (*Don*); RHA (*Wolga*); RHYMNUS (*Gasuri*); DAIX (*Ural*); IAXARTUS (*Sihon*); OXUS (*Gihon*).

QUESTIONS.—What seas surround Asia on the north and east?—What are the southern seas of Asia?—How many gulfs does the Mare Rubrum contain?—Their names?—By what different names was the Mediterranean known?—How was it subdivided?—The names of the other seas?—What is said about Mare Caspium?—What about Oxia Palus?—What are the principal mountains of Asia?—The principal rivers?

ASIA MINOR.

§ 3. **General View.**—The term "Asia *Minor*" was not used by the Ancients, the simple designation of ASIA alone being applied by them to the entire region. The modern name is ANATOLIA, or NATOLIA, a designation directly derived from the Greek word 'Ἀνατολή, which signifies *rising*, hence *the East.* Many portions of this extensive peninsula are enriched with scenery of exquisite loveliness, and contain many points admirably fortified by nature. The luxuriant and enchanting plains of the interior are agreeably diversified and fertilized by many water-courses, some of considerable size, such as the Tigris and Euphra'tes; while on the sea-coast are commodious and secure harbors which naturally attracted, at an early period, a large and enterprising population.

Divisions.—It embraced the following countries:

a. Three countries on the ÆGÆAN SEA: (1.) MYSIA. The Ægæan coast south of the Hellespont was called TROAS. (2.) LYDIA. The Northern coast, with the Southern coast of Mysia, was called Æ'OLIS, or ÆOLIA. The remaining portion of the coast, with a small part of Caria, was called IONIA. (3.) CARIA. Its south-west coast was called DORIS.

b. Three countries on the *Southern Coast:* (1.) LYCIA; (2.) PAMPHYLIA; (3.) CILICIA.

c. Three countries on the *Euxine:* (1.) CAPPADOCIA; (2.) PAPHLAGONIA; (3.) BITHYNIA.

d. Three countries *in the interior:* (1.) GALATIA; (2.) PHRYGIA, with LYCAONIA; (3.) PISIDIA, with ISAURIA.

QUESTIONS.—§ 3. What is the modern name of Asia Minor?—Whence is the name derived?—What is said of Asia Minor?—How many countries does it comprise?—The names of the three countries on the Ægean Sea?—What countries are on the Mediterranean?—What on the Euxine?—What were the countries of the interior?

At the close of the fourth century of our era, Asia was divided into six parts, viz.:

I. ASIA PROCONSULA'RIS, a strip of territory extending along the coast from Arsus to the Mæander: its *capital*, ÉPHESUS. II. HELLESPONTUS: *capital*, CY'ZICUS. III. LYDIA: *capital*, SARDES. IV. PHRYGIA SALUTA'RIS: the north-east part of Phrygia: *capital*, EUCARPIA. V. PHRYGIA PACATIA'NA: the west part of Phrygia: *capital*, LAODICE'A. VI. CARIA: *capital*, APHRODISIAS.

DIVISION I.

MYSIA. (*Μυσία*, or *Μυσὶς αἶα.*)

§ **4. Name.**—The original signification of this name is *marshy country*. The name is identical with that of *Mœsia*, a country on the Danube. From this latter region Mœsians emigrated, who made settlements in the north-western part of the country to the whole of which, in the time of the Roman Empire, the name of *Mysia* was applied.

Boundaries.—On the North, HELLESPONTUS and PROPONTIS; on the East, BITHYNIA and PHRYGIA; on the South, LYDIA; on the West, the ÆGÆAN SEA.

Divisions.—During the earliest periods of the Roman Empire, it was subdivided into the following districts: (1.) MYSIA MINOR, or Hellespontus, the northern part of the coast; (2.) MYSIA MAJOR, the southern part of the interior; (3.) TROAS, the northern part of the Western coast; (4.) ÆOLIS, the southern part of the coast; (5.) TEUTHRANIA, the southern frontier.

Under the Persian dominion, the term MYSIA was used to designate only the north-eastern division of the country; the

---

QUESTIONS.—Into how many parts was Asia divided at the end of the fourth century?——§ 4. How is Mysia bounded?—What does the name mean?—Into how many parts was Mysia divided?—The names of the divisions?—What did the term Mysia comprise during the Persian dominion?

western part of the coast was called PHRYGIA MINOR, and the southern part of the coast TROAS. Under the Christian Emperors of Rome, the larger part of MYSIA belonged to the province of HELLESPONTUS, while the southern districts were attached to the province of Asia.

Mountains.—The greater part of Mysia is mountainous; it is traversed by the north-western branches of the TAURUS. Its main branches, which incline toward the west, are IDA; TEMNUS (*Demirji-Dagh*); OLYMPUS (*Tumandji-Dagh*).

Rivers.—MYSIA has many small rivers which are not navigable; the most celebrated are, (1.) GRANI'CUS, which takes its rise from one of the heights of Mount Ida, and flows in a northerly direction into the Propontis, which it reaches east of Parium. It is commemorated in the Iliad, and immortalized by the first victory of Alexander over the armies of Darius Codomannus, last king of Persia (May 22, B.C. 334): (2.) SI'MOIS and SCAMANDER, or XANTHUS (see § 6): (3.) RHY'NDACUS (*Lupad*); ÆSE'PUS (*Satoldere*); EVE'NUS (*Sandarli*); CAÏ'CUS (*Ak-Su*).

§ 5. **Productions.**—It was distinguished for its excellent wheat and oysters—*Pontus et ostriferi fauces tentantur Abydi* (VIRG. Georg. I. 207). Of minerals, the most noted was the *lapis Assius*, a species of limestone, found in great abundance in Assus, a township of Troas, whence it derived its name. It was used for coffins on account of its peculiar property of causing a rapid decomposition of the human body.

Inhabitants.—The MYSIANS had immigrated into Asia from Europe either before, or soon after, the Trojan war. They were a race of peace-loving and inoffensive shepherds. By the incursions of such warlike tribes as the PHRYGIANS, the TROJANS, and ÆOLIANS, they were forced to retire further toward the interior.

QUESTIONS.—To what provinces did Mysia belong under the Christian Emperors of Rome?—What mountains traverse Mysia?—What were its main branches?—What is said of the rivers?—Who was slain near the Granicus?—§ 5. What is said about the productions of Mysia?—What about its inhabitants?—Where did they come from?

Cities.—1. ABY'DOS (Ἄβυδος), at the narrowest point of the Hellespont, nearly opposite to SESTOS, the scene of the romantic story of Leander and Hero.

2. LAMP'SACUS (Λάμψακος), on the Hellespont. Alexander resolved to destroy this city on account of the vices of its inhabitants; but it was saved by Anaxi'menes, who, knowing that Alexander had sworn to deny any request he might make, begged him to destroy it.

3. PERCO'TE (Περκώτη). Artaxerxes bestowed three rich cities on Themis'tocles, to supply his wants: PERCO'TE to furnish him with supplies of meat; MAGNESIA, with bread; and LA'MPSACUS with wine.

4. SCEPSIS (Σκῆψις). In this city the original writings and library of Aristotle were discovered. The library was ultimately removed by Sylla to Athens.

5. CHRYSA (Χρύσα), or SMINTHIUM, contained the temple of Apollo Smintheus.

6. DAR'DANUS (Δάρδανος), at the entrance of the Hellespont, a point which still retains the ancient name altered into *Dardanelles.*

7. Other noted cities were PARIUM, CYZ'ICUS, APOLLONIA, ZELIA, ALEXANDRI'A TROAS, ASSUS, ADRAMYTTIUM, THEBE, TROJA, PER'GAMUM, and the Æolian cities. (See § 8.)

§ 6. TROAS AND ILIUM. (Τρωάς; Ἴλιος, Ἴλιον.)

The north-west part of MYSIA received the name of TROAS, from TROIA, TROJA, a place of great importance in the annals of the human race, whose name has been made immortal in the verse of Homer.

The chieftains engaged in the long and memorable siege of Troy, have been for three thousand years objects of admiration

QUESTIONS.—Name six celebrated cities of Mysia.—Where is Abydos situated?—What is said of Lampsacus?—How many cities were given to Themistocles?—*Who was Themistocles?*—What is said of Scepsis?—Where was Dardanus situated?——§ 6. Where was Troas situated?—What is said concerning it?

and interest among all civilized nations. By their magnanimity, their heroism, their physical power, and their friendships, they richly merited the renown which Homer has conferred upon them. Through their means, Asia and Europe formed their first durable relations, and the Grecian tribes were first united in the bonds of a common enterprise. The extensive region of TROAS seems to include the territory west of an imaginary line, drawn from the north-east corner of the Adramyttian gulf to the Propontis at Parium. The whole territory is intersected by the mountain spurs connected with Mount IDA, two of the summits of which bore the special names of COT'YLUS and GAR'GARA.

TROJAN WAR.

The coast lying between SIGE'UM (*Tomb of Achilles*) and RHŒTE'UM (*Tomb of Ajax*) was the naval station of the Greek

---

QUESTIONS.—Name the boundaries of Troas.—What mountains intersect the country?—Where was the naval station of the Greeks?

squadrons during the siege. Here emptied the united rivers SI'MOÏS and SCAMANDER, the latter of which, according to the representation of Homer, was called by the Gods XANTHUS: ὃν Ξάνθον καλέουσι θεοί, ἄνδρες δὲ Σκάμανδρον.—Iliad xx. 74. The SCAMANDER had its source in two springs, rising near the city of Ilium, one of which was warm and the other cold. It was a large and deep stream, which, after its junction with the SIMOÏS, still retained the name of SCAMANDER. The SIMOÏS took its rise in Mount CO'TYLUS. Its present name is *Dumbrek-Chai*, and its course is now so much altered that it is no longer a tributary of the Scamander, but flows directly into the Hellespont.

The city of ILIUM was situated on a small eminence commanding the plain lying between the rivers SCAMANDER (or Xanthus) and SIMOÏS, at a distance of 42 stadia from the coast of the Hellespont. South-east of the city stood a hill, surmounted by the Acropolis, called PER'GAMUM. Troy was more than once rebuilt under the names of TROJA and ILIUM, and on a site nearer to the sea than the ancient city is supposed to have occupied.

PER'GAMUM OR PER'GAMUS. (*Πέργαμον, Πέργαμος.*)

§ 7. An ancient town of TEUTHRANIA (a division of Mysia), built on a hill overlooking the plain and river of the CAÏ'CUS, near its junction with the SELI'NUS and CETIUS, at a distance of 120 stadia from the sea. It was strongly fortified both by nature and art. On this account, LYSI'MACHUS, one of the generals of Alexander the Great, chose PE'RGAMUM as a place of security for the royal treasures, the care of which he intrusted to PHILETÆRUS; the latter, in anger at a slight received from Alexander's wife, declared himself independent (B. C. 283), and

---

QUESTIONS.—What rivers emptied there?—What is said about the Simois and Scamander?—Where was Ilium situated?—Where was Pergamum situated?—Who destroyed the city of Troy?—Was it ever rebuilt?——§ 7. Where was Pergamum situated?—Who selected this city for the safe-keeping of royal treasures?—To whose custody were these treasures intrusted?—Did he remain faithful to Alexander?

remained master of the town and of a small part of the surrounding country until his death (B. C. 263). He was succeeded by his nephew, EU'MENES, who increased his dominions, and left a prosperous country to his cousin, A'TTALUS I., who assumed the title of "King." This kingdom was enlarged by the Romans (B. C. 197–159) so as to embrace *all the countries in Asia*, WEST OF THE TAURUS. This extension of limits was made for the special benefit of EU'MENES II., son of A'ttalus I., who assisted the Romans to defeat Anti'ochus III. of Syria. Eu'menes III. was a liberal patron of the fine arts and the sciences, and founded a famous library in opposition to that of Ptolemy at Alexandri'a. Ptolemy, having, from motives of national jealousy, forbidden the exportation of papy'rus, Eu'menes invented parchment, which, from the residence of its illustrious inventor, derived its name of *pergaména charta*. The library founded by Eu'menes III., containing two hundred thousand volumes, was transported to Alexandria by Antony, and presented by him to Cleopa'tra.

A'TTALUS III. (the second in succession after Eu'menes) bequeathed his kingdom to the Romans in B. C. 133, and after ARISTONI'CUS, a natural son of Eu'menes II., was overthrown by the Consul Perpenna, the kingdom of Pe'rgamum became a Roman province, under the name of ASIA (B. C. 130).

The city continued to be in a flourishing condition even as late as the time of Pliny, who styled it "*longe clarissimum Asiæ Pergamum.*" Pe'rgamum was one of the seven churches mentioned in the book of *Revelation*, ii. 11. It was also the birthplace of the celebrated physician GALEN.

QUESTIONS.—Who assumed the title of king?—By whom was this kingdom enlarged?—What is said of Eumenes II.?—What led to the invention of parchment?—What is said of one of the most celebrated libraries of antiquity?—When did Pergamum become a Roman province?—How is Pergamum mentioned in the Sacred Writings?—Who was born at Pergamum?—Who was Galen?

DIVISION II.

GRECIAN COLONIES.

Before giving an account of Lydia, we shall describe the three celebrated confederacies, which adorned with their thirty cities the coast of Asia Minor, extending from the Sige'an promontory in the north to Cnidus in the south. The three confederacies were, Æ'OLIS, IONIA, and DORIS.

§ 8. Æ'OLIS.

The territory of the old Æolian cities extended northward from the river Hermus to the Caï'cus (embracing the northern coast of Lydia and the southern coast of Mysia), comprising the sea-coast and a narrow tract of land reaching ten or twelve miles inland. TWELVE cities, eleven of which were clustered round the Elæitic Gulf, rose to importance here, the names of which were as follows: Cumæ, Larissa, Neon Teichos, Temnus, Cilla, Notium, Ægiroessa, Pit'ane, Ægææ, Myri'na, Gryne'um, and Smyrna.

(1.) CYME, or CUMÆ (*Κύμη*), was the most powerful of the Æolian colonies. A colony from this city founded the city of Cumæ on the coast of Campania in Italy, the residence of the Cumæan Sibyl.

(2.) SMYRNA (*Σμύρνα*), the twelfth and most southerly, was situated to the south of Mount Si'pylus. At an early period it fell into the hands of the Ionians, and the city was subsequently (B. C. 627) destroyed by the Lydian king, Alyattes; for a period of 400 years, it was deserted and in ruins, when it was rebuilt (twenty stadia southward of the former city) by Anti'gonus, king

---

QUESTIONS.—Name the three Greek confederacies on the Asiatic coast. —How many cities did they comprise?——§ 8. Where was Æolis?—How many confederate cities did Æolis contain?—What colony was founded by colonists from the city Cumæ?—Where is Smyrna situated? —What is said of the city?

of Syria. After its extension and embellishment by Lysi'machus, NEW SMYRNA became a city of extreme magnificence. Beside these twelve cities, most of which were near the coast, there were SIX Æolian cities in LESBOS (see § 52), and ONE in the Island of Ten'edos; others flourished on Mount Ida, along the Hellespont and on the coast of Thrace. The name *Æolic* is often applied to a dialect of the Greek language; but no entire work written in it is extant.

§ 9. IONIA.

It extended from the CUMÆAN GULF on the north to Mount GRIUS and the gulf BASIL'ICUS south of Mile'tus, a distance of not more than one hundred miles in a straight line, but with a coast three times that length, on account of the many gulfs which indent it. Toward the east, Ionia extended only forty miles.

The colonies were founded about 1044 B. C., by Attic Ionians, Ionians from the Peloponne'sus, and emigrants from other parts of Greece whom chance directed to these very beautiful and fertile regions. They drove out the Carian shepherds, who fed their flocks in the meadows of the Mæander. The Caÿster flowed through a marsh, called the Asian marsh, much frequented by water-fowl:

> *Jam varias pelagi volucres et quæ Asia circum*
> *Dulcibus in stagnis rimantur prata Caystri.*—Virg. Georg. I. 383.

The genial climate of Ionia, its verdant hillsides which were the sources of numerous streams, and its coast abounding in safe harbors, attracted a numerous population, who in time became wealthy, refined, and luxurious. The remains of their monuments give evidence of a fine taste for the arts. Greek literature may be said to have originated on this coast of Asia; for poets, philosophers, historians, and artists flourished in the Ionian cities long

---

QUESTIONS.—How many Æolian cities were in Lesbos?—What is said about the Æolic dialect?——§ 9. Where was Ionia situated?—When were its colonies founded?—What is said of the country?—What in regard to its civilization?

before A'ttica attained to any eminence in intellectual pursuits. There existed, at the commencement of *historical* Greece (777 B. C.), TWELVE IONIAN CITIES of note, on or near the coast of Asia Minor, beside a few others of less importance. Enumerated from north to south, they stand thus: PHOCÆA, CLAZOM'ENÆ, CHIOS, ER'YTHRÆ, TEOS, LEB'EDUS, COL'OPHON, EPH'ESUS, SAMOS, PRIE'NE, MYUS, MILE'TUS.

They all formed independent republics with democratic constitutions; but affairs connected with the general government were discussed at regular meetings held at PANIONIUM, the primitive centre of the older Ionian settlements, on the northern slope of Mount MYC'ALE, near Priene, about three stadia from the coast.

(1.) PHOCÆ'A (*Φώκαια*), was built at the end of a peninsula which formed part of the territory of the Æolic Cumæ. The Cumæans were induced to cede it amicably, and to permit the building of the new town. Its inhabitants afterwards deserted it, in order to avoid being subjected to the power of Cyrus. Having sworn never to return till a mass of iron which they had sunk in the sea should rise to the surface, they founded the city of MASSILIA in Gaul (B. C. 540).

Nulla sit hac potior sententia: Phocæorum
Velut profugit exsecrata civitas—
* * * * *
Sed juremus in hæc; simul imis saxa renarint
Vadis levata, ne redire sit nefas.—Hor. Epod. 16: 17, 25.

(2.) CLAZOM'ENÆ (*Κλαζομεναί*), situated on the south side of the Bay of Smyrna. The original settlement was on the mainland, but the fear of attacks from the Persians caused its removal to the island. It was distinguished for being the birthplace of the philosopher Anaxag'oras.

(3.) CHIOS (*Χίος*), an island of the Ægæan Sea, opposite to the peninsula in which Erythræ was situated, five miles from the

---

QUESTIONS.—How many cities were embraced in the confederacy?—What was the political government?—Name the twelve Ionian cities.—Where was Phocæa situated?—For what reason was it abandoned by its citizens?—To what point did they emigrate and settle?—Where was Anaxagoras born?

mainland of Asia. It is one of the twelve reputed birthplaces of HOMER, and has, perhaps, next to Smyrna, the best claim to the honor: on the northern coast of the island, a grotto, known as Homer's School, is yet pointed out. The places which contended for the honor of being the birthplace of Homer are enumerated in those well-known lines:

HOMER.

Septem urbes certant de stirpe insignis Homeri,
Smyrna, Rhodus, Colophon, Salamis, Chios, Argos, Athenæ.

(4.) ER'YTHRÆ (Ἐρυθραί), situated on a capacious bay, on the west side of the Erythræan peninsula, opposite to the island of Chios. It was celebrated as the residence of one of the Sibyls.

(5.) TEOS (Τέως), on the coast of Lydia, on the south side of the isthmus connecting the Ionian peninsula of Mount Mimas with the mainland. In the time of the Persian dominion the greater part of its inhabitants abandoned the city and removed to ABDE'RA in Thrace. It was the birthplace of Anacreon, who on this account is called the Teian bard.

QUESTIONS.—How many cities disputed the honor of being the birthplace of Homer?—Their names?—What two most justly?—*Who was Homer?*—Where was Erythræ?—For what celebrated?—Where was Teos?—Why is Anacreon called the Teian bard?

(6.) LEB'EDUS (Λέβεδος), about fourteen miles north-west of Col'ophon in Lydia. It was nearly destroyed by Lysi'machus, who transplanted its population to E'phesus. In the time of Horace it was entirely in ruins:

> *Scis Lebedus quid sit, Gabiis desertior atque*
> *Fidenis vicus.*—Epist. I. 11, 6.

§ **10.** (7.) COL'OPHON (Κολοφών), about fifteen miles north of E'phesus, and divided from the territory of the latter by a precipitous mountain-range, called Gallesium. It was the native place of Mimnermus and Nicander. The Colophonians at one time possessed an extensive navy and mounted force. This cavalry generally turned the scale on whichever side they fought: hence, *Colophonem addere*, "to put the Co'lophon to it," became, among the Romans, a proverb equivalent to our English expression, "to give the finishing stroke." In the early period of the art of printing, the statement which the printer subjoined at the end of a book, giving the place and date of the edition, being the last thing required to finish the volume, was called the *Co'lophon.*

(8.) E'PHESUS (Ἔφεσος), in Lydia, on the south side of the CAYSTRUS, and situated near its mouth. Its port was called PANORMUS. It was celebrated for its temple of Ar'temis, or Dia'na (ARTEMISIUM), one of the great holy places of the Ionic Helle'nes. This temple was burnt down by Hero'stratus on the night on which Alexander was born (B. C. 356). The temple was rebuilt, but 220 years elapsed before it was finished. The city is often mentioned in the writings and travels of St. Paul, and also in *Revelation*, ii. 1.

(9.) SAMOS (Σάμος), a large island in that part of the Ægæan called the Icarian Sea, at the distance of about a mile from the promontory of Trogylium. It was the birthplace of Pythag'oras. Here Hera (*Juno*) was worshipped in a very large temple (HE-

QUESTIONS.—What is said of Lebedus?——§ 10. Where was Colophon situated?—What is the meaning of the proverbial expression, *Colophonem addere?*—What celebrated temple was in Ephesus?—What is said concerning it?—Where was Pythagoras born?—Where was Samos?

RÆUM), with peculiar honours. Virgil, speaking of Carthage, says:

> *Quam Juno fertur terris magis omnibus unam*
> *Posthabita coluisse Samo.*—Æn. i. 15.

(10.) PRIE'NE (Πριήνη), near the coast of Caria, near the south-eastern slope of Mount My'cale, on a small stream, called Gæson.

(11.) MYUS (Μυοῦς), north of Miletus in Caria, on the southern bank of the Mæander, and the smallest among the Ionian cities, became incorporated with Mile'tus, to which city finally the Myusians transferred themselves.

(12.) MILE'TUS (Μίλητος), on the northern part of the coast of Caria, opposite the mouth of the Mæander, was once an important and flourishing state, which sent out no less than seventy-five colonies. The most remarkable of these were ABY'DOS, LAMP'SACUS, and PARIUM, on the Hellespont; PROCONNE'SUS and CYZ'ICUS, on the Propontis; SINO'PE and AMI'SUS, on the Euxine. However extensive and beautiful the city of Mile'tus may have been, we have now no means of forming any idea of its topography, since its site and its whole territory have been changed into a pestilential swamp by the muddy deposits of the Mæander. Thales, one of the wisest of the seven contemporary Grecian sages, was a native of this place, as were also Anaxi'menes, Anaximander, the historian Hecatæus, and several other distinguished men.

§ 11. DORIS.

An Amphictyony, or federal republic, on the Triopian promontory, or south-western corner of Asia Minor, constituting an hexapolis, including HALICARNASSUS, CNIDUS, COS, LINDUS, IAL'YSUS, CAMI'RUS.

(1.) HALICARNAS'SUS (Ἁλικαρνασσός), on the Cerami'cus Sinus, or Ceramic Gulf, built on the slope of a precipitous rock,

---

QUESTIONS.—Where were Priene and Myus situated?—Where was Miletus situated?—How many colonies did it send out?—Name some of them.—What great men were born at Miletus?——§ 11. Where was Doris situated?—How many cities did it contain?—Name them.

the largest and most powerful city of Caria, and once the residence of the Carian kings. Here was the splendid tomb, built by Artemisia, queen of Caria, for her husband Mauso'lus (*Mausolé'um*). It was the birthplace of the two historians, Hero'dotus and Dionysius. It was excluded from the Doric league in consequence of the bad conduct of one of its citizens, who, having gained a tripod as a prize, carried it home to adorn his own house, and thus violated the municipal regulation, which required that the tripod should always be consecrated as an offering in the Triopian temple. The city is memorable also for the long siege it maintained against Alexander, under the skilful command of Memnon, the general of Darius.

(2.) Cnidus (*Κνίδος*), at the western extremity of a long peninsula, which forms the southern side of the Cerami'cus Sinus. It was the birthplace of Ctesias, the historian of Persia. Here was the celebrated statue, the Aphrodi'te (*Venus*) of Praxi'teles, the most exquisite creation even of Grecian genius:

> *Quæ* [i. e., *Venus*] *Cnidon*
> *Fulgentesque tenet Cyclades et Paphon*
> *Junctis visit oloribus.*—Hor. Od. iii. 28, 13.

(3.) Cos (*Κῶς*), an island in the Myrto'an sea, nearly opposite the Gulf of Halicarnassus. Here was the Asclepiē'um, or temple of Æsculapius, to which was attached a kind of Medical College. It was the birthplace of Apelles and Hippo'crates. It was known in the old world for its ointment and purple dye, but more especially for its wines.

(4.) Lindus, Ial'ysus, and Cami'rus were three ancient cities on the island of Rhodus, *Rhodes*, which afterward (B. C. 408) became united under the name of Rhodus. (See Rhodus.)

Questions.—What city was the birthplace of Herodotus?—Where was Halicarnassus?—What was the Mausoleum?—Why was Halicarnassus excluded from the Doric league?—Where was the Aphrodite of Praxiteles? —What is said of Cos?—What three towns formed the city of Rhodus?

DIVISION III.

LYDIA. (Λυδία.)

§ 12. **Boundaries.**—North, MYSIA; East, PHRYGIA; South, CARIA; and West, IONIA. In the time of Crœsus, it embraced the whole of Asia Minor, between the Ægæan sea and the river Halys, with the exception of Cilicia and Lycia.

Mountains.—It was intersected by mountain chains, running from east to west. The MESSO'GIS and TMOLUS, both outlying ranges of the Taurus, divided it into two extensive valleys.

Rivers.—Through the southern valley (between the Messo'gis and Tmolus) flows the CAYSTRUS; through the northern the HERMUS, with its tributaries, the HYLLUS and PACTO'LUS.

NAVAL BATTLE.

QUESTIONS.—§ 12. How was Lydia bounded?—Name the chief mountains.—Name the largest rivers.

Capes.—MYC'ALE is the most distinguished, where the Persians were defeated by the Grecian fleet under Leoty'chides and Xantippus, on the same day that Pausanias conquered at Platææ (September, 479 B. C.).

Productions.—Wine, saffron, and gold. The fertility of Lydia, and the salubrity of its climate, are frequently mentioned by ancient writers, and this account is confirmed by the reports of modern travellers.

Inhabitants.—The Lydians were a gifted nation; they cultivated the arts, and differed in refinement but little from the Greeks. They are said to have been the first to establish inns for travellers, and to coin money. Their commercial industry was the great source of their national prosperity.

Cities.—(1.) SARDES (*Σάρδεις*), the ancient capital, situated at the foot of Mount Tmolus, in a fertile plain, twenty stadia from the river Hermus. The river Pacto'lus flowed through the *a'gora*, or public market-place. After the overthrow of the kingdom of Lydia, it became the residence of the Persian Satraps of Western Asia. The attack on this city by the Ionians, assisted by the Athenians (504 B. C.), was the origin of the Persian wars. In its neighborhood was Gygæus Lacus (*λίμνη Γυγαίη*), an artificial lake surrounded by the tombs of the Lydian kings.

(2.) MAGNESIA, near Mount Sip'ylus (*Μαγνησία ὑπὸ Σιπύλῳ*); to be distinguished from the Æolian city of the same name in Ionia. It is celebrated for the victory gained by the two Scipios over Anti'ochus the Great (190 B. C.), who was forced from the last foothold in Western Asia.

(3.) THYATI'RA and PHILADELPHI'A, both mentioned in the Revelation.

QUESTIONS.—Who were defeated at the cape of Mycale?—Name the principal productions of Lydia.—What is said of the Lydians?—What was the capital of Lydia?—What were the consequences of the attack made on this city by the Ionians and Athenians?—Who conquered at Magnesia?—What cities are mentioned in the book of Revelation?

DIVISION IV.

CARIA. (*Καρία.*)

§ 13. **Boundaries.**—North, Lydia; East, Phrygia and Lycia; South and West, the Ægæan Sea. It is separated from Lydia by the Mæander. Its southern coast was colonized by, and belonged to, the Rhodians, and was hence called Peræa Rhodiorum (*Πέραια τῶν Ῥοδίων*).

Mountains.—Messo'gis on the north. The Cadmus range runs through its entire length, rendering the face of the country extremely rugged and broken.

Rivers.—Mæander and Calbis.

Productions.—Excellent grain, figs, olives, wine, and oil. It was noted also for its sheep and for its limestone.

Inhabitants.—The Carians were a warlike and mercenary race, selling their services in time of war to the highest bidder. They lived in small towns or villages, and formed a general confederation, common religious rites being paid to Zeus Chrysa'oreus. The confederacy was called Chrysaoreum.

Towns.—On the southern coast, Caunus (*Καῦνος*), the chief town of the Caunii, who differed in manners and customs from the Carians and from every other people; Phœnix; Alabanda; Stratonice'a (*Στρατονίκεια*), on the south of the river Marsyas, founded by Anti'ochus Soter, was one of the most important towns.

Questions.—§ 13. Name the boundaries of Caria.—What river separates it from Lydia?—Name the principal mountains and rivers.—What are its productions?—What is said of the inhabitants?—What was the name of the confederacy formed by the inhabitants?—What is said of the Caunii?—Who was the founder of Stratonicea?

DIVISION V.

LYCIA. (Λυκία.)

§ **14. Boundaries.**—North, PHRYGIA and PISIDIA; East, PISIDIA and PAMPHYLIA; South, *Mediterranean*, and to a great extent also on the West and East; West, CARIA.

Mountains.—It is a mountainous country. The TAURUS has numerous connecting chains of mountain-spurs, the principal of which are DÆD'ALA, CRAGUS, MASSICY'TES rising to the height of 10,000 feet, and CLIMAX.

Capes.—PROMONTORIUM SACRUM; PROMONTORIUM CHELIDONIUM.

Rivers.—Most of the rivers flow in a southerly direction. The most important are XANTHUS in the West, and LIM'YRUS or ARICANDUS in the East.

Productions.—Lycia was the smallest, but, in proportion to its extent, the richest and most fertile country of Asia Minor. It produced wine and corn in great abundance; its cedars, firs, and plane trees were particularly celebrated.

Inhabitants.—They are said to have come from CRETE, and to have subdued the ancient native tribes of the SOL'YMI and MULYÆ. A portion of the population was of Greek origin. The Lycians were a peaceable and honorable race, and took no part in the piracies of their maritime neighbors. They adopted and practised to a great extent the Grecian arts.

Cities.—Lycia contained formerly as many as seventy cities, thirty-two of which belonged to the Lycian confederacy. The six largest were, XANTHUS, PAT'ARA, PIN'ARA, OLYMPUS, MYRA, and TLOS.

QUESTIONS —§ 14. What are the boundaries of Lycia?—What are the principal mountains?—Name the capes.—What is said of the rivers?—Name the principal ones.—Describe the productions of the country.—Who were the earliest inhabitants?—Who conquered them?—What is said about the inhabitants?—How many towns did Lycia formerly contain?—How many of them belonged to the Lycian confederacy?—Name the six largest towns.

(1.) XANTHUS (Ξάνθος) was destroyed by Har'pagus, general of Cyrus (540 B. C.). It was subsequently rebuilt; and five centuries later, it was burned by its inhabitants, who took this patriotic course rather than permit the city to fall into the hands of Brutus.

(2.) PAT'ARA (Πάταρα) was a little south of the former city. During one-half of the year (the six winter months), it was the reputed residence of Apollo, who there had a celebrated temple and oracle: *Phœbe, qui Xantho lavis amne crines.*—Hor. Od. iv. 6, 26. *Delius et Patareus Apollo.*—Hor. Od. iii. 4, 64.

(3.) OLYMPUS (Ὄλυμπος), is near the Promontorium Sacrum. Above it is the Dorian colony, PHASE'LIS. Near this point, a steep ridge of the Taurus, called *Climax*, juts into the sea. The army of Alexander was, by reason of the narrow pass, placed in the utmost danger, and compelled to wade a whole day, waist deep, in water.

ALEXANDER'S ARMY PASSING CLIMAX.

QUESTIONS.—Who destroyed Xanthus for the first time?—Who for the second time?—What is said of Patara?—What celebrated ridge touches the sea-coast near Phaselis?

(4.) MYRA (*Μύρα*), the capital of all Lycia, when part of the Roman Empire. St. Paul touched there on his voyage to Rome.

DIVISION VI.

§ 15. PAMPHYLIA. (*Παμφυλία.*)

PAMPHYLIA was a narrow strip of coast, extending in a sort of semi-circle around the bay, which is called after it, Mare Pamphylium (*Bay of Adalia*).

Boundaries.—North, PISIDIA; East, CILICIA; South, GULF OF PAMPHYLIA; West, LYCIA.

Mountains.—The country is generally very mountainous. It is traversed by connecting ridges of the TAURUS.

Rivers.—CATARRHACTES, CESTRUS, MELAS, and EURYM'E-DON. At the mouth of the last named, Cimon destroyed the fleet and army of the Persians (469 B.C.).

Inhabitants.—The PAMPHY'LI (*Πάμφυλοι*, i. e. *all races*, or all kinds of races) were a mixture of different Semitic and Hellenic races. They were daring navigators and notorious robbers.

Towns.—(1.) PERGE (*Πέργη*), a town in the interior of the country, situated between the rivers Catarrhactes and Cestrus. It was renowned for the worship of A'rtemis (*Dia'na*). A temple sacred to her stood on a hill outside the town, and in her honor annual festivals were celebrated. It was the first town in Asia visited by St. Paul.

(2.) SIDE (*Σίδη*, i. e. *a pomegranate*), the most ancient colony founded by Cumæ in Æ'olis. The colonists soon forgot the Greek language, and formed an idiom peculiar to themselves. SIDE became, at one time, a principal seaport for the resort of pirates.

QUESTIONS.—What was the capital of Lycia under the Roman sway? ——§ 15. Describe Pamphylia.—What are the boundaries of Pamphylia? —What is the face of the country?—Name the rivers.—Who conquered the Persians at the Eurymedon?—And when?—What are the chief cities of Pamphylia?—Where was Perge situated?—What was Perge celebrated for?—What is said of Side?

TEMPLE OF DIANA.

It was one of the principal seats of the worship of Athe'na (*Minerva*).

(3.) The other towns of note were Olbia, Attalia, Aspendus, Syllium.

Under the Roman Empire, Pamphylia formed a Roman province in connection with Pisidia, Isauria, and a part of Lycia.

DIVISION VII.

CILICIA. (*Κιλικία.*)

§ **16. Boundaries.**—North, LYCAONIA and CAPPADOCIA; East, range of AMA'NUS; South, MARE CILICIUM; West, PAMPHYLIA and PISIDIA.

Divisions.—I. CILICIA PROPER, or Cilicia *beyond the Taurus*, was divided in two parts: CILICIA AS'PERA or TRACHI'A

QUESTIONS.—What were the names of the remaining towns?—— § 16. How is Cilicia bounded?—How is it divided?—How is Cilicia Proper subdivided?

(*Κιλικία ἡ Τραχεῖα*), the western and mountainous part; CILICIA CAMPESTRIS or PEDIAS (*Κιλικία ἡ Πεδιάς*), a considerable extent of level country.

II. CILICIA *within the Taurus* belonged to Cappadocia.

Mountains.—The ridges of the TAURUS, of which the most important is the AMA'NUS. Above Tarsus, the Cydnus forms the famous pass called the PYLÆ CILICIÆ, or the gates of Cilicia. By this pass the younger Cyrus penetrated to Tarsus (401 B. C.), and Alexander the Great to Cilicia (333 B. C.).

Capes.—MYLÆ, or MYLAS (*Cavaliere*); MAGARSUS (*Karadash*).

Rivers.—CYDNUS, the stream in which Alexander the Great nearly lost his life, and on which Cleopatra, in her royal barge, paid her celebrated visit to Antony (34 B. C.); CALYCADNUS, SARUS, and PYR'AMUS, which is the largest of the Cilician rivers.

CLEOPATRA'S BARGE.

QUESTIONS.—What part belonged to Cappadocia?—What is said about the mountains?—Describe the Pylæ Ciliciæ.—What historical events are connected with it?—Name the capes.—Name the rivers.—What is said of the Cydnus?

Climate.—The climate of CILICIA was generally warm and sultry. During the season of winter the temperature was unusually mild. Hence the amazing fertility of the eastern plains.

Productions.—Timber, saffron, and cloth made from goats' hair (*Cilicium*).

Inhabitants.—The Cilicians belonged to a branch of the Arame'an, or Chaldean, race. When their country fell under the sway of foreigners (Greeks and Romans), they maintained themselves in the mountains under the name of Free Cilicians (*Eleu'thero-ci'lices*). Cicero, who was pro-consul of Cilicia, describes them as a fierce and warlike race.

Cities.—(1.) TARSUS (*Ταρσός*), on the Cydnus, the birthplace of St. Paul, and so celebrated for the learning and refinement of its citizens, that it rivalled the fame of Athens and Alexandria.

CICERO.

QUESTIONS.—Describe the climate.—The productions.—What is said of the Eleuthero-cilices?—Who was once pro-consul in Cilicia?—*Who was Cicero?*—Name five towns of Cilicia.—Where was St. Paul born?—What is said of Tarsus?

(2.) SELEUCI'A TRACHI'A (Σελεύκεια), anciently the principal city of Cilicia Trachi'a, and noted for a celebrated temple of Apollo.

(3.) SELI'NUS (Σελινοῦς). The emperor Trajan died here (A.D. 117), in consequence of which it was afterward called Trajano'polis.

(4.) SOLŒ or SOLI (Σόλοι). Pompey here settled the Cilician pirates, to whom he had granted an amnesty. He gave it the name of Pompeïo'polis. It was the birthplace of the philosopher Chrysippus, and of the poet Ara'tus. The *patois* of the inhabitants, which was Greek corrupted by the language of Cilicia, perhaps gave rise to the grammatical term *solecism;* but by some the origin of this term is connected with the town of *Soli*, in Cyprus.

ALEXANDER'S ARMY.

(5.) ISSUS (Ἰσσός), situated close upon the borders of Syria, a little to the north of the river Pin'arus. It was the scene of the victory of Alexander over Darius (333 B.C.).

QUESTIONS.—What is said of Seleucia Trachia?—For whose temple was it celebrated?—On what occasion did Solœ change its name into Pompeiopolis?—What distinguished characters were born in Solœ?—What is the origin of the word "solecism?"—Where was Darius conquered?—And when?

(6.) Of the other towns worthy of mention may be noted CORACESIUM, CELEN'DERIS, COR'YCUS, CLAUDIOP'OLIS, MALLUS, MOPSUCRE'NE, ADA'NA, MOPSUVESTIA, ANAZARBUS.

DIVISION VIII.

CAPPADOCIA. (*Καππαδοκία.*)

§ **17.** Originally it comprised the whole of the north-eastern part of Asia Minor, between the eastern bank of the Halys and Mount Taurus. Under the Persian dominion, this extensive country was subdivided into two satrapies, which after Alexander's death became separate kingdoms.

(A.) The northern part formed the satrapy of *Cappadocia ad Pontum*, or, simply, PONTUS.

(B.) The southern part formed the satrapy of *Cappadocia ad Taurum*, or, simply, CAPPADOCIA.

In A. D. 16, the two parts again were united, and a part of Armenia, lying between the Anti-taurus and Euphra'tes, was incorporated with them.

Mountains.—The principal mountain-chain is the TAURUS, which forms the southern boundary. Two other important chains, the ANTI-TAURUS and PARY'ADRES, run in nearly parallel lines from Armenia into the centre of Cappadocia. The highest point in the country is MONS ARGÆUS, from the summit of which both the Euxine and Mediterranean seas might, it was said, be seen.

Rivers.—(1.) CAP'PADOX, from which the whole country was said to have derived its name.

QUESTIONS.—Name some of the other towns.——§ 17. Give the original boundaries of Cappadocia.—How was it divided under the Persian dominion?—What kingdoms arose afterward from those divisions?—At what time were they re-united?—What was the southern boundary of Cappadocia?—What other important mountain chains run through it?—What are the two most important rivers?

(2.) THERMO'DON, the banks of which stream were frequented by the far-famed Amazons:

Cum flumina Thermodontis
Pulsant et pictis bellantur Amazones armis.—Virg. Æn. XI. 659.

(3.) There were other rivers of some importance, viz.: HALYS, IRIS, LYCUS, SCYLAX, CARME'LUS, EUPHRA'TES, SARUS, PYR'AMUS.

Productions.—CAPPADOCIA was one of the richest territories of Asia Minor, and characterized by extensive plains of great fertility. It was in general deficient in timber, but well adapted for the cultivation of grains of all kinds. Some parts of it produced excellent wine.

Inhabitants.—By the Persians they were called Cappadocians; by the Greeks, Leuco-Syrians (*White Syrians*), because they resembled the inhabitants of Syria and spoke the same language, but were of lighter complexion. They are remarkable as a nation, for having refused independence when it was offered to them, preferring to live under the rule of their own kings. The tribes of the interior were wild and ferocious in disposition. Cappadocia was noted as *one* of *the three bad kappas,* the remaining two of the infamous trio being Cilicia and Crete, the initial letter of which, in Greek, was *K*, *kappa*. The coast of the Euxine was dotted with many Greek colonies, who diffused the light of culture and civilization around them.

Division.—(A.) The southern part; *Cappadocia ad Taurum.* (B.) The northern part; *Cappadocia ad Pontum.*

QUESTIONS.—Who lived on the shores of the Thermodon?—What are the principal productions?—What name was given to the ancient inhabitants by the Persians?—What name was given them by the Greeks?—Why?—What were they remarkable for?—What three countries were designated as "the three bad *kappas?*"—What is said of the coast of the Euxine?—What are the divisions of Cappadocia?

§ 18. (A.) Cappadocia ad Taurum.

To this part were added, about 333 B. C.,

I. Cataonia, a district situated between Cilicia and Comma'gene.

II. Melite'ne, a tract of land along the Euphrates, between the Anti-taurus and Ama'nus.

III. Armenia minor, added to it A. D. 16.

Boundaries.—North, Galatia and Pontus; East, Armenia major; South, Cilicia and Syria; West, Lycaonia and Galatia.

Towns.—(1.) Ty'ana (*Τύανα*), by Xenophon called Dana; the birthplace of the impostor, Apollonius (A. D. 90). On the borders of a lake, in its immediate neighborhood, was a famous temple of Jupiter Asbamæus, thus called from a bubbling spring of hot water (*Asbamœum*) which had no visible outlet.

(2.) Coma'na, (*Κόμανα*), which contained a large and rich temple of Bello'na.

(3.) Melite'ne (*Μελιτηνή*), situated between the rivers Melas and Euphra'tes. Constantine the Great made it the capital of Armenia minor.

(4.) Nicop'olis (*Νικόπολις*, i. e. *City of Victory*) was built by Pompey after he had forced Mithridates across the Euphrates.

(5.) Maz'aca, the ancient residence of the Cappadocian kings, called Cæsare'a (*Καισάρεια*) in the time of Tiberius.

(6.) The names of other towns are Cybistra, Castaba'la, Archela'is, Nazianzus, Nysa, Nora, Parnassus, Sat'ala.

(B.) Cappadocia ad Pontum.

Commonly called Pontus (*Πόντος*). It is first mentioned in Xe'nophon (Anab. 5, 6, 15).

Questions.—§ 18. What countries were added to Cappadocia ad Taurum?—What were its boundaries?—Its chief towns?—What is said of Tyana?—Of Melitene?—Of Nicopolis?—Of Mazaca?—How was Cappadocia ad Pontum generally designated?

Boundaries.—It formed a long and narrow tract of land on the sea-coast in the extreme north-east of Asia, extending from the river Halys to the river Ophis; but in the western part it extended somewhat further south, or inland.

Divisions.—I. The North-west: PONTUS GALA'TICUS, bestowed (65 B.C.) on the Galatian Deio'tarus.

II. The North-east: PONTUS POLEMONI'ACUS, given to Polemon, grandson of Mithrida'tes.

III. The South-east: PONTUS CAPPADOCIUS, being transferred by Polemon's widow to Archela'us of Cappadocia.

Under Constantine the Great, PONTUS was divided into two parts:

I. The Western part: HELENOPONTUS, in honor of the emperor's mother.

II. The Eastern part: PONTUS POLEMONI'ACUS.

Towns.—(1.) AMI'SUS (*Ἀμισός*), a flourishing Greek colony, besieged by Lucullus (69 B.C.).

(2.) AMASI'A (*Ἀμάσεια*), situated in the interior, upon the banks of the Iris. It was the birthplace of Mithrida'tes and Strabo.

(3.) ZELA (*τὰ Ζῆλα*), where Cæsar overcame Phar'naces, the son of Mithrida'tes, in reference to which he sent to Rome the famous despatch: *veni, vidi, vici.*

(4.) COMA'NA (*Κόμανα*), celebrated for the great temple of Ma (Mâ, the *moon*-goddess; comp. *Μήν*, the *moon*-god); to this temple were attached several thousand female slaves (*hierodu'li*).

(5.) CER'ASUS (*Κερασοῦς*), from whence Lucullus introduced the first *cherries* (*cerasi*) into Italy, about 70 B.C.

(6.) TRAPE'ZUS (*Τραπεζοῦς*, *Trebisond*), a branch of the Greek colony SINO'PE. It was the first Greek city entered by Xenophon on his famous retreat, and afterwards (till A.D. 1460) the capital of the Greek empire of the Comneni.

(7.) Other cities were Polemonium, Coty'ora, Pharnacia, Sebastia, Cabi'ra, or Neo-cæsare'a.

QUESTIONS.—Name its boundaries.—Its divisions?—How was it divided by Constantine the Great?—Name its chief towns.—For what is Zela celebrated in history?—Comana?—What is said of Cerasus?—Of Trapezus?

DIVISION IX.

PAPHLAGONIA. (*Παφλαγονία.*)

§ 19. **Boundaries.**—North, PONTUS EUXI'NUS; East, PONTUS; South, GALATIA; West, BITHYNIA. The river PARTHENIUS divided it from BITHYNIA; the HALYS, from PONTUS.

Mountains.—It is traversed by three chains of mountains running in nearly parallel lines from west to east. The highest, and most southerly, is called the OLGASSYS.

Rivers.—The rivers, with the exception of the HALYS, are inconsiderable in size; they are SE'SAMUS, AM'NIUS, and others.

Productions.—Timber was abundant. Numbers of mules and sheep were reared. Paphlagonia was particularly famous for its horses.

Inhabitants.—The Paphlagonians are of Syrian origin, and the inhabitants of the interior are described as superstitious, ignorant, and coarse in manners. They were, however, brave soldiers, and fought particularly well on horseback. The coast was inhabited by Greek colonists. To the north were the HEN'ETI, who are said to have passed over into Italy, after the Trojan war, where they established themselves under the name of Ve'neti.

Towns.—The chief towns were the Greek colonies situated on the coast of the Euxine.

(1.) SINO'PE (*Σινώπη*, *Sinoub*), a colony of the Milesians, for many centuries one of the most flourishing commercial towns in the Euxine, itself the parent city of several colonies, such as Trapezus, Ce'rasus. Mithrida'tes the Great made it the

---

QUESTIONS.—§ 19. Name the boundaries of Paphlagonia.—What bounded it on the side of Bithynia?—On the side of Pontus?—What is said of the mountains?—Of the rivers?—For what was the country particularly famous?—What is said of the Paphlagonians?—Who inhabited the coast?—Who lived toward the north?—Where did they establish themselves afterward?—Where were the chief towns of Paphlagonia situated?—What is said of Sinope?—Who made it the capital of his empire?

capital of his dominions, and adorned it with many public buildings. It was the birthplace of the philosopher Dio'genes.

(2.) AMASTRIS and CYTO'RUM, both mentioned by Homer (Iliad, ii. 855).

(3.) Other cities are Pompeïo'polis and Gangra.

DIVISION X.

BITHYNIA. (*Βιθυνία.*)

§ **20. Boundaries.**—North, PROPONTIS, BOS'PORUS THRACIUS, and PONTUS EUXI'NUS; East, PAPHLAGONIA; South, PHRYGIA and GALATIA; West, MYSIA. It is separated from Mysia by the RHYN'DACUS on the west. The eastern boundary is very uncertain. By ancient authors the river PARTHENIUS is often spoken of as the boundary.

Mountains.—The principal mountain-range in BITHYNIA is that of OLYMPUS, which extends eastward from the RHYN'DACUS.

Capes.—POSIDIUM, NIGRUM, and ACHERUSIA. He'rcules was said to have dragged Cer'berus from hell through a cavern in this promontory.

Rivers.—RHYN'DACUS, SANGARIUS, which next to the Halys was the largest river in Asia Minor; BILLÆUS and PARTHENIUS.

Lakes.—West of the river SANGARIUS are two considerable lakes; ASCANIUS (*Isnik*), APOLLONIA'TIS.

Productions.—The coast was rich in every kind of natural productions, excepting the olive. The forests were principally of oak.

Inhabitants.—The earliest inhabitants were called BEBRY'CES, i. e. Phrygians (hence the country was termed BEBRYCIA). They

---

QUESTIONS.—Which of the Paphlagonian cities are mentioned by Homer?——§ 20. How is Bithynia bounded?—What is the boundary toward Mysia?—What is the principal mountain-range?—What are the principal capes?—Which of them is connected with the story of Hercules?—In what way?—What is said of the Sangarius?—Mention the other rivers.—What fruit did not grow in Bithynia?—What kind of timber abounded in its forests?—What were the earliest inhabitants of Bithynia called?—What was the former name of the country?—

were afterwards conquered by a Thracian immigration of the Thyni (Θυνοί), who settled on the shore of the Euxine from the Bosporus to the Sangarius, where they still retained their own original name, while a part of them went to the interior and were called Bithy'ni. East of the Sangarius were the MARIANDY'NI; north-east of these the CAUCO'NES. Pliny the Younger, the celebrated friend of Trajan, was pro-consul of Bithynia, and from his epistles we derive a great deal of information respecting its condition during the first century of the Christian era.

Cities.—The large towns of Bithynia were all west of the Sangarius; the towns east of the river were of little note, the chief of them being the Greek settlements on the coast.

(1.) PRUSA AD OLYMPUM, (now called *Brusa*, or *Broussa*,) which gave the title of Prusias to the kings of Bithynia. It was the capital of the Ottoman Empire before the capture of Constantinople, and is still one of the most flourishing towns of Anatolia.

(2.) NICÆA (*Isnik*), on the shores of the lake Ascanius, where the Nicene creed was drawn up (325 A. D.). It was the birthplace of the historian Dio Cassius.

(3.) NICOMEDIA, founded by Nicome'des I., was the birthplace (A. D. circ. 100) of Arrianus, the celebrated author of the *Anabasis Alexandri*; it was the chief residence of the Bithynian kings.

(4.) LIBYSSA, which contained the tomb of the Lybian general Hannibal, the Carthaginian.

(5.) CHALCE'DON, at the entrance of the Propontis, called, by way of derision, *the city of the blind*, from the fact of its founders having overlooked the more delightful and advantageous situation of Byzantium, on the opposite side of the Strait; on

---

QUESTIONS.—By whom were they conquered?—What is the difference between Thyni and Bithyni?—Who lived east of the Sangarius?—Who north-east of the Sangarius?—Who was pro-consul in Bithynia in the beginning of the second century?—Where were the large towns situated?—Name five towns of Bithynia.—What is said of Prusa?—Of what empire did it become the capital?—Where was Nicæa situated?—For what is it celebrated in the history of the church?—Who was born here?—Who was buried at Libyssa?—Where was Chalcedon situated?—Why was it called "the city of the blind?"

the Bosporus there was a temple of JUPITER URIUS, the dispenser of favorable wind (οὖρος).

(6.) Other cities of note were Dascylium, Cius, Heracle'a Pon'tica, and Bithynium, afterwards called Claudiop'olis.

DIVISION XI.

§ 21. GALATIA or GALLO-GRÆCIA.

(*Γαλατία* or *Γαλλογραικία.*)

Name.—This country derived its name GALATIA from the settlement of a large body of *Gauls* in it (279 B. C.). In consequence of some dissensions in the army with which Brennus invaded Greece, a considerable number of the troops left their countrymen and marched into Thrace; thence they proceeded to Byzantium, and crossed over into Asia at the invitation of Nicome'des, king of Bithynia, who was anxious to secure their assistance against his brother Zibœtes. With their aid, Nicome'des was successful, and the Gauls received a considerable share of the conquest. After being subdued by A'ttalus I. of Per'gamus, they settled themselves permanently (239 B. C.) in the north of Phrygia and Cappadocia, where, having mingled with some Grecian colonies, the country they inhabited obtained the name of GALLO-GRÆCIA, or GALATIA.

Boundaries.—North, PAPHLAGONIA and BITHYNIA; East, PONTUS; South, CAPPADOCIA and LYCAONIA; West, PHRYGIA.

Divisions.—It was divided among three tribes; each tribe was subdivided into four parts, and each of these twelve divisions was governed by a tetrarch, who appointed all other magistrates and military officers. In the time of Theodosius the Great, Galatia

QUESTIONS.—What temple was in its neighborhood?——§ 21. Whence did Galatia derive its name?—How did these Gauls come to Asia Minor?—*Who was Brennus?*—Describe the course of the Gauls from Greece to the northern parts of Phrygia.—How was Galatia bounded?—How divided?—How subdivided?—How was it divided in the time of Theodosius the Great?

was subdivided into two provinces—GALATIA PRIMA; Capital, ANCY'RA. GALATIA SECUNDA; Capital, PESSI'NUS.

Mountains.—OLYMPUS, and DIN'DYMUS, where Cy'bele was worshipped, hence called *Dindyme'ne.*

> *Non Dindymene, non adytis quatit*
> *Mentem sacerdotum incola Pythius*
> *Non Liber æque.*—Hor. Od. i. 16, 5.

Rivers.—SANGARIUS and HALYS, which traversed it from South to North.

Productions.—The natural productions were wheat, barley, and forests of valuable timber. Of domestic animals, sheep and cattle were reared in abundance.

Inhabitants.—When the GALLI settled in the country, it was inhabited by PHRYGIANS, GREEKS, PAPHLAGONIANS, and probably a few CAPPADOCIANS. The PHRYGIANS formed the largest element, and occupied the Western portion of the centre of Galatia. The GREEKS were also numerous at the time of the Gallic occupation; their language became the common language of the country. The three Gallic tribes were TROCMI, TECTOS'AGES, and TOLISTO'BOGI. They were a nation of herdsmen, shepherds, and cultivators of the soil, and continued to speak the Keltic language even in the days of St. Jerome, six hundred years after their emigration. St. Paul's epistle to the Galatians was not addressed to them, but to the Greek inhabitants of Galatia, and some of the *hellenized* Galli.

Cities.—(1.) PESSI'NUS (*Πεσσινοῦς*) North-east of the river SANGARIUS, near Phrygia, a considerable trading point, with a magnificent temple, sacred to the mother of the gods, who was

---

QUESTIONS.—Name the mountains.—Who was worshipped at Mount Dindymus?—What were the principal rivers?—The productions.—What inhabitants did the country contain before the settlement of the Gauls?—What nation was the most numerous?—What became the language of the country?—Name the three Gallic tribes.—What kind of people were they?—What language did they speak?—To whom was St. Paul's epistle to the Galatians addressed?—Name the chief towns.—Where was Pessinus situated?—What temple was there?

there worshipped under the name of Agdistis. The famous image of the goddess, which was believed to have fallen from heaven, was carried to Rome in the time of the second Punic war, and there worshipped under the name of Cyb′ele.

(2.) Gordium (*Γόρδιον*), formerly the capital of the Phrygian monarchy. Here Alexander cut the Gordian knot, respecting which there was an ancient tradition, that the person who could untie it should possess the empire of Asia.

CUTTING THE GORDIAN KNOT.

(3.) Ancy′ra (*Ἄγκυρα*) (*Angouri*), from whence the celebrated shawls and hosiery made of goat's hair were originally brought. Here was discovered (1544 A. D.) the celebrated Monumentum Ancyra′num, a copy made on marble slabs of the bronze records at Rome, of the life of Augustus.

(4.) Gangra (*Γάγγρα*), the residence of Cicero's friend, king Deiotarus.

(5.) Tavium (*Ταουΐον*), a place of considerable commercial importance, situated in the eastern part of the country.

Questions.—What is said of the image of the goddess?—What is said of Gordium?—What was the chief manufacture of Ancyra?—What is the Monumentum Ancyranum?—What is said of Gangra?—What of Tavium?

DIVISION XII.

§ 22. PHRYGIA WITH LYCAONIA. (*Φρυγία, Λυκαονία.*)

Boundaries.—PHRYGIA, or, more properly, PHRYGIA MAJOR, formed the central country of Asia Minor. On the North were BITHYNIA and PAPHLAGONIA; on the East, CAPPADOCIA; on the South, PISIDIA and CILICIA; on the West, MYSIA, LYDIA, CARIA. The eastern boundary was formed by the river HALYS, the southern by Mount TAURUS. Formerly Galatia also belonged to it (see § 21). The Mysian coast, from the river CIUS to SESTUS, was called PHRYGIA MINOR, or Phrygia Hellespontus, from which circumstance the Roman poets constantly called the Trojans *Phrygians.*

Divisions.—North, VALLEY OF THE SANGARIUS, the most important part; it was also called Phrygia Epicte'tus (*ἐπίκτητος,* i. e. *acquired in addition*); South, PARORIOS (*Παρόριος,* i. e. *adjacent to the mountains*), which was a high table-land; West, KATAKEKAU'MENE (*Κατακεκαυμένη χώρα,* i. e. *the burnt country*), lay partly in Phrygia, partly in Lydia; it contained districts of the greatest beauty, and was the most populous part, but suffered severely from earthquakes; East, LYCAONIA, a rugged district in the South-east, united during the Persian monarchy with the satrapy of Cappadocia, but in Strabo's time, a part of Phrygia.

QUESTIONS.—§ 22. How is Phrygia bounded?—In what part of Asia Minor was it situated?—What river formed the eastern boundary?—What mountain-chain the southern?—What country formerly belonged to it?—Where is Phrygia Minor situated?—Why did the Roman poets call the Trojans "Phrygians?"—What part of Phrygia was the most important?—Why was it called Epictetus?—What does the name Parorios signify?—What part of Phrygia was so called?—How was the western part of Phrygia called?—What does that name signify?—What is said about it?—Name the three principal parts of Phrygia.—Where was Lycaonia situated?—To what satrapy did it belong during the Persian dominion?

Mountains.—PHRYGIA is a high table-land, extending on the south to Mount TAURUS, and on the north to the high range of mountains which runs from west to east, under the names of IDA and TEMNON in Mysia, and OLYMPUS in Bithynia.

Lakes.—The country in the southern and eastern parts is covered with salt marshes, or lakes. Of these salt-lakes, the most curious is the one called TATTA (*Tus* or *Tuzla*), which is forty-five miles in length, and supplies a vast tract of country with salt.

Rivers.—HERMUS, MÆANDER; MARSYAS, on whose banks the musician of that name is said to have been flayed alive by Apollo (Xen. Anab. 1, 2, 8); SANGARIUS, LYCUS.

Productions.—The country was rich in minerals, gold, and marble. It was famous for its wine and sheep. King Amyntas is said to have kept no less than 300 flocks of sheep. The Phrygian wool was very celebrated.

Inhabitants.—The Phrygians, who are generally described as the most ancient inhabitants of Asia Minor, came, most probably, from the Armenian highlands. TROJANS, MYSIANS, MÆONIANS, etc., were all branches of the great Phrygian race. Their name signified, in the Lydian tongue, *freemen*. The nation, though bearing this name, appears from historic records to have been of a pacific disposition, and unable to resist foreign impressions and influences. It deserves remark that the Phrygians never took or exacted an oath. In very early times a highly civilized people, they subsequently became proverbial both for their servility and stupidity.

Cities.—The most important cities were situated in the South-Western part.

QUESTIONS.—What is said about the mountains of Phrygia?—What about the lakes?—What is said about the lake Tatta?—Name the five principal rivers.—What of the river Marsyas?—What was the chief produce of Phrygia?—What is said of the origin of the Phrygians?—What nations belonged to the Phrygian race?—What did their name signify?—Did they really deserve that name?—What was the state of civilization among the Phrygians?—In what part of the country were its most important cities situated?

(1.) LAODICE'A (*Λαοδίκεια*), (*Ladik*), one of the seven churches mentioned in the book of *Revelation*. It was celebrated for its sheep.

(2.) CIB'YRA (*Κιβύρα*), a considerable trading city. It possessed a greatly mixed population. In Strabo's time no less than five languages were spoken there. The town was the capital of the district Cibyra'tis, which was governed by native princes.

(3.) CELÆNÆ (*Κελαιναί*), one of the most ancient cities near the sources of the rivers Mæander (which took its rise in the palace) and Catarrhactes. It was one of the residences of Cyrus the Younger, who had there a palace and a park full of wild animals (*παράδεισος*).

(4.) SYN'NADA (*Σύνναδα*), a small town which, during the time of the Roman Empire, rose to a place of considerable commerce and traffic. It was situated on the highroads to Galatia and Cilicia. Near Syn'nada, the Lapis Synnad'icus, a beautiful kind of white marble, with red spots, was procured; slabs and columns of it were frequently transported as far as Rome.

(5.) IPSUS (*Ἴψος*) lies toward the west of Celænæ; here the battle was fought between the surviving generals of Alexander (301 B.C.).

(6.) COLOSSÆ (*Κολοσσαί*). St. Paul addressed one of his Epistles to this place. It was destroyed by an earthquake, together with Hierap'olis and Laodice'a, in the ninth year of the reign of Nero, but was rebuilt and became, during the middle ages, a place of considerable importance under the name of CHONÆ.

(7.) Other cities worthy of mention were Dorylæum, Amorium, Antiochi'a (later, Cæsare'a), Seleuci'a, Cibo'tus (later, Apame'a), Hierap'olis, Eumenia, Cadi, Æza'ni, and Cotyæum.

QUESTIONS.—Name six principal towns of Phrygia.—What is said of Laodicea?—What of Cibyra?—How many languages were spoken there?—Where was Celænæ situated?—Who possessed a palace there?—What is said of Synnada?—What was found in its neighborhood?—What is said of Ipsus?—How did Colossæ become celebrated?—How was it destroyed?—What towns were destroyed with it?—What was its name during the middle ages?

LYCAONIA contained the following small towns: LAODICE'A COMBUSTA, ANTIOCHI'A, ICONIUM, DERBE, and LYSTRA. These last three places are mentioned by St. Luke (*Acts*, xiii. xiv.). Iconium rose afterwards to great power and importance. In the middle ages it was the most important city of Asia Minor, and was very celebrated at the time of the Crusades.

§ 23. PISIDIA WITH ISAURIA. (*Πισιδία, Ἰσαυρία.*)

Though it was nominally treated as a part of Pamphylia till the fourth century, when it was acknowledged as a separate country, it was, in fact, an independent nation, and maintained its liberty while Pamphylia was a Roman province.

Boundaries.—North, PHRYGIA; East, CILICIA and LYCAONIA; South, PAMPHYLIA; West, PHRYGIA, CARIA and LYCIA.

Mountains.—SARDEMI'SUS and CLIMAX, both ranges of the TAURUS.

Rivers.—CESTRUS and EURYM'EDON.

Productions.—Salt (*iris*), from the root of which a perfume was manufactured. The wine of Am'blada was also very celebrated.

Inhabitants.—They were hardy and warlike mountaineers. None of the successive rulers of Asia Minor could subdue them in their mountain fastnesses. The Isaurians were nominally conquered by Publius Servilius, in the time of the Mithridatic war, who hence obtained the surname of Isau'ricus (78 B. C.).

Divisions.—The eastern part of PISIDIA was called ISAURIA. The western portion, including the north-east part of Lycia, was called MILYAS.

QUESTIONS.—Name some towns of Lycaonia?—What is said of Iconium?——§ 23. To what part of Asia Minor did Pisidia nominally belong?—What was it in reality?—When was it acknowledged as a separate country?—How was it bounded?—Name the mountains.—The rivers.—The productions.—What is said of the inhabitants?—Who conquered the Isaurians?—Give the date of this conquest.—What name was given to the eastern part?—What name to the western part?

Towns.—(1.) CRETOP'OLIS, situated in the western part of the country. It was, during the Crusades, called Sozop'olis.

(2.) TERMESSUS (*Τερμησσός*), situated in a pass of the Taurus. Alexander the Great was not able to conquer it.

(3.) SELGE (*Σέλγη*), the chief mountain fortress in the interior. It was a colony of the Lacedæmonians.

(4.) ISAURA (*Ἴσαυρα*), the capital of Isauria, a wealthy, populous and well-fortified city. It was once destroyed by its own citizens (322 B. C.), and a second time by the Romans (78 B. C.).

(5.) MILYAS (*Μιλυάς*), the South-Western part of Pisidia, contained the following *four towns:* Cib'yra, Œnoanda, Balbu'ra, and Bubon, which formed the Cibyratian *Tetra'polis*

QUESTIONS.—Give the names of four principal towns.—What is said of Isaura?—What towns constituted the Cibyratian Tetrapolis of Milyas?

ASIA ORIENTA'LIS.

§ **24. Divisions.**—I. The countries between the Euxine and Caspian Seas: (1.) SARMATIA ASIAT'ICA; (2.) COLCHIS, IBERIA, and ALBANIA; (3.) ARMENIA MAJOR.

II. The countries between the Euphra'tes and the Tigris: (1.) MESOPOTAMIA; (2.) BABYLONIA and CHALDÆA.

III. The countries between the Mediterranean and Erythræan Seas: (1.) SYRIA, subdivided into, (*a*) *Syria*, (*b*) *Phœni'ce*, (*c*) *Palæsti'na*; (2.) ARABIA, subdivided into, (*a*) *Petræa*, (*b*) *Deserta*, (*c*) *Felix*.

IV. The countries between the Tigris and the Indus: (1.) ASSYRIA; (2.) MEDIA; (3.) PERSIS; (4.) SUSIA'NA; (5.) ARIA'NA.

V. The countries east of the Indus: (1.) INDIA; (2.) SE'RICA; (3.) SINÆ.

VI. The countries between the Caspian Sea and Scythia: (1.) HYRCANIA; (2.) MARGIA'NA; (3.) BACTRIA'NA; (4.) SOGDIA'NA.

VII. SCYTHIA.

§ 25. SARMATIA ASIAT'ICA. (ἡ ἐν Ἀσίᾳ Σαρματία.)

Boundaries.—SARMATIA was the name of a large country lying in Europe and Asia. The boundaries of the Asiatic portion are as follows: on the North, AN UNKNOWN COUNTRY;

QUESTIONS.—§ 24. What name is given to the other part of Asia?—Into how many natural parts is it divided?—Name the countries between the Euxine and Caspian Seas.—Between the Euphrates and Tigris.—Between the Mediterranean and Erythræan Seas.—Between the Tigris and Indus.—Name the countries east of the Indus.—Between the Caspian Sea and Scythia?——§ 25. What is said about Sarmatia?—What are the boundaries of Sarmatia Asiatica?

5*

East, SCYTHIA and the CASPIAN SEA; South, The CAU'CASUS; West, CIMMERIAN BOS'PORUS, PALUS MÆO'TIS, and TANAIS.

Mountains.—MONTES CORA'XICI and HIP'PICI; and MONTES HYPERBOREI (*Ural*).

Rivers.—TANAIS (*Don*); ANTICI'TES (*Kuban*); RHA (*Wolga*).

Towns.—There existed only a few Greek colonies on the coast of the Palus Mæo'tis. (1.) PHANAGORIA, situated on the Asiatic coast of the Cimmerian Bos'porus, which became afterwards the residence of the kings of Bos'porus; (2.) PITYU'SA, SINDA (*Anapa*), CEPUS.

§ 26. COLCHIS, IBERIA, AND ALBANIA.

Boundaries.—North, CAU'CASUS and SARMATIA; East, CASPIAN SEA; South, ARMENIA; West, EUXINE.

Divisions.—I. COLCHIS, on the shore of the Euxine. The greater part of this small territory was covered by marshes, and throughout its entire extent heavy rains were of frequent occurrence. The plains were intersected by numerous channels, on the banks of which the inhabitants built their dwellings, which were generally supported on wooden piles. This province was the celebrated scene of the fable of the Golden Fleece and the Argonautic expedition.

II. ALBANIA (*'Αλβανία*) was situated on the western shores of the Caspian Sea. It is rich in rivers and extremely fertile, but its inhabitants were warlike, and neglected the culture of the soil.

III. IBERIA (*'Ιβηρία*). A district surrounded on all sides by mountains through which there were only four passes. It comprised the central part of the country between the Euxine and

---

QUESTIONS.—Name the mountains.—The rivers?—What is said of the towns?—Name some of their towns.——§ 26. Where are Colchis, Iberia, and Albania situated?—Where was Colchis situated?—What is said of Colchis?—Where is Albania situated?—What is said of Albania?—Where is Iberia situated?—What is said of Iberia?

Caspian seas. It was very fertile; hence its modern name, *Georgia*, derived from the Greek γεωργεῖν, *to till the earth*.

Mountains.—CAU'CASUS, and the MONTES MOS'CHICI.

Passes.—PYLÆ CAUCASIÆ, *the Gates of the Cau'casus* (*Pass of Dariel*), lying about midway between the Euxine and Caspian Seas; PYLÆ ALBANIÆ or CASPIÆ, known in history as the *Iron Gate*, now *Derbent*.

Rivers.—PHASIS, in Colchis, CYRUS, AR'AGUS, CAMBY'SES, and ARAXES, in Iberia and Albania.

Productions.—Gold, timber, flax, oil, and wine. The linen of Colchis was very celebrated.

Inhabitants.—Various tribes, differing in degrees of civilization. The inhabitants of Colchis attained, by means of commerce, a degree of opulence and culture which rendered them very widely celebrated in ancient times.

Cities.—In Colchis; PHASIS, whence came the *aves Phasia'næ*, *pheasants*. CYTA, the birthplace of Mede'a, who from this circumstance is called *Cytæis*.

In Iberia; HARMOZI'CA, and in Albania; ALBA'NA (*Derbent*).

§ 27. ARMENIA MAJOR.

('Αρμενία ἡ μεγάλη, *or*, 'Αρμενία ἡ ἰδίως καλουμένη)

Boundaries.—North, ALBANIA, IBERIA, COLCHIS, and PONTUS; East, MEDIA; South, MESOPOTAMIA and ASSYRIA; West, ARMENIA MINOR.

Divisions.—It was divided into fifteen provinces and one hundred and eighty-seven subdivisions.

QUESTIONS.—Whence is its modern name derived?—What mountains traverse those three countries?—Name the two celebrated passes of the Caucasus.—Name the rivers.—The chief productions.—For what is Colchis celebrated?—What is said about the inhabitants?—Whence do pheasants derive their name?—Why is Medea called Cytæis?—Name one city of Colchis, of Iberia, and of Albania.——§ 27. What are the boundaries of Armenia?—How was it divided and subdivided?

Mountains.—The country is intersected by numerous ranges of mountains, of which the chief peak is AR'ARAT, from which the mountain ranges diverge. It is nearly equidistant from the BLACK and CASPIAN seas. The principal of these mountain ranges are: PARY'ADRUS, MONTES MOSCHI'CI, MONS CAPOTES.

Rivers.—A number of rivers are constantly fed by the snow with which the high mountains are covered. The most important are the HALYS, ARAXES, ACAMPSIS, TIGRIS, CENTRI'TES, and EUPHRA'TES.

Lakes.—LACUS ARSE'NE and LACUS LYCHNI'TIS.

Productions.—The country is in many parts exceedingly fertile as well as highly picturesque, especially near the shores of the Araxes. It is principally distinguished for its horses, precious stones and metals, grain, oil, and wine.

Climate.—Owing to the height of the table-land, and the extreme elevation of the mountains, the temperature is much lower than in other regions situated on the same parallel of latitude.

Inhabitants.—The Armenians were one of the most ancient branches of the Indo-Germanic family. They carried on a considerable trade with the southern nations, especially with the Phœnicians.

Cities.—ARTAX'ATA, a celebrated city strongly fortified, and usually the residence of the kings; TIGRANOCERTA, built by Tigra'nes during the Mithridatic war, and afterward taken by Lucullus; AR'XATA, the ancient capital of Media; Armo'sata or Arsamos'ata, A'mida, Theodosiop'olis.

QUESTIONS.—What is said of the mountains?—What of Mount Ararat?—What is said of the rivers?—Name some of the larger rivers.—Name two large lakes.—What is said of the productions?—What of the climate?—To what family of nations did the Armenians belong?—Name some of the most important towns.

§ 28. MESOPOTAMIA. (*Μεσοποταμία.*)

Name.—The name does not occur until about 200 B. C. Under the Persian empire, it formed a division of the satrapy of Babylonia. The name is composed from two Greek words, *μέσος* and *ποταμός*, and signifies a country *between rivers.* In the Sacred Writings it is called *Aram-Naharaim*, i. e. *Syria between the rivers.*

Boundaries.—North, TAURUS and ARMENIA; East, the TIGRIS, which separates it from ASSYRIA; South, MEDIA and BABYLONIA; West, the EUPHRA'TES, which divides it from SYRIA.

Divisions.—*a.* The Northern part was subdivided into the following two parts: OSRHOE'NE, the north-west part, and MYGDONIA or ANTHEMUSIA, the eastern part.

b. The Southern part was subdivided into four parts: CHALCE'TIS, GAUZANI'TIS, ACAB'ENE, and ANCOBARI'TIS.

Mountains.—MASIUS (*Kardscha-Dagh*).

Rivers.—EUPHRA'TES, TIGRIS, CHABO'RAS, and MASCA.

Inhabitants.—They belonged to the Semitic division of the human family.

Productions.—Timber and different kinds of grain; also fruits and spices. Its luxuriant meadows furnished a fine grazing ground for large herds of cattle.

Cities.—(1.) EDESSA (*Urfah*), the capital of *Osrhoe'ne.* In the Scriptures it is called *Ur.*

(2.) BATNÆ, where an annual fair was held for the sale of Indian and Syrian merchandise.

QUESTIONS.—§ 28. Whence is the name derived?—When does the name occur for the first time?—To what satrapy did it belong?—How is it called in the Scriptures?—What are the boundaries?—How was it divided?—How was the northern part subdivided?—How the southern part?—Name the mountains.—Name the rivers.—What is said of the inhabitants?—Describe the productions.—How is Edessa called in the Scriptures?—What is said of Batnæ?

(3.) CIRCESIUM, where Necho, king of Ægypt, was conquered by Nebuchadnezzar (601 B.C.). A little to the south of Circesium was the tomb of the younger Gordian, killed A.D. 245.

(4.) NIS'IBIS, one of the easternmost fortresses of the Roman empire. In the Scriptures it is perhaps called *Zoba*.

(5.) CAR'RHÆ (the *Charran* of the Scriptures), the point from which Abraham departed for the land of Canaan. Here Crassus lost his life in his Parthian expedition (53 B.C.).

Miserando funere Crassus
Assyrias Latio maculavit sanguine Carrhas.—Lucan i. 104.

(6.) Other towns of note were Nicephorium, Phaliga, An'themus, Dura, Resæna, Sin'gara, Atræ, Apame'a.

§ 29. BABYLONIA AND CHALDÆA. (*Βαβυλωνία.*)

It comprehended originally the country in the immediate vicinity of the city of BABYLON, but in later times included the southern part of MESOPOTAMIA. By Greek and Roman writers it is frequently confounded with ASSYRIA and MESOPOTAMIA. In the Sacred Writings it is called *the land of the Chaldees*, and also *the land of Shinar*, the latter designation being the most ancient.

Boundaries.—North, MESOPOTAMIA; East, SUSIA'NA; South, GULF OF PERSIA; West, ARABIA PETRÆA. It was separated from Mesopotamia by the Median wall, which was twenty parasangs in length, twenty feet in breadth, and one hundred in height, firmly built of brick. It was said to have been built by Semir'amis as a protection against the Medes.

Rivers.—EUPHRA'TES and TIGRIS, which were united by

QUESTIONS.—What occurred near Circesium?—What tomb was in its vicinity?—What is said of Nisibis?—What of Carrhæ?——§ 29. What did Babylonia originally comprehend?—With what countries is it often confounded by Greek and Roman writers?—How was it called in the Scriptures?—What were its boundaries?—What separated it from Mesopotamia?—Name its dimensions.—Who built it?—What rivers are in Babylonia?—How are they united?

numerous artificial channels, not excavated like modern canals, but made by earthen embankments constructed on the surface of the ground, four of which were navigable for vessels suited to carry grain. The most important of these aqueducts were: (1.) Naarsares (*Νααρσάρης*), which ran on the West of the Euphra'tes parallel to it: (2.) Naarmalcha, i. e. *the royal river* (*ποταμὸς βασιλεως* or *διῶρυξ βασιλική*), extending from the Euphra'tes to the Tigris.

Productions.—The periodical inundation of the rivers caused a remarkable fertility of soil. Hero'dotus says that the average return of wheat was from two hundredfold to three hundredfold; that millet and sesame grew to a great size; that the gigantic date-palm, the only kind of tree that adorned the land, was indigenous throughout its entire extent; and that bread, wine, and honey were made from the dates.

Climate.—The climate in ancient times was more temperate than it is at present.

Inhabitants.—They are called BABYLONIANS and CHALDÆANS. The latter were originally a distinguished caste among the native population, comprising the priests, magicians, soothsayers, and astrologers of the country—a circumstance which eventually gave name to the main body of the people. The main body, the Babylonians, belonged entirely to the Semitic race. The Chaldæans were a race of conquerors who had come down from the mountain-ranges in the South of Armenia.

Cities.—(1.) SELEUCI'A (*ἡ Σελεύκεια ἐπὶ τῷ Τίγρει*), founded by Seleucus Nica'tor about 322 B. C., a little above Babylon, on the western bank of the Tigris, at the point where the caravans from the East and West met. It was connected with the Euphra'tes by the canal Naarmalcha. This admirable situation made it one of the most flourishing cities of Western Asia. It quickly rose to unusual wealth and splendor, and soon eclipsed Babylon itself.

QUESTIONS.—Name two aqueducts.—Describe Babylonia.—What is said about the climate?—What is the difference between Babylonians and Chaldæans?—Who formed the ruling caste?—What is said of Seleucia?

The Parthian kings founded CTES'IPHON on the opposite side, and deprived Seleuci'a of some of its advantages. Nevertheless, the latter city contained, in the time of Titus (80 A. D.), still 600,000 inhabitants. In the wars between the Parthians and Romans, both cities were often taken and burnt. They are now called AL MODAIN, i. e. *the two cities*.

(2.) CUNAXA (*Κούναξα*), a small town on the eastern bank of the Euphra'tes, where Cyrus the Younger was defeated and slain by his brother Artaxerxes (401 B. C.).

(3.) SIT'ACE (*Σιτάκη*), a flourishing city near the western bank of the Tigris.

The southern part of Babylonia bore the name of Chaldæa. It contained many flourishing towns; the most celebrated among them are: (1.) BORSIPPA (*Βόρσιππα, Boursa*), situated to the south of Babylon, and noted as the chief residence of the Chaldæan astrologers. It was also noted for its manufactures of linen. (2.) ORCHOË (*Ὀρχόη*), the native appellation of which was UR.

§ 30. BA'BYLON. (*Βαβυλών.*)

Babylon was one of the most ancient cities in the world, and the capital of the Babylonio-Chaldæan empire. It extended along *both* sides of the Euphra'tes, which divided it in the centre. The city was quadrangular in shape, each side 120 stadia in length (15 miles). It was surrounded by a wall of 50 cubits thick, and 200 cubits high, and also by a wide ditch. Each half of the city was further protected by a second brick wall running parallel with the outer wall. At the river edge the two walls were connected by masonry built parallel with the river. The streets were straight, and intersected each other at right

---

QUESTIONS.—In what battle was Cyrus the Younger defeated?—In what year?—What name did the southern part of Babylonia bear?—What towns did it contain?——§ 30. Of what empire was Babylon the capital?—What river flowed through the city?—In what form was it built?—How many walls surrounded it?—Describe the outer wall.—Describe the inner wall.—How were the streets laid out?

angles. On the river side they were closed by gates of brass. The two parts of the city were connected by a bridge. The houses were built three and four stories in height. Each half of the city contained a celebrated building within a spacious enclosure: in the eastern part was the royal palace; in the western the temple of Belus, which consisted of a series of eight towers, one built upon another. The so called hanging gardens, were terraces rising one above another, covered with earth and laid out as gardens; and are generally considered as one of the wonders of the ancient world. Babylon was at the height of its glory in the beginning of the seventh century B. C., when it became the capital of the eastern world. Under Nebuchad-

HANGING GARDENS.

QUESTIONS.—How many bridges connected the two parts of the city?—What building was contained in the eastern part of the city?—What building in the western part?—What was the temple of Belus or Baal?—What is said of the hanging gardens?—When did it become the capital of the eastern world?

nezzar, its power was extended over all the countries lying between Persia and Egypt. But it was taken by the Persians in 538 B. C., according to the prediction of the Jewish prophets. Two centuries later it opened its gates to Alexander the Great, who deemed the city not unworthy to become the capital of his mighty empire. But after the foundation of Seleuci'a (322 B. C.), it was abandoned by many of its inhabitants. The inhabitants of Babylon were noted for their luxury and great licentiousness.

§ 31. SYRIA.

Name.—The classical name for the country was SYRIA. Its ancient native appellation was ARAM, and it is known in modern times as *Esh-Sham.* In its widest sense it embraced, in the East, both Mesopotamia and Assyria, and extended Westward to the Mediterranean and Egypt.

Boundaries.—North, separated from CILICIA by the range of AMA'NUS and TAURUS; East, from MESOPOTAMIA and BABYLONIA by the EUPHRA'TES; South, THE GREAT DESERT OF ARABIA; West, the MEDITERRANEAN.

Divisions.—SYRIA, PHŒNI'CE, and PALÆSTI'NA.

SYRIA. (*Συρία.*)

Boundaries.—North, CILICIA; East, MESOPOTAMIA and BABYLONIA; South, ARABIA; West, PALÆSTI'NA, PHŒNI'CE, and the MEDITERRANEAN.

Mountains.—TAURUS, AMA'NUS, CASIUS, LIB'ANUS; and

QUESTIONS.—Over what countries did it extend its sway?—When was it taken by the Persians?—When by Alexander the Great?—When did the city decline?—What is said about the vices of the citizens? ——§ 31. What is the native appellation of Syria?—What did it include, according to the classical authors?—Name the chief divisions. —What are the boundaries of Syria in its restricted sense?—Name the principal mountains.

east from it, ANTILIB'ANUS, which is considerably higher than the LIB'ANUS. In the Scriptures no distinction is made between Lib'anus and Antilib'anus; both are comprised under the name of *Lebanon.*

Rivers.—ORONTES, CAP'PADOX, CHRYSORRHOAS or BARDI'NES, and CHALUS.

Productions.—The Northern part of the country was more fertile than the Southern. The chief productions were timber, grain, rice, figs, dates, wine, cotton, assafœtida. Of domestic animals, sheep and cattle were raised in abundance. The valleys of the North and South were, in ancient times, far more fertile than they are now; and the Eastern part, which formerly contained many cities, forms now part of the desert. Lebanon was long noted for its splendid forests of cedar trees, of which only a few small groves remain.

Inhabitants.—The population consists of agricultural and nomadic tribes which belong to the Aramæan branch of the Semitic race. This branch comprises the whole population between Egypt, the Mediterranean, the Halys, the Euxine, and the mountain ranges of the Zagrus and Paracho'athras. The Syrians were successively under Hebrew (in the reign of David), Assyrian, Babylonian, Persian, and Macedonian dominion. After the beginning of the fourth century, B. C., it formed the nucleus of the great empire of the Seleu'cidæ. This empire comprised, under its founder, the greater part of Asia, from the remote provinces of Bactria and Sogdia'na to the coasts of Phœnicia, and from the Paropami'sus to the central plains of Phrygia. After an existence of upwards of 200 years, it was conquered by Tigra'nes (79 B. C.), with whose dominions it was, fifteen years later, added to the Roman empire (64 B. C.).

QUESTIONS.—What is said of the name Lebanon?—Name the rivers.—Name the productions.—What is said of the Syrians?—To what race do they belong?—To what branch of that race?—Under what dominion were the Syrians?—When did it form the nucleus of the empire of the Seleucidæ?—Name the boundaries of that empire?—When was it added to the Roman empire?

Divisions.—I. In the earliest times, Syria was divided into a number of independent states among which DAMASCUS was the most powerful.

II. Under the Macedonians the country was divided into two parts, Mount Lebanon constituting the boundary between them:

a. The northern part, called SYRIA PROPER, or UPPER SYRIA.

b. The southern part, called CŒLE SYRIA (ἡ κοίλη Συρία, i. e., *Hollow Syria, the Syrian Vale*).

III. Under the Romans the northern part was divided into the following nine districts: COMMAGE'NE, CYRRHES'TICE, PIERIA, SELEUCIS, CHALCID'ICE, CHALYBONI'TIS, PALMYRE'NE, APAME'NE, and CASIO'TIS.

IV. After Theodosius the Great, into SYRIA PRIMA and SYRIA SECUNDA.

§ **32. Cities.**—(1.) In COMMAGE'NE:

a. SAMOS'ATA (Σαμόσατα), situated on the right bank of the Euphrates, the capital of COMMAGE'NE, and the birthplace of Lucian.

b. Other towns: GERMANICIA, DOL'ICHE, and ANTIOCHI'A AD TAURUM.

(2.) In CYRRHES'TICE:

a. HIERAP'OLIS (Ἱερὰ πόλις, i. e. *sacred city*), was called MABOG by the natives. Under the Seleu'cidæ, Syria, from its central position between Antioch and Seleuci'a, on the delta of the Tigris, became a great emporium. It was the chief seat of the worship of the Syrian goddess, Astarte, the mythic personification of the passive powers of nature

b. Other towns: BERŒA (*Aleppo*), ZEUGI'NA, GIN'DARUS.

QUESTIONS.—How was Syria divided in the earliest times?—How under the Macedonians?—How under the Romans?—How after Theodosius the Great?——§ 32. What is said of Samosata?—What was the native appellation of Hierapolis?—What goddess was worshipped at Hierapolis?

(3.) In SELEU'CIS, or the Tetra'polis:

a. SELEUCI'A PIERIA (Σελεύκεια Πιερία), situated on the sea between Cilicia and Phœnice, to the north of the mouth of the Orontes, and at the southern extremity of Mount Pieria. It was founded by Seleucus (300 B. C.), who was himself buried here in a splendid mausole'um.

b. ANTIOCHI'A AD ORONTEM (Ἀντιόχεια ἐπὶ Ὀρόντῃ or Δάφνῃ, i. e. *on the Orontes* or *by Daphne*), situated on the left bank of the Orontes. It was the capital of the Greek kings of Syria, and one of the most important cities of the ancient world. Here the disciples of our Lord were first called Christians, and it was one of the earliest strongholds of the Christian religion.

c. The two other cities of the Tetra'polis were APAME'A and LAODICE'A These four cities were called the sister-cities, being all founded by Seleucus Nica'tor, and called by the names respectively of himself, his father, his wife, and his mother-in-law; that bearing his father's name being the largest, that bearing his own, the strongest.

(4.) In APAME'NE:

E'MESA (Ἔμεσα), situated on the eastern bank of the Orontes, where there was a famous temple of Heliogab'alus (or of the Sun), a priest of which, only a youth of fourteen, was made emperor by the licentious Roman soldiers (A. D. 218). In its neighborhood Zenobia was defeated by the emperor Aurelian (273 A. D.).

(5.) In CŒLE SYRIA:

a BAALBEC, or HELIO'POLIS (Ἡλιούπολις; in Hebrew, *Baalath*), where are still to be seen the ruins of a most magnificent temple of Baal (whom the Greeks identified with Helios, or the Sun), built by Antoni'nus Pius.

b. DAMASCUS (Δαμασκός), one of the most ancient and cele-

QUESTIONS.—Name the four sister-cities founded by Seleucus.—What is said about their names?—Where was Seleucia situated?—When was it founded?—What was the capital of the Greek kings of Syria?—For what was Emessa famous?—What is said of Baalbec?

brated cities of all Asia. It was beautifully situated in the valley of the Chrysorrhoas, one of the most fertile of the Syrian plains. The famous manufactory of Damascus blades was established there by Diocletian.

§ 33. PALMY'RA. (*Πάλμυρα.*)

It was situated in an O'asis of the Syrian desert, nearly midway between the rivers ORONTES and EUPHRA'TES. Its names, PALMY'RA and TADMOR, derive their origin from the palm-trees which once adorned its neighborhood. In 2 *Chronicles*, viii. 4, we read that Solomon "built TADMOR in the wilderness." This city was most probably destroyed by Nebuchadnezzar. But soon a new TADMOR arose, which, in the time of Pliny (A. D. 100), was the chief emporium of traffic between the Eastern and Roman empires. It afterward became allied to the Roman empire as a free state, and was greatly favored by the Antonines, under whom it attained its greatest splendor (A D. 150). ODENA'THUS, a native of Palmy'ra, assumed afterward (A. D. 250), with the consent of the Romans, the title of king. He drove (A. D. 260) the Persians out of Syria, and for this service was rewarded by Gallie'nus with the title of Augustus. After his death (A. D. 266) his wife, ZENOBIA, a woman of heroic valor and extraordinary endowments, both of mind and body, assumed the title of *Queen of the East*, and asserted her sovereignty over Mesopotamia and Syria. She opposed the emperor Aurelian, whom she nearly defeated on the plains of Syria, at the head of 700,000 men, but was finally forced to succumb, and carried captive to Italy (A. D. 273), where she had large possessions, suitable to her imperial rank, assigned her near

QUESTIONS.—In what valley was Damascus situated?——§ 33. Where is Palmyra situated?—Whence is the name derived?—How is it called in the Scriptures?—When did it attain its greatest splendor?—When did Odenathus assume the title of king?—When did he receive the title of Augustus?—Of whom?—When did he die?—Who succeeded him?—What was her design?—Who defeated her?—Where?—When?

ZENOBIA.

Tibur. Her minister, or secretary of state, was the celebrated Longi'nus, the author of the well-known critical treatise, *On the Sublime*. He fell a sacrifice to the fury of the Roman soldiery on the capture of the city, which was ruthlessly plundered, and afterward partially destroyed during an insurrection of its citizens. It has been in a ruined and desolate state during the last four or five centuries, ever since its capture and pillage in 1400 by the army of Tamerlane. The ancient site is still occupied by a small tribe of Bedouin Arabs, who have built their hovels in the peristyle of the great temple.

§ 34. PHŒNI'CE. (*Φοινίκη.*)

Name.—By the classic Greek and Roman authors it was called PHŒNI'CE; by later writers, PHŒNICIA. Its signification is literally *the land of palms,* the name being directly derived from the Greek word *φοίνιξ*, *a palm.* By the Phœnicians

QUESTIONS.—Who was her secretary?—What is said of him?—Describe the present state of the city.——§ 34. What does the name *Phœnice* signify?

themselves, and by their neighbors of the land of Israel, it was called CANAAN, i. e. *Low-land.*

Boundaries.—Even in the most flourishing period of its history, it was insignificant in size, being nowhere more than twelve miles in breadth. It extended along the eastern coast of the Mediterranean, from the town of AR'ADUS and the river ELEU'THERUS on the north, to Mount CARMEL, or DORA, on the south. It was bounded on the east by the LIB'ANUS and ANTILIB'ANUS.

Division.—It was divided into several small independent kingdoms, or rather cities, which were sometimes united together, and at other times in hostility to each other.

Mountains.—LIB'ANUS.

Capes.—PROMONTORIUM ALBUM (*Cape Blanc*); CARMEL.

Rivers.—Numerous rivers had their source in the LIB'ANUS, and rendered the land exceedingly fertile; the principal of them were the ELEU'THERUS, SABBA'TICUS, ADO'NIS, LEO or LEONTES.

Productions.—Cedar, pine, fir, and cypress; corn, peaches, grapes, oranges, figs, dates, and other fruits; sugar, cotton, and silk; iron and copper.

Climate.—The climate is sensibly affected by the close proximity of LEBANON, whose summits are capped with snow during the greater part of the year. Hence the temperature is much lower than is usually found in corresponding latitudes.

Inhabitants.—They were a branch of the great Semitic family of nations, and originally dwelt either on the Red Sea or the Persian Gulf. They surpassed all the other nations of antiquity in commercial enterprise. They were also the inventors of glass, of purple dye, of coinage, and of the alphabetic characters which afterward were adopted in the languages of Europe.

QUESTIONS.—What is the literal meaning of *Canaan?*—How was it bounded?—How divided?—Name the mountain range.—Name the capes.—What is said of the rivers?—Name some of the productions?—What is said of the climate?—Why is the temperature lower than might be expected from the latitude?—What is said of the inhabitants?

Cities.—The brief extent of sea-coast was dotted with numerous towns, which were more or less celebrated for their arts and manufactures.

(1.) AR'ADUS (*Ἄραδος*: in the Hebrew, *Arvad*), situated on an island in the northern part, founded by exiles from Sidon. In the time of the Seleu'cidæ it was the third city in magnitude and importance, being outrivalled only by Tyrus and Sidon.

(2.) TRIP'OLIS (*Τρίπολις*, *Tripoli*) consisted of *three* distinct *towns*, founded respectively by TYRE, SIDON, and A'RADUS.

(3.) BERY'TUS (*Beirut*), a very ancient town, celebrated for its law school.

(4.) ACA, later PTOLEMA'IS (*St. Jean d'Acre*), which the Israelites did not succeed in conquering, though it was included in the division of the Holy Land made by Joshua.

(5.) Other towns of note were Byblus, Sarepta, Tyrus, and Sidon. (See below.)

§ 35. SIDON (*Σιδών*) AND TYRUS (*Τύρος*).

SIDON was a very ancient and important maritime city of PHŒNICIA. It stood on the coast of the Mediterranean, in a plain nearly a mile in breadth. It possessed a fine harbor, and, at a very early period, became distinguished for its immense commerce. Joshua speaks of it, as early as 1444 B. C., as *Great Sidon*.

It was renowned for its glass, which was made from the fine sand on the coast near Mount Carmel. Its inhabitants are also often mentioned in the Bible as skilful builders. They paid religious worship to the goddess *Ashtaroth*, whose image is commonly found upon Phœnician coins. During the earlier periods of Phœnician history, Sidon appears to have been the

---

QUESTIONS.—Name four Phœnician cities.—What is said of Aradus?—Of Tripolis?—What celebrated school was at Berytus?—What is said of Aca?——§ 35. Where was Sidon situated?—What was the chief article of manufacture?—What goddess was worshipped at Sidon?—When was Sidon the chief city of Phœnicia?

first city in point of importance; but after its capture by the king of A'scalon and the subsequent emigration of many of its inhabitants, Tyre became dominant, and retained the supremacy until the Persian conquest. In 352 B. C., it resolved to throw off the Persian yoke. The loss of a large fleet, and of forty thousand lives, was the result. The cruelty of the Persians left a painful remembrance which was not wholly effaced when

SIDON.

twenty years later, Alexander having entered Phœnicia, Sidon hastened to open her gates to him. After Alexander's death, it was subject alternately to the kings of Egypt and Syria, until it finally fell under Roman sway.

TYRUS.

TYRUS was the most celebrated city of Phœnicia. By the Israelites it was called TSOR, *Rock*, but by the Tyrians them-

---

QUESTIONS.—In what year was the attempt made to throw off the Persian yoke?—What was the result of it?—What is said of Sidon in connection with Alexander?—What was Tyrus called by the Israelites?—By the Tyrians?

selves SOR, or SUR, as its ruins are still called. It was a colony of Sidon, but it soon exceeded the mother-city in importance. It was built partly on an island, partly on the mainland. That part which lay on the mainland was called PALÆ'-TYRUS, or *Old Tyre.* The island contained only forty acres. The smallness of this area was, however, compensated by the great height of the houses. The island-city was much improved by King Hiram, the celebrated friend of Solomon. Its powerful navies found ample and admirable accommodation in two excellent harbors, one on the north, the other on the south side of the island.

Tyrus was repeatedly besieged; by Shalmane'ser (B. C. 727), Nebuchadnezzar (B. C. 595), Alexander (B. C. 333), and Anti'gonus (B. C. 315). The attack of Alexander was the most remarkable. The city, famed for its merchant princes, sustained a seven months' siege, and was only entered by the conqueror after a mole, or causeway, had been built, connecting the island with the mainland. The city was burnt, and most of the inhabitants either killed or sold into slavery. It was repeopled by Carians. Eighteen years sufficed to restore in a great measure its ancient wealth and power; but it had a formidable rival to encounter in Alexandri'a. Under the Roman empire it rose to metropolitan glory, and its harbor became the most important naval station on the Syrian coast. The staple manufacture of Phœnicia was the *purple* dye, produced from an animal juice, found in a shell-fish called in Greek, πορφύρα; in Latin, *púrpura* or *murex.* The superiority of the Tyrian purple depended on the quality of the fish, which varied on different coasts, and probably also on some chemical secret. The trade was confined to Tyre; under the Roman dominion Tyre enjoyed the exclusive privilege of manufacturing the imperial purple.

QUESTIONS.—Describe Tyrus.—Who improved the island-city?—How many harbors did it contain?—How often was Tyrus besieged?—By whom?—Which was the most remarkable siege?—How long did that siege last?—By what nation was Tyrus repeopled?—What became its rival?—What is said of the staple manufacture of Phœnicia?

Colonies.—Starting from a narrow coast on the Syrian sea, the Phœnicians visited all the shores of the Mediterranean; they peopled Thasos and many other islands in the vicinity of Greece; they made settlements also in Bœotia, the north of Africa, and on the coast of Spain. Their principal colonies were CYPRUS, RHODES, the CYC'LADES, a certain portion of GREECE (*Bœotia*), parts of Asia Minor (BITHYNIA), the north-west corner of SICILY, MEL'ITE (*Malta*), SARDINIA, SOUTHERN SPAIN (*Tartessus*), CASSITE'RIDES (the *tin*-islands—κασσίτερος, *tin*—now probably the *Scilly Islands* on the coast of *Cornwall*), and the middle part of the northern coast of Africa, where they founded U'TICA, LEPTIS, HIPPO, HADRUME'TUM, and CARTHA'GO.

§ 36. PALÆSTI'NA.

Though for a long period shut up within the confines of a limited territory, and exposed to the antipathy and contempt of more powerful and cultivated nations, the people of Palestine, after the fall of their capital, exerted a far more general and permanent influence over the human race, through the agency of the Christian religion, than their Roman conquerors with all the prestige of their three hundred and twenty triumphs.

Name.—PALÆSTI'NA, in its original and proper sense, comprised merely that part of the Syrian coast inhabited by the ancient Philistines. In its wider acceptation, it is applied by the Christian world as a classical name to the territory of *Canaan*, or *Judæa*. Among sacred authors the name Palæstina was used by the prophet Isaiah, to denote the promised inheritance of the seed of Abraham, and the scene of the birth, sufferings and death of our Lord. It is now usually designated by the title of THE HOLY LAND.

QUESTIONS.—What is said of Phœnicia's colonies?—Name some of the principal colonies.——§ 36. What did Palæstina originally comprise?—What, in a wider sense?—Which of the sacred writers employs the name Palæstina?—What other names are used to designate the same country?—Why is it called The Holy Land?

Boundaries.—North, LEBANON, which divided it from Phœnicia and Cœle-Syria; East, The ARABIAN DESERT; originally, however, by the JORDAN and its lakes; South, The RIVER OF EGYPT (*El-Arish*), which divided it from Arabia Petræa; West, The GREAT SEA (*Mediterranean*). Its frontier towns were DAN on the north, and BEER'SHEBA on the south.

Divisions.—I. *Before the conquest by the Israelites*, it was divided among *seven* tribes: *Canaanites, Hittites, Amorites, Perizzites, Hivites, Jebusites*, and *Girgashites.*

II. *After the conquest*, it was divided among the Twelve Tribes: (*a*) West of the river Jordan: *Judah, Simeon, Dan, Benjamin, Ephraim, Manasseh west of the Jordan, Is'sachar, Asher, Ze'bulon, Na'phtali;* (*b*) East of the Jordan: *Reuben, Gad*, and the other half of *Manasseh.*

III. *After the death of Solomon*, in consequence of the revolt of Jeroboam, it was divided into the two kingdoms of JUDAH and ISRAEL, of which the former included the tribes of JUDAH, BENJAMIN, DAN, and SIMEON; and the kingdom of ISRAEL all the rest (B. C. 975).

IV. The kings of Syria divided the land of Israel, west of the Jordan, into the provinces of Galilæa, Samaria, and Judæa. The country east of the Jordan was called Peræa (*Περαία, Πέραν τοῦ Ἰορδάνου, Beyond the Jordan*). These divisions were adopted by the Romans, when they conquered the country, B. C. 63; and were recognised in the time of our Saviour.

V. Under Constantine the Great (A. D. 333), Palestine was divided into *Prima* (the middle part), *Secunda* (the northern part), and *Tertia* (the southern part).

Extent.—The whole country contained about eleven thousand

QUESTIONS.—Give its boundaries.—Among how many tribes was it divided before the conquest?—Among how many after the conquest?—How many tribes were west of the Jordan?—Their names?—How many east of the Jordan?—Their names?—How was it divided after Solomon's death?—What tribes were included in Judah?—What tribes in Israel?—How was it divided under the Romans?—How was it divided under Constantine the Great?—What is said of its extent?

square miles. By the conquests of David (B.C. 1050), the territory of the Hebrews was extended to the EUPHRA'TES and the ÆLANITIC GULF.

§ 37. **Mountains.**—The face of the country, toward the East, rises in the form of a lofty mountain chain, including the whole space between the coast and the valley of the Jordan. On the other side of the Jordan, a steep mountain range rises like a wall. The most celebrated mountain summits are CARMEL, TABOR, GE'RIZIM, NEBO, and HERMON. The hill country of Judæa reaches its greatest point of elevation in the vicinity of HEBRON, being there 3250 feet above the level of the Mediterranean. The lands lying along the Mediterranean are generally level.

Valleys.—The VALLEY OF THE JORDAN, which is the principal one, traverses the whole length of the country from North to South. In GALILÆA, lie the valleys of ABILE'NE, ZE'BULON, NAZARETH, and JEZREEL. The last-named was the great battle field of the East, the scene of the combats of Gideon, Saul, Godfrey of Boulogne, and Napoleon. In SAMARIA, the valleys of JENNIN, SHECHEM (watered by three hundred and sixty-five springs), and LEBAN. In JUDÆA, the valleys of BETHEL, JEREMIAH, ELAH (the scene of David's victory over Goliath), JEHOS'APHAT, REPHAIM, MAMRE (*Sepulchre of Abraham*), and SOREK.

Rivers and Lakes.—The most important river is the JORDA'NES, or JORDAN, i. e. *the flowing, the river*. The sources, three in number, are in the north of Palæsti'na, and first meet in

---

QUESTIONS.—How far did David extend his empire?——§ 37. What is said of the mountains?—Name the most celebrated summits.—Which is the highest peak?—What portion of the country is level?—Which is the principal valley?—What valleys are in Galilee?—What is said of the valley of Jezreel?—What valleys are in Samaria?—What is said of the vale of Shechem?—What valleys are in Judea?—What is said of Elah?—What of Mamre?—What is the most important river?—What does the name signify?—From how many sources does the river take its rise?

the small lake, called in the sacred writings *the Waters of Merom*. Thence the river flows through the SEA OF TIBERIAS (*Lake of Gennesareth*, or *Sea of Galilee*) into the Dead Sea. This very remarkable salt-lake occupies the site of the plain of *Siddim*, in which lay SODOM, and the other cities which

THE DEAD SEA.

were destroyed by fire from heaven in the time of Lot (*Gen.* xiv. 3; xix. 24, 25). The surface of the lake is 1312 feet below the level of the Mediterranean, it being thus by far the deepest known fissure on the earth's surface. Its waters are thoroughly impregnated with salt, and it has not been proved that any animal exists in them.

Productions.—It is described in the book of *Deuteronomy* (viii. 7–9) as "a land of brooks of water, of fountains, and depths that spring out of valleys and hills; a land of wheat and barley, and vines and fig-trees, and pomegranates; a land of oil-olive, and honey; a land wherein thou shalt eat bread

---

QUESTIONS.—Where do the head-waters intermingle for the first time?—Through what lake does the river flow into the Dead Sea?—Describe the Dead Sea.—Describe the productions.—Where do we find this description?

without scarceness, thou shalt not lack anything in it; a land whose stones are iron, and out of whose hills thou mayest dig brass."

Climate.—The climate is mild and the temperature equable. There are but two seasons, the rainy and the dry season. The former lasts from October to April, the latter from June to September.

Inhabitants.—The children of Israel were a nation of shepherds and agriculturists. In early times the most distinguished individuals cultivated the soil; and agriculture continued at all times to be the basis of national prosperity. Their institutions were of such a nature as to seclude them from intercourse with other nations, and their attachment to the law of Moses was equalled only by their detestation of foreign religions. They were forbidden to contract any marriages or alliances with other nations. The population probably did not at any time exceed four millions, even if it reached that number. Only three millions entered Canaan, under the conduct of Joshua.

§ 38. GALILÆA. (*Γαλιλαία.*)

In this country our Saviour chose his disciples; and he resided there so long that he was himself styled a Galilæan (Matt. xxvi. 69). Many of his miracles were wrought there, and thither he directed his disciples to repair, to meet him after the resurrection (Matt. xxviii. 7–16). It formed the Northern part of Palestine.

Boundaries.—North, LEBANON; East, JORDAN, and its lakes; South, SAMARIA; West, PHŒNI'CE.

Divisions.—It included the territories of Asher, Is'sachar, Naph'tali, and Zeb'ulon. It was divided into two parts:

QUESTIONS.—Describe the climate.—What was the chief employment of the children of Israel?—Had they intercourse with the rest of mankind?—How great was their number when they entered Canaan?—Did it increase much?——§ 38. What are the boundaries of Galilæa?—What tribes did it comprise?—Into how many parts was it divided?

I. UPPER GALILEE, or *Galilee of the Gentiles*, being inhabited by Syrians, Greeks, Phœnicians, and Egyptians, as well as by Jews.

II. LOWER GALILEE.

Population.—The inhabitants, on account of their heathen origin, were despised by the purer Jews of Judæa. They spoke a corrupt dialect, which grated harshly on the ears of their more polished neighbors. The Apostle Peter was detected by his Galilæan accent (*Mark*, xiv. 70). Galilæa comprised some of the most fertile and populous districts of Palestine.

TOWNS MENTIONED IN THE OLD TESTAMENT.

I. In LOWER GALILEE, which contained Asher and Issachar, and which extended along the coast of the Mediterranean:

a. In the tribe of *Asher*, which contained twenty-two towns:

(1.) ZAR'EPHATH, the residence of the prophet Elijah during the prevalence of famine in the land of Israel, and the place where he restored the widow's son to life (1 *Kings*, xvii. 9–22).

(2.) MIS'REPHOTH-MA'IM, HELKAH, ACHSAPH, BETH'REHOB.

(3.) Within the boundaries of Asher were included the Phœnician cities of TYRUS, SIDON, and ACCA.

b. In the tribe of *Is'sachar*, which comprehended the valley of the Jordan on the North, from Jericho to Mount Tabor, and the Eastern part of the plain of Esdraë'lon, and which contained sixteen towns:

(1.) MEGIDDO, on the river Kishon, famous for the battles fought in the extensive plain near it: here the army of Jabin was destroyed by Barak (*Judges*, iv. 15); Ahazi'ah died of the wounds received in battle against Jehu (2 *Kings*, ix. 27), and Josiah was defeated and slain by Necho (2 *Kings*, xxiii. 29).

QUESTIONS.—What was Upper Galilee often called?—Why?—What is said of the population?—What tribes did Lower Galilee contain?—Name some cities of the tribe of Asher.—What Phœnician cities were situated within its boundaries?—How many towns did the tribe of Asher contain?—Where was the territory of Issachar situated?—How many towns did it contain?—What is said of Megiddo?

(2.) SHUNAM was the place where the prophet Elijah restored to life the son of the Shunamite woman (2 *Kings*, iv. 35).

(3.) JEZREEL, for many years the capital of the kingdom of Israel.

(4.) DOTHAM, where Joseph was sold by his brethren to the Ish'maelite merchants (*Gen.* xxxvii. 28).

II. In UPPER GALILEE, which comprised the tribes of Zebulun and Naph'tali:

a. In the tribe of *Zeb'ulun*, situated West of the Sea of Tiberias. It contained twelve towns.

(1.) GATH-HE'PHER, the native place of the prophet Jonah (2 *Kings*, xiv. 25).

(2.) BETHULIA and JOKNEAM.

b. In *Naph'tali*, the northernmost of the tribes. It contained nineteen towns.

(1.) KEDESH. It belonged to the Levites, and was one of the cities of refuge. It was the birthplace of Barak and Tobi'as.

(2.) ABEL-BETH-MA'ACHAH and HAZOR.

TOWNS MENTIONED IN THE NEW TESTAMENT.

(1.) CAPERNAUM (*Καπερναοῦμ*), situated on the North-Western shore of the lake of Tiberias. It was often the residence of our Saviour. Here he performed many miracles, and in its neighborhood he delivered the sermon on the Mount; yet its inhabitants "repented not," and for this reason their city was included with Chorazin and Bethsa'ida in the fearful denunciation uttered by our Lord (*Matt.* xi. 21–24). Capernaum is nowhere mentioned in the Old Testament.

(2.) TIBERIAS (*Τιβεριάς*), situated on the Western shore of the lake, which derived its name from the town. It was built

---

QUESTIONS.—Name some other towns.—What tribes did Upper Galilee contain?—Where was Zebulun situated?—How many towns did it contain?—Name some of them.—Where was Naphtali situated?—How many towns did it contain?—Name some of them.—What towns are noted in New Testament times?—What is said of Capernaum?—Who was the founder of Tiberias?

by the tetrarch Hero'des An'tipas, in honor of the Roman emperor Tiberius, from whom it derived its name. After the destruction of Jerusalem, Tiberias was famous for its Academy of learned Jews. In its immediate neighborhood were the celebrated hot springs of Emmaus.

(3.) CANA (*Κανᾶ*), where Christ performed his first miracle (*John*, ii.). It was also the birthplace of Nathanael.

(4.) NAIN (*Ναΐν*), the scene of the raising of the widow's son (*Luke*, vii. 15).

(5.) NAZ'ARETH (*Ναζαρέθ*) (i. e. prob. *sprout*, *branch*), where our Saviour resided with Joseph and Mary, until He commenced his public ministry; hence He was styled Jesus of Nazareth.

(6.) BETHSA'IDA (*Βηθσαϊδά*), the birthplace of the Apostles Peter, Andrew, John, James, and Philip.

(7.) SEPPHO'RIS (*Σέπφωρις*). After the times of Hero'des An'tipas, it was the capital of Galilee, and was called Dio-Cæsare'a, in honor of Cæsar Augustus. It was the seat of one of the three great Councils (*συνέδρια*, *Sa'nhedrim*).

§ 39. SAMARIA. (*Σαμάρεια.*)

It was situated between Galilæa and Judæa, and was the smallest among the provinces on the West of the Jordan. Samaria included the territories of Ephraim and the Western half-tribe of Manasseh.

Population.—When the ten tribes were carried away captive by the Assyrians, the land of Israel was left nearly desolate, but was soon repeopled by heathen colonists and such Israelites as returned from the adjacent countries. These mixed races were called Samaritans; they adopted the religion of Moses, but mingled with it idolatrous rites and ceremonies. Hence they were regarded by the Jews with extreme aversion, and denied the

---

QUESTIONS.—What were in its neighborhood?—What signifies the name Nazareth?—What is said of Sepphoris?——§ 39. What is said of the situation of Samaria?—What tribes did it comprise?—What is said of the Samaritans?—Of their religion?

privilege of worshipping at Jerusalem: the Samaritans, therefore, built a temple for themselves on Mount Ger'izim, near Shechem, and worshipped there.

TOWNS MENTIONED IN THE OLD TESTAMENT.

a. In the tribe of *Ephraim*:

(1.) SAMARIA (in Hebrew, *Shomron*), the capital of the kingdom of Israel, founded by Omri (919 B. C.), and destroyed afterwards by the Assyrians (729 B. C.), but subsequently rebuilt.

(2.) SHECHEM, or SICHEM, the residence of Jacob. It was the chief seat of the Samaritan religion.

(3.) SHILOH, where the ark and tabernacle were first established.

(4.) JOPPA was the only seaport of the Israelites; from hence Jonah took ship to go to Tarshish.

b. In the tribe of *Manasseh*, West of the Jordan:

(1.) ISRAEL, or JEZREEL (later, *Esdraë'la*), the residence of Ahab and Joram.

(2.) THIRZA, until the time of Omri, the residence of the kings of Israel.

(3.) ENDOR, where Saul visited the witch (1 *Sam.* xxviii. 7).

(4.) OPHRAH, the birthplace of Gideon.

TOWNS MENTIONED IN THE NEW TESTAMENT.

(1.) SAMARIA (*Σαμάρεια*). It was granted to Herod the Great by Augustus, and was converted by him into a Roman city, under the name of Sebaste. The imperial name, *Augustus*, was rendered by *Σεβαστός*; hence, *Augusta* by *Σεβαστή*. It is sometimes extremely difficult, in passages of the New Testament, to decide whether, under the name Samaria, the *city* or the

---

QUESTIONS.—What towns were situated in the tribe of Ephraim?—What is said of Samaria?—Of Sichem?—Of Shiloh?—What was the only seaport?—What towns were situated in West Manasseh?—What is said of Jezreel?—Of Thirza?—Of Endor?—Of Ophrah?—What towns were noted in New Testament times?—Who converted Samaria into a Roman city?—Under what name?

SAMARIA.

country is meant. The magnificent city of Herod the Great is now a total ruin, a remarkable fulfilment of the prophecy of *Micah* (i. 6): "I will make Samaria as an heap of the field, as plantings of a vineyard, and I will pour down the stones thereof into the valley, and I will discover the foundations thereof."

(2.) CÆSARE'A (*Καισάρεια*), a maritime city, founded by Herod the Great, on the site of the Greek colony Turris Strato'nis, and named Cæsare'a, in honor of Cæsar Augustus. It was the chief town of Samaria in New Testament times. Here Cornelius, the Roman centurion, was converted under the Apostle Peter, and here also the Apostle Paul defended himself against the Jews (*Acts*, xxiv.).

(3.) SYCHAR (*Συχάρ*), the Sichem of the Old Testament, situated between Mount Ebal and Mount Ger'izim. Near the city was Jacob's Well, where our Saviour held the memorable conversation with the woman of Samaria (*John*, iv.). The

QUESTIONS.—What is said about the prophecy of Micah?—What was the chief town of Samaria in New Testament times?—What is said of it?

emperor Vespasian greatly improved the town, and called it Neap'olis (*Νεάπολις*, i. e. *Newtown*), which has been since corrupted into *Naplous*. It was the birthplace of Justin Martyr.

(4.) JOPPA (*Ἰόππη*). In New Testament times it was the chief port of the Israelites, subsequent to the foundation of Cæsare'a. The apostle Peter resided here for some time.

(5.) LYDDA, ANTIP'ATRIS, and ÆNON.

§ 40. JUDÆA. (*Ἰουδαία.*)

It nearly coincided with the ancient kingdom of Judah. The interior was rugged and mountainous; but on the coast the land was more level and fertile. It was less fertile than either Samaria or Galilee, but was of larger extent than either, and contained a more numerous population. It comprised the territories of JUDAH, BENJAMIN, DAN, and SIMEON.

Boundaries.—North, SAMARIA; East, JORDAN, and the DEAD SEA; South, The RIVER OF EGYPT, and the DESERT; West, The GREAT SEA, i. e. the Mediterranean.

TOWNS MENTIONED IN THE OLD TESTAMENT.

a. In the tribe of *Judah*. Judah comprised one hundred and six towns. It was the native tribe of David and Solomon as well as of our Lord, and to it was made the prophetic promise, "the sceptre shall not depart from Judah until Shiloh (i. e. *rest*, *peace*, through the Messiah) come" (*Gen.* xlix.)

(1.) BETH'LEHEM, or BETH'LEHEM E'PHRATAH, was the birthplace of David.

(2.) HEBRON, David's first capital; he reigned here upward of seven years before he took Jerusalem.

QUESTIONS.—From whom did it receive the name of Neapolis?—What is said of Joppa?——§ 40. What is said of Judæa?—What territories did it comprise?—Give the boundaries of Judæa.—How many towns did Judah possess?—What is said of Judah?—What towns did it contain?

(3.) TEKO'AH, the birthplace of the prophet Amos.

(4.) MARE'SHAH, where an Ethiopian army, of a million of men, under Zerad, was defeated by Asa, king of Judah.

(5.) BETH'SHEMESH, ADULLAM, EPHES-DAMMIN.

b. In the tribe of *Benjamin.* It possessed twenty-six towns (*Josh.* xviii. 11–28).

(1.) JERUSALEM; built chiefly on three hills, Zion, Moriah, Acra, between the valley of Jehoshaphat on the East, and that of Gihon on the West and South. Judah acquired it by conquest. The chief ornament of the city was the magnificent temple of Solomon, built on Mount Mori'ah. This temple was destroyed by Nebuchadnezzar (588 B C.).

(2.) JER'ICHO; the first conquest of the Israelites after they crossed the Jordan. It was destroyed by Joshua, five centuries afterward rebuilt, and then became a school of the prophets.

(3.) GIBEAH was the residence of Saul. At ZELAH he was buried.

(4.) BETHEL (i. e. *House of God*), or LUZ, famous for the Ægyptian worship of the Golden Calf, instituted by Jeroboam.

(5.) AN'ATHOTH was the birthplace of the prophet Jeremiah.

(6.) GILGAL, GIBEON, NAROTH.

c. In the tribe of *Dan.* It was the North-Western part of the tribe of Judah. This territory, being of small dimensions, the tribe was induced to send out some of its people in search of other settlements (*Judges,* xviii.). They accordingly took LAISH, situated near the river Jordan, and changed its name to DAN. It was for a long time the most Northern town in Israel.

In *Dan* were situated the Philistine towns ASHDOD, EKRON, and GATH.

d. In the tribe of *Simeon.* It comprised seventeen towns in the South of Judah.

QUESTIONS.—How many towns did Benjamin possess?—What is said of Jerusalem?—What of Jericho?—Name some other towns.—Where was Dan situated?—Where was the town of Dan situated?—What Philistine town was in Dan?—How many towns belonged to Simeon?

(1.) Beer'sheba and Gerar, both residences of Abraham and Isaac.

(2.) Gaza and As'calon, towns of the Philistines.

TOWNS MENTIONED IN THE NEW TESTAMENT.

(1.) Jerusalem (*Ἱερουσαλήμ*, or *Ἱεροσόλυμα*), as it existed in the time of our Saviour, was the city built by the Jews, who returned from Babylon. But neither the city nor the temple approached its first magnificence until the reign of Herod, who began, about the year 16 B.C., to adorn the former with many spacious buildings, and repaired the latter from its very foundations, in a substantial and splendid manner.

(2.) Beth'lehem (*Βηθλεέμ*), the birthplace of our Lord and Saviour.

(3.) Jer'icho (*Ἱεριχώ*), one of the principal towns, and the residence of Herod the Great.

(4.) Em'maus (*Ἐμμαούς*), visited by our Lord with two disciples after his resurrection.

(5.) Juttah, Ephraim, Arimathe'a.

§ 41. PERÆA. (*Περαία, Πέραν τοῦ Ἰορδάνου.*)

Its situation was favorable to commerce and industry. It comprised the territories of Reuben, Gath, and the eastern half of Manasseh.

Boundaries.—North, Lebanon; East and South, Arabia; West, Jordan, its lakes, and the Dead Sea.

Division.—It was divided into two tetrarchies:

I. The Northern comprised the districts Trachoni'tis with Ituræa, Gauloni'tis, Batanæa, and Gamali'tica.

Questions.—What towns were the residences of Abraham and Isaac? —What towns were in the country of the Philistines?—What is said of Jerusalem in New Testament times?—What other towns are noted in New Testament times?——§ 41. What is said of Peræa?—What territories did it comprise?—Give the boundaries.—Give the divisions.—Give the subdivision of the northern part.

II. The southern comprised PERÆA PROPER, and was governed by the tetrarch of Galilæa.

TOWNS MENTIONED IN THE OLD TESTAMENT.

a. In the tribe of *Reuben*, situated on the East side of the Dead Sea. This territory was celebrated for its cattle, sheep, and goats.

(1.) HESHBON, the capital of the Amorites. It is often mentioned by the prophets.

(2.) Other towns worthy of mention were: MED'EBA, AR'OER, DIBON, KEDE'MOTH, and BEZER.

b. In the tribe of *Gath.* It contained JABESH GILEAD and RAMOTH GILEAD, MAHANA'IM, PENU'EL.

c. In the tribe of *Manasseh beyond Jordan.* It contained DAN (already mentioned), GESHUR, ARGOB, ASH'TAROTH, EDREI.

TOWNS MENTIONED IN THE NEW TESTAMENT.

In the northern part was the district called DECAP'OLIS, so named from its containing *ten towns*, which were situated at some distance one from another. They were all in Peræa, except BETHSHEAN or SCYTHOP'OLIS, which lay in Samaria. The other towns of the Decap'olis were: DAMASCUS, PHILADELPHI'A, RHAPHANA, GAD'ARA, HIPPOS, DIOS, PELLA, GALASA, CAN'ATHA. Their inhabitants were chiefly Greeks, who received various important privileges from the Romans. Multitudes of people came from these cities to hear the preaching of our Lord, and in some of these places He performed several miracles.

(1.) GAD'ARA (*Γαδαρά*), where our Lord met and healed two persons possessed of devils.

(2.) CÆSARE'A PHILIPPI, or PANE'AS (*Πανειάς*), where our Lord gave the remarkable rebuke to Peter.

(3.) BETHSAIDA, MAG'DALA, BETHAB'ARA.

QUESTIONS.—Where was the tribe of Reuben situated?—What is said of it?—What is said of Gath?—What of Manasseh?—What is said of Decapolis?—What is said of its inhabitants?—Name some of the towns.

§ 42. JERUSALEM.

This was the ancient capital of the Holy Land subsequent to the time of David (1050 B. C.). The origin of this designation is uncertain. By the Rabbies it is formed of the latter part of the title Jehovah-*jireh* (i. e. God *will provide;* comp. *Gen.* xxii. 8) and Salem, the earlier name; according to Reland it is *Yarash-salem* (i. e. *possession of peace*). The classical name was HIEROSOL'YMA, and, after it was rebuilt by Hadrian, it was called ÆLIA CAPITOLI'NA. The modern name is *El-Kuds*, i. e. *the Holy* (City). The site of the city is an elevated piece of ground within an amphitheatre of gently sloping hills two thousand feet above the level of the sea. It has a gradual descent from West to East, so that the town is fully displayed like a panorama to those who view it from the East. In the South-West is Mount SION; North-East of this, separated from it by a valley, is Mount ACRA (or Salem); and East of this, Mount MORI'AH; West, is the valley of Gihon; and South, Hinnom; East, the valley of Jehoshaphat. The several parts of the city were enclosed by distinct walls. The upper city was surrounded by the old wall built by David and Solomon, and fortified by their successors. On its North-West angle was the celebrated palace of Herod, entirely surrounded by a wall thirty cubits high. The lower city was surrounded by another wall, and the third wall, built only thirty years before the destruction of the city, enclosed the new city (Be'zetha), which was North and West of the older city. The temple stood on Mount MORI'AH, called generally in the Scriptures the *Mountain of the Lord's*

QUESTIONS.—§ 42. When did Jerusalem become the capital of the Holy Land?—What does Jerusalem signify?—What was its classical name?—What was its last Roman name?—Describe the situation of the city in general.—What is the most favorable point from which to view the city?—Describe the situation of the three hills.—What valleys were between them?—What is said of the old wall?—Where was the palace of Herod situated?—Where stood the temple?

house. The city seems to have been, even in Canaanitish times, a religious, as well as a political centre. David, after his conquest, made it the capital of his kingdom, and Solomon selected it also as the ecclesiastical head of the nation. He erected the first temple. This temple and all the buildings of Jerusalem were destroyed by fire, and its walls completely demolished by Nebuchadnezzar (588 B. C.). Fifty years afterward, Cyrus, king of Persia, permitted the restoration of the temple, which, in consequence of numerous vexatious interruptions, occupied one hundred and twenty years (418 B. C.). Again after fifty years the city passed into the hands of Alexander, after whose death Judæa became the frontier province of Syria and Egypt. The city suffered no material diminution of its prosperity, notwithstanding the occasional changes in its dynasty as it became the prize successively of contending military rivals. Internal factions subjected it at last to the dominion of Anti′ochus Epiph′anes, whose tyranny resulted in a national revolution (175 B. C.), which secured the independence of Jerusalem until its capture by the Romans (63 B C). From this time, though nominally subject to a native prince, it was virtually a mere dependency of the Roman government.

Be′zetha, or *Newtown*, was built up about this period by Agrippa, the grandson of Herod. At this time the city is supposed to have attained its greatest extent and population; it was upwards of four miles in circuit, and had from 100,000 to 150,000 inhabitants. On the death of Herod the Great, Judæa became a Roman province within the prefecture of Syria, and was governed by a procura′tor, Pontius Pilate (A. D. 26–36), under whom the Jews crucified the SAVIOUR OF MANKIND on

QUESTIONS.—Who built the temple?—Who destroyed it?—Who permitted its restoration?—When was the second temple finished?—When and by whom was this temple destroyed?—What was the fate of Jerusalem after the death of Alexander the Great?—When did it become independent?—When was it taken by the Romans?—What was its fate under Roman supremacy?—When did Jerusalem attain its highest prosperity?—What was its government after the death of Herod?—What happened under Pontius Pilate?

TITUS BEFORE JERUSALEM.

the hill of CALVARY. The terrible siege and destruction of the city by the Roman army under Titus, occurred A. D. 70. Sixty years afterward, it was rebuilt by Hadrian, under the name of Ælia Capitoli'na. A temple built to Jupiter Capitoli'nus occupied the once sacred enclosure on Mount Mori'ah, and over the site of the Holy Sepulchre rose a temple in honor of Venus. Two hundred years afterward, the city recovered its name and became a Christian bishopric, and (A. D. 400) a patriarchate. In the first half of the seventh century (A. D. 634) it was invested by the Saracens, and after a defence of four months capitulated to the Khalif Omar in person. Since that time it has followed the vicissitudes of the various dynasties which have swayed the destinies of Western Asia.

QUESTIONS.—When was the city destroyed by Titus?—When rebuilt?—Under what name?—By whom?—What temples were erected at Jerusalem, and where?—When did Jerusalem regain its sacred character?—When did the city fall into the hands of the Saracens?

§ 43. ARABIA. (Heb. *Arab*; Ἀραβία.)

Name.—The name Arab first occurs after the time of Solomon. The native tradition derives it from *Yarab*, the son of Joktan, the father of the race. According to Gesenius, it is from the Heb. *arab* = *arid*, sterile. It may, however, be connected with the Heb. *ereb*, *eve*, evening (ἔρεβος, *E'rebus* = nether gloom); pr. *the Evening* Land, with reference to the position of Arabia to the West of the Euphra'tes, and the earliest abodes of the Semitic race; just as Italia was called Ἑσπερία, *the Evening* Land, *the West*, relatively to Greece. Compare the use of the Gr. ἑσπέρα, the Latin *Occidens*, the Germ. *Abend*, and also the Egyptian *Amenti*, Hades, and *Ement*, the West.

Boundaries.—North, JUDÆA, SYRIA, and MESOPOTAMIA; East, South, and West, the ERYTHRÆAN SEA, with its two gulfs.

Divisions.—ARABIA DESERTA, ARABIA FELIX, ARABIA PETRÆA.

Capes.—POSEIDONIUM, between the two gulfs of the Red Sea; PALIN'DROMUS (*Bab-el-Mandeb*), at the entrance of the Red Sea; SY'AGRUS, on the extreme East, and MACE'LA, North-West of the former.

Mountains.—The mountain-range, which runs from North-West to South-East, parallel to the Red Sea, may be regarded as a continuation of the Lebanon range. The chains running along the other sides of the peninsula resemble it in character.

Rivers.—It is entirely destitute of navigable rivers.

Productions.—Spices and various drugs, sugar, indigo, tamarinds, grapes, figs. In the open desert, wood is so scarce that the dried manure of camels is the only fuel. The classics commonly do not distinguish between the productions of Arabia, India, and the Eastern Islands.

QUESTIONS.—§ 43. What is said of the origin of the name Arab?—How is Arabia bounded?—How divided?—Name the capes.—What is said of the mountains?—What is said of the rivers?—What of the productions?

Climate.—The atmosphere of Arabia is one of the driest in the world. On the mountain-slopes the climate varies from that of the tropics to that of the lower latitudes of the temperate zone.

Inhabitants.—The Arabians comprise the greater part of the Semitic race, and were closely akin to the Israelites. They have in general preserved their national characteristics and independence from the days of the Patriarchs to the present hour. During many centuries, they received subsidies of gold from foreign nations, but never as a nation submitted to a foreign yoke. Although sometimes serving as Persian auxiliaries, they were never subjected to the Persian empire, but they showed their friendship for *the Great King*, by an annual present of a thousand talents' worth of frankincense. Augustus sent an army into Arabia Felix under Ælius Gallus, 24 B.C. This expedition, which the geographer Strabo accompanied, proved more successful in its contributions to science than in military conquests. A small part of Western Arabia was formed into a Roman province, A.D. 105, which was at a later period somewhat enlarged (A.D. 195).

§ 44. I.—ARABIA PETRÆA. (*ἡ πετραία Ἀραβία.*)

It comprised the peninsula of Sinai, between the two gulfs of the Red Sea.

Name.—Its name was derived from the city of Petra, i.e. *Rock*, and not from its physical character, which, however, corresponds in the main with this designation.

Mountains.—A sandy desert nearly two hundred leagues in extent stretches from the borders of Egypt toward the mouth of the Euphra'tes. At the point where the two arms of the Sinus Ara'bicus diverge and extend into the land, rise the two lofty

---

QUESTIONS.—What is said of the climate?—To what race do the Arabians belong?—Describe the Arabians.—What is said about the expedition of Ælius Gallus?—Who accompanied this expedition?——§ 44. Whence does Arabia Petræa derive its name?—What is said about the mountains?—Between what gulfs were they situated?

mountains, SINAI and HOREB, separated from each other by a deep valley. Here, amid the emphatic and impressive thunders of Heaven, Israel received her sacred Law.

Gulfs.—I. The Eastern Gulf was called Ælani'ticus Sinus, from the city of Æla'na (*Αἴλανα*) at its Northern point (*Gulf of Akaba*).

II. The Western Gulf was called Heroöpoli'tes, from the city of Heroö'polis (*Ἡρώων πόλις* or *Ἡρώ*), situated near its head, on the canal made by Necho to connect it with the Nile.

Inhabitants.—The tribes of Arabia Petræa, in the North, such as the Amalekites, Midianites, Edomites, Moabites, are frequently mentioned in the Old Testament. The classical authors call them by one common name Nabathæi.

(1.) Amalekites dwelt in the desert, South of the land of Canaan. They attacked the Israelites at Rephidim, where Joshua defeated them. Long afterward they were routed by Gideon, and then by Saul.

(2.) The Ammonites inhabited the part of the country which lay East of Palestine. They were conquered by David (2 *Sam.* viii.; xii. 31), but afterward they regained their independence.

(3.) The Moabites lived South of the Ammonites, and East of the Red Sea. They were conquered by the Maccabees (B. C. 78).

(4.) The Edomites lived South of the Dead Sea. They were rendered tributary to David.

(5.) The Midianites occupied in part the country East of Edom, and partly the East coast of the Red Sea. Moses, after he fled from Egypt, resided forty years among them, and kept the flocks of his father-in-law, Jethro.

Towns.—(1.) PETRA (*Πετρά*), *Wady Musa*, in the Old Testament called SELAH, the noted capital of the Idumæans, which was taken by Amaziah, who changed its name to Joktheel (2 *Kings*, xiv. 7). In the times of the Romans, it was a great com-

---

QUESTIONS.—By what tribes is it inhabited?—What is said of the Amalekites?—Moabites, Edomites, Midianites?—What is the principal town of Arabia Petræa?—How is it called in the Old Testament?—When did it become a great emporium?

mercial emporium. In the reign of Trajan it belonged to the Roman empire, and afterward it became the capital of Palæsti'na Tertia (the eastern part of Arabia Petræa). During this period probably the temples and mausole'a were made, the remains of which have so arrested the attention of modern travellers.

(2.) EZIONGE'BER (afterward Bereni'ce) and ELATH, were noted seaports on the eastern gulf of the Red Sea, whence the fleets of Solomon and Hiram sailed to Ophir and Tarshish.

II.—ARABIA DESERTA. (*ἡ ἔρημος Ἀραβία.*)

The great SYRIAN desert between the EUPHRA'TES on the East and SYRIA on the North, was entirely inhabited by nomad tribes, called by the ancients *A'rabes Sceni'tæ*, from their dwelling in *tents*, and *No'madæ* from their mode of life, which was that of *wandering herdsmen* (the modern *Bedouins*).

Three great caravan roads crossed the desert:

I. From Egypt and Petræa Eastward to the Persian Gulf.

II. From Palmy'ra Southward into Arabia Felix.

III. From Palmy'ra South-East to the mouth of the Tigris.

III.—ARABIA FELIX. (*ἡ εὐδαίμων Ἀραβία.*)

The name of this region, probably originating with the Arabs of the North, was *El-Yemen*, the country on *the Right;* i.e. *the South*, as the face was supposed by the Oriental geographers to be turned toward *the East.* Since the Greeks, however, in taking the auspices turned toward *the North*, the Eastern or *fortunate* (*εὐδαίμων*) side was on *the right;* hence from *El-Yemen*, *ἡ εὐδαίμων Ἀραβία;* the Roman, *Arabia Felix;* and our, *Araby the Blest.*

QUESTIONS.—Of what country did it become the capital?—Mention the two seaports on the eastern gulf.—What is said of them?—What is said of Arabia Deserta?—What is the origin of the designation Arabia Felix?

Boundaries.—It included the peninsula proper, to which the name was extended from the South-Western parts, and was divided amongst various tribes (SABÆI, NABATHÆI, etc.).

Cities.—(1.) On the coast of the Arabian Gulf: MODIA'NA, LEUCE-COME, HIPPOS.

(2.) In the interior: LATHRIPPA (*El-Medi'neh* = the city), MACO'RABA (*Mecca*).

(3.) South are the MINYÆ, with the city CARNA, and the SABÆI, with SABA (Heb. *Sheba*), famous for its frankincense.

(4.) On the Southern coast are the commercial towns MUSA, ARABIA FELIX, or EDEN (*Aden*), CANE, SAB'BATHA.

(5.) On the Eastern shore: GERRHA, and the islands AR'-ADUS and TYLUS, both Tyrian colonies.

§ 45. ASSYRIA. (Heb. *Ashur; 'Ασσυρία; Kurdistan.*)

In the Cuneiform Inscriptions this country is called *Asura*. Originally it was perhaps only a district North-East of the junction of the Tigris and Zab'atus.

Boundaries.—North, ARMENIA; East, MEDIA; South, BABYLONIA; West, MESOPOTAMIA and BABYLONIA.

Mountains.—It was generally a mountainous region. The most important mountain-ranges are TAGRUS and CHO'ATRAS, which divided it from Media.

Rivers.—The principal river is the TIGRIS (*Τίγρις*), which divided it from Mesopotamia and Babylonia. Its Eastern branches are: LYCUS, or ZAB'ATUS (*Λύκος*, or *Ζάβατος*, the Great *Zab*), and CAPRUS (*Κάπρος*, the Little *Zab*).

Cities.—(1.) NINUS, or NIN'IVE (*Νίνος, Νινευή, Nin'eveh*), on the East bank of the Tigris. It was one of the great capitals of antiquity, and is described, by some writers, as being forty-eight, and by others fifty-five, miles in circumference. Its

---

QUESTIONS.—Name the boundaries.—What cities were on the Arabian Gulf?—Name some of the island cities.—What towns were on the southern coast?——§ 45. What is said of the name Assyria?—What was its territory at first?—How is it bounded?—Name the mountains.—What are the principal rivers?—What is said of Nineveh?

walls were built of brick, one hundred feet in height, and so wide that on the top three chariots could be driven abreast. They were moreover protected by fifteen hundred lofty towers, each two hundred feet in height. The prophets often speak of its greatness, wealth, and luxury. It was destroyed 625 B. C. Numerous sculptures and inscriptions have been brought to light by the recent discoveries of Dr. Layard, Col. Rawlinson, and other modern travellers.

(2.) ARBE'LA (*Ἄρβηλα*), opposite the plain of Gaugame'la (*Γαυγάμηλα, Karmelis*), where the third and decisive battle was fought between Alexander and Dari'us (331 B. C.).

(3.) CTES'IPHON (*Κτησιφῶν*), a large city on the East bank of the Tigris, which grew on the decay of Seleuci'a, as the latter had risen on the fall of the earlier capital, Babylon. It was not a place of great importance until the Parthian empire was firmly established. It became then the winter residence of the Parthian kings, who passed their summers at Ecbat'ana. In the Old Testament, Assyria is called *Ashur*. Nothing special is said of it in Scripture from its first settlement until the time that the prophet Jonah visited Nin'eveh (825 B. C.) (*Jonah*, i. 2). About fifty years afterward, Pul, the king of Assyria, rendered the kingdom of Israel tributary, and the succeeding line of royal rulers executed the threatenings of Jehovah against the rebellious house of Israel (2 *Kings*, xvii. 6).

THE EMPIRE OF ASSYRIA, the most ancient of the Four Great Empires of the world, varied very much, both in power and extent, according to the individual influence and conquests of particular kings. As a geographical term, the name, *Assyria*, is used in different acceptations. Greek and Roman historians commonly employ it as a general designation for the countries of BABYLONIA, MESOPOTAMIA, and ASSYRIA PROPER; but frequently they make it embrace even a part of ASIA MINOR.

QUESTIONS.—Who was conquered at Gaugamela?—What is said of Ctesiphon?—How is Assyria called in the Scriptures?—When is it first spoken of in the Scriptures?—Who rendered Israel tributary?—What is said of the Assyrian empire?

§ 46. MEDIA. (*Μηδία, Irak Aghami;* comp. Heb. *Madai.*)

Boundaries.—North, CASPIAN SEA; East, HYRCANIA and PARTHIA; South, PERSIS and SUSIA'NA; West, ASSYRIA. It forms the extreme Western portion of the great table land of Iran.

Divisions.—GREAT MEDIA, or the South; ATROPATE'NE, or the North-West; and THE NORTH.

Mountains.—TAGRUS. The most mountainous division was that on the North-West, or Atropate'ne.

Productions.—Great Media was a rich and fertile plain. It produced wine, figs, oranges, citrons, and honey.

Inhabitants.—It was inhabited by a branch of the Indo-Germanic family, which was nearly allied to the Persians and Indians. They were divided, according to Hero'dotus, into six tribes. The terms *Mede* and *Medes* are often used, by Greek authors, for Persian. In general, the name, *Medes*, was applied by them to the nations on the east of the river Tigris.

Cities.—(1.) ECBAT'ANA (*'Εκβάτανα, Hamadan*), the ancient capital of the Median monarchy, and afterward the summer residence of the Persian and Bactrian monarchs. The city was two hundred and forty stadia in circumference, and was surrounded by seven walls.

(2.) RHAGÆ (*'Ράγαι, Rhey*), afterward ARSACIA, mentioned in the history of *Tobit.* Near this town are the PYLÆ CASPIÆ, a strongly fortified pass leading from North-Western Asia into the North-Eastern provinces of Persia. Through this pass Alexander the Great pursued Dari'us. In its neighborhood was the celebrated Nisæan plain (Nisæus Campus), the pasture-ground for the horses belonging to the royal family.

(3.) HERACLE'A, founded by Alexander the Great.

QUESTIONS.—§ 46. What are the boundaries of Media?—How is it divided?—What is said about its productions?—What about its inhabitants?—What do the Greek authors mean by the term Medes?—What cities are situated in Media?—What was the ancient capital?—What is said of Rhagæ?—What are the Pylæ Caspiæ?—What plain was in its neighborhood?

The empire of Media, under its third king, Cyax'ares (B. C. 635–595), extended its boundaries as far West as the Halys. As a geographical term, among the Greeks, it represented the country East of the Tigris.

§ 47. PERSIS. (*Περσίς, Farsistan.*)

Boundaries.—North, MEDIA and PARTHIA; East, CARMANIA; South, PERSIAN GULF; West, SUSIA'NA.

Mountains.—PARACHO'ATHRAS and OCHUS.

Rivers.—ARAXES, MEDUS, and CYRUS (*Kur*).

Productions.—The mountain districts possess excellent pasture for horses and camels; the middle slopes are rich in fruit, but the coast contains only a few palms.

Inhabitants.—The Persæ belonged to the Indo-Germanic race, and their language was nearly connected with the classical Sanskrit. Their generic name was *Paraca.* They called themselves, however, like the Medes, *Arii.* As a nation, they were divided into three great classes: WARRIORS, HUSBANDMEN, and NOMADS. The PASAR'GADÆ were the most important tribe of the first class. The ACHÆMEN'IDÆ, from whom their well-known line of kings descended, was one of the families of the Pasar'gadæ.

Cities.—(1.) PASAR'GADA (*Πασαργάδα*, i. e. acc. to Ouseley, *Habitation of the Persians*), was its earliest capital, and contained the tomb of Cyrus the Great.

(2.) PERSEP'OLIS (*Περσέπολις, Chel-Minar*), the sacred city of the empire, the burial-ground of the Persian monarchs. It

---

QUESTIONS.—How far did the empire of Media extend under Cyaxares?—What does Media signify as a geographical term?——§ 47. What are the boundaries of Persis?—Mountains?—Rivers?—Productions?—What was the generic name of the inhabitants?—How did they call themselves?—Into how many classes were they divided?—Name the most important tribe of the first class.—What celebrated family of that tribe?—Name three cities.—What is said of Pasargada?—What of Persepolis?

was situated on the north side of the Araxes. It became known to the Greeks by the expedition of Alexander the Great, in the course of which he burnt it.

(3.) GABÆ (*Γάβαι*), one of the residences of the kings, situated near the borders of Carmania.

THE PERSIAN EMPIRE, under Dari'us Hystaspes (500 B.C.), extended from India to the Mediterranean. The three royal residences were: ECBA'TANA, for the Summer; SUSA, for the Spring; and BABYLON, for the Autumn and Winter.

SUSIA'NA. (*ἡ Σουσιανή, Khuzistan.*)

Boundaries.—North, MEDIA; East, PERSIS; South, PERSIAN GULF; West, MESOPOTAMIA and ASSYRIA.

Rivers.—TIGRIS: CHOASPES, whose waters were so excellent that the kings of Persia would drink no other (*regia lympha Choaspes*, Tibullus, IV. 1, 140).

Cities.—(1.) SUSA (*Σοῦσα, Sus;* prob. from the Persian *susan*, lily) situated on the Choaspes, was the Spring residence of the Great King. The city was two hundred stadia in circumference.

(2.) SELEUCI'A and A'ZARA, famous for their temples.

§ 48. ARIA'NA. (*ἡ Ἀριανή, Iran.*)

Name.—ARIA'NA (Hindu *Arya*, distinguished; comp. *Ἄρης, ἥρως, ἀρετή, ἄριστος*) was a district of wide extent in Central Asia, comprehending nearly the whole of the ancient Persian monarchy. Its inhabitants belonged to the great Indo-Germanic family, and called themselves *Arii.*

QUESTIONS.—How far did the Persian empire extend under Darius Hystaspes?—What were the three royal residences?—What are the boundaries of Susiana?—What is said of the Choaspes?—Name three cities.—What is said of Susa?——§ 48. With what is the name of Ariana connected?—Where was it situated?

Boundaries.—North, BACTRIA'NA, MARGIA'NA, and HYRCANIA; East, INDUS; South, ERYTHRÆAN SEA; West, MEDIA.

Divisions.—GEDROSIA, DRANGIA'NA, ARACHOSIA, PAROPAMI'SADÆ, ARIA, PARTHIA, CARMANIA.

Mountains.—PAROPAMI'SUS, and its different branches.

Rivers.—ARIUS (*Herat*), SUASTUS (*Sewad*).

Productions.—Excepting in certain valleys where the vine flourished, Aria'na was, for the greater part, a desert swept by constant simooms of moving sand. These simooms caused the destruction of the Assyrian and Persian armies of Semir'amis and Cyrus, and almost annihilated the army of Alexander.

Almost the whole of this extensive region fell under the dominion of the Parthians (256 B. C.—A. D. 226) .who, at the height of their power (B. C. 40), extended their sovereignty from the Euphrates to the Oxus, and from the Caspian to the Arabian Sea. The first capital was HECATOM'PYLOS; but afterwards CTES'IPHON became the winter, and ECBA'TANA the summer, residence of the Parthian kings. In classical authors a constant confusion is noticeable in the use of the names *Persian* and *Parthian*, the exact limitations of application of either term not being very definitely settled.

Towns.—I. In *Gedrosia* (*Γεδρωσία*), the most South-Easterly province of the Persian empire: TARSIS, the capital.

II. In *Drangia'na* (*Δραγγιανή*): the capital, PROPHTHASIA, situated on the North of the lake called Aria Lacus (*Zarah*).

III. In *Arachosia* (*Ἀραχωσία*): ALEXANDROP'OLIS, the capital.

IV. In *Paropami'sadæ* (*Παροπαμισάδαι*), on the Southern slopes of Mount Paropami'sus: ORTOS'PANA.

V. In *Aria* (*Ἀρία*): ARTACOA'NA, the ancient capital.

VI. In *Parthia* (*Παρθυαία, Παρθία*): HECATOM'PYLOS, the first residence of the Parthian kings.

QUESTIONS.—Name its boundaries.—How many countries did it comprise?—Name those countries.—Name the mountains.—The rivers.—Productions.—What armies were destroyed in its deserts?—When did Ariana fall under Parthian dominion?—Name some of the towns.

VII. In *Carmania* (*Καρμανία*): CARMA'NA, the capital, and HARMOZIA, on the river A'namis, the place where Nearchus landed on his return from India.

THE COUNTRIES BETWEEN THE CASPIAN SEA AND SCYTHIA.

Boundaries.—North and East, SCYTHIA; South, PAROPAMI'-SUS, and its Western branches; West, CASPIAN SEA.

Divisions.—(1.) HYRCANIA, between the CASPIAN SEA and the OCHUS.

(2.) MARGIA'NA, between the OCHUS and OXUS.

(3.) BACTRIA'NA, BACTRIA, between the OXUS and Mount PAROPAMI'SUS.

(4.) SOGDIA'NA, between the OXUS and IAXARTES.

Rivers.—OCHUS, OXUS, IAXARTES, and MARGUS.

Productions.—Timber, grapes, and corn. Over many sections of the territory wild animals roamed in abundance. Alexander is said to have hunted down four thousand of them in Sogdia'na alone.

Inhabitants.—They were for the greater part rude mountaineers, and served constantly in the Persian armies. In the middle of the third century B. C. the various tribes were united under the Greek empire of Bactria, which lasted about two hundred years.

Cities.—In *Hyrcania* (*Ὑρκανία*): ZADRACARTA.

In *Margia'na* (*Μαργιανή*): ANTIOCHI'A MARGIA'NA, where the captured soldiers of Crassus were transported. Many of them intermarried with the inhabitants, and hence were unwilling to return to Rome when ordered back by Augustus.

QUESTIONS.—Where is Hyrcania situated?—Between what rivers is Margiana situated?—Between what rivers is Bactriana?—Between what rivers is Sogdiana?—What is said of the productions?—What is said of the inhabitants?—When were they united?—How long did the Bactrian empire last?—Name the chief cities.—What is said of Antiochia Margiana?

In *Bactria'na* (*Βακτριανή*): BACTRA, the capital.

In *Sogdia'na* (*Σογδιανή*): MARACANDA (*Samarkand*), where Alexander killed Clitus.

§ 49. INDIA. (*ἡ Ἰνδική* or *Ἰνδία.*)

Name.—The names *Indus*, *India*, are without doubt derived from the Sanskrit designation of the river, *Sindhu*, which in the plural form means also the people who dwelt along its banks. The form *Hendu* is found in the Zend or old Persian; *Hoddu* in Hebrew; in Greek *Σίνθος* occurs; Pliny says, *Indus* incolis *Sindus* appellatus; and hence also *Hindoo*, *Hindostan*.

The term, *India*, denoted the country East of Aria'na.

Boundaries.—North, IMAUS and MONTES EMO'DI; East, SINÆ and OCE'ANUS ORIENTA'LIS; South, OCE'ANUS IN'DICUS; West, INDUS.

Divisions.—INDIA INTRA GANGEM (*Hindostan*), and INDIA EXTRA GANGEM (*Siam* and *Malacca*).

Mountains.—PAROPAMI'SUS, which the Macedonians, in order to flatter Alexander, called Cau'casus In'dicus; IMAUS and MONTES EMO'DI; MONTES SEMANTHI'NI; MERUS (*Meru*) the residence of the gods, as was Mount Olympus among the Greeks.

Capes.—PROMONTORIUM MAGNUM, PROMONTORIUM AUREÆ CHERSONE'SI, PROMONTORIUM COLIAS, COMARIA (*Comorin*).

Rivers.—INDUS, SERUS, DOA'NAS, GANGES, DYAR'DANES (*Brahma-putra*), HY'PHASIS, and HYDASPES, on the Eastern shore of which Alexander erected altars in memory of his progress eastward.

Productions and Commerce.—The commerce of India, including the Northern and Southern districts, may be considered as an epitome of the trade of the world, there being few productions which may not be found within its vast area.

QUESTIONS.—§ 49. What is said of the name of India?—How is it bounded?—How is it divided?—What was the Caucasus Indicus?—Name some other mountains.—Name the promontories.—Name the rivers.—What is said of the Hydaspes?—What is said of the commerce of India?

Cities.—The number of cities in India, known to the ancient world, was quite large, yet ancient authors furnish very meagre details in regard to them. In fact, we have scarcely anything beyond a mere list of names. Of these the following are the most noticeable:

AORNOS, a fortress thought to be impregnable till its capture by Alexander; NICÆA (*Νίκαια*), built by Alexander in honor of his victory over Porus; BUCEPH'ALA (*Βουκέφαλα*), built by him in memory of his horse Buceph'alus; PERIM'ULA (*Malacca*); CALINGA (*Calingapatam*).

SE'RICA (*Σερική*) AND SINÆ (*οἱ Σῖναι*).

Boundaries.—North, unknown; East, OCE'ANUS ORIENTA'LIS; South, INDIA; West, SCYTHIA.

Mountains.—MONTES AUXACII and AN'NIBI (*Altai*).

Rivers.—ŒCHARDES and BANTES.

Cities.—SERA (*Kan-tcheon*).

In the East of Se'rica were the SINÆ, who were probably settled in the province of *Shensi*, the most Western province of China.

SCYTHIA:

A vast area in the Eastern half of Northern Europe, and in Western and Central Asia Its limits were variously stated, according to the different degrees of information on the part of its geographers.

Division.—GREAT, MIDDLE, and LESSER SCYTHIA; or *Scythia intra Imaum*, and *Scythia extra Imaum*.

Mountains.—MONTES HYPERBOREI, OXII, and SOGDII.

QUESTIONS.—What is said about the towns?—Give the names of some of them.—What are the boundaries of Serica?—The mountains?—The rivers?—The towns?—Where lay the country of the Sinæ?—Where is Scythia situated?—How is it divided?—Name the mountains.

Rivers.—PAROPAMI'SUS, RHYMNUS, DAIX, IAXARTES, and OXUS.

Lakes.—PALUS OXIA'NA—(*Lake of Aral, the Lake of Karakoul*).

Inhabitants.—The name by which the Scythians called themselves was SCO'LOTI (*Σκόλοτοι*, Hdt. IV. 6), and the Greek name *Σκύθαι*, SCYTHÆ, is perhaps allied to it. They were an Asiatic people, who were partly driven from their settlements to the North of the Araxes by the Massa'getæ, and after crossing that river descended into Europe.

QUESTIONS.—Name the rivers of Scythia.—What lake does it contain?—What is said of the inhabitants?

§ 50. ISLANDS OF ASIA.

I. In the Mediterranean Sea: CYPRUS, RHODUS, COS, SAMOS, CHIOS, LESBOS, TE'NEDOS, PATMOS, and smaller islands, as *Casus, I'carus.*

II. In the Propontis: PROCONNE'SUS, OPHIUSSA.

III. In the Pontus Euxi'nus: I'NSULÆ CYANEÆ.

IV. In the Indian Ocean: TABROBA'NE, IABADIUS.

CYPRUS (*Κύπρος*):

A large island in the Mediterranean, on the South of Cilicia, colonized by the Phœnicians at a very early period. Although lying in that sea, which was the peculiar nurse of the Grecian race, CYPRUS never developed the nobler features of Hellenic culture and civilization. The exuberant generosity of nature served only to invite a sensuality which effectually extinguished the better sentiments of the human heart. The Semitic Astarte, *Venus,* was chiefly worshipped here, under the form of a *rude conical stone,* and Venus was hence called *Cypria.*

Mountains.—The OLYMPUS, whose peaks reach the height of 7000 feet, runs through the entire length of the island.

Rivers.—They are scarcely more than mountain torrents; the largest of them was the PEDIÆUS, which watered the extensive plain of Mes'saræ.

Productions.—It possesses many beautiful and fertile valleys. Its principal article of commercial value, however, was copper.

QUESTIONS.—Name the islands of Asia in the Mediterranean Sea.—In the Propontis.—In the Pontus Euxinus.—In the Indian Ocean.—Where was Cyprus situated?—What is said about its civilization?—What of its religion?—What mountain chain runs through the island?—What is said of the rivers?—What is the chief produce?

The Romans called this metal after the island, *Cyprium æs*, *Cyprium;* and later, *cuprum;* whence our word *copper*.

Cities.—(1.) SAL'AMIS (*Σαλαμίς*), founded on the South-Eastern part of the coast by Teucer,

> *Salamina patremque*
> *Cum fugeret.*—Hor. Od. I. 7, 21.

It was the most important city of the island, and was the acknowledged capital of the Eastern part. Under Constantine the Great, it suffered severely from an earthquake; the emperor rebuilt it under the name of Constantia, and made it the capital of the island.

(2.) CARPASIA (*Καρπασία*), situated to the North-East, facing the promontory of Sarpe'don, on the Cilician coast. East of it was the summit of Olympus, crowned by a temple of Venus, which women were forbidden to enter.

(3.) CITIUM (*Κίτιον*), situated on the South coast, the birth-place of Zeno the Stoic. Cimon, the celebrated Athenian general, died there.

(4.) SOLI (*Σόλοι*), situated on the North coast. The inhabitants were called *Solii* (*Σόλιοι*), to distinguish them from the citizens of *Soli* in Cilicia, who were called *Σολεῖς* (see page 37).

(5.) Other towns: PAPHOS, in the South-West, the peculiar seat of the worship of Venus, hence called *regina Paphi*, *Paphie*, *Paphia Venus;* IDALIUM or IDALIA, with a forest sacred to Venus, who was hence called Venus *Idalia;* AM'ATHUS, GOLGUS, MARIUM, LA'PETHUS.

QUESTIONS.—Name four important cities.—What is said of Salamis?—What temple was near Carpasia?—Where is Citium situated?—What is said of Soli?—What of Paphos and Idalium?

§ 51. RHODUS. (Ῥόδος.)

Name.—As the *rose*, ῥόδον, appears as a symbol on the coins of the island, *Rhodus* is supposed to mean, the Island of *Roses*. It was one of the chief islands of the Ægæan Sea, South of the coast of Caria. A branch of the Doric race, having taken possession of the island, quietly developed its resources, and rose to great prosperity and affluence. Its important towns were all situated on the coast. The three most ancient were LINDUS (*Λίνδος*), IAL'YSUS (*Ἰαλυσός*), and CAMI'RUS (*Κάμειρος*), which formed, with Cos, Cnidus, and Halicarnassus, the Doric Hexap'olis. (See Doric Colonies, page 26.) The three towns were united (408 B. C.), and formed the large city of RHODUS. Here was the celebrated Colossus of the Sun, seventy cubits in height. It stood at the entrance of one of the ports, but the statement that it stood astride over the entrance, and that the largest ships could sail between its legs, is in all probability an exaggeration. It was the work of Chares, the pupil of Lysippus. It was erected about 280 B. C., and thrown down by an earthquake about 224 B. C. In this state it continued till sold by the Saracens to a Jew (A. D. 672), who broke it up and loaded nine hundred camels with the bronze. Rhodus was the birthplace of the poet Apollonius, and the philosopher Panætius. Lindus was the birthplace of Cleobu'lus, one of the seven wise men of Greece. Rhodus reached its highest degree of importance during the wars between the Macedonians and Romans, and remained constantly faithful to the latter.

QUESTIONS.—§ 51. Describe the situation of Rhodus.—What is said of its inhabitants?—What three ancient towns were to be found at Rhodus?—What cities formed the Doric Hexapolis?—What is said of the city of Rhodus?—What of the Colossus?—What celebrated men were born at Rhodus?—When did Rhodus reach its highest prosperity?

COS. (*Κῶς*, *Stanco*, i. e. *ἐς τὰν Κῶ*.)

It lies in the mouth of the Gulf of CER'AMUS. Its principal city, which was immediately opposite to Halicarnassus, bore the same name. It was destroyed by a severe earthquake. Cos was colonized from Epidaurus, and the new settlers introduced the worship of Æsculapius. A school of physicians was attached to its temple, the great collection of votive models in which made it a kind of museum of anatomy and pathology. Cos was the birthplace of Hippo'crates, of Apelles, and of Ptolemæus Philadelphus. Its wines, unguents, and purple dyes, were famous throughout Greece.

§ 52. SAMOS. (*Σάμος*, *Samo.*)

The name denotes *a height*, especially one situated near the sea-shore. This island rises conspicuous South-East of Chios, opposite Mount My'cale, from which it is separated by a narrow strait, the scene of the battle of My'cale (479 B. C.). It is a very rugged, though picturesque and productive island. There is good timber on the hills, which have abundant and valuable quarries of white marble. It was celebrated for its pottery. The population was a mixture of Carians, Lesbians, and Ionians. They were eminent in sculpture, bronze-casting, architecture, painting, and ship-building. Their coins are very numerous and worthy of attention. Samos was in very ancient times governed by tyrants, the most celebrated of whom was Poly'crates (555 B.C.), who had a larger navy than any other Grecian prince or state of his time, and extended his sway over many of the neighboring states. After his death it became subject to Persia. The city

---

QUESTIONS.—Where is the island of Cos situated?—What worship was introduced there?—What is said of its temple?—Who were born at Cos?—For what was Cos especially celebrated?——§ 52. What does the word Samos mean?—Where is the island situated?—Describe the island.—What is said of its population?—What of its government?—What is said of Polycrates?—To whom was the island subject after his death?

of SAMOS belonged to the Ionian confederacy. It founded the following five colonies: SAMOTHRA'CE, ANŒA, PERINTHUS, BISANTHE, and AMORGOS. Samos was the birthplace of Pythag'oras. Juno was the chief divinity of the island.

CHIOS. (*Χίος, Scio.*)

This is an island in the Ægæan Sea, opposite ER'YTHRÆ. It is very rocky, ill provided with water, and rain seldom falls there. It produced, however, corn and excellent wine. The Chian wine was exported to Italy and is often mentioned by the Roman writers. The *town* of Chios was on the Eastern side of the island. It belonged to the Ionian confederacy, and was one of the places that claimed to be the birthplace of Homer. A rock on the Northern coast of the island is still called HOMER'S SCHOOL.

LESBOS. (*Λέσβος, Mitylen.*)

It is a mountainous and very healthy island, situated near the coast of Mysia, exactly opposite the opening of the Gulf of ADRAMYTTIUM. It contained six cities which, even in Homer's time, were populous and flourishing: MITYLE'NE, PYRRHA, ERESSUS, ANTISSA, ARISBA, and METHYMNA.

Inhabitants.—The Æolians of Lesbos were among the most cultivated and refined of the Greeks, and were distinguished as well for their mercantile enterprise and bravery as for their marvellous attainments in the art of poetry conjoined with music. Lesbos produced the poets Alcæus, Sappho, Ari'on, Terpander; and the philosophers Pit'tacus and Theophrastus.

QUESTIONS.—To what confederacy did the city of Samos belong?—How many colonies did it found?—Give the names.—Who was born at Samos?—What goddess was worshipped there?—Where is Chios situated?—What are its productions?—Where was the town of Chios?—To what confederacy did the island belong?—What is Homer's School?—Where is Lesbos situated?—How many flourishing cities did it contain?—Name those cities.—What is said about the inhabitants?—What celebrated men were born at Lesbos?

Towns.—(1.) MYTILE'NE (*Μυτιλήνη*) was the most important city on the island, and has continued without intermission to flourish, up to the present day. It was originally built upon a small island, and possessed two harbors. The beauty of the ancient city and the strength of its fortifications are celebrated both by Greek and Roman writers. It was the birthplace of Sappho and Alcæus.

(2.) METHYMNA (*Μήθυμνα*) was situated on the Northern shore of the island. It was chiefly celebrated for the excellent wine produced in its neighborhood:

> *Non eadem arboribus pendet vindemia nostris,*
> *Quam Methymnæo carpit de palmite Lesbos.*—Virg. Georg. II. 89.

Methymna was the birthplace of the poet and musician Ari'on.

§ 53. TE'NEDOS. (*Τένεδος.*)

This is a small island near Troas, which acts a prominent part in the Trojan legend. During the wars of the Macedonians with the Romans, Te'nedos, owing to its situation near the entrance of the Hellespont, was an important naval station. In the war against Mithrida'tes, Lucullus fought a great naval battle near Te'nedos. In Virgil's time it had fallen into insignificance:

> *Est in conspectu Tenedos notissima fama*
> *Insula, dives opum, Priami dum regna manebant,*
> *Nunc tantum sinus, et statio malefida carinis.*—Æn. II. 21.

QUESTIONS.—Describe Mytilene.—Describe Methymna.—Who was born there?—Describe Tenedos.—What battle was fought in its neighborhood?

PATMOS. (*Πάτμος*, *Patmo.*)

Patmos was one of the Spo'rades in the South-Eastern part of the Ægæan Sea. This little island is celebrated as the place to which St. John was banished toward the close of the reign of Domitian, and where he wrote the *Revelation*. The cave is still shown where the Apostle is said to have received the revelation.

PATMOS.

I'NSULÆ ARGINU'SÆ. (*αἱ Ἀργινοῦσαι.*)

These are three small islands near the mainland of Æ'olis, opposite Cape Malea. Off these islands the ten commanders of the Athenians, after a severe struggle, gained a victory over the Spartans, in which battle Callicra'tidas, the brave Spartan king, was slain (406 B. C.).

The other islands of Asia in the Mediterranean are CAR'PATHUS, CHALCIA, TELOS, CALYMNA, LEPSIA, CASUS, SYME, NISY'RUS, LEROS, PSYRA, I'NSULÆ CORASSIÆ and IC'ARUS, with the towns, Istri and Œni.

QUESTIONS.—What is said of Patmos?—Where are the Arginusæ situated?—Who were conquered in its neighborhood?—What other islands of Asia were situated in the Mediterranean?

THE ISLANDS OF ASIA IN THE PROPONTIS:

OPHIUSSA, HALO'NE, PROCONNE'SUS (*Mar'mora*), celebrated for its *marble* (Lat. *marmor*), BES'BICUS and DEMONE'SI.

THE ISLANDS OF ASIA IN THE PONTUS EUXI'NUS:

I'NSULÆ CYANEÆ, or PETRÆ, two rocks at the entrance of the Bos'porus Thracius, THYNIAS, I'NSULA CI'LICUM, ARETIAS.

THE ISLANDS IN THE OCE'ANUS IN'DICUS.

TAPROBA'NE (*Ceylon*) was the only one of the East Indian islands which was known to any great extent to the ancient geographers.

Mountains.—MONTES GA'LIBI and MONS MALEA.

Rivers.—PHASIS, GANGES, AZA'NUS.

Cities.—ANUROGRAMMUM and MAAGRAMMUM.

Other islands: IABADIUS (*Java*), I'NSULÆ SATYRO'RUM (*Anamba islands*), and some of the Laccadives and Maldives.

QUESTIONS.—What islands of Asia are situated in the Propontis?—In the Euxinus?—What islands in the Oceanus Indicus?—What is said of Taprobane?

§ 54. LI'BYA. (ἡ Λιβύη.)

This was the general term applied to the Southern coast of the Mediterranean, between the mouth of the Nile and the shores of the Atlantic. It was sometimes regarded by ancient authors as an independent division of the earth's surface, and sometimes as a part of Asia, and even of Europe.

The name, *Libya*, comprised—

I. In the HOMERIC AGE (1000 B. C.), all that portion of the African Continent lying to the west of Ægypt:

II. In the TIME OF HERO'DOTUS (444 B. C.), the Southern coast of the Mediterranean, between the Isthmus of Suez and the Red Sea in the East, and the Oce'anus in the West and South. Hero'dotus (iv. 42) states that some Phœnicians at the order of Necho, king of Ægypt, set sail out of the Red Sea, coasted along the shores of Ægypt and Æthiopia, passed into the Ocean, and at the expiration of three years reached the waters of the Nile. The mariners, who took part in the voyage, reported the phenomenon of the sun appearing on their right hand, i. e. to the North, as they sailed round Li'bya. This expedition probably set out about 600 B. C. From the facts furnished by those engaged in it, Hero'dotus was led to determine the boundaries as above given:

III. In the TIMES OF PTOLEMY (200 A. D), the account of the voyage mentioned by Hero'dotus appears either to have been forgotten, or to have lost credit. The Western coast was then known as far as the In'sulæ Fortuna'tæ (prob. the *Canaries*),

---

QUESTIONS.—§ 54. What is said of Libya?—What did it comprise in Homer's time?—What in the time of Herodotus?—Give the boundaries of Herodotus.—How did he arrive at this determination?—What are the boundaries as stated by Ptolemy?—Are his boundaries better or worse defined than those of Herodotus?

but the Southern portion was believed to be joined to the Eastern part of Asia, and the Indian Ocean was supposed to be a vast salt lake.

Divisions.—ÆGYPTUS, ÆTHIOPIA, MEROË, MARMAR'ICA, CYRENA'ICA, AF'RICA, NUMIDIA, MAURITANIA, LI'BYA INTERIOR.

§ 55. ÆGYPTUS. (ἡ Αἴγυπτος.)

From the Northern extremity of the delta formed by the waters of the Nile, a long valley ascends along the course of the river beyond Memphis, to the spot where Luxor displays its astonishing ruins. Another valley extends from this point to the rocks over which the Nile falls in a succession of rapids. To the West lie deserts of sand; to the East, mountains whose bases are washed by the Arabian Gulf. The Delta and these valleys comprise the whole of Ægyptus. Ægyptus is remarkable as one of the most universally fruitful countries of the earth, and as the abode of a very ancient people.

Name.—It was called by the earliest inhabitants CHEMI (*Black* Land); in the Old Testament MAZOR or MIZRAIM (*Border*, or *Borders*, acc. to Gesenius; acc. to Bochart, *the Fortified*); by the Arabs, MESR; in the classics, ÆGYPTUS; and in the Coptic, EL-KEBIT (*the Inundated Land*).

Boundaries.—North, the MEDITERRANEAN; East, ISTHMUS OF ARSINOË and SINUS ARABI'CUS; South, ÆTHIOPIA; West, MARMAR'ICA and LIB'YCI MONTES.

Divisions.—DELTA, subdivided into ten districts, or provinces, called *nomes* (νομοί, i. e. *divisions*); HEPTA'NOMIS, into seven; and THEBA'ÏS, into ten. In earlier times, the number of *nomes* was only twelve; afterward they were increased to forty-five. Each *nome* had its peculiar creed, temple, priesthood, and magistrates.

QUESTIONS.—Name the different countries of Libya.——§ 55. Describe Ægyptus.—What is said of its name?—Give the boundaries of Ægyptus.—How was it divided?—What was a nome?

Extent.—Ægypt is that portion of the valley of the Nile between the islands of Philæ and Elephanti'ne, and the Mediterranean Sea. The average breadth of this valley is about seven miles, only five of which contain arable land. The broadest part, between Cairo and Edfou, is about eleven miles, and the narrowest, including the river, about two miles. The length is about 526 miles; its area about 11,000 square miles (a little larger than the state of Vermont).

§ **56. Mountains.**—MONTES ARA'BICI, MONTES LI'BYCI, MONS CASIUS, on the Western flank of which was the tomb of Pompe'ius Magnus.

Capes.—DREP'ANUM and LEPTE.

River.—NILUS (*the Nile*). (See page 118.)

Lakes.—LACUS TANIS, LACUS BU'TICA, LACUS MAREO'TIS, LACUS MŒ'RIDIS (see page 120), LACUS SIRBO'NIDIS, which Milton describes as

that Serbonian bog
'Twixt Damiata and Mount Casius old,
Where armies whole have sunk.—Par. Lost, II. 293.

This vast tract of morass was the scene of the partial destruction of the Persian army 350 B. C.

Productions.—Wheat, onions, beans, melons, cotton, papy'rus, lotus, olives, and figs. The following animals were native to the soil: oxen, horses, turtles, alligators, serpents, ichneumons, the ibis, tro'chili, and various kinds of fishes.

Climate.—The climate of the Delta is not so hot as Upper Ægypt, which belongs to the tropical regions.

Population.—No nation has bequeathed to us so many or such accurate memorials of its history and national characteristics as the Ægyptians have done. They were darker in hue than the Greeks or the neighboring Asiatics, but were not a negro

---

QUESTIONS.—What is the length and breadth of Ægypt?—How many square miles does it contain?——§ 56. Name the mountains.—The capes.—The rivers.—The lakes.—Describe Lacus Sirbonidis.—What army was destroyed there?—Name the chief productions.—What is said about the climate?—What is said of the Ægyptians?

race; this is proved by osteology and by their monumental paintings, where negroes often appear, but always either as tributaries or captives. The valley of the Nile contained probably three races, with an admixture of a fourth. On the Eastern shores were ARABIANS; on the Western, LIBYANS. The ruling caste was an elder branch of the Syro-Arabian family. The fourth class was the mixed race of the ruling caste and the Libyans. The number of its inhabitants varied from four millions to six millions.

§ **57. Cities.**—I. In ÆGYPTUS INFERIOR (*ἡ κάτω χώρα; El-Rif*), LOWER ÆGYPT:

(1.) CANO'BUS, or CANO'PUS (*Κάνωβος*, or *Κάνωπος*), near the Western (Canopian) mouth of the Nile. Before the foundation of Alexandri'a, it was an important commercial town. It was celebrated for the temple and oracle of Sera'pis.

(2.) SAÏS (*Σαΐς*), on the Eastern bank of the Canopian arm of the Nile. It was the ancient capital of Lower Ægypt, and contained the tombs of the Pharaohs.

(3.) NAU'CRATIS (*Ναύκρατις*), a colony of Mile'tus, and settled as early as 550 B.C. It was the only place in Ægypt where the Greeks were allowed to settle or foreign merchants to resort (Hdt. ii. 178, 179). It was the birthplace of Athenæus and Julius Pollux.

(4.) BUSI'RIS (*Βούσιρις*), celebrated for an immense temple dedicated to Isis.

(5.) BUBASTUS (*Βούβαστος*), noted for the temple and festivals maintained in honor of Dia'na Bubastis.

(6.) PELUSIUM (*Πηλούσιον*), on the Eastern side of the Easternmost mouth of the Nile, which derived its name from the town. In the Scriptures it is called *Sin*, and "the strength of Egypt" (*Ezek*. xxx. 15), on account of its strong fortifications.

QUESTIONS.—How many races did the valley of the Nile contain?—Describe them.—What was the number of its inhabitants?——§ 57. Where was Canobus situated?—What was the ancient capital of Lower Ægypt?—What is said of Naucratis?—What temple was at Busiris?—What at Bubastus?—Where was Pelusium situated?—What is it called in the Scriptures?

It was often the scene of battles and sieges, from the epoch of the defeat of Sennacherib (713 B.C.) down to its capture by Octavia'nus (31 B.C.). It was the birthplace of Ptolemy, the geographer.

(7.) HELIOP'OLIS (Ἡλιούπολις), in the Sacred Writings called *On*, or *Beth'shemesh;* the chief seat of the worship of the Sun. The priests attached to this worship were reputed to be very learned. Joseph married Asenath, the daughter of one of the priests of On (*Gen.* xli. 45).

(8.) HEROÖP'OLIS (Ἡρώων πόλις, or Ἡρῶ), the residence of the ancient shepherd kings. In the neighborhood of this town was Goshen, the rich pastoral district in which the Israelites first dwelt. It was situated along the Eastern bank of the Nile.

(9.) ONEION, founded by the Hebrew priest, Onias (173 B.C.). The city and temple existed for nearly two hundred and fifty years.

(10.) ARSINOË (Ἀρσινόη, *Suez*), at the entrance of the canal which connected the Red Sea with the Nile.

(11.) CERCASO'RUS (Κερκάσωρος), situated at the point where the Nile separated into different channels.

(12.) Other towns: NICOP'OLIS, HERMOP'OLIS, ANDROP'OLIS, GYNÆOÖP'OLIS, MENDES, TANIS, BUTO, BABYLON.

(13.) ALEXANDRI'A (see page 123).

Delta, the name of the fourth letter of the Greek alphabet, was given by the Greeks to that part of Lower Ægypt which was comprised between the Canopian and Pelusian branches of the Nile and the sea, and which had a triangular form, somewhat resembling the Greek letter *Delta*, Δ.

§ **58.** II. In MIDDLE ÆGYPT, or HEPTA'NOMIS (ἡ μεταξὺ χώρα, or Ἑπτανομίς; *Wusta'ni*), which extended from the division of the Nile at Cercaso'rus to Chemnis:

QUESTIONS.—Who was born at Pelusium?—What was the chief seat of the worship of the Sun?—Where was Goshen situated?—What is said of Oneion?—What of Arsinoe?—Of Cercasorus?—What is the Delta?—Why was this name given to the northern part of Ægypt?—§ 58. How far did Heptanomis extend?

(1.) MEMPHIS (*Μέμφις; Memf*). After the fall of Thebes, this was the capital of Ægyptus, and in the time of Psammet'ichus it became the royal residence. From this period until its destruction by Camby'ses, it enjoyed its greatest prosperity. It was the centre of inland commerce, and also of the religion of Apis and Sera'pis. From the priests attached to the national worship, the Greeks derived their knowledge of Ægyptian annals, and the rudiments also of their philosophical systems. At Busi'ris in the neighborhood of Memphis were the three highest pyramids. (See page 120.)

(2.) CROCODILOP'OLIS (later, *Arsinoë, 'Αρσινόη*), the seat of the worship of the Crocodile. In the North-West part of the city was the famous Labyrinth (*Λαβύρινθος*). It contained no less than three thousand apartments, of which fifteen hundred were subterranean, and an equal number were above ground, the whole being surrounded by a massive wall. It was divided into courts, each of which was surrounded by colonnades of white marble. Hero'dotus, who saw the upper part of it, was not allowed to enter the subterranean passages, which were the burial-places of its royal founders, and of the sacred Crocodiles. The whole arrangement of the edifice was a symbolical representation of the zodiac and the solar system.

(3.) Other cities: ACANTHUS, NILOP'OLIS, HERACLEOP'OLIS, HERMOPOLITA'NE PHY'LACE.

In this part of Ægypt are included three O'ases (*'Οάσεις, Αὐάσεις;* prob. the Coptic *Ouah*, a resting-place)—fertile spots in the Libyan desert—which, in the Roman time, were used as places of banishment.

QUESTIONS.—What city became the capital of Ægypt after the fall of Thebes?—When did Memphis become the royal residence?—What temples were in Memphis?—What influence did they exercise upon Greece?—What is said of Crocodilopolis?—Describe the Labyrinth.—What are Oases?—Whence probably the name?—Where are they situated?—For what purpose were they used by the Roman government?

III. In UPPER ÆGYPT, or THEBA'ÏS (Θηβαΐς or οἱ ἄνω τόποι; *Said*). It extended from Chemnis to Sye'ne, where Æthiopia begins:

(1.) ABY'DUS (Ἄβυδος). Here was the celebrated tomb of Osi'ris. The celebrated list of the Pharaohs, known as *the Tablet of Aby'dus*, now in the British Museum, was found at Aby'dus.

(2.) TEN'TYRA (Τέντυρα, *Den'derah*), where still exist the best preserved remains of an ancient Ægyptian temple. A portion of the ceiling, which was adorned with a representation of the zodiac, was taken down and transported to Paris. From this zodiac an extravagant idea of the antiquity of the temple was entertained, until the key to the interpretation of hieroglyphics was discovered.

(3.) COPTUS (Κοπτός, *Kuft;* whence probably the modern *Kubt, Copts*, i. e. the people of Ægypt mainly descended from the ancient *Ægyptians* as distinguished from foreigners; compare the word Αἴ-γυπτ-ος) was noted for its extensive commerce. A road led from the city to Bereni'ce (Βερενίκη), by which the merchandise of India was transported to the Nile. Its neighborhood was celebrated for emeralds and other precious stones.

(4.) SYE'NE (Συήνη, *Assouan*), at the Southern boundary of Egypt, near the rapids of the Nile.

(5.) ELEPHANTI'NE, and PHILÆ (Ἐλεφαντίνη, Φιλαί), two islands in the Nile, celebrated, the former for its rock-hewn temples; the latter, for its rich architectural remains.

(6.) Other towns: LYCOP'OLIS, APHRODITOP'OLIS, PTOLEMA'IS HERMII, HERMONTHIS, LATOP'OLIS, CHEMNIS, later PANOP'OLIS.

(7.) THEBÆ. (See page 122.)

QUESTIONS.—How far did Thebais extend?—What is said of Abydos?—What is said of Tentyra?—What of its zodiac?—For what is Coptus noted?—What is said of the name?—What was found in its neighborhood?—What two celebrated islands were situated in the Nile?

§ 59. NILUS (*Νεῖλος*), *Nile; El-Bahr* or *Bahr Nil.*

As Ægypt was the principal resort of the scientific men of Greece, the Nile has been more accurately examined and described by classical authors than any other river of the ancient world.

Name.—The Scripture designation *Sihor* (*Jer.* ii. 18), the Coptic *Chemi* (used both of the country and the river, as in Gr. *ὁ Αἴγυπτος*, the Nile; *ἡ Αἴγυπτος*, Ægypt) and the old Latin *Melo* (*μέλας*) were applied to it with reference to its color imparted by the *dark* slime. Virgil says of it:

Et viridem Ægyptum nigra fecundat arena.—Georg. iv. 291.

The name *Νεῖλος*, *Nilus*, *Nil*, *Nile* is probably the Hebrew *Nahal*, river, in which language it was also termed *Nahal*-Mizraim, River of Egypt.

The river is formed by the confluence of two head-streams, the As'TAPUS, or *Blue River* (*Bahr-el-Azrek*), and the *White River* (*Bahr-el-Abiad*). These two streams meet at a point near the site of the modern Khartoom. Here the united waters, after passing through a gloomy defile, traverse the immense plains of Meroë. At the extremity of the peninsular tract of Meroë, the Nile receives its last tributary, the ASTAB'ORAS (*Tacazze*). Between this point and Sye'ne, a distance of some seven hundred miles, occur the Cataracts of the Nile, in reference to which the ancients invented, or credited, many astounding marvels. There are seven cataracts in all, none of them remarkable for their height. The descent of the second, or great cataract, is but eighty feet in a space of five miles.

At Sye'ne the Nile enters Ægypt. Between SYE'NE and LA-

QUESTIONS.—§ 59. What information do we possess in regard to the Nile?—What two rivers unite to form the Nile?—What is said of its various names?—What river does the Nile receive beyond Meroë?—How long is the region of the Cataracts?—What is said of the rapids?—Where does the Nile enter Ægypt?

TOP'OLIS the country is sterile and unattractive, because deprived of the fertilizing benefits of the periodical inundations, in consequence of the high and rocky character of the river banks. Beyond Latop'olis, descending the stream, the shores become less rugged, and allow a broader verge for the earthy deposits of the river, and at Thebes the banks present a broad plain on each side, little elevated above the ordinary level of the water. Near DIO'SPOLIS PARVA (*How*) starts the CANAL OF JOSEPH (*Bahr-Yussouff*), which flows in a direction parallel with the river through Arsi'noë. A little below Memphis, the rocks on both sides of the river diverge again, and the river expands into the wide alluvial plains of the Delta. At CERCASO'RUM the river put forth two main branches, and beside these, five others. These seven arms of the Nile were known by the following names, going from East to West: the PELUSIAN, the TANITIC, the PHATNITIC, the SEBENNYTIC, the BOLBITIC, and the CANOPIAN. Of these only two—at Damietta and Rosetta—are now navigable. The three main arms were the PELUSIAN, SEBENNYTIC, and CANOPIAN.

Upper and Lower Ægypt, during the periodical inundations from the beginning of July to the beginning of November, present the appearance of a vast inland lake, and the Delta, of a wide gulf. These inundations are caused by the torrents of rain in the month of May in Æthiopia. The rise of the river, which was ordinarily from fifteen to sixteen cubits, was carefully noted on instruments called Nilo'meters, at Primis, Elephanti'ne, and Memphis; and its rising or falling was reported by letters to different parts of Ægypt, in order that the farmers might calculate the time for the commencement of sowing.

The Nile, as the sole sustainer of life in a seeming valley of death, was worshipped with divine honors.

QUESTIONS.—Where does the valley of the Nile commence?—What was the Canal of Joseph?—Where does the separation of the Nile begin?—What are the three main arms?—Describe the inundation of the river.—What was the use of the Nilometers?—Why was the state of the river reported throughout the country?—Why was the Nile worshipped?

§ 60. LAKE MŒRIS. (*Μοίριδος λίμνη, Birket-el-Kerun.*)

This was the most extensive and remarkable of all the Ægyptian lakes, and connected with the Nile by the Canal of Joseph. Its area was not less than two hundred and ten square miles. It was regarded by Hero'dotus (ii. 149) as an artificial lake, but more correctly by Strabo as a natural basin. The name of ARSI'NOË was originally applied to a limestone valley, in the Southern part of which was this lake. In remote periods, the entire valley was a reservoir for the waters descending from the surrounding hills. As the waters gradually subsided, the highest points of land were cultivated, so that the whole of the lake was diversified by fertile islands and peninsulas, all of which disappeared during the annual inundations.

According to Hero'dotus, there were two pyramids in the lake itself, each rising three hundred feet above the surface of the water, and sinking to an equal depth below it. On the top of each was a colossal human figure of stone, seated on a throne.

PYRAMIDS.

The Pyramids are only found in Central Ægypt. They are quadrilateral piles of masonry, consisting of a series of platforms, rising one above the other, each smaller than the one on which it rests, and consequently presenting, where the smooth casing of stone has been removed as material for building, the appearance of steps which diminish in length from the bottom to the top. The pyramids are built in groups, some of which lie at a considerable distance from each other. It has been supposed that

---

QUESTIONS.—§ 60. What is the most remarkable of the Ægyptian lakes?—How is it connected with the Nile?—What is its extent?—Is it an artificial lake?—In which nome was it situated?—Describe the lake during the time of the inundation.—What is said about the pyramids in the lake?—Where are the Pyramids to be found?—What kind of structures are they?—Are they built separately?

they were intended for royal sepulchres, and also as places of observation for astronomical purposes. They range in a line running exactly North and South; and while the direction of the faces to the East and West might have served to fix the return of a certain period of the year, the shadow cast by the sun, or the time of its coincidence with their slope, might have been observed for a similar purpose. The length of one of the sides of the base of the greatest pyramid, if multiplied five hundred times, is exactly equal to a geographical degree. The cube of the Nilo'meter, if multiplied two hundred thousand times, gives precisely the same measurement.

The most important group of pyramids is near the modern village *El-Gizeh*, distant about seven miles from the banks of the Nile. Here is also the largest pyramid. Hero'dotus was informed by the priests of Memphis that this was built by Cheops, king of Ægypt (900 B.C.); that the body of Cheops was placed in a room beneath the base of the pyramid; and that the chamber was surrounded by a vault, to which the waters of the

---

QUESTIONS.—What were the Pyramids intended for?—Describe how they were placed.—In what relation are the sides of their base to a geographical degree?—Which is the most celebrated group?—Which is the largest pyramid?—Mention the particulars that are known of this pyramid.

Nile were conveyed by a subterranean passage. The entrance to the pyramid is in the North face. Within are passages leading to chambers lined with granite, in one of which is a sarco'phagus of red granite, supposed to be the tomb of Cheops.

§ 61. THEBÆ (Θῆβαι) AND ITS NECROP'OLIS.

Thebes was the religious capital of all who worshipped Ammon, from Pelusium to Axu'me, and from the O'ases of Li'bya to the Red Sea. In the Sacred Writings it is called NO, or NO-AMMON; its native appellation was T-APE, i. e. *the Head*, whence its classical name THEBÆ: it was also designated in the classics, DIO'SPOLIS MAGNA. Situated in an extensive plain, it occupied both banks of the Nile. On the eastern bank the population was densely crowded, while the western was more especially appropriated to the numerous temples with their avenues of sacred Sphinxes. Rumors of its greatness had reached the Greeks of Homer's age, who called it the *hundred-gated* (Θήβας—αἵθ' ἑκατόμπυλοί εἰσι—Il. ix. 381 seqq.), which expression may not have been intended as an allusion to the gates of the *city* (as the city was not surrounded with any wall), but employed to indicate the number of *temple*-gates.

The power and prosperity of Thebes are to be ascribed to three causes:

First, its TRADE: in ancient times it was the great emporium of Eastern Africa.

Second: its MANUFACTURES of linen, glass, and pottery.

Third: its RELIGION. Thebes was to Ægypt and to Æthiopia what Rome was to mediæval Christendom. When the stream of commerce had turned to Alexandri'a, and its manufactures

---

QUESTIONS.—§ 61. What was the religious capital of Ægypt?—How was it called in the Sacred Writings?—What was its native appellation?—What its classical?—Where was it situated?—How was it divided?—What was the difference between its two divisions?—How is it called by Homer?—What does this appellation signify?—Name the sources of the prosperity of Thebes.—Which of these sources operated the longest?

had fallen into decay, Thebes still remained the headquarters of the Ægyptian priesthood, and the principal retreat of old Ægyptian manners and customs. The remains of the monuments of Thebes, exclusive of its sepulchral grottoes, cover on both sides of the river a large space, of which the extreme length from North to South is about two miles, and the extreme breadth from East to West about four. The most remarkable buildings are the collection of temples called *El-Karnak*, after a modern village in the vicinity. They lie on the Eastern bank of the river, and consist of a large temple and several smaller structures, surrounded by a massive brick wall.

Another striking object is the VOCAL MEMNON, the most Northerly of two gigantic statues, which formerly gave forth at sunrise certain sounds, probably due to some unexplained physical cause. On the Western bank was the Necrop'olis, *the City of the Dead*. Here are found the rock-hewn painted tombs, *the Tombs of the Kings*, whose sculptures so copiously illustrate the history, the arts, and the social life of Ægypt. Here also are the famous OBELISKS, pillars of stone square at the base and terminating in a point, generally formed out of a single block of granite. Several of them have been taken to Europe and erected in Rome, Paris, and London.

§ 62. ALEXANDRI'A.

(*Ἀλεξάνδρεια*, Alexandria, *El-Skanderish.*)

The capital of the empire of the La'gidæ, so called from Lagus, the father of Ptolemy, the founder of the Ægyptian monarchy. It was the Hellenic capital of Ægypt. It was founded (332 B. C.) at the North-East angle of the Lake Mareo'tis, by Alexander the Great, who himself traced the

QUESTIONS.—How great was the extent of the city?—Describe the temples of *El-Karnak*.—What was the Vocal Memnon?—Where was the Necropolis situated?—Describe the tombs of the kings.—What is an obelisk?——§ 62. What was the Hellenic capital of Ægypt?—Who was its founder?

ground-plan. It was not completed until the reign of Ptolemæus Philadelphus, and received embellishments and additions from nearly every potentate of the Lagid dynasty. The city was situated on a narrow strip of land between the Lake Mareo'tis and the sea, and was laid out in parallelograms, the streets crossing each other at right angles. The whole city was divided into three parts: the Greek, Ægyptian, and Jewish quarters, each of which was surrounded by its own walls. The Greek quarter contained the most conspicuous of the public buildings. Here was the far-famed LIBRARY and MUSEUM, enriched with 700,000 volumes, a part of which were placed in the temple of SERA'PIS in the Ægyptian quarter. Here were also deposited the 200,000 volumes of the library of Per'gamus, presented by Marcus Antonius to Cleopa'tra. The library of the Museum was destroyed while Julius Cæsar was blockading the Greek quarter (48 B. C.); that of the Serapeion is said, but without any very positive proof, to have been destroyed by the Saracens at the command of the Caliph Omar (A. D. 650). The collection was begun by Ptolemæus Soter, and largely augmented by his successors. They retained all the original manuscripts which were brought to Alexandri'a, and gave copies of them to their proper owners. Among the professors and pupils of the institution were EUCLID, CTESIBIUS, CALLI'MACHUS, ARA'TUS, ARISTO'PHANES, and ARISTARCHUS, the last-named of whom was considered the most distinguished critic of antiquity.

In the Greek quarter also stood the MAUSOLE'UM of the Ptolemies, or the SOMO, containing also the remains of Alexander the Great. The population of Alexandri'a was about half a mil-

---

QUESTIONS.—Who completed his work?—Where was the city situated?—How was the city laid out?—Into how many parts was it divided?—What part contained the bulk of the public institutions?—Describe the library.—Where was a part of the library placed?—When was the library of the Museum destroyed?—When the Serapeion?—How did they come in possession of manuscripts?—Name some of the men of learning whose names are associated with the Museum.—What was the Mausoleum?—What was the Somo?—What is said of the population?

TOWER OF PHAROS.

lion, and consisted of people from all parts of the world. They formed a very gay, yet very industrious, population. Beside the exporting trade, the city had numerous manufactories of paper, linen, glass, and muslin. It had four harbors, the largest of which was sheltered from the North winds by the island of Pharos. On this island, and named after it, was the celebrated Tower of the Pharos. It consisted of several stories and is said to have been four hundred feet in height. It was built about 300 B.C., and the architect, as the inscription stated, was So'stratus of Cnidus. A telescopic mirror of metal was placed at its summit, in which vessels might be discerned at a very great distance. The old lighthouse of Alexandria still occupies the site of its ancient predecessor.

QUESTIONS.—What is said of the trade of the city?—What of the Pharos?

§ 63. ÆTHIOPIA.

(ἡ *Αἰθιοπία*, *Habesch*, *Kordofan*, and *Nubia*.)

Æthiopia, as an ethnic designation, comprised those who dwelt between the equator, the Red Sea, and the Atlantic. Strabo gives the Æthiopians the epithet Hesperian, and Herodotus treats of them as inhabiting all South Libya. The name Æthiopians (*Αἰθίοπες*, *Æthi'opes*) is probably Semitic, but the Greek geographers deduced it from *αἴθω-ὤψ*, and accordingly applied it to all the *sun-burnt*, *dark-complexioned* races above Ægypt.

Boundaries.—North, ÆGYPTUS and MARMAR'ICA; East, SINUS ARAB'ICUS and MARE RUBRUM; South, and West, unknown.

Mountains.—GAR'BATA, E'LEPHAS, MONTES ÆTHIOP'ICI, and MONTES LUNÆ.

Rivers.—AS'TAPUS, ASTAB'ORAS, and NILUS.

Inhabitants.—The Greeks gave them the following names: ICHTHYO'PHAGI (*Ἰχθυοφάγοι*, *Fish-eaters*), inhabiting the shores of the Sinus Ara'bicus, South-East of Sye'ne; TROGLO'DYTÆ (*Τρωγλοδύται*, *Cave-dwellers*); HYLO'PHAGI (*Ὑλοφάγοι*, *Wood-eaters*); ELEPHANTO'PHAGI (*Ἐλεφαντοφάγοι*, *Elephant-eaters*). These tribes belonged to the Semitic race, and spoke a language closely allied to the Arabic. They were never wholly conquered by the most powerful rulers of Egypt or of Rome, while in the earliest times the Æthiopians often invaded Egypt, and even subdued it for a time. In the reign of Augustus, an Æthiopian queen, Can'dace, defeated C. Petronius. One of her officers of state was baptized by the evangelist Philip (*Acts*, viii. 36).

QUESTIONS.—§ 63. What is said of the origin of the names Æthiopia and Æthiopians, and how were they used?—Name the boundaries of this land.—The mountains.—The rivers.—The tribes.—To what race did they belong?—What language did they speak?—Who conquered them?—What is said of Candace?—What of one of her officers?

In the Old Testament Æthiopia stands for the Heb. *Cush* (the name of the son of Ham), which designates Eastern Arabia and the region South of Ægypt (with *Ham*, Heb. *Cham*, *hot*, comp. the Coptic name of Ægypt, *Chemi*, i. e. *black*, *hot*, and the Heb. designation of Ægypt, *the Land of Ham*, *Ps.* cv. 23).

The Æthiopia of the New Testament was South of Ægypt on the Nile, including the island of Me'roë, and corresponded to the modern Nubia and the adjacent parts of Abyssinia, forming a separate kingdom governed by a succession of females, all bearing the name Can'dace (*Κανδάκη*). Compare the designation *Pharaoh*, i. e. *the King*, the common title of the Ægyptian monarchs down to the time of the Persian invasion.

MEROË. (*ἡ Μερόη.*)

Me'roë was in fact a peninsula situated between the NILE, AS'TAPUS, and ASTAB'ORAS. It is described, however, by the ancient geographers as an island.

Productions.—Gold, iron, and copper were among its minerals, and date-palms and almond trees among its valuable trees. It contained large meadows, affording fine grazing for cattle, and also forests abounding with wild beasts and game.

From the remotest times MEROË was the principal seat of commercial intercourse between Æthiopia and the Red Sea; afterward it was one of the chief centres of the great trade carried on between Carthage, the East, and the interior of Libya.

Inhabitants.—The military caste of Egypt, having left their country on account of some injustice received from the king, settled in Me'roë (650 B. C.), brought the natives of that region under their sway, and established a system of government somewhat similar to that of Egypt, but differing from it in the

---

QUESTIONS.—What does Æthiopia signify in the Sacred Writings?—Where was Meroë situated?—What is said of its productions?—What of its commerce?—Who settled in Meroë?—Why?—What was the difference between the governments of Egypt and Æthiopia?

restraints put upon the power of the kings and in the greater influence of the priestly caste.

Cities.—In Me'roë and Æthiopia:

(1.) AUXU'ME (*Αὐξούμη*), and ADU'LE (*Ἀδούλη, Azoole*), two commercial towns. In the latter the *Monumentum Adulita'num* was found (A. D. 535). It is a Greek inscription in which the conquests of Ptolemy Euer'getes are recorded.

(2.) PTOLEMA'IS THERON, the chief mart for the ivory trade.

(3.) MEROË (*Μερόη*), the religious capital of Æthiopia and Me'roë, which contained one of the largest temples of Ammon.

(4.) Other towns: NAPA'TA, BERENI'CE PANCHRY'SOS (i. e. the *all-golden*, from its vicinity to *Jebel Allaki*, the principal gold mines of the Ægyptians), and BERENI'CE EPIDI'RES.

§ 64. MARMA'RICA (*ἡ Μαρμαρική*) AND THE AMMONIUM.

Boundaries.—North, the MEDITERRANEAN; East, ÆGYPTUS; South, LIBYA INTERIOR; West, CYRENA'ICA.

Inhabitants.—MARMA'RIDÆ. The tribes in the interior were entirely different from those on the coast. The latter closely resembled the Egyptians.

Cities.—CHERSONE'SUS MAGNA, TAPOSI'RIS, and PARÆTONIUM (*Παραιτόνιον*), also called Ammonia, a large city which was a dependency of Egypt.

South of Marma'rica, in the midst of the sands of the Libyan Desert, was a small and beautiful spot, an O'asis (now *Siwah*), rich in fountains and shade, and luxuriant with verdure, in which stood the celebrated temple of AMMON, the ram-headed god of Thebes. In a grove of dates South of the Ammonium, was the FONS SOLIS, the high temperature of which is not

---

QUESTIONS.—What was the capital of Meröe?—What is the Monumentum Adulitanum?——§ 64. What are the boundaries of Marmarica?—What is said of its inhabitants?—What of its towns?—Where was the Oasis of Ammon situated?—What was Ammon?—Describe the Fons Solis.

observed during the heat of the day, but at night it is perceptibly warmer than the surrounding atmosphere:

> *Esse apud Ammonis fanum fons luce diurna*
> *Frigidus, at calidus nocturno tempore fertur.*—Lucretius, VI. 848.

Here also was the ancient and much-famed oracle (*Ammonium*), so difficult and dangerous of access through the Libyan deserts. It was consulted by Alexander the Great, whom it saluted as *the Son of Ammon.* In honor of this event, Alexander is represented on some of his medals as bearing a ram's horn in his hand.

CYRENA'ICA (ἡ Κυρηναία) or PENTAP'OLIS.

Boundaries.—North, the MEDITERRANEAN; East, MARMA'RICA; South, LIBYA INTERIOR; West, REGIO SYR'TICA with the ARÆ PHILÆNORUM.

Capes.—PROMONTORIUM BORION and PHYCUS.

Mountains.—The country is dotted with mountains of considerable elevation, which reach their highest point of altitude near Cyre'ne. The valleys are very productive, though frequently traversed by ravines which carry off to the sea the winter freshets, and which at no season of the year are destitute of water.

River.—LATHON.

Inhabitants.—These were Theræan colonists who married Libyans. Colonists afterward came from all parts of Greece, principally from Pelopone'sus, Creta, and the other islands of the Ægæan Sea.

Cities.—The *five* principal *cities* from which the country derives its name of Pentap'olis are: (1.) CYRE'NE (Κυρήνη), the chief city; (2.) BERENI'CE (Βερενίκη), previously Hes'peris;

QUESTIONS.—Who consulted the Ammonium?—How is Cyrenaica bounded?—Name the capes.—Describe the character of the country.—What is said of the inhabitants?—What five cities constituted the Pentapolis?

(3.) BARCA (Βάρκα), from which most of the inhabitants retired to Ptolema'is on the coast to enrich themselves by commerce; (4.) ARSINOË (Ἀρσινόη), earlier Tauchi'ra; (5.) APOLLONIA (Ἀπολλωνία), the harbor of Cyre'ne, and birthplace of Eratos'-thenes.

Cyre'ne was the chief city of the Libyan Pentap'olis. It was founded by Battus, who led thither a Lacedæmonian colony from THERA, one of the Cy'clades (630 B.C.). Five centuries later, Cyre'ne, with the whole territory of the ancient Pentap'olis, was bequeathed to the Romans by the last of the Ptolemies, surnamed Apion (97 B.C.) It was afterward formed into one province with Creta. Cyre'ne was the birthplace of ARISTIPPUS and CALLI'MACHUS. A part of its inhabitants left it and founded BARCA, in the interior (560 B.C.), which became a powerful state, and extended its dominion over the whole of Western Cyrena'ica. Fifty years later, the city was taken by the Persians.

§ 65. AF'RICA or AFRICA PROVINCIA. (ἡ Καρχηδονία.)

Name.—Africa is the name by which the quarter of the world still called *Africa* was known to the Romans, who received it from the Carthaginians and applied it first to that part of Africa with which they first became acquainted, the part namely about Carthage, and afterward to the whole continent.

Boundaries.—North, the MEDITERRANEAN; East, CYRENA'-ICA; South, LIBYA INTERIOR; West, NUMIDIA. The Western limit was the river TUSCA.

Divisions.—It was divided into three parts:

(1.) REGIO SYR'TICA, or TRIPOLITA'NA—now *Tripoli*—the South-Eastern part.

QUESTIONS.—What was the chief city?—When and by whom was it founded?—When and by whom was it bequeathed to the Romans?—Who were natives of Cyrenaica?—What is said of Barca?——§ 65. What did the name of Africa mean in its early and restricted sense?—How was this country bounded?—What river formed the western boundary?—How was it divided?

(2.) ZEUGITA'NA (which embraced the modern *Frigeah*, probably a corruption of the ancient *Africa*), the Western part.

(3.) BYZACIUM, a narrow strip of land along the Eastern coast.

Mountains.—MONS GIGLIUS and MONS CIRNA.

Capes.—PROMONTORIUM CEPH'ALÆ, PROMONTORIUM MERCURII, PROMONTORIUM CAN'DIDUM (Cape *Blanco*).

Gulfs.—SYRTIS MAJOR and SYRTIS MINOR.

Rivers.—CIN'YPHUS, TRITON, BAG'RADA.

Productions.—Grain and fruit in abundance. Precious stones were among its mineral treasures. The plains of Zeugita'na and Byzacium were always proverbial for their fertility.

Inhabitants.—The original inhabitants were Caucasians, and not negroes. At an early period colonists from the Western coast of Asia, chiefly from Phœnicia, settled on these shores.

Cities.—I. In Regio Syr'tica:—

LEPTIS MAGNA, a Sidonian colony, the birthplace of Septimius Seve'rus; O'EA and SA'BRATA. From these *three cities* the country derived the name of TRIPOLITA'NA.

II. In Zeugita'na:

ADES, South of Carthage. Hanno was conquered here by Re'gulus (258 B.C.); U'TICA, the oldest Phœnician colony, was the scene of Cato's suicide (47 B.C.).

III. In Byzacium:

CAPSA, in an O'asis. It was the place where Jugurtha deposited his reserved treasures. It was destroyed by Marius.

Islands.—In the Syrtis Minor are the islands MENINSE and CERCI'NA.

QUESTIONS.—Name the mountains.—Capes.—Gulfs.—Rivers.—What is said of the productions?—What of the fertility of the soil?—What of the inhabitants?—What three towns were in Regio Syrtica?—What towns in Zeugitana?—In Byzacium?—What islands in Syrtis Minor?

§ 66. CARTHA'GO. (ἡ Καρχηδών.)

Urbs antiqua fuit, Tyrii tenuêre coloni,
CARTHAGO, *Italiam longe Tiberinaque contra*
Ostia, dives opum, studiisque asperrima belli;
Quam Juno fertur terris magis omnibus unam
Posthabita coluisse Samo.—Virg. Æn. I. 12.

Name.—The name Cartha'go is of Phœnician origin and means *Newtown.* The city seems to have been so called to distinguish it from another Phœnician city in its neighborhood, *U'tica* which is the Phœnician for *Old-town.*

Carthage, according to tradition, was founded 814 B. C. by a Phœnician colony from Tyre under the conduct of the princess Dido. The city was situated on a peninsula where the African shore juts out into the Mediterranean and approaches nearest to the opposite coast of Sicily. Its citadel, BYRSA, surrounded by a triple wall, and crowned at its summit by a magnificent temple dedicated to Æsculapius, was built upon the narrow isthmus of this peninsula. In the fourth century B. C. its empire extended eastward as far as the Altars of the Philæni, near the Great Syrtis, and westward along the coast to the Ocean. CARCHEDONIA (the part subject to its dominion) comprised only Zeugita'na and, further south, the strip of coast along which lay Byzacium and the Emporia. Its inhabitants were called Liby-Phœnicians, a mixed population formed by the intermarriage of Phœnician settlers with the natives. At the beginning of the wars with Rome it contained 700,000 inhabitants. In its infancy an agricultural state, it soon became the greatest commercial emporium of the world. Manufactures were established and the mechanic arts cultivated; great wealth flowed into the

---

QUESTIONS.—§ 66. What is said of the name of Carthage?—When was it founded?—By whom?—Where was it situated?—What was Byrsa?—Where situated?—How far did the empire of Carthage extend?—What is said of its inhabitants?—What were the sources of its wealth?

CARTHAGE.

city by the import of the precious metals. The dependencies were all obliged to pay a heavy tribute, mostly in produce. The military system of Carthage grew out of the necessity for foreign conquest which was entailed upon the state by the extension of her commerce. Her armies were composed of her Libyan subjects, who served by compulsion; of the mercenaries from the Nomadic tribes; and finally of her slaves. Such soldiers had never any real attachment to the cause in which they fought, nor to the commanders under whom they served. The city is immortalized on account of the three wars it sustained against Rome, each characterized by an imperishable name:—

I. B.C. 264—241: RE'GULUS.

II. B.C. 219—202: HAN'NIBAL.

III. B.C. 149—146: SCIPIO the Younger.

The third Punic war terminated with the total defeat and demolition of CARTHAGE by Scipio Africa'nus Minor. A century

QUESTIONS.—Describe the military system of Carthage.—How many wars did it sustain against Rome?—What was the result of those wars?

afterward it was rebuilt, and again became a flourishing city, only second in size to Rome. Ecclesiastically it was one of the most important of the numerous bishoprics of Africa. Among the great names associated with Carthage are Cyprian, its celebrated bishop, and Tertullian, who was probably a native of the city. It was taken by Genseric, A. D. 439, and made the capital of the VANDAL KINGDOM in Africa. It was retaken by Belisarius, A. D. 533, and finally destroyed by the Arabs under Hassan, A. D. 647. Even the ruins of CARTHAGE are now buried or have almost perished; and its site might be totally unknown, if some broken arches of an aqueduct did not serve to guide the footsteps of the inquisitive traveller.

§ 67. ARÆ PHILÆNO'RUM.

This was an elevated table-land, very near the base of the Great Syrtis on the North coast of Africa, which marked the boundary between the territories of CARTHAGE and CYRE'NE. The name is derived from the following story: The citizens of Carthage and Cyre'ne having had much dissension respecting the boundaries of the two states, resolved to fix them at the point where their respective envoys, sent forth at the same time, should meet. Two brothers, named Philæni, were appointed for this service on the part of the Carthaginians and advanced much further than the Cyrenæans. Valerius Ma'ximus states that they set forth before the time agreed upon; but Sallust merely says that they were accused of the trick by the Cyrenæans because they had themselves mismanaged the affair, and that they would consent to the boundary being fixed at the place of meeting only on condition that the Carthaginian envoys should submit to being buried alive on the spot. The Philæni accepted the proposal and sacrificed their lives for their country. *The*

QUESTIONS.—When was Carthage rebuilt?—Name two celebrated men of Christian Carthage.—When did it become the capital of the Vandal Kingdom?—When was it finally destroyed?——§ 67. What were the Aræ Philænorum?—How is the name said to have originated?

Altars of the Philæni, ARÆ PHILÆNO'RUM, were erected to mark the scene of their heroic deed.

NUMIDIA. (ἡ *Νομαδία*, i. e. land of *Nomades; Algiers.*)

Boundaries.—North, the MEDITERRANEAN; East, AFRICA; South, LIBYA INTERIOR; West, MAURETANIA.

Mountains.—THAMBES, AURASIUS.

Gulf.—SINUS NUMID'ICUS.

Capes.—PROMONTORIUM HIPPI, STOBORRUM.

Rivers.—RUBRICA'TUS, AMP'SAGA, and TUSCA.

Productions.—Olives, oranges, dates, grain; it was indeed one of the principal granaries of Rome. Its marble also was much esteemed.

Inhabitants.—The Numidians were a faithless, merciless, unscrupulous race, a nation of horsemen, who formed the chief cavalry of the Carthaginians. King Massinissa, who, till the age of ninety, could mount his horse with agility, represents the true Numidian.

Cities.—The number of towns must have been considerable, as Numidia had in the fifth century one hundred and twenty-three episcopal sees: HIPPO REGIUS, residence of St. Augustine; VAGA, a large commercial town; CIRTA (*Constantine*), the capital of the ancient Numidian kings; ZAMA, the memorable scene of the victory obtained by Scipio Africa'nus Major over Ha'nnibal (202 B. C.).

QUESTIONS.—What are the boundaries of Numidia?—Name the mountains.—Gulfs.—Capes.—Rivers.—Productions.—What is said of its inhabitants?—Who was the type of a true Numidian?—Did it contain many towns?—How many episcopal sees did it possess in the fifth century?—What was the residence of St. Augustine?—What was the ancient capital?—Who was defeated at Zama?—When?

§ 68. MAURETANIA. (*ἡ Μαυρουσία, Morocco, Fez.*)

Name.—This country was from the earliest times inhabited by a people called *Maurusii* (*Μαυρούσιοι, Μαυρήνσιοι*), *Mauroi* (*Μαῦροι*, from *μαυρός*, *black;* whence *Moor*, *Morocco*), and thus originated the name *Mauretania*, as it is spelt in inscriptions and on coins.

Boundaries.—North, the MEDITERRANEAN; East, NUMIDIA; South, GÆTULIA; West, OCE'ANUS.

Divisions.—MAURETANIA CÆSARIENSIS, the Eastern part, and MAURETANIA TINGITA'NA, the Western.

Mountains.—ATLAS, from which the *Atlantic* Ocean derives its name. The name, *Atlas*, however, was, by the ancients, given only to the mountains in Mauretania Tingita'na.

Cape.—PROMONTORIUM APOL'LINIS.

Rivers.—PHUTH, SUBUR, CHINALAPH.

Productions.—Grain, timber, precious stones, and metals.

Cities.—IGIL'GILIS, SALDÆ, ICOSIUM (*Algiers*—*Cæsare'a*); SIGA, the ancient residence of Syphax; TINGIS (*Tangier*); SALA, the remotest Roman city on the Western shore. Off the Western coast, the I'NSULÆ FORTUNA'TÆ (prob. the *Canaries*) were not fully known to the ancients until 72 B. C., and below them HESPE'RIDUM I'NSULÆ, possibly the *Bissagos*, lying a little above Sierra Leone.

QUESTIONS.—§ 68. What is said of the name of Mauretania?—What of its boundaries?—How is it divided?—What mountain range is in Mauretania Tingitana?—What cape?—What rivers?—Productions?—Towns?—What island groups were situated off the western coast?

GÆTULIA. (ἡ Γαιτουλία.)

Boundaries.—North, MAURETANIA; East, GARAMANTES; South, NIGER; West, OCE'ANUS.

Strabo employs the term *Gætulia* as a general designation for Central Africa. He speaks of the Gætulians as the chief element of the population of Libya.

Inhabitants.—The *Gætulians* and the *Libyans* constituted the *two* great races who originally inhabited the North-Western regions of Africa. When various tribes from Asia invaded the coast on the North, and formed permanent settlements, the Gætulians were forced to retire into the interior, toward the regions lying South of Mount Atlas. They led a nomadic life upon the O'ases of the *Western* part of the great desert of Sahara. There was no correspondence of physical characteristics between the Gætulians and the Negro race. The former are described as warlike in disposition, savage in manners, subsisting mainly on the flesh of animals whose skins served for garments, dwelling in tents, or wandering at large without any settled abode. The tribes who inhabited the Eastern part of the Desert were called Garamantes, of the same generic type with the Gætulians. The large trade carried on with Libya Interior was mainly in the hands of the Gætulians and Garamantes. The extreme South-Western portion of Africa, as well as the South-Eastern portion, was believed to be inhabited by Æthiopians.

QUESTIONS.—What are the boundaries of Gætulia?—What did Strabo comprise under the term Gætulia?—What is said of the Gætulians?—By whom were they driven into the desert?—Were they negroes?—How are they described?—Who were their eastern neighbors?—What is said of their trade?—Who inhabited the interior of Africa?

§ 69. EURO'PA. (ἡ Εὐρώπη.)

Euro'pa, as known to the Ancients, corresponded with the modern continent, neither in respect of boundaries, divisions, physical aspect, nor population.

Name.—The earliest use of this name to designate a division of the Earth, is in the Homeric Hymn to Apollo (vv. 250, 251), where in distinction from Peloponne'sus and the Greek islands it seems to denote *the long and deeply embayed line* of the Thracian shore, hence called, according to Hermann, *Euro'pa*, from εὐρύς-ὤψ, the *Broad-faced* Land. Bochart thinking the term had a Phœnician origin, pointed out its resemblance to the Heb. *Ereb*, as if it were, the *Evening* Land. With this view compare the remarks on the derivation of *Arab*, *Arabia*, page 89. The Mythologers, as is well known, said that this continent took its name from Euro'pa, the *broad-browed* daughter of the Phœnician king Age'nor, who was carried to Crete by Jupiter.

Boundaries.—They were different at different epochs. At the downfall of the Roman republic they were as follows: North, OCE'ANUS SEPTENTRIONA'LIS; East, TANAIS and PALUS MÆO'-TIS; West, OCE'ANUS HESPERIUS, or MARE ATLAN'TICUM; South, MARE, or MARE INTERNUM (Mediterranean).

Seas, Straits, and Gulfs.—(1.) MARE SARMA'TICUM, or SCY'-THICUM (*Baltic Sea*).

(2.) MARE SUE'VICUM, or SINUS CODA'NUS (*the Two Belts*).

(3.) MARE GERMAN'ICUM, or CIM'BRICUM (*German Ocean*).

(4.) FRETUM GAL'LICUM, or BRITAN'NICUM (*Strait of Dover*).

QUESTIONS.—§ 69. Does ancient Europe correspond with the modern continent?—What is said of the derivation of the name?—What were the boundaries at the close of the Roman republic?—Name some seas.—Some straits.—Some gulfs.

(5.) MARE BRITAN'NICUM (*British Channel*).

(6.) MARE CANTAB'RICUM (*Bay of Biscay*).

(7.) FRETUM GADITA'NUM, or HERCULEUM (*Strait of Gibraltar*).

The Mediterranean Sea contained the following Gulfs and Straits :

(1.) MARE IBE'RICUM, or BALEA'RICUM, along the Eastern coast of Spain.

(2.) SINUS GAL'LICUS (*Gulf of Lyons*).

(3.) MARE SARDO'UM, West and South of Sardinia.

(4.) LIGU'STICUM MARE (*Gulf of Genoa*).

(5.) MARE TYRRHE'NUM, or IN'FERUM, West of Italy.

(6.) MARE SIC'ULUM, or AUSO'NIUM, along the Eastern coast of Sicily.

(7.) SINUS TARENTI'NUS (*Gulf of Taranto*).

(8.) MARE ADRIAT'ICUM, or SU'PERUM (*the Adriatic*).

(9.) MARE IONIUM, along the Western coast of Greece.

(10.) MARE ÆGÆUM (*the Archipelago*), subdivided as follows :

a. Mare Thracium : the Northern part, North of the Island of Eubœa.

b. Mare Myrto'um: South of Eubœa, At'tica, and Ar'golis.

c. Mare Ica'rium: the South-East part of the Ægæan, along the coasts of Caria and Ionia.

d. Mare Cre'ticum, along the Northern coast of the Island of Creta.

§ **70. Extent.**—The surface of Europe, inclusive of the islands, is in fact nearly four millions of square miles. In the time of the Roman Empire it was estimated to contain but three millions of square miles; its length being supposed to range between 26,800 and 30,800 stadia, and its breadth between 9,200 and 12,700 stadia.

QUESTIONS.—What gulfs and straits did the Mediterranean contain? How is the Mare Ægæum subdivided?——§ 70. What is said of the extent of Europe?

Principal Mountains.—ALPES; PYRENÆI MONTES; HÆMUS (*Balkan*); MONTES CAR'PATES (*Carpathian Mountains*); SYLVA HERCYNIA—the general appellation for the mountains of Southern and Central Germany; MONS SEVO (*Mount Kjölen*).

Largest Rivers.—ISTER, or DANUBIUS (the latter name was mostly applied to the upper part); BORYS'THENES, or later, DAN'APRIS (*Dnieper*); TYRAS, or later, DANASTRIS (*Dniester*); RHENUS (*Rhine*); VIS'TULA (*Weichsel*). These rivers all flow through more than one country.

Climate.—The mean temperature of Spain, Italy, and Greece, was formerly lower than at the present day; while Gaul and Germany experienced in some measure the rigors of an arctic winter. The horns of the moose-deer, which are occasionally dug up in parts of Southern Germany, attest the presence of arctic animals in those regions in ancient times.

Productions.—Asia and Africa liberally afforded means of luxury; but Europe furnished a steady and bountiful supply of the necessaries of life. The productions of Europe were corn, wine, and oil, timber and valuable building stone, iron and copper, and even the more precious metals, gold and silver.

Inhabitants.—They belonged to the Japhetic, or Indo-Germanic family of nations, and were divided into

(1.) *Iberians*, in Hispania;

(2.) *Kelts*, in Gallia, Britannia, some parts of Hispania and Southern Germania, and Northern Italia;

(3.) *Teutons*, in Middle and North Germania;

(4.) *Thracians*, in Thracia, Dacia, Mœsia, and Pannonia;

(5.) *Pelasgo-Helle'nes*, in Hellas, Epi'rus, Macedonia, the South of Italy, and Etruria;

(6.) *Old Italians*, in the middle part of Italy;

(7.) *Scythians*, in Sarmatia and Scythia.

QUESTIONS.—Name the principal mountains of Europe.—What are the largest rivers?—What is said of the climate?—Of the productions?—Of the inhabitants?—What were the chief nations who inhabited Europe?

Languages.—The educated Romans were very familiar with the Greek language; the Greeks generally cultivated only their own. The dialects of the other races of Europe, being neither refined nor fixed by a native literature, gradually vanished. In the Gallic and Spanish provinces of Rome the Keltic gave way in great measure to the Latin; and even the Germans beyond the Rhine adopted the language of their enemies.

Divisions.—GRÆCIA, MACEDONIA, THRACIA, ILLYR'ICUM, ITALIA, HISPANIA, GALLIA, GERMANIA, VINDELICIA, RHÆTIA, NOR'ICUM, PANNONIA, MŒSIA, DACIA, and SARMATIA EUROPÆA.

§ 71. GRÆCIA (ἡ Ἑλλάς, *Hellas* and *Morea*): GREECE.

Name.—Originally confined to a small district in Thessaly, the town and district of Hellas in Phthio'tis, the Helle'nes gradually spread over the rest of Greece and the countries adjacent. To the countries thus settled they applied the general name, *Hellas*, which term therefore did not indicate a particular tract of country, but in general *any country settled by Helle'nes.* In its more restricted sense it signified all the land South of the Ambracian Gulf and the mouth of the river Pene'us, as far as the Isthmus of Corinth. But in its wider acceptation, in which it will here be used, it denoted all the country South of the Cambunii Montes, in opposition to the land of the barbarians.

The word, *Græci* (Γραικοί), first occurs in Aristotle as the name of a tribe about Dodo'na in Epi'rus; and may have been at one period in very general use on the Western coast, and so have become the particular title by which its inhabitants were known to the Italians on the opposite side of the Ionian Sea. In this

QUESTIONS.—What language beside their own was used by the educated Romans?—What is said of the Greeks?—Why have the other languages died out?—Give the divisions of Europe.——§ 71. What did Hellas originally comprise?—What did it afterward comprise?—What is the more restricted meaning of the word *Hellas?*—What author first uses the term *Græci?*—Where was the original abode of that tribe?—How may this name have passed into Italy?

manner the Roman designations, *Græci*, *Græcia*, are supposed to have arisen. After the conquest of Greece by the Romans (146 B.C.), Hellas bore, in official language, the name of *Achaia*, in consequence of the *Achæan* league.

Boundaries.—North, OLYMPUS, and the extension of the Cambunian Mountains; East and South, ÆGÆAN SEA; West and partly South, IONIAN SEA.

Extent.—Its greatest length from Mount Olympus to Cape Tæ'narus was 250 miles; its greatest breadth from the Western coast of Acarnania to Ma'rathon in Attica, 180 miles. Its area, excluding Epi'rus, but including Eubœa, is only 21,121 square miles. The small extent of the surface of Greece will be better conceived by comparing it with the area of some of the States of our Union. Indiana has 33,000 square miles; South Carolina, 29,000; Pennsylvania and New York, each about 46,000.

Mountains.—(1.) In the North of Greece are the CERAUNII, or ACROCERAUNII MONTES (*Κεραύνια* or *'Ακροκεραύνια ὄρη*), with their Eastern branch, the *Cambunii Montes*, terminating with Mount Olympus (*Ὄλυμπος*, *Elympo*), 9,754 feet high, believed to be the residence of Zeus and the other gods.

(2.) This Northern mountain-chain is intersected at right angles about midway between the Ionian and Ægæan Seas by the long and lofty range of PINDUS (*Πίνδος*), running from North to South, and constituting the backbone of Greece. Its different ramifications to the East and West were: OTHRYS (*Ὄθρυς*), ŒTA (*Οἴτη*), PARNASSUS (*Παρνασός*), HE'LICON (*Ἑλικών*).

(3.) The mountain system of Peloponne'sus has no connection with the rest of Greece. The loftiest peaks are in Arcadia, the central district of Peloponne'sus. Mount CYLLE'NE (*Κυλλήνη*, *Zyria*) rises to the height of 7,788 feet above the level of the

---

QUESTIONS.—What name did Greece bear after the Roman conquest?—What are the boundaries of Greece?—What is the greatest length of Greece?—What the greatest breadth?—What is its area?—What mountains are in the north of Greece?—By what chain are they intersected?—Name some of its branches.—What is remarked about the mountain system of Peloponnesus?—From what point does it radiate?—What is the highest mountain?

sea, and was regarded by the ancients as the highest mountain in Peloponne'sus; but one of the summits of Taÿ'getus reaches the elevation of 7,902 feet. The ERYMANTHUS (Ἐρύμανθος) forms the westernmost point of this chain.

§ 72. **Capes.**—(1.) On the Western coast of Northern Greece, ACROCERAUNIA (τὰ Ἀκροκεραύνια); ACTIUM (Ἄκτιον).

(2.) On the Southern coast of Northern Greece, ANTIR'-RHIUM (Ἀντίρριον).

(3.) On the Northern coast of Peloponne'sus, RHI'UM (Ῥίον); CHELONA'TAS (Χελωνάτας).

(4.) On the Southern coast of Peloponne'sus, ACRI'TAS (Ἀκρίτας); TÆ'NARUS or TÆ'NARUM (Ταίναρος or Ταίναρον, *Cape Matapan*), the southernmost point of Europe; MA'LEA (Μαλέα).

(5.) On the Eastern coast, SCYLLÆUM (Σκύλλαιον); SUNIUM (Σούνιον); SEPIAS (Σηπιάς).

Gulfs.—(1.) SINUS AMBRA'CIUS (Ἀμβράκιος κόλπος—Gulf of *Arta*), between Epi'rus and Acarnania.

(2.) SINUS CORINTHI'ACUS (Κορινθιακὸς κόλπος—Gulf of *Lepanto*), between Hellas and Peloponne'sus.

(3.) SINUS MESSENI'ACUS (Μεσσηνιακὸς κόλπος—Gulf of *Koron*), between Messenia and Laco'nica.

(4.) SINUS LACON'ICUS (Λακωνικὸς κόλπος—Gulf of *Kolokythia*), between Tæ'narus and Malea.

(5.) SINUS ARGOL'ICUS (Ἀργολικὸς κόλπος—Gulf of *Napoli di Romania*), between Laco'nica and Ar'golis.

(6.) SINUS SARON'ICUS (Σαρωνικὸς κόλπος—Gulf of *Egina*), between Peloponne'sus and Hellas.

(7.) SINUS THERMÆUS (Θερμαῖος κόλπος—Gulf of *Saloniki*), between Thessalia and Macedonia.

QUESTIONS.—Where is the Erymanthus situated?——§ 72. What capes are to be found on the western shores of northern Greece?—What cape on its southern shores?—What capes on the northern shores of Peloponnesus?—What capes are on the eastern shores of Greece?—Name the seven principal gulfs.—Give the situation of Sinus Ambracius.—Sinus Corinthiacus.—Sinus Messeniacus.—Sinus Laconicus.—Sinus Argolicus.—Sinus Saronicus.—Sinus Thermæus.

Rivers.—None of the rivers of Greece are navigable. Most of them are merely winter torrents to which the Greeks gave the name of *Χειμαρροῦς*, or *winter-flowing* streams. The most considerable rivers are:

A. In *Northern Greece* and *Hellas:*

(1.) Ao'us (*Ἄωος*). It was the chief stream of Il'lyris Græca.

(2.) Thy'amis (*Θύαμις*), which formed the boundary between Cestri'na and Thesprotia in Epi'rus.

(3.) Arach'thus (*Ἄραχθος*), the chief river of Epi'rus.

(4.) Achelo'us (*Ἀχελῷος*), the largest river of all Greece, and the boundary between Acarnania and Ætolia.

(5.) Eve'nus (*Εὔηνος*), which flows principally through Ætolia.

(6.), (7.) Pene'us (*Πηνειός*), flowing through the vale of Tempe, and Sperche'us (*Σπερχεῖος*), both in Thessalia.

B. In the *Peloponne'sus:*

(1.) Alphe'us (*Ἀλφειός*), the chief river of the peninsula.

(2.) Pene'us (*Πηνειός*), in Elis.

(3.) Euro'tas (*Εὐρώτας*), the chief river of Laco'nica.

§ **73. Lakes.**—Though there are few rivers of considerable size in Greece, the nature of the soil is favorable to the formation of marshes and lakes. From some of these the waters find an outlet through the cavities of limestone mountains, called *katavo'thra* by the modern Greeks; and after disappearing under ground for a greater or less distance, rise again to the surface. The most remarkable lakes are:

(1.) Lacus Pambo'tis (*Παμβῶτις λίμνη*), in Molossia in Epi'rus.

Questions.—What is said of the rivers of Greece?—What was the main stream of Illyris Græca?—What rivers were in Epirus?—What was the largest river of all Greece?—What rivers were in Thessalia?—What is the principal stream of the Peloponnesus?—What river was in Elis?—What was the chief stream of Laconica?——§ 73. What is said of the lakes of Greece in general?—What are *katavothra?*—Name four large lakes.

(2.) Bœbe'ïs (*Βοιβηΐς*), in Thessalia.

(3.) Tricho'nis (*Τριχωνίς*), in Ætolia.

(4.) Co'païs (*Κωπαΐς*), in Bœotia, the largest in Greece.

Productions.—The most fertile districts were Thessaly, Bœotia, and a part of Peloponne'sus; the least fertile were Arcadia and At'tica. Wheat, barley, flax, wine, and oil were the chief productions. The hills afforded excellent pasture for cattle, and supplied timber in abundance. The domestic animals were horses, asses, mules, oxen, swine, goats, and sheep. Bears, wolves, and boars frequented the mountains. The best marble quarries were at Carystus in Eubœa, at Pentel'icus and Hymettus in At'tica, and in the island of Paros. Gold was found in the island of Thasos. The most productive silver mines were at Laurium in the South of At'tica. Both copper and iron were found near Chalcis in Eubœa; there were also iron mines in Mount Tay'getus in Laconia.

Climate.—Owing to the inequalities of its surface, the climate varies greatly in different districts. On the highlands, in the interior, the winter is often long and rigorous, the snow lying upon the ground till late in the spring; while in the lowlands, near the seacoast, there is very rarely any severe weather, snow being almost entirely unknown there.

Inhabitants.—Among the earliest inhabitants were the Pelasgi. In historical times (subsequent to 777 B.C.) the country was settled by the Helle'nes, a branch of the Pelasgi, who, by their superior mental and physical endowments, were able to conquer their kinsmen in other parts of Greece. The four great divisions of the people were the *Dorians*, *Æolians*, *Achæans*, and *Ionians*.

Questions.—What were the most fertile districts of Greece?—What districts were the least fertile?—Name the chief productions of Greece.—Name some of the domestic animals.—Some of the wild animals.—Where were the best marble quarries to be found?—What island produced gold?—Where were the richest silver mines?—Where were iron mines?—What is said of the climate?—Who were the oldest inhabitants of Greece?—Which branch of them gained the supremacy?—What were the subdivisions of the Hellenes?

Divisions.—NORTHERN GREECE.

(1.) EPI'RUS:	(2.) THESSALIA:
Atintania,	*Thessalio'tis,*
Chaonia,	*Phthio'tis,*
Thesprotia,	*Pelasgio'tis,*
Molossia,	*Hestiæo'tis,*
Athamania.	*Magnesia.*

HELLAS PROPER.

(1.) ACARNANIA,	(4.) DORIS,	(7.) AT'TICA,
(2.) ÆTOLIA,	(5.) PHOCIS,	(8.) ME'GARIS.
(3.) LOCRIS,	(6.) BŒOTIA,	

PELOPONNE'SUS.

(1.) ACHAIA,	(4.) CORINTHIA,	(7.) MESSENIA,
(2.) ELIS,	(5.) SICYONIA,	(8.) LACON'ICA.
(3.) ARCADIA,	(6.) AR'GOLIS,	

§ 74. EPI'RUS (ἡ Ἤπειρος), part of ALBANIA.

Name.—The Greek word Ἤπειρος, *Epi'ros,* signified the *mainland,* and was the name originally given to the whole of the western part of Greece extending from the Acroceraunian promontory as far as the entrance of the Corinthian gulf, in contradistinction to Corcy'ra, and the Cephallenian Islands. Epi'rus, especially toward the North, was scarcely recognised as a Grecian state. It is a wild and mountainous country, and has in all ages been the resort of half-civilized tribes of robbers.

Boundaries.—North, MONTES ACROCERAUNII; East, PINDUS; South, ÆTOLIA and ACARNANIA; West, MARE IONIUM

QUESTIONS.—Name the two divisions of Northern Greece.—The eight divisions of Hellas Proper.—The eight divisions of Peloponnesus.——§ 74. What does the word Epirus signify?—To what part of Greece was this name originally given?—Was it a Greek state?—Name the boundaries.

Divisions.—ATINTANIA, CHAONIA, THESPROTIA, MOLOSSIA, and ATHAMANIA.

Mountains.—The ACROCERAUNII and PINDUS.

Capes.—POSIDIUM and ACROCERAUNIUM:

Infames scopulos Acroceraunia.—Hor. Od. I. iii. 20.

Rivers.—(1.) AO'US, which flows through the Fauces Antigonenses, where Philip V., king of Macedonia, in vain attempted to arrest the progress of the Roman Consul, Titus Quintius Flamini'nus (199 B. C.).

(2.) ACH'ERON, which passed through the lake Acherusia, and after receiving the river Cocy'tus, flowed into the Ionian Sea. In mythology they are both transferred to the lower world, on account of the dark color of their waters.

(3.) ACHELO'US and CHA'RADRUS.

Inhabitants.—It was inhabited by fourteen tribes, which were not of pure Hellenic origin.

Cities.—(1.) BUTHRO'TUM (*Βουθρωτόν*), a commercial seaport opposite Corcy'ra.

(2.) NICOP'OLIS (*Νικόπολις*), situated North of the entrance of the Ambracian Gulf, opposite to Actium, was built by Augustus on the site of his camp, in honor of the decisive victory which he gained there. After the time of Constantine the Great, it became the capital of the province of Epi'rus.

(3.) DODO'NA (*Δωδώνη*), celebrated for the oracular oaks, and for the most ancient oracle of Zeus in Greece. It is said that the temple of Dodo'na stood at the foot of Mount Toma'rus, on the confines of Thesprotia and Molossia. After the rise of Delphi, the oracle here was consulted chiefly by the neighboring tribes.

(4.) Other towns in Epi'rus: *Ambracia, Pandosia, Casso'pe, Onchesmus, O'ricum* or *O'ricus.*

QUESTIONS.—Name the divisions of Epirus.—Its mountains.—Name its capes.—Give the names of four rivers of Epirus.—What happened at the Fauces Antigonenses?—What is said of the Acheron and Cocytus?—How many tribes inhabited Epirus?—Name three cities of Epirus.—Who founded Nicopolis?—Why?—Where was the oldest oracle of Zeus?

§ 75. THESSALIA. (ἡ Θεσσαλία)

Name.—It received its name from the *Thessalians*, a Hellenic people, who came hither from Thesprotia, conquered the plain of the Pene'us, and expelled the Æolians, who at that time formed the great body of the population.

Boundaries.—North, PENE'US and OLYMPUS; East, SINUS THERMÆUS; South, SINUS MALI'ACUS and ŒTA; West, PINDUS.

Divisions.—Aleuas (600 B. C.) divided the country into the following tetrarchies: THESSALIO'TIS (Θεσσαλιῶτις), PHTHIO'TIS (Φθιῶτις), PELASGIO'TIS (Πελασγιῶτις; comp. Πελασγοί, *Pelasgi*), and HESTIÆO'TIS (Ἑστιαιῶτις). Later there was a fifth division called MAGNESIA (*Μαγνησία*).

Mountains.—MONTES CAMBUNII; OLYMPUS, with the celebrated vale of Tempe (τὰ Τέμπη); PINDUS; OSSA; PELION; OTHRYS and ŒTA, with the famous pass of Thermop'ylæ (Θερμόπυλαι, *Hot-Gates*, so called from the *hot springs* at the point where the pass was fortified). This pass, situated on the Sinus Mali'acus, was guarded by Mount Œta on the West, and by deep morasses and the sea on the East. Here Leon'idas and his three hundred Spartans made their memorable stand against Xerxes and the Persian host (Aug. 7, 480 B. C.). Of the brave band of Spartans all perished but two.

Rivers.—PENE'US, ENI'PEUS, APIDA'NUS, and PAMI'SUS.

Gulfs.—SINUS PAGASÆUS and SINUS MALI'ACUS.

Productions.—The plain of Thessaly was the most fertile portion of Greece. It produced grain plentifully and nourished cattle in abundance. It contained a numerous population in the towns, and was noted especially for its rich and proud aristocracy.

QUESTIONS.—§ 75. Whence is the name Thessalia derived?—What are its boundaries?—Who divided the country?—Into how many parts?—Name those parts.—What celebrated vale was in Thessalia?—What was Thermopylæ?—Where situated?—Name the rivers.—Gulfs.—What is said of the productions?—What of the population?

The Thessalian horses were the finest in Greece, and the Thessalian cavalry were celebrated for their efficiency.

Cities.—(1.) LARISSA (*Λάρισσα*), the birthplace of Achilles; it was the ancient Pelasgian capital, and the residence of the noble family of the Aleu'adæ. After the time of Constantine, it was the capital of the province.

(2.) PHARSA'LUS (*Φάρσαλος*), situated near the confluence of the Apida'nus and Eni'peus, the scene of the famous battle between Cæsar and Pompey, in which Cæsar obtained the empire of the Roman World (48 B. C.).

(3.) PHERÆ (*Φεραί*), situated in the South-Eastern part of the Thessalian plain, the residence of Jason, the celebrated chief of Thessaly (374 B. C.).

(4.) LAMIA (*Λαμία*), situated near the Maliac Gulf, the scene of the Lamian war of the Greek states against Macedonia (323 B. C.).

(5.) SCOTUSSA (*Σκοτοῦσσα*), in the vicinity of which were the hills called Cynosce'phalæ (*Κυνὸς Κεφαλαί, Dog-heads*), where Philippus IV. of Macedonia was conquered by T. Q. Flamini'nus (197 B. C.).

(6.) IOLCOS (*Ἰωλκός*), the place of rendezvous of the Argonauts.

(7.) Other towns: *Phthia, Larissa, Cremaste, Heracle'a, Echi'nus, Hy'pata, Gomphi, Iricca, Gonnus, Demetrius.*

§ 76. HELLAS PROPER. (*Livadia.*)

Boundaries.—North, THESSALIA and EPI'RUS; East, MARE ÆGÆUM; South, SINUS SARON'ICUS and CORINTHIUS; West, MARE IONIUM.

Mountains.—In its Western half is a branch of Mount Pindus, which extending from Mount Tymphrestas in a South-Westerly

QUESTIONS.—Name some towns of Thessalia.—What was the residence of the Aleuadæ?—Where was Pharsalus situated?—Who was conquered there?—Where was Pheræ situated?—Who resided there?—What celebrated hills were in the neighborhood of Scotussa?——§ 76. What are the boundaries of Hellas Proper?—What is said of its mountains?

direction, finally unites with the continuation of the Epi'rot Mountains, and forms rugged and inaccessible highlands, which have been at all times the haunt of tribes of robbers. The South-Easterly continuation of Mount PINDUS passes through Phocis, Bœotia, and At'tica, under the names of Parnassus, He'licon, Cithæron, and Hymettus, till it touches the seacoast at Sunium.

Divisions.—ACARNANIA, ÆTOLIA, LOCRIS, DORIS, PHOCIS, BŒOTIA, AT'TICA, ME'GARIS.

ACARNANIA. (*ἡ Ἀκαρνανία.*)

Boundaries.—North, EPI'RUS; East, ÆTOLIA; South, MARE IONIUM; West, SINUS AMBRACIUS.

Mountains.—CRANIA and THY'AMUS. It is a very rough country; there are, however, here and there a few broad and fertile plains through which the Achelo'us flows.

Rivers.—ACHELO'US, on the confines of Acarnania and Ætolia, and IN'ACHUS.

Cape.—ACTIUM, the scene of the battle between Antony and Augustus, which decided the fate of the Roman Empire (31 B.C.).

Towns.—ACTIUM (*Punta*), with a temple of Apollo; AMBRACIA, with a temple of Athe'na (*Minerva*); THYRE'UM; ARGOS AMPHILO'GICUM; STRATUS, the capital; ANACTORIUM; LIMNÆA; DIORYCTUS; PALÆRUS; AS'TACUS; ŒNI'ADÆ. The Corinthians founded several colonies on the coast.

ÆTOLIA. (*ἡ Αἰτωλία.*)

Boundaries.—North, EPI'RUS and THESSALIA; East, WESTERN LOCRIS; South, SINUS CORINTHIUS; West, the ACHELO'US, which separated it from ACARNANIA.

Mountains.—The Northern part is very rugged, but its coast was fertile.

QUESTIONS.—Name the eight divisions of Hellas Proper.—Give the boundaries of Acarnania.—Its mountains.—Its rivers.—What battle was fought near Actium?—Name some of its towns.—Give the boundaries of Ætolia.—The mountains.

Rivers.—ACHELO'US (*Aspropotamo*), the largest river in Greece, EVE'NUS, SPERCHE'US, and PARACHELOI'TIS.

Lakes.—TRUCHO'NIS and HYRIA were two large lakes which communicated with each other.

Productions.—In the plains excellent corn was grown, and the slopes of the mountains produced good wine and oil. It was also celebrated for its horses.

Inhabitants.—Pelasgi and Helle'nes. Some of the mountaineers of Ætolia are described by Thucy'dides as eating raw flesh and speaking a language very unintelligible.

Divisions.—OLD ÆTOLIA and ACQUIRED ÆTOLIA (*ἡ ἀρχαία Αἰτωλία* and *ἡ ἐπίκτητος Αἰτωλία*).

Towns.—(1.) THERMUM (*Θέρμον*), near the mountains; PANÆTO'LUS (*Παναίτωλος*), where the Ætolians held the meetings of their league.

(2.) CA'LYDON (*Καλυδών*), mentioned by Homer; PLEURON (*Πλευρών*), also mentioned by Homer, where was a temple sacred to Athe'na. The prominent part which the Ætolians took in the expulsion of the Gauls from Greece (279 B. C.) made them one of the three great powers in Greece, the other two being the Macedonians and Achæans.

§ 77. LOCRIS. (*ἡ Λοκρίς.*)

In historical times the Locrians were divided into two distinct tribes, differing from each other in customs, habits, and civilization.

The Eastern Locrians, called the Opuntii and Epicnemidii, were the more ancient and refined. They dwelt upon the Eastern coast of Greece, opposite the island of Eubœa.

QUESTIONS.—Name the rivers of Ætolia.—Lakes.—Productions.—What is said of its inhabitants?—Name some of the towns.—What is said of Thermum?—What of Calydon?—What of Pleuron?—In what manner did the Ætolians become one of the great powers in Greece?—Name the two other great powers.——§ 77. How were the Locrians divided?—How were the Eastern Locrians called?—Where did they dwell?

The Western Locrians are said to have been a colony from the former. They are not mentioned until the time of the Peloponnesian war, and even then are represented as a semi-barbarous race. They inhabited the country around the Corinthian Gulf.

EASTERN LOCRIANS.

Boundaries.—North, THESSALIA; East, OPUNTIC GULF; South, BŒOTIA; West, PHOCIS.

The portion of the country occupied by them was a narrow slip of coast extending from the pass of Thermop'ylæ to the mouth of the river Cephi'sus.

Divisions.—The Locrians North of the territory of Daphnus were called *Epicnemidii*, from Mount *Cnemis*, and those South of this territory were called *Opuntii*, from the city *Opus*, which was regarded as their chief town. It was the birthplace of Patro'clus.

Towns.—THRONIUM, and CNEMI'DES, both situated in the territory of the Epicnemidian Locrians, and the latter on Mount *Cnemis*.

WESTERN LOCRIANS, or LOCRI OZ'OLÆ.

Boundaries.—North, DORIS and ÆTOLIA; East, PHOCIS; South, SINUS CORINTHIUS; West, ÆTOLIA.

Name.—The origin of the epithet Oz'olæ is uncertain. Some derived it from ὄζειν, *to smell*, from the *strong-smelling* sulphur springs at the foot of Mount Taphiassus; the Locrians themselves referred it to the branches (ὄζοι) of a vine which was produced in their country in a marvellous manner.

Towns.—(1.) AMPHISSA (Ἄμφισσα), razed to the ground by Philip of Ma'cedon, when acting as general of the Amphictyons (338 B. C.).

QUESTIONS.—What is said of the Western Locrians?—Where did they dwell?—What were the boundaries of Eastern Locris?—How was Locris divided?—What territory formed the boundary between the Opuntii and Epicnemidii?—What were the boundaries of Western Locris?—Why were the inhabitants called Ozolæ?—What is said of Amphissa?

(2.) NAUPACTUS (*Ναύπακτος*, *Lepanto*). In the time of Pe'ricles it fell into the hands of the Athenians; during the Peloponnesian war (431—404 B. C.) it was the headquarters of the Athenians.

§ 78. DORIS (*ἡ Δωρίς*), previously, *Dry'opis.*

It is a narrow plain between Parnassus and Œta.

Boundaries.—North, THESSALIA; East, LOCRIS and PHOCIS; South, LOCRIS; West, ÆTOLIA.

River.—CEPHI'SUS or CEPHISSUS, which flows through the plain of Phocis and Bœotia.

Towns.—*Four* in number; hence the name *Tetrap'olis Do'rica:* PINDUS (*Πίνδος*), ERY'NEUS (*Ἐρινεός*), CYTINIUM (*Κυτίνιον*), BŒUM (*Βοιόν*).

Doris founded many Grecian states and colonies. From this plain the Dorians are said to have descended to the conquest of Peloponne'sus.

PHOCIS. (*ἡ Φωκίς.*)

Boundaries.—North and East, LOCRIS; East, BŒOTIA; South, SINUS CORINTHIUS; West, WESTERN LOCRIS and DORIS.

Mountains.—PARNASSUS, upward of 7,000 feet high, the highest mountain in central Greece, was sacred to Apollo and the Muses. Midway up the mountain, above the town of Delphi, were two lofty cliffs sacred to Diony'sus (*Bacchus*), between which flows the Castalian Fount (*Fountain of St. John*) from

---

QUESTIONS.—What is the modern name of Naupactus?—For what is the town celebrated?——§ 78. Where was Doris situated?—Give its boundaries.—Its rivers.—Why was it called Tetrapolis Dorica?—Name the four towns—What is said of the Dorians?—In what relation did Doris stand to many of the Grecian states?—How is Phocis bounded?—What is said of Parnassus?

the upper part of the mountain. These cliffs are often called by the poets and later writers *the two peaks of Parnassus :*

Mons ibi verticibus petit arduus castra duobus,
Nomine Parnassus, superatque cacumine nubes.
Ovid, Met. I. 316 seq.

The Southern extremity of the Parnassian ridge was He'licon, also the abode of Apollo and the Muses. Mount Cnemis formed the boundary between Phocis and the Locri Epicnemidii.

Rivers.—CEPHI'SUS and CASTALIA, or FONS CASTALIUS. The Castalia was the holy water of the Delphian temple. All who visited Delphi for any religious object purified themselves at this sacred fountain, which seems to have been done chiefly by bathing the hair. This Apollo himself is said to have done :

Qui rore puro Castaliæ lavit
Crines solutos.—Hor. Od. III. 4, 61 seq.

As Apollo was protector of the Muses, the Roman poets in later times represented this spring as imparting poetic inspiration to those who drank of it:

Mihi flavus Apollo
Pocula Castalia plena ministret aqua.
Ovid, Am. I. 15, 35 seq.

Hence also the designation of the Muses :

Sili, Castalidum decus sororum.—Martial, IV. 14.

Towns.—The towns were situated on both sides of the Cephi'sus.

(1.) DELPHI. (See page 155.)

(2.) DAULIS (Δαυλίς), the residence of king Tereus, and the scene of the story of Procne and Philome'la.

QUESTIONS.—What name does the southern extremity of Parnassus bear?—What was the boundary between Phocis and the Locri Epicnemidii?—What river was in Phocis?—Why were the Muses called *Castalides?*—Where were the towns situated?—Name some towns.

(3.) ELATE'A (Ἐλάτεια) was the largest city; the surprise of this by Philip produced a shock at Athens, very finely described by Demos'thenes in his Oration on the Crown.

(4.) CRISSA (Κρίσσα), with its harbors, CIRRHA (Κίρρα) and ANTICIRRHA (Ἀντίκιρρα), celebrated for its hellebore, the great remedy for madness among the ancients.

§ 79. DELPHI. (*Δελφοί*, earlier, *Πύθω*, *Pytho; Kastri.*)

A town in Phocis, and one of the most celebrated places in the Hellenic world, in consequence of its oracle of Apollo. It lies in the narrow vale of the Pleistus, which is shut in on one side by Mount Parnassus, and on the other by Mount Cirphis. It was surrounded by mountains on all sides except on the South, and on that side it was fortified by a line of walls.

The oracle of Delphi belonged originally to the Phocian town of Crissa, which possessed a fertile and valuable territory, extending down to the Corinthian Gulf, on which it had a port, called Cirrha. This port soon became of more importance than Crissa, from being the landing-place of most of the strangers who came to consult the oracle. The exorbitant tolls levied by them on visitors, in addition to other outrages, brought upon them the punishment of the Amphictyons, who, after a ten years' war, levelled the guilty city with the ground, and consecrated its fertile territory to the god of Delphi (585 B.C.). The spoils were employed in founding the Pythian games, which after that epoch were celebrated every four years. About the same time, the sanctuary of the god fell into the hands of the Dorian tribe of the Delphians, who came from Lycorei'a, the highest summit

---

QUESTIONS.—What was the largest town of Phocis?—What is said about it? —What was the hellebore?—Where was it found?——§ 79. What was Delphi?—What caused its renown?—Describe its situation. —To what town did the oracle originally belong?—What was the port of Crissa?—Why was Crissa destroyed?—To whom was its territory given?—What use was made of the spoils?—What tribe took the oracle from the Phocians?—To which of the Greek tribes did they belong?

of Parnassus; and thereafter a violent antipathy existed between the Phocians and Delphians.

The circuit of the town was only a little more than two miles. The most striking object among these holy places was the great temple dedicated to Apollo. After the old temple had been burnt down (548 B. C.), the Amphictyons determined that it should be rebuilt on a scale of magnificence suited to the

MOUNT PARNASSUS.

sanctity of the spot. The front of this new temple was of Parian marble, while the rest was of ordinary building-stone. It was divided into three parts: Prona'us (πρόναος), Cella (ναός), and A'dytum (ἄδυτον, μαντεῖον). In the Prona'us was a bronze statue of Homer, while the walls of the interior were adorned by celebrated sayings of the Seven Wise Men, such as *Know thyself*, *Moderation in all things*. In the Cella were the statues of the two goddesses of Fate, surrounded by the altars of Poseidon, Zeus, and Apollo. Here was also the iron chair on which Pindar

---

QUESTIONS.—What was the circuit of the town of Delphi?—What was the most remarkable building at Delphi?—When was the first temple burnt down?—Into how many parts was the new temple divided?—Name those parts —Describe the Pronaus —Describe the Cella.

is said to have sung his hymns to Apollo. A perpetual fire burned on the hearth, and near it was the Om′phalos, or *Navel-Stone*, which was supposed to mark the middle-point of the earth. In the A′dytum was the golden statue of Apollo, and in front of it a fire of fir-wood constantly burning. Laurel garlands covered its roofs, and laurel furnished the incense of its altar; in its centre was a deep fissure in the ground (*χάσμα*), over which stood the tripod of the Pythia, or priestess of Apollo. The vapor rising from under this tripod was supposed to inspire her, and under this inspiration she uttered the revelations of the god. No religious institution of antiquity obtained so paramount an influence, and that not only in Greece, but throughout the countries around the Mediterranean. Its priests formed for the Hellenic world a sort of hierarchical senate which proved itself undoubtedly the wisest legislative body known in history till the beginning of the Peloponnesian war. For at this time the partiality for Sparta became so manifest that the Ionians began to lose all reverence and esteem for it, though it always had a leaning toward the Greeks of the Doric race. It continued to flourish, but without exercising political influence, to the times of the Emperor Julian; and then gradually falling into decay, it was entirely done away with by Theodosius.

§ 80. BŒOTIA.

Boundaries. North, EASTERN LOCRIS; East, MARE EUBŒUM; South, AT′TICA, MEG′ARIS, and the SINUS CORINTHIUS; West, PHOCIS.

Extent.—It contained about 1,000 square miles, being a little smaller than Rhode Island (1,306 square miles), the smallest state of the United States.

QUESTIONS.—Describe the Adytum.—What is said of the influence of the oracle?—When did that influence cease to exist?—For what reason?—At what time was the oracle entirely abolished?——§ 80. What are the boundaries of Bœotia?—What is its extent?

14

Mountains.—HEL'ICON, PARNASSUS, PARNES, CITHÆRON, which separated Bœotia from Me'garis and At'tica; its summit was sacred to Zeus and Diony'sus; and was the scene of the metamorpho'sis of Actæon, the death of Pentheus, and the exposure of Œ'dipus.

Rivers.—CEPHI'SUS, celebrated by Pindar; ISME'NUS, ASO'PUS, PERMESSUS, and TRITON.

Fountains.—AGANIPPE: HIPPOCRE'NE, the verse-inspiring fountain, said to have been formed by the hoof of Peg'asus.

Lakes.—COPAÏS and HY'LICA, which were united by a subterranean passage. In the marshes of the Copaïs grew the *aule'tica*, or flute-reed.

Productions.—The plain of the Copaïs was particularly distinguished for its fertility. Grain, vegetables, and fruit were cultivated with great success, and in this part of Greece the vine was first planted. The mountains yield black and gray marble, and iron; the Bœotian sword-blades were very celebrated.

Climate.—The air is thick and heavy in consequence of the vapors rising from the valleys and lakes. The winters are generally cold and stormy.

Inhabitants.—The oldest inhabitants were of *Pelasgian* origin. In addition to these, two other tribes appear as ruling Bœotia in the heroic ages: the *Minyæ* and the *Cadme'ans*, or *Cadmeo'nes.* Sixty years after the Trojan war, these primitive tribes were conquered by the Bœotians, an Æolian people from Phthio'tis in Thessalia. Though this people were reproached with stupidity, especially by their lively neighbors, the Athenians, yet Pindar, the greatest lyric poet, and Epaminondas, the

---

QUESTIONS.—Name some of the mountains of Bœotia.—Rivers.—Fountains.—What is said of Hippocrene?—What does the name signify?—What lakes are in Bœotia?—How were they connected?—What grew in the marshes?—Name some of the productions.—What is mentioned in regard to the vine?—What of the iron?—How was the climate?—Who were the earliest inhabitants?—What tribes dwelt in Bœotia beside the Pelasgians?—By whom were they conquered?—Where did the Bœotians come from?—How were they regarded in Greece?—Give the names of celebrated Bœotians.

most accomplished general of the Greeks, were Bœotians; as were also Hesiod, Corinna, and Plutarch.

§ **81. Cities.**—(1.) THEBÆ (Θῆβαι), said to have been founded by *Cadmus*, who called it *Cadme'a*, a name afterward confined to its citadel; situated almost in the centre of Bœotia, on the little river Isme'nus. It was the scene of the sufferings of Œ'dipus, and the birthplace of Pindar, whose house and descendants were spared when Thebes was utterly destroyed by Alexander (335 B. C.). It was rebuilt by Cassander more than twenty years afterward. Under its renowned citizen, Epaminondas, it rose to a commanding influence in Greece.

(2.) CORONE'A (Κορώνεια), where Agesila'us conquered the allied forces of Greece (394 B. C.).

(3.) ORCHO'MENUS (Ὀρχομενός), the old capital of the Minyæ. It was a very ancient, wealthy and powerful city. It was finally destroyed by Thebes (367 B. C.).

(4.) CHÆRONE'A (Χαιρώνεια), the scene of the victory of Philip, by which he became master of Greece (338 B. C.). It was also the birthplace of Plutarch.

(5.) AULIS (Αὐλίς), a harbor on the East coast of Bœotia, where the Greeks were detained, when they had assembled for their expedition against Troy, until Agamemnon had appeased Diana by the sacrifice of his own daughter, Iphigeni'a.

(6.) DELIUM (Δήλιον); the Athenians were here defeated by the Thebans (424 B. C.). Soc'rates fought at this battle and saved the life of Xen'ophon.

(7.) TANA'GRA (Τάναγρα), the scene of a victory of the Lacedæmonians over the Athenians (457 B. C.).

QUESTIONS.—§ 81. Where is Thebæ situated?—By whom was it founded?—How was it known in mythology?—What poet was a native of Thebæ?—When was the city destroyed?—Who rebuilt the city?—When?—Under whom was it at the head of Greece?—Who were conquered near Coronea?—What is said of Orchomenus?—What battle was fought near Chæronea?—Who was a native of Chæronea?—Where was Aulis situated?—What happened at Aulis?—Who were defeated at Delium?—Who fought in this battle?—Who were conquered near Tanagra?

(8.) HALIARTUS (Ἁλίαρτος), destroyed by the Romans in the first Macedonian war (171 B. C.).

(9.) THESPIÆ (Θεσπιαί), destroyed by Xerxes in the last Persian war (480 B. C).

(10.) LEUCTRA (Λεῦκτρα), the scene of the victory of Epaminondas, by which Thebes attained her national supremacy (371 B. C.).

(11.) PLATÆÆ (Πλαταιαί), where the Persian general, Mardonius, was defeated by Pausanias, on the same day that the Persian fleet was defeated off My'cale (Sept. 479 B. C.).

(12.) LEBADEI'A (Λεβάδεια). *Livadia*, the Northern part of the modern kingdom of Greece derives its name from this city. It possessed the celebrated statue of Zeus by Praxi'teles.

(13.) ASCRA, the residence of Hesiod, MYCALESSUS, ANTHE'DON.

§ 82. AT'TICA. (ἡ Ἀττική, also Ἀκταία, and earlier, Ἀκτική.)

Name.—The name is probably derived from *Acte*, *Coast*-Land (ἀκτή), as being a projecting peninsula, in the same manner as the peninsula of Mount Athos was also called Acte.

Boundaries.—North, BŒOTIA; East and South, MARE ÆGÆUM; West, ME'GARIS.

Divisions.—The oldest division was into twelve independent communities, which were afterward united into one state by Theseus. There existed another division into four tribes (φυλαί), which arrangement was abolished by Cleis'thenes (510 B. C.), who formed ten new tribes, which were augmented to twelve in 307 B. C., and afterward to thirteen. Each tribe was subdivided into ten *demes* (δῆμοι), in some one of which every Athenian citizen was obliged to be enrolled.

QUESTIONS.—When was Haliartus destroyed?—When Thespiæ?—What battle was fought near Leuctra?—Who was defeated at Platææ?—When?—What is said of Lebadeia?——§ 82. What is the origin of the name Attica?—Give the boundaries.—What is the oldest division?—Who united the twelve tribes?—What other division existed?—Who abolished this division?—What was the division of Cleisthenes?

Extent.—The area of At'tica is about 700 square miles, exclusive of the island of Sa'lamis, which is about forty more. So that the state of A'ttica, the sovereign of the sea, and surpassing the world in point of intellectual supremacy, had an area comprising only about one-third of that of the small state of Delaware (2,120 square miles).

Mountains.—The CITHÆRON, with its branches Parnes, Pentel'icus, and Hymettus; LYCABETTUS and LAURION.

Capes.—COLIAS, ZOSTER, and SUNIUM, with the celebrated temple of Athe'na *Sunias*.

Plains.—The ELEUSINIAN and ATHENIAN plains (sometimes simply *τὸ Πέδιον*): the plain of MAR'ATHON in the Diacria (*Διακρία*) or Highlands, where the Athenians, under the generalship of Milti'ades, defeated the Persian army (Sept. 28, 490 B.C.). The MESOGÆA (*Μεσόγαια*), or Midland district, and the PARALIA (*Παραλία*), or the Southern coast.

Rivers.—The rivers of At'tica are little more than mere mountain torrents, almost entirely dry in summer, and only full in winter, or after heavy rains. The Athenian plain is watered on the West by the Cephi'sus and on the East by the Ilissus, the former being the larger stream.

Climate.—The climate is dry, with an exceedingly pure and transparent atmosphere.

Productions.—It was originally not a very productive country, so that *Attic poverty* became a proverbial expression; but the energy of its inhabitants made it one of the gardens of earth. Its chief mineral was white and blue, or black marble; the former variety from Pentel'icus and Hymettus, the latter from Eleusis. It was an important article of export. Laurium contained valuable silver mines. The soil is better adapted for fruits than for grain, which latter was imported; figs were abundant, and olives

---

QUESTIONS.—What is said of the extent of Attica?—Name the mountains.—The capes.—The five plains.—What is said about the rivers?—What was the most important river?—Was it very fertile?—What made it a desirable residence?—Where was marble found?—Where were the silver mines?—Was it rich in grain?

were an article of exportation. Sheep and goats formed a large part of the wealth of the husbandmen. Mount Hymettus was celebrated for its bees :

nisi Hymettia mella Falerno
Ne biberis diluta.—Hor. Sat. ii. 2. 15.

§ **83. Inhabitants.**—The inhabitants of At'tica were Ionians, who were divided, down to the time of Cleis'thenes (510 B.C.), into four tribes, called, from the respective occupations of their members,

Geleontes, or *Teleontes*, the Cultivators;
Hople'tes, the Warriors;
Ægi'cores, the Goatherds;
Ar'gades, the Artisans.

Cleis'thenes formed ten tribes instead of four, and this number remained till 307 B. C, when two were added, and finally under Hadrian the number was thirteen.

The population of At'tica, about 317 B. C., was nearly 527,000, of whom about 127,000 were free, and 400,000 slaves. This would give a population of about 700 to a square mile. Massachusetts, comparatively the most populous of the United States, contains but 126 inhabitants to a square mile.

Towns.—(1.) ACHARNÆ (Ἀχαρναί), the principal *deme* of At'tica, which has given name to a play of Aristo'phanes.

(2.) ELEUSIS (Ἐλευσίς), on the high-road from Athens to the Isthmus, which was lined with numerous monuments, and along which all the sacred processions travelled. It was the chief seat of the worship of Deme'ter and Perse'phone, and of the mysteries celebrated in honor of these goddesses, which were called the Eleusinia. They lasted 1800 years, and were abolished by the

---

QUESTIONS.—What domesticated animals were found in Attica?—For what was Hymettus celebrated?——§ 83. What is said of the inhabitants of Attica?—Into how many tribes were they divided?—What is said of the population?—What was the greatest *deme* of Attica?—Where was Eleusis situated?—What goddess was worshipped there?—What were the Eleusinian mysteries?—How long did they last?—By whom were they abolished?

Emperor Theodosius. The penalty of revealing these mysteries was death:

Vetabo qui Cereris sacrum
Vulgarit arcanæ, sub isdem
Sit trabibus, fragilemque mecum
Solvat phaselum.—Hor. Od III. 2. 26 seqq.

(3.) PHYLE (Φυλή), the fort held by Thrasybu'lus and the Athenian exiles who expelled the Thirty Tyrants from Athens after the Peloponnesian war (401 B.C.).

(4.) DECELE'A (Δεκέλεια), garrisoned by the Lacedæmonians in the Peloponnesian war (414 B C.).

(5.) MAR'ATHON (Μαραθών), a small plain in the North-Eastern part of At'tica. On the North and South are marshes; the heights of Brilessus form the Western boundary. On the East is the bay. It comprised four towns, Mar'athon, Probalinthus, Tricor'ythus, and Œ'noë, which originally formed the Tetrap'olis, one of the twelve districts into which At'tica was divided before the time of Theseus. In the plain of Ma'rathon the tumulus still exists which was erected to the hundred and ninety-two Athenians who were slain in the memorable battle (490 B.C.), and whose names were inscribed upon ten pillars, one for each tribe, placed upon the tomb. There was a separate monument to Milti'ades.

(6.) Other towns: PÆANIA, ELEU'THERÆ, SUNIUM, RAMNUS, ALOPEÆ, ORO'PUS, BRAURON, PRASIÆ.

§ 84. ATHE'NÆ.

(αἱ Ἀθῆναι, *Atiniah*, or *Settines*, that is, ἐς Ἀθήνας.)

Athe'næ, the capital of At'tica, is situated four or five miles from the sea-coast, in the central plain of At'tica which is enclosed by mountains on every side except on the South, where it is open to the sea. After the rebuilding of the city (479 B.C.) it con-

---

QUESTIONS.—What is said of Phyle?—What of Decelea?—Describe the situation of Marathon.—What battle was fought there?——§ 84. Describe the situation of Athens.

tained, including its three port-towns, 10,000 houses and 180,000 inhabitants. The circuit of the city was almost twenty miles.

It comprised within its boundaries the following four celebrated hills: Acrop′olis, Areiop′agus, Pnyx, and Muse′um.

(1.) Acrop′olis (ἀκρόπολις), a square craggy rock rising abruptly about 150 feet, with a flat summit of 1000 by 500 feet. It stood in the centre of the city, the heart of Athens. It formed the original *city:* therefore, in historical times, it was often called Polis (πόλις). After the Persian wars it was not inhabited as a place of residence, but served as the fortress, the sanctuary, and the museum of the city. The rock was covered with temples, sanctuaries, or monuments, the whole forming a vast array of architecture, sculpture, and painting. The buildings stood on platforms communicating with each other by steps. The Acrop′olis was entered by—

a. The *Propulæa* (τὰ προπύλαια), a marble vestibule built under the administration of Per′icles (437 B. C.), the northern wing of which is still tolerably perfect.

b. On the highest part of the Acrop′olis stood the *Par′thenon* (Παρθενών), the temple of *Athena the Virgin* (Ἀθηνᾶ Παρθένος), so called as *the invincible goddess of war.* This most perfect production of Grecian architecture also was built under the administration of Per′icles, on the site of the old Hecatom′pedon. It was built entirely of Pentelic marble, and rested upon a rustic basement of ordinary limestone. Its architecture was of the Doric order. The whole building was adorned within and without with the most exquisite pieces of sculpture executed by different artists under the direction of Phidias. The colossal statue of the goddess, about forty feet in height, was the work of his own hand. The statue itself was of ivory; the dress and ornaments of solid

---

QUESTIONS.—How many houses did Athens contain?—What was the number of its inhabitants?—Name the four celebrated hills.—Describe the Acropolis.—Describe the entrance to it.—What temple occupied the highest part of the Acropolis?—Describe the Parthenon.—Under whose supervision was the sculpture executed?—What was the work of Phidias himself?—Describe the statue of the virgin goddess.

gold. It represented the goddess standing, clothed with a tunic which reached to the ankles; her left hand holding her spear, while her right sustained an image of Victory, six feet high. She was represented girded with the ægis, a helmet on her head, and her shield supported on the ground by her side.

c. The most revered of all the sanctuaries of Athens was the *Erechthe'um* (Ἐρέχθειον), the temple of Poseidon (*Neptune*), built over the well of salt water produced, according to the ancient myth, by the stroke of the trident. It contained also the sanctuary of Athe'na Polias, *Athe'na* the Guardian *of the City*, and the olive-tree from which the Moriæ, or sacred olive-trees in the Academi'a were derived, and from these again all other olive-trees which grew in the precincts of the temples and the grounds of private persons. The original Erechthe'um, with all the other buildings, was burnt down by the Persians. About 400 B.C. the new building of the Ionic order was completed.

THE ACROPOLIS.

QUESTIONS.—Describe the Erechtheum—What is said of the sacred olive trees?

These were the chief buildings of the Acrop'olis, but its summit was covered with other temples, altars, statues, and works of art.

(2.) Immediately west of the Acrop'olis is the *Areiop'agus* (*Ἄρειος πάγος*, *Hill of Ares, Mars*). On its South-Eastern summit the council of Areiop'agus met. This hill possesses peculiar interest to Christians as the spot from which the Apostle Paul preached to the men of Athens.

(3.) To the South-West rises a third hill, the *Pnyx* (*Πνύξ*), the place of assembly of the Athenian people, which formed part of the surface of a low rocky hill. In the middle point of this wall of rock a solid rectangular block projects, hewn from, but adhering to it on one side. This is the celebrated Bema (*Βῆμα*, i. e. *step* which one mounted), often called *the Stone* (*ὁ λίθος*), whence the orators addressed the multitude in the semicircular area before them.

(4.) To the South of the Pnyx is the *Muse'um*. At the eastern foot of this hill are three ancient excavations in the rock, one of which is said to have been the prison of Soc'rates.

§ **85.** Beneath the southern wall of the Acrop'olis was the theatre of Diony'sus, built of stone, in which all the great productions of the Grecian drama were performed. Near it was the Music Hall (Ὠιδεῖον). North of the Areiop'agus was the *These'um*, at the same time temple and tomb, containing the bones of Theseus. It is the best preserved of all the monuments of ancient Athens. South-East of the Acrop'olis was the Olympie'um, sacred to Zeus Olympius, the greatest temple not only of Athens but of all Greece. It was one of the four most celebrated specimens of architecture in marble, the other three being the temples of Eph'esus, Bran'chidæ, and Eleusis. It was

---

Questions.—Describe the Areiopagus.—What peculiar interest does it possess for Christians?—Where was the hill Pnyx situated?—What was the Bema?—What was the Museum?——§ 85. Where were the great productions of the Greek drama performed?—Describe the Theseum.—Describe the Olympieum.—Name the four places which contained the greatest temples of Greece.

commenced by Pisis'tratus and nearly seven hundred years afterward finished by Hadrian. West of the Acrop'olis was the *A'gora* (Ἀγορά), which formed a part of the Ceramei'cus (*Κεραμεικός*, pr. *Potters' Quarter*). The A'gora had an enclosure at its southern entrance, containing the House of the Senate and the temple dedicated to the Mother of the gods. On the south-west side of the square were the statues of the Epo'nymi, or ten heroes, from whom the ten tribes of At'tica were named. At the eastern gate were two porticos, one of which, known as the Porch of the *Hermæ*, contained three statues of *Hermes* (Mercury), bearing the names of those soldiers who had distinguished themselves in the battles against the Persians; and the other, called the *Pœ'cile* (ἡ Ποικίλη στοά), adorned with fresco painting of the battle of Mar'athon by Polygno'tus, was the place where Zeno the founder of the *Stoic* philosophers taught. In the A'gora was the court of the Archon, near the statues of the Epo'nymi. Here, too, was the police-station of the Scythians employed by the government in the maintenance of the peace of the city. At the north-eastern angle of the Acrop'olis was the *Prytane'um* (Πρυτανεῖον), where the Pry'tanes, the presiding officers of the Senate and the Assembly had their meals, and where distinguished citizens and the children of those who fell in battle were often entertained. Here also the laws of Solon were kept.

§ **86.** We have now to mention the three celebrated schools in the suburbs, the *Academi'a*, the *Cynosarges*, and the *Lyce'um:*

(1.) The *Academi'a* (Ἀκαδήμια or Ἀκαδήμεια), on the north-west, derived its name from the hero Acade'mus, the original owner of the grounds. It was afterward converted into a Gymnasium. The beauty of the surrounding plane trees and olive plantations was particularly celebrated. The Academy was the

---

QUESTIONS.—Who commenced the building of the Olympicum?—Who finished it?—Describe the principal edifices of the Agora?—What was the Pœcile?—Where was the court of the Archon?—Describe the Prytaneum.——§ 86. What three celebrated schools were at Athens?—Describe the Academia.

school of Plato, and his successors continuing to teach in the same spot, were hence called the Academic Philosophers.

(2.) The *Cynosarges*, on the east, was a sanctuary of Her'cules and, at the same time, a Gymnasium. Antis'thenes, the founder of the Cynic school, taught here.

(3.) The *Lyce'um*, also on the east, was the chief of the Athenian Gymnasia, and was dedicated to Apollo Lyce'us. This was the place in which Aristotle and his disciples taught, who were called *peripatetics* from their practice of *walking about* in this Gymnasium while delivering their lectures.

Athens had three port-towns. The *Piræus* (Πειραιεύς) was the principal port and was connected with the city by means of two walls, called *the long walls*. East of the Piræus was the second port called *Munychia* (Μουνυχία); and still further East the *Phale'ron* (Φάληρον), the least frequented of the three. The walls, which connected the Piræus with the city, were forty stadia (about five miles) in length, probably sixty feet high, and about twelve feet thick, if we may judge from the foundations of the northern wall. These walls were begun by Themis'tocles and finished by Cimon and Per'icles, and were one of the causes of the Peloponnesian war (431—404 B.C.), which ended with the capture of Athens by the Peloponnesians and Bœotians, and the loss of the Athenian supremacy. In the seventy-fifth year after the battle of Sa'lamis, the sovereignty of Athens received its calamitous termination.

But the intermediate times had done much toward awakening the genius of the people of Athens; and the love of the sciences and of the fine arts, which had sprung up among them, was now the foundation of lasting fame. In no city were the festivals and theatrical entertainments so magnificent and various. In

---

QUESTIONS.—Describe the Cynosarges.—The Lyceum.—Name the three port-towns of Athens.—Which was the most important one?—Describe the walls by which it was connected with the city.—Who built these walls?—What war was caused by them?—When did the war begin?—When did it end?—How long was it after the battle of Salamis?—What was the character of Athens after the destruction of her supremacy?

manners, the people were most polished, and their enjoyments of life the most multiplied and refined. Commerce flourished in Athens, and strangers, eager for knowledge, flocked thither in great numbers. The public walks of Athens, the groves of the Lyce'um and the Academy, became the seat of a more glorious empire than the fate of arms could bestow or take away; and the victory of the Peloponnesians at Ægospo'tami destroyed only the material sway, not the genuine greatness, of Athens.

§ 87. ME'GARIS. (*ἡ Μεγαρίς.*)

Boundaries.—North, BŒOTIA; East, AT'TICA; South, CORINTHIA and SINUS SARO'NICUS; West, SINUS ALCYO'NICUS.

Extent.—It occupied the greater part of the isthmus which connects Hellas with Peloponne'sus. The area of the country is 143 square miles.

Mountains.—It is a rugged and mountainous country, and contains no plain except the one in which its capital, Me'gara, was situated. The mountains were called GERANEI'A, one of whose passes, *the Scironian Rocks* (*αἱ Σκειρωνίδες πέτραι*), was named from the robber Sciron.

Cape.—ÆGIPLANCTUS.

Town.—Me'garis contained but one town of importance, ME'GARA, with its harbor Nisæa (*Νίσαια*). In the seventh century before the Christian era, it was one of the most flourishing commercial cities of Greece, and it founded some of the earlier Grecian colonies, both in Sicily and Thrace: Me'gara in Sicily, As'tacus in Bithynia, Cy'zicus in the Propontis, Chalce'don at the mouth of the Bos'porus, and Byzantium opposite Chalce'don. Me'gara was celebrated on account of its School of philosophy, which was founded by Eucli'des, a disciple of Soc'rates, and

---

QUESTIONS.—§ 87. What are the boundaries of Megaris?—What is said of its extent?—What is said of its mountains?—What cape was in Megaris?—What was the only town of importance?—Give the name of its harbor.—What colonies were founded by Megaris?—Who was the founder of the school of the Megarici?—Whose disciple was Euclides?

which distinguished itself chiefly by the cultivation of dialectics. The philosophers of this school were called the Mega'rici.

Other towns of note were: Rhus, on the North of Me'gara; and Pegæ and Ægos'thena, on the Corinthian Gulf.

§ 88. PELOPONNE'SUS. (*ἡ Πελοπόννησος, Morea.*)

Boundaries.—The peninsula forming the lower part of Greece below the Sinus Corinthi'acus and the Sinus Saro'nicus was called the Peloponne'sus (*Πελοπόννησος,* i. e. *Island of Pelops*).

Extent.—Its area is 7,777 square miles, or not quite as large as the state of Massachusetts.

Mountains.—The mountains of Peloponne'sus have their origin in Arcadia, the central district of the country, which is encircled by an irregular ring of mountains forming a kind of natural wall, from which lateral branches extend in all directions toward the sea. The principal mountain ranges are ERYMANTHUS, LYCÆUS, TAY'GETUS.

Capes.—CHELONA'TAS, ICHTHYS, TAE'NARUS, and MA'LEA.

Rivers.—The chief river is the ALPHE'US in Arcadia and Elis, next in size are the EURO'TAS in Lacon'ica, the PAMI'SUS in Messenia, and the PENE'US in northern Elis.

Volcanic Changes.—Earthquakes have, in all ages, been of frequent occurrence in Peloponne'sus. The earthquake of 464 B. C. destroyed almost the whole city of Sparta, and a century later (373 B. C.) two cities of Achaia, He'lice and Bura, were swallowed up by the sea.

Divisions.—The central district was called ARCADIA. South of it were LACON'ICA and MESSENIA; on the West ELIS; on the North, ACHAIA, and on the East, AR'GOLIS, which was subdivided into CORINTHIA, PHLIASIA, SICYONIA, AR'GOLIS and CYNURIA.

QUESTIONS.—§ 88. What is the modern name of Peloponnesus?—What are its boundaries?—What is its extent?—Describe its mountains. Its capes.—Its rivers.—What is said about volcanic changes?—What cities were destroyed by the earthquake of 464 B. C.?—Give the divisions of Peloponnesus.—How was Argolis subdivided?

§ 89. ARCADIA. (ἡ Ἀρκαδία.)

Boundaries.—North, ACHAIA; East, AR'GOLIS; South, MESSENIA and LACON'ICA; West, ELIS.

Extent.—Next to Lacon'ica it was the largest country in Peloponne'sus. Its area was about 1,700 square miles.

Mountains.—It was surrounded and traversed by different ranges of mountains. It has been aptly called the Switzerland of Greece, and was a celebrated pastoral country of the poets. Virgil makes a boastful shepherd say:

Pan etiam, Arcadia mecum si judice certet,
Pan etiam Arcadia dicat se judice victum.
Ecl. IV. 58 seq.

The most celebrated mountains are CYLLE'NE, which the ancients thought was the highest in the Peloponne'sus, an honor which is now known to belong to one of the summits of Tay'getus; ERYMANTHUS, MÆ'NALUS, LYCÆ'US.

Rivers.—The ALPHE'US and its tributary, the LADON.

Lake.—STYMPHA'LUS (Στύμφαλος), the residence of the Harpies, the destruction of which monsters was one of the twelve labors of Her'cules. The lake discharged its waters through a mountain chasm and reappeared in Ar'golis as a river.

Climate.—The winter is often long and rigorous; even in March the weather is intensely cold.

Productions.—The Northern mountains were covered with forests and abounded in game. The Eastern region is intersected by mountains of lower elevation, between which there are several small and fertile plains, producing corn, oil, and wine. Of all

---

QUESTIONS.—§ 89. What are the boundaries of Arcadia?—What is its extent?—With what modern country has it often been compared?—Why?—Name some of its mountains.—Some of its rivers.—What remark is made in regard to Lake Stymphalus?—What is said of the climate?—What were the chief productions?

the productions of Arcadia, the best known were its asses, which were in request in every part of Greece.

Persius bears testimony to their vigor:

Arcadiæ pecuaria rudere credas.—Sat. III. 9.

Inhabitants.—It was inhabited by the same race of people from the earliest historical times. The Arcadians regarded themselves as the most ancient inhabitants of Greece. They were a strong and hardy race of mountaineers, and, like the Swiss in modern Europe, constantly served as mercenaries. They were very fond of music; Hermes is said to have invented the lyre in their country and the syrinx, or shepherd's pipe, was regarded as a contrivance of Pan, their tutelary god. The simplicity of the Arcadian character was exaggerated by the Roman poets into an ideal excellence, and its shepherds were represented as living in a state of perfect innocence and virtue.

Towns.—The chief towns were situated in the Eastern valleys. The other parts contained only villages.

(1.) TE'GEA (*Τεγέα*), which, after a long struggle, was obliged to acknowledge the authority of Sparta.

(2.) MANTINE'A (*Μαντίνεια*), the largest and one of the most ancient of the Arcadian towns, the scene of the victory and death of Epaminondas (362 B.C.).

(3.) MEGALOP'OLIS (*Μεγαλόπολις*), founded by Epaminondas (371 B.C.), in order to check the inroads of the Lacedæmonians, was the birthplace of Philopœmen and Polybius, the historian.

(4.) LYCOSU'RA (*Λυκόσουρα*), at the foot of Mount Lycæus. It was considered by the Greeks as the most ancient city in the world.

(5.) CLITOR (*Κλείτωρ*), in which territory was the celebrated

---

QUESTIONS.—What is said of the asses of Arcadia?—What is said of the inhabitants?—How are they described by the Roman poets?—Where were the chief towns of Arcadia situated?—Mention some of them.—What is said of Tegea?—Who died at Mantinea?—When?—Who founded Megalopolis?—What celebrated men were natives of Megalopolis?—What was found in the neighborhood of Clitor?

fountain, of whose waters those who drank lost for ever their taste for wine:

> *Clitorio quicumque sitim de fonte levarit,*
> *Vino fugit, gaudetque meris abstemius undis.*
> Ovid. Met. XV. 322.

(6.) Other places of note were: ORCHO'MENUS, PHENEUS, PSOPHIS, CAPHYÆ, THELPU'SA, PALLANTIUM, and PHIGALIA.

§ 90. LACON'ICA. (ἡ Λακεδαίμων or Λακωνική.)

COAST OF LACONIA.

Name.—The most ancient name was *Lacedæmon* (Λακεδαίμων), given as well to the country as to its capital. The usual name in Greek authors was LACON'ICA; the Romans called the country LACON'ICA, LACON'ICE, or LACONIA. Some modern scholars are of opinion that the root of the word is LAC, connected with

QUESTIONS.—§ 90. What is the most ancient name of Laconica?—What does the name signify?

λάκος, λάκκος, Lat. *lacus*, *lacuna*, Eng. *lake*, and that it was given to the central region from its being *sunk* between mountains.

Boundaries.—North, CYNURIA, AR'GOLIS, and ARCADIA; East, MARE MYRTO'UM (*Μυρτῷον πέλαγος*) and SINUS ARGOL'ICUS; South, SINUS MESSENI'ACUS and LACON'ICUS; West, MESSENIA.

Extent.—It is a long valley surrounded on three sides by mountains, and open only on the fourth to the sea: it contains about 1,900 square miles.

Mountains.—The Western range which terminated in Cape Tæ'narum was called TAY'GETUS; the Eastern range terminating in Cape MA'LEA was known by the names of PARNON (*Πάρνων*), THORAX, and ZARAX.

Volcanic Changes.—Lacon'ica was called *the easily shaken* (*ἐύσειστος ἡ Λακωνική*). In the terrible earthquake of 464 B.C. not more than five houses are said to have been left standing at Lacedæmon; more than 20,000 persons were believed to have perished, and huge masses of rock were rolled down from the highest peak of Tay'getus.

River.—The whole drainage of the valley empties into the river EURO'TAS (*Εὐρώτας*, called *Basili-potamo*, below the Spartan plain), which flows from the highlands of Arcadia into the Laconic Gulf.

Climate.—The orange-tree flourishes in the valley of Sparta while the summits of Tay'getus are wrapped in snow.

Productions.—The slopes of Tay'getus are clothed with forests of pine. This mountain-range is rich in iron, marble, and green porphyry. The soil is generally poor, difficult to plough, and better suited to the cultivation of olives than of grain.

Inhabitants.—The oldest inhabitants were the *Le'leges*, who

QUESTIONS.—What are the boundaries of Laconica?—What is the extent?—What is said about the mountains?—When was Sparta destroyed by an earthquake?—Were earthquakes common there?—What is the only remarkable river of Laconica?—What is said of the Eurotas?—What is said of the climate?—What of the productions?—Who were the oldest inhabitants?

were succeeded by the *Achæans*. Eighty years after the fall of Troy, Lacon'ica was conquered by the Dorians. The population of Lacedæmon was hence divided into the three classes of Spartans, Periœci (*Περίοικοι*), and Helots (*Εἵλωτες*). The Spartans lived in the city of Sparta or Lacedæmon and were the ruling Dorian class; the Periœci lived in the different townships in Lacon'ica, and though freemen, had no share in the government, but received all their privileges from the ruling class at Sparta; the Helots were serfs bound to the soil, who cultivated it for the benefit of the Spartan proprietors, and the Periœci.

The number of the citizens of Sparta, at the time of the Persian wars, was about 8,000. After this time it gradually but steadily declined, so that, about two and a half centuries later, it did not contain more than 700 inhabitants.

Towns.—There were no towns of any importance in Lacon'ica except the capital.

(1.) SPARTA or LACEDÆMON (*Σπάρτη* or *Λακεδαίμων*), the capital, on the right bank of the river Euro'tas, at the foot of Mount Tay'getus. The appearance of the city was much inferior to its fame, as there was a comparative absence of elegant temples or private residences. The Spartans, protected by the lofty ramparts of mountains, continued to dwell in the midst of their plantations and gardens, with their original rural surroundings. This rural freedom formed the chief charm and beauty of the city of Sparta. It is at present a heap of shapeless ruins near the modern town of Mistra.

(2.) One of the most ancient towns was AMY'CLÆ (*Ἀμύκλαι*), the residence of the Achæan kings. Apollo was here worshipped with peculiar solemnities, and his temple was superior to any other in Lacon'ica. Here *the Hyacinthia*, a festival in honor of

---

QUESTIONS.—When was Laconica conquered by the Dorians?—What three parts did it contain since that time?—What is said of the Spartans?—Who were the Periœci?—Who were the Helots?—What was the number of citizens (Spartans) during the Persian wars?—Did the population decrease or increase after that time?—What was the capital of Laconica?—Where was it situated?—What was the appearance of the town?—What was its chief charm?—What is said of Amyclæ?

Hyacinthus, was celebrated. Amy'clæ was said to have been called *tacitæ*, or the *Silent:*

tacitis regnavit Amyclis,
Virg. Æn. X. 564:

from the fact of the inhabitants having made a law, which forbade the mention of the approach of their enemies, the Spartans. They afterward fell victims to their absurd statute.

(3.) GYTHIUM (*Γύθιον*), South-West of the mouth of the Euro'tas, was the naval station of the Spartans. In its neighborhood was Helos (*Ἕλος*), whose inhabitants the Lacedæmonians reduced to slavery, whence their slaves were called *Helots*, according to the historian Eph'orus; but others more plausibly make *Helot* synonymous with *captive*, as if derived from *ἑλεῖν*.

(4.) SELLASIA (*Σελλασία*), where Cleom'enes, the last of the royal line of the Heracli'dæ, was defeated and expelled by Anti'gonus (222 B. C.).

(5.) THERAPNE, EPIDAURUS, LIME'RA, CURIÆ.

§ 91. MESSENIA. (*ἡ Μεσσηνία.*)

Boundaries.—North, ELIS and ARCADIA; East, LACON'ICA; South, SINUS MESSENI'ACUS; West, MARE IONIUM.

Extent.—Its area was nearly 1,200 square miles. The most fertile and most populous part is the basin of the Pami'sus (*Πάμισος*). This basin is divided into two distinct parts, which are separated from each other by Mount Itho'me (*Ἰθώμη*) and connecting highlands. The upper part was called *Stenycle'rus*, and the lower part, *Macaria*.

Mountains.—The mountains on the Western coast of Messenia are much less rugged than on the Eastern coast of Lacon'ica.

QUESTIONS.—What was the naval station of the Spartans?—What is said of Helos and of the origin of the name Helot?—What battle was fought near Sellasia?——§ 91. What are the boundaries of Messenia?—What is its extent?—What is said of the basin of the Pamisus?—What is said about the mountains?

The chief mountain-chain was called AIGALEON, the Northern range ELAI'ON, and the Western range TAŸ'GETUS. In the middle were the two great natural fortresses, Itho'me and Ira (Εἶρα), the former commanding the entrance to the lower plain, and the latter situated in the mountains in the Northern part of the upper plains. Ira held out against the Spartans, when they ejected the Messenians (671 B. C.), and was not finally reduced till three centuries later.

Capes.—ACRI'TAS, CYPARISSIUM, CORYPHASIUM.

Bays.—SINUS CYPARISSIUS and SINUS MESSENI'ACUS. On the Western coast is the deep Bay of Pylos (*Navarino*), the best, and only really good harbor of the Peloponne'sus, celebrated both in ancient and modern history. The Athenians here made prisoners of a hundred and twenty of the first Spartan families, and thus impaired the strength of the old notion that the Spartans would rather die than yield; and in recent times a great battle was won in this bay by the combined fleets of England, France, and Russia, in conflict with the Turkish fleet (Oct. 20, 1827).

Rivers.—The PAMI'SUS flows through the entire length of the country, from North to South, fertilizing cultivated and extensive plains which constitute the largest portion of the whole country. The principal river in the upper plain was called BAL'YRA (Βαλύρα). At its junction with the AM'PHITUS is a celebrated triangular bridge, the foundations and piers of which are of great antiquity.

Climate.—The climate is often praised by the ancients as temperate and soft, especially on the lower plain, which was hence called *Macaria* (ἡ Μακαρία), *the Blest.* It is described as neither too hot in summer, nor too cold in winter.

QUESTIONS.—What were the great natural fortresses?—Which of these fortresses commanded the lower plain?—Which the upper plain?—When was Ira taken?—Name some promontories of Laconica.—Some of the bays.—Where is the Bay of Pylos situated?—What happened there?—What are the principal rivers?—What is said of the Pamisus?—What was the principal river of the upper plain?—What is at the junction of the Balyra and Amphitus?—What is said of the climate?

§ 92. **Productions.**—It was the most fertile part of the Peloponne'sus. It was watered by very numerous streams, and abounded in fruits and flocks.

Inhabitants.—The oldest inhabitants were LEL'EGES, who, with the rest of the Peloponnesians, were conquered by the Dorians. In the middle of the eighth century before the Christian era, a series of disputes and skirmishes occurred on the borders of Messenia and Lacon'ica, which gave rise to a confirmed hatred between the two kindred nations. Bloody wars followed, and the result was the incorporation of Messenia with Lacon'ica (666 B.C.), while the inhabitants were reduced to the condition of Helots. The majority of freemen, however, withdrew from Messenia and settled in various parts of Greece. A large number, under the two sons of Aristom'enes, sailed to Italy and settled at Rhegium. They afterward obtained possession of Zancle, on the opposite coast of Sicily, and called it Messa'na, which has retained the same name to the present day.

Towns.—(1.) ANDANIA (*Ἀνδανία*), the capital of the Messenian kings before the Dorians.

(2.) STENYCLA'RUS (*Στενύκλαρος*), the capital of the Dorian conquerors.

(3.) MESSE'NE (*Μεσσήνη*), founded by Epaminondas at the foot of Mount Itho'me, on the summit of which was the citadel, one of the strongest places in the Peloponne'sus.

(4.) IRA or EIRA (*Εἶρα*), where the citizens maintained themselves during the second Messenian war.

QUESTIONS.—§ 92. What is said of the fertility of Messenia?—Of its productions?—Who were the oldest inhabitants?—By whom were they conquered?—With which of their kindred neighbors did these conquerors go to war?—What was the result?—When did this incorporation happen?—Did the whole population submit to their conquerors?—Whither did they go?—Under whose conduct did they sail to Italy?—Where did they settle first?—Where afterward?—Name some Messenian towns.—What was the ancient residence of the Messenian kings?—What became the capital of the Dorian conquerors?—Where was Messene situated?—Who was its founder?

(5.) PYLUS (Πύλος), and METHO'NE (Μεθώνη), were the chief towns on the Western coast. The former was the residence of king Nestor, famed for his wisdom and eloquence (Il. I. 247 seqq.).

(6.) Other towns: CORO'NE, CYPARISSUS.

§ 93. ELIS. (Ἦλις.)

Name.—The Doric name of ELIS was *Alis*, or, written with the digamma, *FAΛIΣ*, perhaps connected with the Latin *vallis*, *a vale*, *valley*, and so signifying originally, a hollow.

Boundaries.—North, MARE IONIUM; East, ACHAIA and ARCADIA; South, MESSENIA; West, MARE IONIUM.

Divisions.—(1.) The Northern part, or ELIS PROPER, or Hollow Elis;

(2.) The middle part, or PISA'TIS, district of *Pisa;* and

(3.) The Southern part, or TRIPHYLIA, i. e. the country of the *three tribes*, Minyæ, Ele'ans, Cauco'nes.

Capes.—The coast of Elis is a long and almost unbroken sandy level, interrupted only by three rocky promontories, ARAXUS, CHELONA'TAS, and ICHTHYS, of which Chelona'tas is the largest.

Mountains.—Elis has no mountain system of its own, but only hills and plains. Its chief mountain, PHOLOË, was celebrated in ancient poetry and mythology. This name comprised all the highlands North of the river Alphe'us.

Valleys.—The plain of the Pene'us, being the level portion of Hollow Elis. Its mountain region was called Acrore'a. The South-West part of the plain of the Pene'us is called the plain

---

QUESTIONS.—What were the chief towns on the western coast of Messenia?—Where was the residence of Nestor?——§ 93. What is the Doric form of Elis?—How is it written with the digamma?—With what Latin word does it correspond?—With what English word?—What does Elis signify?—How is it bounded?—How divided?—What does Triphylia signify?—What is said of the mountains?—What is the chief mountain?—Name the principal valleys.

of Gastu'ni, and Pisa'tis comprises the lower valley of the Alphe'us.

Rivers.—The principal rivers are the ALPHE'US, which flows along a broad and fertile valley through the centre of Elis; and the river PENE'US (*Gastuni*), beside a great many smaller streams. Along the coast of Triphylia were many lagoons.

Productions.—The country was very populous and more fertile than any other in the Peloponne'sus, and is said to have been the only one in Greece which produced flax. Horses, cattle, and oxen were reared within its limits in large numbers; it was also full of timber, mostly oak.

Inhabitants.—The most ancient inhabitants of Elis appear to have been *Pelasgians*, who were called Cauco'nes, Epe'ans, Pylians, and Ele'ans. The Ele'ans were the first people in the Peloponne'sus who experienced the effects of the Dorian invasion, their territory being the landing-place of the invaders.

Towns.—ELIS (*Ἦλις*) was the residence of the Dorian invaders. It was the only fortified town in the country. The rest of the towns were all unwalled villages, inhabited by the Pelasgians, who all rendered obedience to the ruling class at Elis. The harbor of Elis was called Cylle'ne (*Κυλλήνη*). In Triphylia was the town of SCILLUS, given by the Lacedæmonians to the historian Xen'ophon, then an exile from Athens, who lived here more than twenty years. Other towns were: PYLOS, PISA, LEPREUM, SA'MICUM, OLYMPIA (see § 94)

§ 94. OLYMPIA. (*ἡ Ὀλυμπία.*)

It lay on the right bank of the Alphe'us, nearly in the centre of Elis, and was properly not a town, but only a collection of

---

QUESTIONS.—Name the two largest rivers of Elis.—What is said of the productions?—What product was entirely confined to Elis?—What Pelasgian tribes inhabited Elis?—Where had been the landing-place of the Dorian conquerors?—What was the only fortified town of the country?—What was its harbor?—What is said of Scyllus?——§ 94. Describe the situation of Olympia.—Was it really a town?

sacred buildings. It belonged originally to Pisa, and the plain in which it stood was called, in more ancient times, the plain of Pisa; but after the destruction of this city by the Ele'ans (572 B.C.), the name of Olympia was extended to the whole district. This district comprises a plain surrounded on all sides by hills except on the West, where it opens toward the sea. Here was the celebrated sacred grove which surrounded the temple of Zeus. Olympia lay partly within and partly outside of the sacred grove. This grove bore the name of Altis, and was surrounded by a wall with several gates, but with only one entrance, situated in the middle of the western side, and called the Pompic Entrance. On the right hand of this gate, within the wall, was the sacred olive from which a boy with a golden knife cut the olive branches destined to adorn the head of the conqueror in the games. In the immediate neighborhood of this tree was the *Olympe'um*, or temple of Zeus Olympius. It was of the Doric order. Its length was two hundred and thirty feet, its breadth ninety-five feet, and its height sixty-eight feet. It had six columns in front, and thirteen on the sides. These columns were fluted, and seven feet four inches in diameter, and larger than any known to have belonged to any ancient temple of Greece. In its interior construction it resembled the Par'the-non at Athens. In this temple was the colossal statue of Zeus Olympius, the master-work of Phidias, which surpassed even his celebrated statue of Athe'na in the Par'thenon. The statue was formed of gold and ivory, fifty-eight feet in height, seated on a throne and almost touching the roof of the temple. Upon the head of the god was an olive crown; in his right hand he bore a winged figure of Victory, also of gold and ivory, crowned, and holding a wreath. In his left hand was a lofty sceptre sur-

---

QUESTIONS.—To what town did Olympia originally belong?—What was the ancient name of the plain?—When did it receive the name of Olympia?—When was Pisa destroyed?—By whom?—Describe the plain. —What was the Altis?—How many gates did it possess?—What was its name?—What is said of the sacred olive?—Describe the temple of Zeus Olympius.—Describe his statue.—Whose work was it?

mounted with an eagle. His sandals and robe were of gold, the latter painted with animals and flowers, particularly lilies. The throne was formed of ivory and ebony, inlaid with gold, set with precious stones, and sculptured with graceful figures. The faces of the steps bore bas-reliefs of classic myths, and the foot-stool rested upon four lions couchant. In making this statue Phidias himself said he followed the model expressed by Homer:

So did he speak, and, at pausing, he sign'd with his shadowy eyebrows,
And the ambrosial curls from the Head Everlasting were shaken,
And at the nod of the King deep trembled the lofty Olympus.
Il. I. 528 seqq.

The next important sites were the Stadium and Hippodrome, which together formed the place of exhibition for all the Olympic contests, usually called the Olympic Games, the greatest of the national festivals of the Helle'nes. Those contests consisted of various trials of strength and skill in foot races and horse races, wrestling and boxing. In the beginning probably confined to the Peloponnesians, the Olympic games became at length a festival for the whole nation, not only of Hellas, but of all the colonies. No one was allowed to contend in the games but persons of pure Hellenic blood. After the conquest of Greece by the Romans, the latter were permitted to take part in the games. No women were allowed to be present. As persons from all parts of the Hellenic world were assembled together at the Olympic games, it was the best opportunity, not only for carrying on commercial transactions with persons from distant places, but also for the artist and the author to make their works known. Before the invention of printing, the easiest and surest mode of publishing the works of an author was to read them to as large an assembly as could be obtained, and this was a favorite practice

---

QUESTIONS.—What model did Phidias follow in making the statue of Zeus Olympius?—Where were the Olympic games celebrated?—By whom were they celebrated?—Was everybody allowed to contend in them?—What foreigners were afterward permitted to participate in them?—In what did the games consist?—What opportunity did they afford to merchants?—What opportunity did they afford to authors?

of the Greeks and Romans. It is said to have been done by Hero'dotus, Hippias, Lysias, Dion Chrysos'tomus. Painters and other artists also exhibited their works at Olympia.

These Games were celebrated about midsummer, at the conclusion of every fourth year, or rather of every forty-ninth month, and were held for five successive days. This period of four years elapsing between the celebrations of the Olympic Games was called an *Olympiad* (ἡ Ὀλυμπιάς), and the Olympiads began to be reckoned from the victory of Corœbus in the foot-race in the year 776 B. C., which thus forms the epoch of Greek history. The Games were totally abolished (A. D. 394) during the reign of Theodosius the Great.

§ 95. ACHAIA. (Ἀχαΐα, earlier Ἀχαιΐς.)

Name.—It was originally called ÆGI'ALUS, or ÆGIALE'A (*Αἰγιαλός, Αἰγιάλεια*, i. e. *the Coast*). It was nothing more than a narrow slip of coast, lying upon the slope of the Northern range of Arcadia, only a little broader toward the West.

Boundaries.—North, SINUS CORINTHIUS; West, ELIS and MARE IONIUM; South, ARCADIA and ELIS; East, SICYONIA and PHLIASIA.

Extent.—The extent was only 650 square miles.

Mountains.—From the Arcadian mountain range, numerous ridges descend, running toward the sea-coast, and separated from it by narrow plains. The highest mountain is called PANACHA'ICUS.

Capes.—Each river has a promontory, which is in general nearly opposite to the openings at which the rivers emerge from

---

QUESTIONS.—What authors made use of the opportunity afforded by the Olympic Games?—When were they celebrated?—What is an Olympiad?—When were the Games abolished?——§ 95. What was the original name of Achaia?—What is its signification?—What are the boundaries?—What is the extent?—What is said about the mountains?—What is the highest mountain?—What is said about the capes?—What are the most conspicuous promontories?

the mountains. The most conspicuous are DRE'PANUM, RHIUM, ARAXUS.

Rivers.—The plains are drained by numerous streams; but, in consequence of the proximity of the mountains to the sea, the course of these torrents is necessarily short, and most of them are dry in summer. Out of its fourteen rivers there are only two of any importance: the CRATHIS and the PEIRUS.

Inhabitants.—The original inhabitants were Pelasgians. The Ionians subsequently settled the country and called it Ionia. They remained in possession of the country till the invasion of Peloponne'sus by the Dorians, when the Achæans, who had been driven out of Argos and Lacedæmon by the invaders, marched against the Ionians in order to obtain new homes for themselves in the country of the latter. They were successful, and the country was thenceforth called after them, *Achaia.* These Achæans, mentioned by Homer as the ruling people of the Peloponne'sus, are rarely noticed during the flourishing period of Grecian history; but by means of the celebrated Achæan League they again became first among the Greeks in the last days of the nation's independence. Their particular importance may be traced to the influence of Ara'tus (251—213 B. C.), whose main object was to liberate the Peloponnesian cities from their tyrants. After the Roman conquest of Greece (146 B. C.), the term, Achaia, received an extension in its signification, principally due to the importance which the Achæan league had obtained. The *Roman* province of Achaia comprehended all Peloponne'sus with Northern Greece South of Thessaly, perhaps, not inclusive of Acarnania. Hence *Achæus,* in Latin, was synonymous with *Græcus.*

QUESTIONS.—What is remarked of the rivers of Achaia?—Name the principal rivers.—Who were the original inhabitants?—Who settled the country afterward?—By whom were they driven out?—Where did they come from?—Why did they leave it?—How many times did the Achæans play a conspicuous part in Greek history?—Who was the great leader of the Achæan League?—What was his object?—What did the term Achaia signify during the Roman dominion?—What did the Roman province Achaia comprehend?

Towns.—The Ionians are said to have dwelt in hamlets or small villages. The cities in the country are supposed to have been first built by the Achæans. Several of these original villages were united into one town, and twelve of the towns formed the league. In the time of Hero'dotus, the twelve towns were Pelle'ne, Ægeira, Ægæ, Bura, He'lice, Ægium, Rhypes, Patræ, Pharæ, O'lenus, Dyme, and Tritæa.

Leontium and Cerynei'a afterward took the place of Rhypes and Ægæ, which had fallen into decay.

(1.) HE'LICE (*Ἑλίκη*), the old capital, was destroyed by an earthquake (373 B. C.).

(2.) ÆGIUM (*Αἴγιον*) became afterward the seat of the central government.

§ 96. CORINTHIA. (*ἡ Κορινθία.*)

Boundaries.—North, ME'GARIS and the SINUS CORINTHIUS; East, SINUS SARO'NICUS; South, AR'GOLIS; West, SICYONIA and PHLIASIA.

Extent.—It was a small, but wealthy and powerful district, and was situated upon the isthmus which connects the Northern part of Greece with the Peloponne'sus. Its area was about 300 square miles.

Mountains.—The mountains to the North of the Isthmus, which bore the name of GERANEI'A, extend across the Isthmus from sea to sea. The mountains to the South of the Isthmus were called the *Oneian* Ridge (*τὸ Ὄνειον*), from their resemblance to the back of an ass (*ὄνος*). In the centre is a plain from which the solitary rock of *Acrocorinthus* rises to the height of 1,886 feet.

QUESTIONS.—Were the Ionians in the possession of towns?—Who founded the towns?—How many towns formed their league?—Name the twelve towns which formed the ancient Achæan league?—What was the old capital?—What became afterward the seat of government?—— § 96. What are the boundaries of Corinthia?—Where was it situated?—What was its extent?—What mountains did it contain?—What solitary rock stood in the centre?

Capes.—Promontorium Olmiæ and Heras, with a celebrated temple of Hera (*Juno*).

Productions.—The only arable land in the territory of any extent is the plain upon the coast, lying between Corinth and Sicyon, and belonging to these two cities. The fertility of this plain is praised in the highest terms by the ancient writers: and such was its value that to own *what lies between Corinth and Sicyon* became a proverbial expression for the possession of great wealth. It furnished Corinth and its port-towns with fruit and vegetables, but could not have yielded any large supply of corn. The wine of Corinth was proverbially bad.

Inhabitants.—The oldest settlers were Æolians, Ionians, and also Phœnicians. It was afterward conquered by the Dorians, who, though the ruling class, appear to have formed only a small proportion of the population of Corinth. Five centuries after the Dorian conquest (666 B. C.), the power of the Æolians was restored by Cyp'selus and his son Periander, one of the Seven Wise Men of Greece. The inhabitants were naturally led to try their fortune on the sea to which their situation invited them.

City.—Corinthus (*Κόρινθος*, most anciently *'Εφύρη*) was built on a level rock to the North of the Acrocorinthus, which served as a citadel and was included within the walls. It had two ports. The northern, on the Corinthian Gulf, was called *Lechæum*, and was connected with the city by two parallel walls, twelve stadia in length, which were partly destroyed by the Spartans (393 B. C.). The south-eastern port, *Cenchreæ*, seventy stadia distant, on the Saronic Gulf, does not appear to have been connected with the city by walls. It was, however, a more considerable place than Lechæum, and contained several temples.

Questions.—Name the capes of Corinthia.—What temple adorned Cape Heras?—Where was the only arable portion of the territory?—What is said of its fertility?—What was its principal produce?—What is said of its wine?—Name the oldest inhabitants of Corinthia.—By whom were they conquered?—Who restored the power of the Æolians?—When?—What was the principal occupation of the inhabitants?—What was the capital of Corinthia?—Describe its situation.—What were its ports?—Which of them was the more considerable?

CORINTH.

The insults which the Corinthians had offered to the Roman embassy, led to the plunder and destruction of the town by L. Mummius (146 B.C.) according to an express decree of the Roman senate. All the males were slain; the women and children were sold as slaves; and, after the Roman soldiers had pillaged what then was the richest city in all Greece, at a given signal the place was set on fire and reduced to ashes. This act marks the subjugation of Greece to Roman sway. Corinth remained in ruins for a century. The site on which it had stood was devoted to the gods, and was not allowed to be inhabited. The greater part of its commerce passed over to Delos. A century after its destruction, it was restored by Julius Cæsar, who sent thither a numerous colony, consisting of his veterans and freedmen. It soon rose again to be a populous and prosperous city, and when St. Paul visited it a century after its restoration,

---

QUESTIONS.—What led to the plunder of the city of Corinthus?—By whom?—When?—How long did it remain in ruins?—What place inherited its commerce?—Who restored the city?—Who preached the Gospel there?—What was its condition at that time?

it was the capital of the province of Achaia. Two of the epistles of St. Paul are addressed to the flourishing Christian church which he founded in Corinth.

The city was one of the earliest seats of Grecian art. Painting, architecture, and sculpture flourished here, and it was particularly celebrated for its works in bronze (*Æs Corinthi'acum*). Its vases of terra-cotta were among the finest in Greece. In the time of Periander (600 B. C.), poetry was likewise much cultivated, but afterward little attention was paid to letters. The favorable position of Corinth for commerce made it the emporium of the trade between the East and the West, and, as a natural consequence, it became the most opulent city in Greece; but this accession of wealth, giving rise to luxury and sensual indulgence, made it at the same time the most licentious. The patron goddess of the city was Aphrodi'te (*Venus*), who had a splendid temple on the Acrocorinthus.

The colonies of Corinth were very numerous. With the exception of the colony that founded Potidæa on the coast of Chalci'dice, they were all sent out from Lechæum, and confined to the seas West of the Isthmus. The most celebrated were Syracu'sæ and Corcy'ra.

§ 97. PHLIASIA. (*ἡ Φλιασία.*)

Boundaries.—North, SICYONIA; East, CORINTHIA; South, ARCADIA and AR'GOLIS; West, ACHAIA.

Extent.—This territory is a small valley about nine hundred feet above the level of the sea, surrounded by mountains from which streams flow down on every side, joining the river Aso'pus in the middle of the plain. Its area was about fifty square miles.

QUESTIONS.—What arts used to flourish at Corinth?—What was its literary character?—What made it the richest city of Greece?—What was the result of this wealth?—Who was the patron goddess of the city?—Where did her temple stand?—What colony was sent out from Cenchreæ?—From what port were the other colonies sent out?—To what seas were those colonies confined?—Which were the most celebrated Corinthian colonies?——§ 97. How is Phliasia bounded?—What is its extent?

Productions.—The country was celebrated in antiquity for its wine.

Inhabitants.—The oldest inhabitants were Ionians, who, on the arrival of the Dorians, migrated to Samos and Clazo′menæ. The Dorians of Phliasia were in historical times generally allied with Sparta.

Towns.—The old capital of the country is ARÆTHYREA, but the inhabitants subsequently deserted it and built PHLIUS (Φλιοῦς). This city is celebrated in the history of literature as the birthplace of Pra′tinas, the inventor of the Satyric drama, and who contended with Æs′chylus for the prize at Athens.

SICYONIA. (ἡ Σικυωνία.)

Boundaries.—North, SINUS CORINTHIUS; East, CORINTHIA; South, PHLIASIA and AR′GOLIS.

Extent.—It was very small, containing in fact little more than the valley of the Aso′pus. Its area was only 84 square miles.

River.—The ASO′PUS, which, in the upper part of its course, is confined between mountains, but near the sea it opens out into a wide plain, which was called *Asopia.*

Productions.—The plain of Asopia was celebrated for its fertility, and was especially adapted to the cultivation of the olive. The neighboring sea supplied an abundance of excellent fish. The wine of Sicyon was also celebrated.

City.—SICYON (Σικυών) was one of the most important cities of the Peloponne′sus and was situated upon a table-land at a distance of about two miles from the Corinthian Gulf. It consisted of three parts: the acropolis, on the hill; the lower-town, at its

QUESTIONS.—What are the productions of Phliasia?—Who were the oldest inhabitants?—To what place did they migrate?—With what state was it generally allied in historical times?—What is the old capital?—What is the new capital?—For what is Phlius celebrated?—How is Sicyonia bounded?—What is its extent?—What is its area?—What part of it was called Asopia?—Whence that name?—Name the chief productions of Sicyonia.—Where was Sicyon situated?—Describe the town.

foot; and a well fortified port-town upon the coast. It was the birthplace of Ara'tus, the celebrated general of the Achæan League, through whom it became one of the most important cities in the Peloponne'sus. The conquest of Corinth by the Romans was also a favorable event for Sicyon, but after the restoration of this city by Julius Cæsar, Sicyon rapidly declined, till an earthquake completed its ruin. For a long time it was one of the chief seats of Grecian art, and was celebrated alike for its painters and its sculptors. It was also one of the most ancient seats of the plastic art.

§ 98. AR'GOLIS or ARGOS. (ἡ Ἀργολίς or τὸ Ἄργος.)

Name.—Argos is said by Strabo to have signified *a plain*, in the language of the Macedonians and Thessalians, and it is, therefore, not improbable that it contains the same root as ἀγρός, the Latin *ager*, English *acre*. The Greek writers use the term Argos, to designate the city, and sometimes to designate the country. Hero'dotus calls the country Ar'golis; other Greek authors more frequently, Argei'a (ἡ Ἀργεία). The Romans included under Ar'golis the whole peninsula between the Saronic and Argolic Gulfs.

Boundaries.—North, CORINTHIA and SICYONIA; East, SINUS SARO'NICUS; South, SINUS HERMIO'NICUS and MARE MYRTO'-UM; West, ARCADIA.

Divisions.—AR'GOLIS Proper, or ARGEI'A; EPIDAURIA, TRŒZENIA, and HERMI'ONIS.

Extent.—Its area was about 450 square miles.

Mountains.—PARNON, PARTHENIUS ARTEMISIUS, ARACH-

QUESTIONS.—Through whom did Sicyon become the most important city in Greece?—When did its decline commence?—What completed its ruin?—In what relation did it stand to Grecian art?—— § 98. Explain the meaning of the word Argos.—What do Argos and Argolis signify in Greek authors?—What did Roman authors mean by Argolis?—How was Argolis bounded?—How was it divided?—What was its extent?—Name its mountains.

NÆUS (Ἀραχναῖον), on which was one of the beacon-lights of Agamemnon, by which he announced the capture of Troy on the same night that it was taken (Æsch. Ag. 281 seqq.).

Capes.—BUCE'PHALA and SCYLLÆUM.

Rivers.—Of these, which are simply mountain-torrents, the principal is the I'NACHUS (Ἴναχος).

Lake.—LERNA, celebrated for the destruction of the Lerne'an Hydra by Her'cules.

Productions.—The only fertile part of the country was the plain of Argos, which now produces corn, cotton, rice, and vines. It was also celebrated for its excellent horses. In summer there is generally want of moisture; hence Homer calls it πολυδίψιον Ἄργος, *very thirsty Argos.*

Inhabitants.—The ancient inhabitants were Pelasgians; afterward, a Phœnician colony settled among them. These nations were subsequently supplanted by Achæans, who, in Homeric times, were the predominant race on the Eastern side of Peloponnes'us. On the conquest of the peninsula by the Dorians, eighty years after the Trojan war, the Achæans were mostly driven out, those who remained being reduced to the condition of a conquered people.

Towns.—(1.) CLEO'NÆ (Κλεωναί), which derived its chief importance from the Neme'an Games being celebrated within its territory in the grove of Ne'mea, between Cleo'næ and Phlius. These Games formed one of the great national festivals of the Greeks, and were celebrated in honor of Zeus regularly twice in every Olympiad.

(2.) MYCE'NÆ (Μυκῆναι), one of the most ancient towns in

QUESTIONS.—What is mentioned of Mount Arachnæus?—Name the capes.—What is remarked of the rivers?—Name the principal river.—What lake was in Argolis?—What are the productions of the country?—What epithet does Homer give to it?—Why?—Name the ancient inhabitants.—Who were its inhabitants in Homer's times?—By whom were they conquered?—When?—Name some of the principal towns.—What festivals were celebrated at Cleonæ?—What were the Nemean games?

Greece, and celebrated as the residence of Agamemnon, under whose government it was regarded as the first city in Greece.

(3.) ARGOS (*Ἄργος*), usually called ARGI (-orum) by the Romans, the most ancient city in Greece. After the Dorian conquest it became also the first city in Pelopon'nesus, and held this rank till about 666 B. C., when Sparta took precedence. Its citadel, *Larissa* (Pelasgic name for *citadel*) was built on an insulated conical mountain 900 feet in height. Its port, Nauplia (*Ναυπλία, Napoli di Romana*) was at a considerable distance (see 5).

§ **99.** (4.) TIRYNS (*Τίρυνς*), one of the most ancient towns in Greece. Its massive walls, which have been regarded with wonder in all ages, are said to have been the work of the Cyclo'pes, and belong to the same age as those of Myce'næ. Their ruins still exist.

(5.) NAU'PLIA appears, in the historical times of ancient history, merely as the port of Argos. In the middle ages, it became a place of considerable importance, and in recent times was the seat of the Greek central government till the king removed his residence to Athens.

(6.) EPIDAURUS (*Ἐπίδαυρος*), the capital of Epidauria, which, throughout the flourishing period of Grecian history, was an independent state. Near it was the temple of Æsculapius, which was frequented by patients from all parts of the Hellenic world.

(7.) TRŒZEN (*Τροιζήν*), the capital of Trœzenia. At an early period it was a powerful maritime state, as is shown by its founding the cities of Halicarnassus and Myndus in Caria.

QUESTIONS.—Who resided at Mycenæ?—When did Argos become the first town in Peloponnesus?—When and to whom was it forced to yield precedence?—What is said of the Larissa?—What was its port of entrance?——§ 99. What remarkable remains are there at Tiryns?—When did Nauplia become a place of importance?—What was the capital of Epidauria?—What temple was in its neighborhood?—What was the capital of Trœzenia?—What colonies were founded by it?

(8.) METHONE (Μεθώνη), fortified by the Athenians in the Peloponnesian war (425 B.C.).

(9.) HERMI'ONE (Ἑρμιόνη), the capital of Hermi'onis. It was the chief seat of the worship of Deme'ter Chthonia.

(10.) LERNA (Λέρνα). In its neighborhood was the Lerne'an swamp where Her'acles (*Her'cules*) slew the many-headed hydra.

CYNURIA. (*ἡ Κυνουρία.*)

Boundaries.—North, AR'GOLIS; East, SINUS ARGO'LICUS; South, LACO'NICA; West, ARCADIA. The exact boundaries cannot be defined, as its inhabitants were only a tribe, and never formed a political body. They were almost confined to the fertile valley of Thyrea'tis.

QUESTIONS.—What is said of Methone?—What goddess was chiefly honored at Hermione?—What is said of Lerna?—Where was Cynuria situated?—Give its boundaries.

§ 100. ISLANDS OF GREECE.

The whole number was *sixty-one*. The most remarkable were:

A. ISLANDS WEST OF GREECE.

CORCY'RA,	ITH'ACA,	ZACYNTHUS,
LEUCAS,	CEPHALLENIA,	SPHACTERIA.
ECHIN'ADES,		

B. ISLANDS EAST OF GREECE.

CYTHE'RA,	ÆGI'NA,	EUBŒA,
CALAUREI'A,	SA'LAMIS,	CRETA.

The other islands were divided into *two* groups:

I. CY'CLADES, so called because fancied to lie in a circle (ἐν κύκλῳ) about Delos, which was the smallest, but most important island. They were *twelve* in number:

CEOS,	SIPHNOS,	DELOS,	MY'CONOS,
CYTHNOS,	PAROS,	RHENEI'A,	TENOS,
SERI'PHOS,	NAXOS,	SYROS,	ANDROS.

II. SPO'RADES (σπείρω, Lat. *spargo*), or *the Scattered* Islands, including all the others, numbering about twenty-five. The most remarkable are:

THASOS,	IMBROS,	AMORGOS.
SAMOTHRA'CE,	LEMNOS,	

QUESTIONS.—§ 100. Name the islands west of Greece.—The islands east of Greece.—Into how many groups were the other islands divided?—What were those groups?—What does the name Cyclades signify?—Give the names of the Cyclades.—What is the signification of the name Sporades?—Give the names of some of the Sporades.

§ 101. ISLANDS WEST OF GREECE.

CORCY'RA. (*Κέρκυρα*; later and on coins, *Κόρκυρα*, *Corfu.*)

The modern citadel is a rock split into two lofty peaks; these were called *Κορυφώ* or *Κορυφοί* (comp. *κορυφή*, *head*, *summit*); and hence has come slightly corrupted, *Κορφοί*, *Corfu*, the modern name of the town and island.

Situation.—In the Ionian Sea, opposite the coast of Chaonia in Epi'rus. Its most ancient name was Dre'pane. Perhaps, also, it is the Scheria (*Σχερίη*) of the Odyssey.

Extent.—It is a mountainous island, containing an area of 227 square miles.

Productions.—It was celebrated for its fertility in antiquity, and was very industriously cultivated by its inhabitants. It produced wine and oil in considerable abundance.

Inhabitants.—The island was peopled by Corinthian settlers (737 B.C.), who soon became in the Western seas of Greece the commercial rivals of the mother country. They founded Epidamnus on the Illyrian coast (616 B.C.). A quarrel with Corinth in regard to this settlement was one of the causes of the Peloponnesian war.

Towns.—CORCY'RA (*Corfu*), the capital, and CASSI'OPE (*Κασσιόπη*), in which there was a temple of Zeus Cassius, at whose altars Nero sang.

LEUCAS. (*Λευκάς*, *Santa Maura.*)

Situation.—In the Ionian Sea, separated by a narrow channel from the coast of Acarnania. Originally a peninsula, it was, in

---

QUESTIONS.—§ 101. What is the modern name of Corcyra?—From what is that name derived?—What was the most ancient name of Corcyra?—With what island of the Odyssey is it identified?—What is the extent of the island?—Who were the settlers of the island?—What city did they found upon the Illyrian coast?—What connection had it with the Peloponnesian war?—What towns did Corcyra contain?—What temple was at Cassiope?—Where was Leucas situated?

the middle of the seventh century B.C., converted into an island by Corinthian settlers, who dug a canal through the isthmus.

Name.—The name of the island is derived from its *white* (λευκός) cliff.

Extent.—The interior of the island is very rugged; it is but little cultivated; its area is about 120 square miles.

Towns.—LEUCAS (Λευκάς), in the Macedonian times, the chief town of Acarnania, and the place in which the meetings of the Acarnanian confederacy were held. The most celebrated spot on the island was the promontory Leuca'tas, rising 2,000 feet and crowned with the temple of Apollo. This cape was much dreaded by mariners. Hence Virgil says:

> *Mox et Leucatæ nimbosa cacumina montis,*
> *Et formidatus nautis aperitur Apollo.*—Æn. III. 274 seq.

At the annual festival of Apollo celebrated at this spot, it was the custom to throw a criminal from the steep precipice of the cape into the sea. This probably gave rise to the story of Sappho's leap from the rocks.

ECHIN'ADES. (*αἱ Ἐχῖναι*, or *Ἐχινάδες, νῆσοι.*)

It is a group of barren and rugged islands off the coast of Acarnania, at the mouth of the Achelo'us, which in Homer's time were inhabited, but afterward deserted.

§ 102. ITH'ACA. (*Ἰθάκη, Thiaki.*)

This island, so celebrated as the kingdom of Ulysses, lies off the coast of Acarnania. Its area is 45 square miles; its general aspect is one of ruggedness and sterility, rendered striking by

---

QUESTIONS.—When and in what way did Leucas become an island?—From what is the name derived?—What is said about the island in general?—What is said of the town of Leucas?—What was the most celebrated spot on the island?—Whose temple was there?—What gave origin to the story of Sappho's leap from this rock?—What are the Echinades?—Opposite to what river were they situated?——§ 102. What is said of Ithaca?—Who resided there?—Where is it situated?

the bold and broken outline of mountains and cliffs, indented by numerous harbors and creeks.

CEPHALLENIA. (*Κεφαλληνία, Cephalonia.*)

This island, called by Homer, *Same*, or *Samos* (*Σάμη, Σάμος*), is the largest in the Ionian Sea, opposite the Corinthian Gulf and the coast of Acarnania. Its area is about 348 square miles. It was a *tetra'polis*, containing the *four towns* of *Same*, *Pale*, *Cronis*, and *Proni*. In Homer's time it was subject to Ulysses.

ZACYNTHUS. (*Ζάκυνθος, Zante.*)

An island in the Sicilian Sea, lying off the Western coast of Peloponne'sus, opposite the promontory Chelona'tas in Elis, and to the South of the island of Cephallenia. It formed part of the dominions of Ulysses. The inhabitants were a colony of Achæans from Peloponne'sus, who attained considerable importance at an early period; two hundred years before the Trojan war, they founded Saguntum in Spain, in conjunction with the Ru'tuli of Ar'dea.

SPHACTERIA. (*Σφακτηρία, Sphagia.*)

It lies across the entrance of the Bay of Pylos (*Navarino*), on the Western coast of Messenia. It is celebrated in ancient history for the defeat and capture of the Spartans by the Athenians, in the seventh year of the Peloponnesian war (421 B.C.). It is minutely described in the third chapter of the fourth book of Thucy'dides.

QUESTIONS.—Where is Cephallenia situated?—How was it called by Homer?—Why was it called a tetrapolis?—Where was Zacynthus situated?—Opposite to what promontory?—Who inhabited this island?—What colony did they found?—To whom were these two islands subject in Homer's time?—Where is Sphacteria situated?—What is its modern name?—Where is it minutely described?—What happened on it?

§ 103. ISLANDS EAST OF GREECE.

CYTHE'RA (-orum). (*τὰ Κύθηρα, Cerigo.*)

An island lying off the South-Eastern extremity of Laco'nica. It was partly settled by Phœnicians, who established here the headquarters of their purple fishery. They brought thither the worship of the Syrian Aphrodi'te (*Venus*), which was thence introduced into Greece; and consequently in the Grecian legends this island is said to have received the goddess after her birth from the foam of the sea. Hence, in the Greek and Latin poets, Cythe'ra is constantly represented as one of the favorite residences of Aphrodi'te, and, for this reason, *Cytherœa* is one of the most frequent epithets applied to her. Cythe'ra contained, in the interior, a town of the same name, of which Scandei'a (*Σκανδεία*) was the harbor.

CALAURIA. (*Καλαυρία, Poro.*)

A small island in the Saronic Gulf opposite Pogon, the harbor of Trœzen. It possessed an ancient temple of Poseidon, a sacred asylum, in which stood the statue of Demos'thenes, and where divine honors were paid to this celebrated orator, who put an end to his life here by poison (321 B.C.), after having fled to this retreat when pursued by the emissaries of Anti'pater.

ÆGI'NA. (*Αἴγινα.*)

It was situated in the Saronic Gulf, and one of the most celebrated islands in Greece. This small island, its area containing but 40 square miles, held, about the year 500 B.C., the empire of the sea, and was for many years the chief seat of Grecian art.

QUESTIONS.—§ 103. Where was Cythera situated?—Who were its first settlers?—What worship did they bring thither?—Why is Aphrodite, or Venus, so often called Cytheræa?—What town did the island contain?—Where was Calaureia situated?—What temple was there?—Who fled to this temple?—When?—Where was Ægina situated?—What is said of the island?—When did it reach its greatest prosperity?

Fifty years later it was subdued by the Athenians, and became a part of their empire, and on the breaking out of the Peloponnesian war (431 B.C.), the entire population was expelled, and by the Spartans transferred to Thyrea. After the battle of Ægospo'tami (404 B.C.), they were restored to their own country; but they never recovered their former prosperity. On a hill in the North-Eastern part are the remains of a magnificent temple of the Doric order, the beautiful sculptures of which, now known as *the Ægi'na Marbles*, found in 1811 buried under the ruins, are preserved at Munich, and casts from them are in the British Museum.

SA'LAMIS. (*ἡ Σαλαμίς, Kuluri.*)

This lies between the Western coast of At'tica and the Eastern coast of Me'garis, and forming the Southern boundary of the Bay of Eleusis. It continued to be an independent state till

THE GULF AND ISLAND OF SALAMIS.

QUESTIONS.—When and by whom was Ægina conquered?—To what place were the population transferred at the beginning of the Peloponnesian war?—When were they restored to their country?—What are the Ægina Marbles? –Where is Salamis situated?

620 B.C., when, through a stratagem of Solon, it fell under the sway of the Athenians. The island is chiefly memorable on account of the great battle fought in the strait between it and the coast of At'tica, in which the Persian fleet of Xerxes was defeated by the Greeks (480 B.C.).

§ **104.** EUBŒA. (*ἡ Εὔβοια; Negropont*, in the middle ages *Egripo*, a corruption of *Euri'pus.*)

Situation.—It is the largest island in the Ægæan, lying along the coasts of At'tica, Bœotia, Locris, and the Southern part of Thessaly, from which countries it is separated by the Eubœan Sea, called, in its narrowest part, the *Euri'pus* (*Εὔριπος*).

Mountains.—It is long and narrow, and throughout its entire extent there runs a range of mountains, which appears to be a continuation of the range of Ossa and Pelion, and of that of Othrys.

Productions.—In the plains of Eubœa a considerable quantity of wheat was grown in ancient times. There is excellent pasture for sheep on the mountain-slopes. The mountains contain copper and iron.

Inhabitants.—The island was inhabited by Ionic Greeks, and the Athenians are said to have taken the chief part in their colonization.

Towns.—There were seven independent cities, upon which a few smaller places were dependent. The most important were:

(1.) CHALCIS (*Χαλκίς*), one of the greatest of the Ionic cities, which at an early period carried on an extensive commerce with almost all parts of the Hellenic world. It planted colonies upon the coasts of Macedonia, Italy, Sicily, and in the islands of

---

QUESTIONS.—When did Salamis fall into the power of the Athenians? —What great battle was fought here?——§ 104. Where is Eubœa situated?—What is the origin of its modern name?—What is the Euripus? —What is remarked about its mountains?—What about its productions? —Which of the Greek tribes inhabited the island?—How many independent towns did it contain?—What was the chief city of the island?—What is said about its colonies?

the Ægæan. It gave name to the peninsula of Chalci'dice, between the Thermaic and Singitic gulfs, in consequence of the large number of cities which it founded in this district. It was the birthplace of the orator Isæus, and there Aristotle died (322 B. C.).

(2.) ERETRIA (Ἐρετρία), next to Chalcis, the most powerful city of the island. At an early period, it was one of the chief maritime states in Greece, and sent five ships to the Athenian fleet which sailed to support Mile'tus and the other Ionic cities in their revolt from Persia (500 B. C.). In consequence of this step the town was utterly destroyed by a Persian force under Datis and Artaphernes, and the inhabitants settled in the Cissian territory. A little further to the South, a new town arose, which soon became a place of considerable importance. It was the seat of a celebrated school of philosophy founded by Menede'mus, a native of the city and a disciple of Plato.

The name of the Northern coast and promontory was Artemisium (Ἀρτεμίσιον), and off this coast the Grecian fleet gained their celebrated victory over the fleet of Xerxes (480 B. C).

§ 105. CRETA. (Κρήτη; Saracenic, *Khandax;* Venetian, *Candia;* now, by its own inhabitants, *Crete.*)

Creta Jovis magni medio jacet insula ponto;
Mons Idæus ubi et gentis cunabula nostrae.
Centum urbes habitant magnas, uberrima regna.
Virg. Æn. III. 104 seqq.

Situation.—It is one of the largest islands of the Mediterranean Sea, and is situated to the South of the Archipelago, between the Morea, Africa, and Asia Minor.

Extent.—The interior is very mountainous and woody. It is intersected by fertile valleys. Its area is about 3,166 square miles.

QUESTIONS.—What peninsula was called after Chalcis?—Why?—Why was Eretria destroyed?—By whom?—Was the city rebuilt?—Where?—What philosophical school was established there?—Where was Artemisium situated?—What battle was fought here?——§ 105. Where is Creta situated?—Give an account of its names.—What is its area?

Mountains.—About the centre of the island was Mount Ida, which rises to the height of 7,654 feet, on which Zeus (*Jupiter*) was said to have been reared. To the West it was connected with the White Mountains (λευκὰ ὄρη), and the prolongation eastward formed the ridge of Dicte (ἡ Δίκτη), sacred to Zeus.

Productions.—According to Pliny everything grew better in Crete than elsewhere. Among the medicinal herbs for which it was famed was the *dictamnon*, *dittany* (so called from Mount *Dicte*), celebrated among physicians, naturalists, and poets. Its forests could boast of the fruit-bearing poplar and the evergreen pla′tanus (both now extinct), the cypress, palm, and cedar; its wines, and especially the *passum* or raisin wine, were highly praised. The island by the bounty of He′racles was free from all wild beasts and noxious animals.

Inhabitants.—During the heroic ages it was peopled by Dorians, who made Crete the headquarters of the worship of Apollo; among these, Phœnicians and Phrygians also settled. They appear to have been hardy and daring corsairs, and this characteristic gave rise to that naval supremacy assigned by Hero′dotus and others to the traditionary Minos and his Cretan subjects. The generous friendship of the heroic ages, which was singularly regulated by law, had degenerated into a frightful license, and as early as 600 B.C., Cretan was a synonym for *a liar and a brute :*

Κρῆτες ἀεὶ ψεῦσται, κακὰ θηρία, γαστέρες ἀργαί.

Epime′nides, quoted by St. Paul, Tit. i. 12.

Crete was also one of the *three bad kappas* (τρία κάππα κάκιστα; see p. 39).

The soldiers had a high reputation as light troops and archers, and served as mercenaries both in Greek and Barbarian armies.

Towns.—Homer (Odyss. XIX. 174) describes it as containing

QUESTIONS.—What is said about the mountains of Creta?—Name some of its productions.—What nations inhabited the island?—What was their principal occupation?—What is said about the moral character of the Cretans?—How many towns did it contain according to Homer?

ninety cities. Many other authors speak of its containing a hundred, as Virgil in the quotation above.

The chief towns were:

(1.) CYDONIA (Κυδωνία), one of the most ancient and important mentioned by Homer. *Quinces* derived their name from this place, being called by the Romans, *mala Cydonia*.

(2.) LEBEN (Λεβήν), the harbor of Gorty'na. It possessed a temple of Asclepius (*Æsculapius*).

(3.) GNOSSUS or CNOSSUS (Γνωσσός or Κνωσσός), was the royal city of Crete, founded by Minos and made his chief residence. The whole district was peculiarly connected with the worship of Zeus. Not only the birthplace, but also the tomb of the god was here shown by the lying Cretans. At an early period it was colonized by Dorians, and from it Dorian institutions spread over the whole island. The well-known Cretan Labyrinth is always associated with this place; the natural caverns and excavated sepulchres still to be seen near Cnossus gave rise most probably to this fable.

(4.) GORTY'NA (Γόρτυνα), was the most important city next to Cnossus, and in early times shared with Cnossus the government of the whole island.

(5.) Other towns were: PHÆSTUS, RHITYMNIA, LYCTOS.

The island became in 67 B.C. a Roman province, and was annexed to Cyre'ne in Africa.

§ 106. CY'CLADES. (αἱ Κυκλάδες.)

DELOS. (ἡ Δῆλος, Delo.)

Delos was the smallest of the Cy'clades and was regarded as

QUESTIONS.—What are the chief towns of Creta?—What fruit was brought into Europe from Cydonia?—What is said of Leben?—What was the chief residence of Minos?—Whose birthplace and tomb were shown here?—What is said about the Cretan Labyrinth?—What is said of Gortyna?—When did the island fall under Roman control?—To what country was it annexed?——§ 106. Give the names of the principal Cyclades.

the birthplace of Apollo and Ar'temis (*Dia'na*), who were hence called *Delius* and *Delia*. In the earliest times it was one of the holiest spots in Hellas, being also the centre of a great periodical festival in honor of the mighty Ionian god, celebrated by all the Ionic cities on the mainland as well as in the islands. In the formation of the confederacy for the purpose of carrying on the war against Persia, Delos was chosen as the common guardian of the public purse (477 B.C.). After the fall of Corinth it had very great commercial importance, and in its slave-mart 10,000 persons are said to have changed hands in one day.

CEOS. (ἡ *Κέως*.)

Ceos was celebrated as the birthplace of Simo'nides, the great lyric poet, who was frequently called emphatically, the *Cean;* and Horace, in like manner, alludes to his poetry under the name of *Ceæ Camenæ* (Carm. IV. 9, 8) and *Cea nænia* (Carm. II. 1, 38), as he also composed *dirges* (*θρῆνοι*), Lat. *næniæ*. Simo'nides of Ceos commemorated in matchless verse some of the greatest deeds of Greece, as her exploits at Ma'rathon and Thermo'pylæ.

CYTHNOS. (ἡ *Κύθνος*, *Thermia*.)

This island lies between Ceos and Seri'phos. After the death of Nero, a false Nero made his appearance here and gathered around him many adherents (A.D. 68).

SERI'PHOS. (ἡ *Σέριφος*, *Serpho*.)

This lay between Cythnos and Siphnos. It is celebrated in mythology as the place where Da'naë and Perseus drifted ashore in the ark in which they had been exposed by Acrisius. By the later writers it was almost always mentioned with contempt on account of its poverty and insignificance (CIC. *de Senect.* 3),

QUESTIONS.—What gave Delos its importance?—When was it chosen the common treasury?—What trade was especially carried on there after the fall of Corinth?—What poet was born at Ceos?—What happened at Cythnos after Nero's death?—Where was Seriphos situated?—How is it mentioned in mythology?

and was therefore employed by the Roman emperors as a place of banishment for state criminals.

PAROS. (ἡ Πάρος.)

Paros was one of the largest of the Cy'clades and famed for its white marble, which was reckoned only second to that of Mount Pente'licus:

> *Quale manus addunt ebori decus, aut ubi flavo*
> *Argentum Pariusve lapis circumdatur auro.*
> Virg. Æn. I. 592 seq.

Here was discovered the famous tablet, known as the Parian Chronicle, one of the Arundelian marbles which are now in the possession of the University of Oxford. During the reign of Charles I. this marble was broken and defaced, but when perfect it contained a chronological account of the chief events of Greek history from the time of Cecrops down to 264 B. C. Paros was the birthplace of the poet Archi'lochus.

NAXOS. (ἡ Νάξος)

Naxos was the largest and the most fertile of the Cy'clades. Off Naxos, Chabrias gained a signal victory over the Spartan fleet, which restored to Athens the empire of the sea (376 B. C.).

The names of the other Cy'clades are as follows: RHENEI'A, SIPHNOS, SYROS, MY'CONOS, TENOS, and ANDROS.

SPO'RADES. (αἱ Σποράδες.)

THASOS (Θάσος), was in the North of the Ægæan Sea, off the coast of Thrace, celebrated for its gold mines. It was the birthplace of the celebrated painter, Polygno'tus.

SAMOTHRA'CE (Σαμοθράκη), in the North of the Ægæan Sea,

QUESTIONS.—What is the Parian Marble?—What poet was born at Paros?—Who gained a victory near Naxos?—Where was Thasos situated?—What mines did it contain?—What painter was born there?—Where was Samothrace situated?

opposite the mouth of the Hebrus, was the chief seat of the worship and the mysteries of the Cabei'ri. It was called Samothra'ce, *Thracian Samos:*

> *Threiciamque Samon quæ nunc Samothracia fertur.*
> Virg. Æn. VII. 208,

to distinguish it from the Icarian Samos.

LEMNOS (*Λῆμνος, Stalimene*), one of the larger islands in the Ægæan Sea, situated nearly midway between Mount Athos and the Hellespont. It was said to be sacred to Hephæstus (*Vulcanus*), who was frequently called *the Lemnian god:*

> *Hæc pater Æoliis properat dum Lemnius oris.*
> Virg. Æn. VIII. 454;

and here Hephæstus himself says he struck when he was hurled down from heaven:

> Πᾶν δ' ἦμαρ φερόμην, ἅμα δ' ἠελίῳ καταδύντι
> Κάππεσον ἐν Λήμνῳ.
> Hom. Il. I. 592 seq.

The whole island still bears the strongest marks of *volcanic* fire, and hence we may account for its connection with *Vulcan.*

AMORGOS (*Ἀμοργός*), chiefly celebrated as the birthplace of the Iambic poet, Simo'nides of Amorgos (777 B. C.).

§ 107. MACEDONIA. (*ἡ Μακεδονία.*)

Boundaries.—North, MŒSIA and THRACIA; East, THRACIA; South, THESSALIA and MARE ÆGÆUM; West, EPI'RUS and ILLY'RICUM.

In the time of Strabo, it included a considerable part of Illyria and Thrace.

Divisions.—It was divided into Upper and Lower Macedonia,

QUESTIONS.—What is said of Samothrace?—Why was it so called?—Where was Lemnos situated?—Who was called the Lemnian god?—Why?—Who was born at Amorgos?——§ 107. What were the boundaries of Macedonia?—How was it divided?

and again subdivided into seventeen parts. The sea-coast was occupied by various tribes.

Gulfs.—(1.) SINUS STRYMO'NICUS, East of the peninsula of Chalci'dice.

(2.) SINUS SINGI'TICUS, between the peninsulas of Acte and Sithonia.

(3.) SINUS TORONA'ICUS, between Sithonia and Palle'ne.

(4.) SINUS THERMÆUS (*Gulf of Saloniki*), West of the peninsula of Chalci'dice.

Mountains.—The face of the country is generally mountainous, being traversed by lateral ridges, or elevations, which are connected with the main range of SCARDUS. From the mountains which divide Illyria and Macedonia, two ranges run toward the South-East; the BERMIUS, which is the most southern, and the DYSO'RUM, the most northern. At the extremity of the peninsula of Acte is the lofty mountain of ATHOS, now covered with Greek monasteries and chapels, noted in ancient times on account of a canal which Xerxes is said to have cut through the isthmus on the north, twelve stadia in breadth according to Hero'dotus, for the passage of the Persian fleet, in order to escape the gales and boisterous seas, which swept constantly around the promontory, and which had wrecked the fleet of Mardonius (492 B.C.). The account of this canal has been rejected as a falsehood by many writers both ancient and modern, and Ju'venal speaks of it as a specimen of Greek mendacity:

creditur olim
Velificatus Athos, et quidquid Græcia mendax
Audet in historia. Sat. X. 174 seqq.

It was, however, believed by Hero'dotus, Thucy'dides, and other ancient writers, and distinct traces of such a work have been discovered by modern travellers. The isthmus is found to be 2,500 yards wide, which agrees very well with the statement of Hero'dotus.

QUESTIONS.—Name some of the principal gulfs of Macedonia.—What is the nature of the country?—What story is related about Acte?

Rivers.—The country is watered by three large rivers: the AXIUS, LYDIAS, and HALIACMON, all flowing into the Sinus Thermæus.

Inhabitants.—The ancients were unanimous in excluding them from the true Hellenic family. Yet they are not to be confounded with the hordes of armed plunderers—the Illyrians, Thracians, and Epi'rots—by whom they were surrounded, as they resembled more closely the Thessalians, and the other ruder elements of the Grecian race. The various sections of the population were swallowed up by those pre-eminently known as the Macedonians, who had their original centre at Ægæ, or Edessa, in Lower Macedonia. This was owing to the energy of those who controlled the dynasty of Edessa, who called themselves Heraclei'dæ and traced their origin back to the Teme'nidæ of Argos. After the reign of Amyntas I. and his son Alexander (about 500 B. C.), who were on friendly terms with the Peisistra'tidæ of Athens, Macedonia became involved directly in Grecian affairs. Philip II. (359—336 B. C.) accomplished the destruction of Grecian liberties, and laid the foundations of the vast empire completed by his son, Alexander the Great. Macedonian settlements were planted almost everywhere, and Grecian manners diffused over the immense region extending from the temple of Ammon in the Libyan O'asis, and from Alexandri'a on the Western arm of the Nile, to the Northern Alexandri'a on the Iaxartes.

Language.—Their language differed from the Greek; but there are many grammatical forms in it which are commonly called *Æolic*, and also many words which are not found in the Greek, but have been preserved in the Latin language.

QUESTIONS.—Name some of the Macedonian rivers.—Did the inhabitants of Macedonia belong to the Hellenic family, or not?—Where was the chief centre of the pure Macedonians?—In what relation did the dynasty of Edessa stand to the kings?—After what time were they in regular intercourse with Greece?—Who was the destroyer of Greek liberty?—Who founded the Macedonian empire?—What were the consequences of its foundation?—What is said of their language?

§ 108. **Towns.**—I. In Mygdonia (*Μυγδονία*), situated on the North of the Chalcidian Peninsula:

Therma, afterward called *Thessaloni'ca* (*Θεσσαλονίκη*, *Saloniki*) most probably by Cassander in honor of his wife who bore that name. The Apostle Paul addressed two epistles to the Christian converts in this town.

II. In Bottiæis (*Βοττιαιίς*):

Pella (*Πέλλα*), which became the residence of the kings. It was the birthplace of Alexander the Great.

III. In Pieria (*Πιερία*), the celebrated seat of the Muses, comprising the country South of the river Haliacmon:

Pydna (*Πύδνα*), a Greek city, in whose neighborhood the battle was fought which decided the fate of the Macedonian monarchy (168 B.C.).

IV. In Emathia (*Ἠμαθία*), which comprised the country North of the river Haliacmon:

Ægæ (*Αἰγαί*), probably *Edessa*, the ancient capital; when it had ceased to be the residence, it still continued to be the burial-place, of the kings. Here Philip, the father of Alexander the Great, was murdered by Pausanias (336 B.C.).

V. In Chalci'dice (*Χαλκιδική*). It was the peninsula South of Mygdonia, between the Thermaic and Strymonic Gulfs, and was called after the Chalcidians of Eubœa, who formed settlements in this country at a very early period. The peninsula of Chalci'dice comprised in the South three smaller peninsulas, Palle'ne, Sithonia, and Acte, which contained several important towns, frequently mentioned in Grecian history:

Questions.—§ 108. Where was Mygdonia situated?—What town was in Mygdonia?—How was it called afterward?—What was the birthplace of Alexander the Great?—Where was Pieria situated?—What battle was fought in the neighborhood of Pydna?—Where is Emathia situated?—What town was there?—Who was murdered here?—Between what gulfs is Chalcidice situated?—Name the three smaller peninsulas which it comprised.

(1.) POTIDÆA (*Ποτίδαια*), a Dorian city, colonized from Corinth, situated on the narrow isthmus connecting Palle'ne with the mainland. During the time of the Athenian supremacy, it was subject to that city; but in 432 B. C. it revolted. After a siege of two years, the Potidæans surrendered and were allowed to quit the place, which was then colonized by a thousand Athenians. Philip of Ma'cedon afterward gave it up to the Olynthians, and extirpated or sold the Greek population. Cassander rebuilt this city and named it *Cassandri'a* (*Κασσάνδρεια*) (300 B. C.).

(2.) OLYNTHUS (*Ὄλυνθος*), at the head of the Toronaic Gulf, between Palle'ne and Sithonia. The city is immortalized by the three *Olynthiac* orations of Demos'thenes, who induced the Athenians to send succors to their ancient foes, inhabitants of *Olynthus*, when the latter were besieged by Philip, who took and destroyed their city (347 B. C.). The fall of Olynthus completed the conquest and destruction of no less than thirty Chalcidic cities, which constituted the Olynthian confederacy.

§ 109. THRACIA. (*ἡ Θρᾴκη*, *Roumelia*, nearly.)

Name.—The etymology adopted by Mure is the most satisfactory, who derives it from *τραχεῖα*, *rugged*, as indicating the geographical character of the various districts to which it was given.

Boundaries.—It comprised formerly all that part of Europe which lies to the North of Greece; hence Hero'dotus calls the Thracians, next to the Indians, *the greatest nation on earth.* In historical times, its boundaries were as follows: North, MŒSIA; East, PONTUS EUXI'NUS and BO'SPORUS THRACIUS; South,

---

QUESTIONS.—Describe the situation of Potidæa?—Of what Grecian city was it a colony?—To what city was it subject?—Who destroyed it?—Who rebuilt it?—Where is Olynthus situated?—What has given celebrity to this city?—Who destroyed the city?—What was the result of the fall of Olynthus?——§ 109. What is the derivation of Thracia?—Where was it situated?—Was it a large country?—What is the remark of Herodotus about it?—What were its boundaries in historical times?

PROPONTIS, HELLESPONTUS, and MARE ÆGÆUM; West, MACEDONIA.

Mountains.—The surface of Thrace is very mountainous. From the chief range of the HÆMUS three chains of mountains branch off toward the South-East, and with their various ramifications occupy nearly the entire country. The most Westerly are the parallel ranges known as the PANGÆUS and RHO'DOPE, the peaks of which latter attain the height of about 8,500 feet.

Rivers.—The rivers all flow from North to South: NESTUS, HEBRUS, ÆGOSPO'TAMI, the scene of the famous defeat of the Athenian fleet by Lysander, which brought the Peloponnesian war to a close (405 B.C.).

Climate.—The climate of Thrace is always spoken of by the ancients as being extremely cold and rigorous. The Hæmus was regarded as the abode of the North wind, and the countries beyond it were believed to enjoy a delightfully mild climate.

Productions.—In ancient times vast quantities of grain and wine were supplied from the valley of the Hebrus. In the Iliad, the ships of the Achæans are described as bringing wine every day to Agamemnon from Thrace; and the Marone'an wine, *vinum Marone'um*, which retained its reputation in the time of Pliny (N. H. xiv. 4. 6), is described in the Odyssey (ix. 196 seqq.). The mountainous parts of the country possessed mines of precious metals. Thrace was also famous for its white horses.

Inhabitants.—The oldest inhabitants of Thrace, the so-called mythical Thracians, were Pelasgians, agreeing in language, religion, and other important respects, with the Greeks. They appear to have made settlements also extensively over Southern Greece. The earliest Greek poets, Orpheus, Linus, Musæus,

---

QUESTIONS.—What is said about the mountains of Thracia?—Name some of the rivers.—What battle was fought at Ægospotami?—What is said about the climate of Thrace?—Where was the fancied abode of the north wind?—What was the general belief about the countries beyond the Hæmus?—What were the chief productions of Thrace?—What is said of the Thracian wines?—Who were the oldest inhabitants of Thrace?—What is said of them?

and others, are all represented as coming from Thrace. These Pelasgian-Thracians were, at a comparatively late period, driven out, or subjugated, by a savage race from the North, which we find recognised in historical times under the title of Thracians. These historical Thracians were a barbarous people, who, like the Cretans, sold their services in war to the highest bidder.

Chersone'sus Thra'cica.—The most important part of Thrace was the peninsula extending in a South-Westerly direction into the Ægæan, between the Hellespont and the Bay of Melas, protected against incursions from the mainland by a wall running across the Isthmus. Its ancient name was Chersone'sus Thra'cica, its modern name, the peninsula of the Dardanelles. It was originally inhabited by Thracians, but was at a very early period colonized by the Athenians.

§ **110. Towns.**—I. In *Chersone'sus Thra'cica:*

(1.) Cardia (*Καρδία*), at the head of the Gulf of Melas, a Greek colony from Mile'tus, Clazo'menæ, and Athe'næ.

(2.) Calli'polis (*Καλλίπολις, Gallipoli*), situated opposite to Lamp'sacus, has given the modern name to the peninsula.

(3.) Elæus (*'Ελαιοῦς*), the most Southern town, a colony of Teos in Ionia. It was celebrated for the tomb, temple, and sacred grove, of the hero Protesila'us.

(4.) Pactye (*Πακτύη*), whither Alcibi'ades retired after the Athenians had for the second time deprived him of the command.

(5.) Sestus (*Σηστός*), the principal town of the Chersone'sus, and the usual point of departure for those crossing over from Europe to Asia. It was the Western terminus of the famous bridge of Xerxes for the passage of his army into Europe.

Questions.—By whom were the Pelasgian-Thracians driven out of Thrace?—What kind of people were the historical Thracians?—What was the most important part of Thrace?—Where is it situated?—What is the modern name?—Who first inhabited it?—By whom was it colonized?——§ 110. Name some of the towns of Chersonesus Thracica.—Where was Cardia situated?—Where Callipolis?—What is said of Elæus?—To what place did Alcibiades retire?—What was the principal town of the Chersonesus?—What is said of it?

II. In *the remaining part of Thrace:*

(1.) AMPHI'POLIS (*Ἀμφίπολις*), founded by the Athenians on the left bank of the Strymon, and regarded by them as the jewel of their empire. Through the supposed inactivity of the commander, Thucy'dides the historian, it fell into the hands of the Spartan general, Bra'sidas. This event led to the banishment of Thucy'dides.

(2.) ABDE'RA (*Ἄβδηρα*), upon the Southern coast of Thrace, a colony of Teos. Demo'critus, the philosopher, was born here (444 B. C.), of whom Se'neca records: *Democritum aiunt nunquam sine risu in publico fuisse. De Ira*, II. 10.

(3.) DORISCUS (*Δόρισκος*), situated in a large plain, where Xerxes numbered his army.

(4.) BYZANTIUM (*Βυζάντιον*; Arabic, *Constanije;* Turkish, *Istambûl* or *Stambûl*, a corruption of *εἰς τὴν πόλιν*), a Greek city which occupied part of the site of modern Constantinople. It was founded by a Doric colony from Me'gara (666 B.C.). Constantine the Great determined to remove the seat of empire from the banks of the Tiber, and impressed with the striking situation of Byzantium, built a new city by the side of it, which he called *Nea Roma.* It was to cover seven hills, like old Rome, and was divided into fourteen wards (*regiones*). It was for more than a thousand years the capital of the Eastern world, and for the last five centuries it has been the capital of the Ottoman Empire. The Ottomans took it in 1453.

(5.) Other Greek colonies: DICÆA, MARONE'A, IS'MAROS, STRYME, MESEMBRIA, ÆNUS.

(6.) Other towns on the Propontis: PERINTHUS, SELYMBRIA (later, EUDOXO'POLIS).

QUESTIONS.—What city was regarded by the Athenians as the jewel of their empire?—Through whom was it lost to the Athenians?—Where was Abdera situated?—What philosopher was born there?—What happened in the plain near Doriscus?—When was Byzantium founded?—Give its names.—Who intended it to be the capital of the Roman empire?—How long was it the capital of the Eastern Roman world?—When was it taken by the Ottomans?

§ 111. ILLY'RICUM.

The Greek name was *I'llyris* (*Ἰλλυρίς*). The Roman *Illy'ricum* was, however, of very different extent from the Greek I'llyris, or Epi'rus Nova.

I'LLYRIS GRÆCA, or, EPI'RUS NOVA.

Philip, the father of Alexander the Great, annexed it to his dominions, whence its name of I'llyris Græca. It was the scene of the first wars between Rome and Macedonia.

Boundaries.—North, I'LLYRIS BA'RBARA; East, MACEDONIA; South, EPI'RUS; West, MARE IONIUM.

Mountains.—ACROCERAUNII and CANDAVII MONTES.

Rivers.—AO'US (*Viosa*), APSUS (*Beratino*).

Inhabitants.—The most accurate among the ancient writers have always distinguished them as a separate nation from the Thracians and Epi'rots. They are described as a religious people, just and kind to strangers, loving liberality, and of a quiet and well-ordered life.

Towns.—(1.) APOLLONIA (*Ἀπολλωνία*), a colony of the Corinthians and Corcyræans. Toward the end of the Roman republic it was celebrated as a seat of learning. Many Roman noblemen, and among them Octavia'nus, went thither for the purpose of studying the literature and philosophy of Greece.

(2.) EPIDAMNUS (*Ἐπίδαμνος*), called by the Roman authors *Dyrrhachium* (now *Durazzo*), a colony of the Corcyræans. The dispute between Corinth and Corcy'ra respecting this city is intimately connected with the celebrated Peloponnesian war. Under the Romans it was an important port; travellers going from Brundisium to the shores of the Bo'sporus, or to any inter-

---

QUESTIONS.—§ 111. What was the Greek name of Illyricum?—When did one part receive the name of Illyris Græca?—Name the mountains.—Rivers.—To what race did the Illyrians belong?—What kind of people were they?—Name the principal towns.—When did Apollonia become most celebrated?—Why?—How was Epidamnus called by the Romans?

mediate place, disembarked here and proceeded by the *Via Egnatia*, which led through Illy'ricum and Macedonia.

(3.) Other towns: AULON, a port, to which persons travelling from Italy to Greece frequently crossed over, and from which they went on their way through Epi'rus into Thessaly; O'RICUM, LY'CHNIDUS.

I'LLYRIS BA'RBARA, or, ROMA'NA.

Boundaries.—North, PANNONIA; East, MACEDONIA and MŒSIA; South, I'LLYRIS GRÆCA; West, ITALIA and MARE ADRIA'TICUM.

Divisions.—TAPYDIA, LIBURNIA, and DALMATIA.

Mountains.—MONTES BEBII, ALBIUS, and SCARDUS.

Towns.—I. In *Tapydia*, METU'LUM (*Μέτουλον*), the capital. The inhabitants of this region followed the custom of the wild Thracian tribes in tattooing their bodies.

II. In *Liburnia*, IA'DERA, the capital, which afterward became a Roman colony. The inhabitants of Liburnia were probably Pelasgians originally.

III. In *Dalmatia*, EPIDAURUS, a maritime city, besieged in the civil war between Pompeius and Cæsar; SCODRA, a fortified place. This country, abounding almost everywhere with the olive and vine, was little noticed by ancient authors, and its real worth not explored, in consequence of the wildness and predatory habits of the inhabitants.

IN'SULÆ LIBUR'NICÆ.

These were small islands near the coast of Illy'ricum.

QUESTIONS.—Give the boundaries of Illyris Barbara.—Give its divisions.—Mountains.—What is the capital of the Tapydians?—What is said of them?—What was the capital of Liburnia?—What is said of the Liburnians?—What is said of Dalmatia?—What small islands were near the coast?

§ 112. ITALIA. (*Ἰταλία.*)

Italy is protected on the East, South, and West by the sea, and on the North by almost impassable mountains. With this protection, and with admirable seaports on both seas, it was situated with regard to the great nations of Western Europe, on the one side, and to Greece and Asia on the other, in such a position that it seemed destined to attain universal dominion.

Name.—The geographical term, *Italia*, comprised different countries, situated on the peninsula of the Pyrenees, which were, however, never politically united until they all fell under Roman sway. The name was first applied to the Southern part of the present peninsula of Calabria, and was afterward extended so as to embrace all as far North as the river Laüs, comprising the countries around the Tarentine Gulf. This was the generally established understanding of the term among the Greeks in the fifth century B. C. In 41 B. C. the name Italia, which in the popular language of the times had been extended so as to take in Gallia Cisalpi′na, comprehended all the country South of the Alps. The word, *Italia*, perhaps signifies *land of cattle*, as being connected etymologically with the form, *vitulus*. The South-West portion was also called Œnotria (*Οἰνωτρία*, perhaps from *οἶνος*, and so properly, *Wine*-land). The countries on the shores of the Tyrrhene Sea, North of the Pondonian Gulf, were known by the names of O′pica and Tyrrhenia. The whole peninsula, lying entirely West of Greece, was called by the Greeks *Hesperia* (*Ἑσπερία*, see p. 89), and by poetical writers,

QUESTIONS.—Describe the situation of Italia.—What did the geographical term, Italia, embrace?—When were they united?—To what part was the name Italia first applied?—What did the term Italia comprise amongst the Greeks in the fifth century B. C.?—What was its signification after 100 B. C.?—What does the word Italia perhaps mean?—How was the south-western portion called?—What may be the meaning of the word Œnotria?—What was the name of the countries on the shores of the Tyrrhenian Sea?—How was it called by the Greeks?—Why?

Ausonia, from the *Au'sones*, a people found in Latium, and *Saturnia*, from having been the fabled residence of Saturn.

Boundaries.—Under the Roman empire, they were as follows: North, ALPES; East, MARE ADRIA'TICUM; South, MARE SI'CULUM, or AUSONIUM; West, MARE LIGU'STICUM and TYRRHE'NUM, and the river VARUS. Until the time of Augustus, Italia was understood to extend only as far as the Ru'bicon on the Eastern, and to the Macra on the Western side.

Extent.—Its area is about 93,600 square miles, or about as large as the states of New York and Pennsylvania, which have together 93,000 square miles. Its greatest breadth from the Tuscan Apennines to the sources of the Adda is about a hundred and fifty miles. The remaining portion, which is the peninsula proper, extends in a South-Easterly direction between the Adriatic and Mediterranean Seas for above five hundred miles, its breadth varying from a hundred and thirty miles to fifty, and in some parts of Calabria it is even less.

§ **113. Mountains.**—APENNI'NUS MONS (*the Apennines*), a chain of mountains traversing almost the entire length of Italy. It may be considered as constituting the backbone of the country, determining its configuration and physical characters. The most remarkable peaks are:

(1.) SORACTE, situated in Etruria, between Falerii and the Tiber. It was consecrated to Apollo, who had a temple on its summit. The god was worshipped here with peculiar religious rites.

(2.) AL'GIDUS, a mountain of Latium, forming part of the volcanic group of the Alban Hills. It was the scene of many conflicts between the Romans and Æquians.

QUESTIONS.—Why was Italia called Ausonia?—Why Saturnia?—What were the boundaries during the empire?—What rivers formed the ancient boundaries toward the north?—What is its area?—What its greatest breadth?——§ 113. What mountain chain traverses Italy?—Name some of its most remarkable peaks.—To what deity was Soracte consecrated?—Where is Algidus situated?—What nations often fought in its neighborhood?

(3.) ALBA'NUS MONS, the highest and central summit of the Alban Hills. It contained the central sanctuary of the Latin nations.

(4.) MAS'SICUS MONS, a range of hills which formed the boundary between Campania and Latium Novum. Its wine was very celebrated.

(5.) MONS SACER, a hill in the neighborhood of Rome. It is mentioned by ancient authors only once, on the occasion of the secession of the Plebeians from Rome (494 B. C.).

(6.) GARGA'NUS, the only projecting headland on the East coast of Italy.

(7.) TABURNUS, a mountain-group of the Apennines, situated in Samnium. At a very short distance from its base were the celebrated *Fu'rculæ Caudi'næ*, famous as the scene of the great disaster of the Romans during the second Samnite war (321 B. C.).

(8.) GAURUS, an extinct volcano in Campania, celebrated as the scene of a great victory gained by the Romans over the Samnites (340 B. C.).

(9.) VESUVIUS. The fearful eruption (after it had been for many centuries in a quiescent state) of the 24th of August, A. D. 79, first gave to Vesuvius the world-wide celebrity it has ever since maintained. That great catastrophe is described in detail in a celebrated letter of the younger Pliny to the historian Ta'citus. The mass of matter thrown out was so vast as not only to bury the cities of Herculaneum and Pompeii, at the foot of the volcano, but to overwhelm the more distant town of Stabiæ, where the elder Pliny perished by suffocation.

QUESTIONS.—Where was the central sanctuary of the Latin nations?—Where was Mons Massicus situated?—For what is Mons Sacer celebrated?—What is said of Mons Garganus?—Where is Taburnus situated?—For what are the Furculæ Caudinæ famous?—Who were conquered near Mons Gaurus?—Where was it situated?—When did the first eruption of Vesuvius, mentioned in antiquity, take place?—Who has described this event?—What cities were destroyed by this eruption?—Who perished by it?

RUINS OF POMPEII.

Capes.—(1.) CIRCÆUM PROMONTORIUM, in Latium on the coast of the Tyrrhene Sea.

(2.) MISE'NUM, on the coast of Campania, and, after the time of Augustus, the permanent station of the Roman fleets. It was the burial-place of the hero Mise'nus:

quo non præstantior alter
Ære ciêre viros, Martemque accendere cantu.
Virg. Æn. VI. 164,

and hence its name:

qui nunc Misenum ab illo
Dicitur, æternumque tenet per sæcula nomen.
Virg. Æn. VI. 234.

(3.) SCYLLÆUM, on the West coast of Bruttii, almost exactly at the entrance of the Sicilian strait, the fabled abode of the monster, Scylla:

QUESTIONS.—Name some of the capes of Italy.—Where was the permanent naval station?—What is said of Scyllæum?

Dextrum Scylla latus, lævum implacata Charybdis
Obsidet, atque imo barathri ter gurgite vastos
Sorbet in abruptum fluctus, rursusque sub auras
Erigit alternos, et sidera verberat unda.
Virg. Æn. III. 420.

(4.) LEUCO'PETRA, the most South-Western point, PROMONTORIUM HE'RCULIS, the most Southern, and ZEPHYRIUM, the most South-Eastern point of Italy.

(5.) LACINIUM formed the Southern limit of the Gulf of Tarentum, as the Iapygian promontory did the Northern one.

§ **114. Lakes.**—(1.) LACUS VERBA'NUS (*Lago Maggiore*), one of the three great lakes of Northern Italy.

(2.) LACUS LARIUS (*Lago di Como*), situated at the foot of the Alps and formed by the river Addua. On its shores were the three celebrated villas of the younger Pliny.

(3.) LACUS BENA'CUS (*Lago di Garda*), the largest of all the lakes in Italy, and also the roughest. Hence, Virgil (Georg. II. 160), in his beautiful description of Italy, says:

Fluctibus et fremitu assurgens Benace marino.

(4.) LACUS TRASIME'NUS (*Lago di Perugia*), the largest of the Etrurian lakes. It was the scene of the great victory obtained upon its shores by Ha'nnibal over the Roman consul, Caius Flaminius (217 B. C.), one of the greatest defeats sustained by the Roman arms during the whole course of their history.

(5.) VADIMO'NIS LACUS (*Laghetto di Bassano*), a small lake of Etruria, the scene of two successive defeats of the combined Etruscan forces by the Romans (309 and 283 B. C.).

(6.) LACUS REGILLUS, a small lake in Latium, celebrated for

QUESTIONS.—Name the three southern points of Italy.—What was the southern limit of the Gulf of Tarentum?——§ 114. Name some of the principal lakes of Italy.—Where is Lacus Larius situated?—By what river is it formed?—What celebrated villas are on its shores?—Which was the largest of the Etrurian lakes?—What battle was fought in its neighborhood?—Who were defeated near Vadimonis Lacus?—When?—For what is Lake Regillus celebrated?

the great battle between the Romans and the Latins under C. Mamilius (496 B. C.).

(7.) POMPTI'NÆ PALU'DES (*Pontine Marshes*), formed principally by the stagnation of the waters of two streams, Amase'nus and Ufens. The marshes occupy a space of about thirty miles in length by seven or eight miles in breadth. They were crossed by the celebrated Appian Way.

(8.) MINTURNENSES PALU'DES, in which Marius concealed himself, and from which he was dragged forth in ignominy with a rope round his neck, to Minturnæ.

(9.) LACUS AVERNUS (*Lago d'Averno*), a small lake in Campania, which occupies the crater of an extinct volcano, which was supposed to be the entrance to the infernal regions. Its name was connected by the ancients with Ἄορνος, i. e. ἀ-ὄρνις, *without birds*, in allusion to the deadly effect produced on birds that approached its vicinity. Hence Lucretius (VI. 741) says:

> *nomen id ab re*
> *Impositum est, quia sunt avibus contraria cunctis.*
> *E regione ea quod loca cum advenêre volantes,*
> *Remigii oblitæ pennarum vela remittunt,*
> *Præcipitesque cadunt molli cervice profusæ*
> *In terram, si forte ita fert natura locorum.*

§ **115. Rivers.**—A. On the *Eastern* coast:

(1.) A'THESIS (*Adige*). On its banks near Vercellæ, the Cimbri were defeated by Marius and Ca'tulus (101 B. C.).

(2.) PADUS (*Po*), the largest river in Italy; hence called *fluviorum rex* by Virgil (Georg. I. 401) Its most remarkable tributaries are:

a. On the Southern, or right, bank:

I. *Trebia*, on whose banks the battle was fought between

QUESTIONS.—What were the Pomptinæ Paludes?—By what Way were they crossed?—Who concealed himself in the Paludes Minturnenses?—Where is Lacus Avernus situated?—From what was its name derived?——§ 115. Name five of the most remarkable rivers on the eastern coast of Italy.—Near what rivers were the Cimbri defeated?—What is the largest river in Italy?—Name some of the southern tributaries to the Padus.—What battle was fought near the Trebia?

Ha'nnibal and Sempronius, which was the second victory in Italy obtained by the Carthaginian general (218 B. C.).

II. *Rhenus* (*Reno*), which is celebrated on account of the interview between Antonius, Octavia'nus, and Le'pidus, which took place on a small island formed by its waters.

b. On the Northern, or left, bank:

I. *Tici'nus* (*Ticino*), whose banks were the scene of the first victory of Ha'nnibal in Italy (218 B.C.).

II. *Addua* (*Adda*), in the neighborhood of which the Gauls were defeated by the Romans.

(3.) RU'BICON, the Northern boundary of Italia Proper. The pause of Cæsar on its banks, though not mentioned by himself, has given a proverbial celebrity to this little stream.

(4.) METAURUS, in Umbria, the scene of the defeat and death of Ha'sdrubal, the brother of Ha'nnibal (207 B. C.).

(5.) AU'FIDUS, the principal river of Apulia. Horace, whose native place, Venusia, was scarcely ten miles distant from the Au'fidus, calls himself (Carm. IV. 9, 2)

Longe sonantem natus ad Aufidum.

B. On the *South-Eastern* coast:

(1.) The SIRIS, in Lucania, famous for the first victory of Pyrrhus, king of Epi'rus (280 B. C.).

(2.) The SAGRAS, North-East of Locri. It is celebrated for the great battle fought on its banks, in which an army of 130,000 Crotonians is said to have been totally defeated by 10,000 Locrians; an event regarded as so extraordinary that it passed into a kind of proverb for the expression of a startling fact that appeared incredible.

QUESTIONS.—What treaty was concluded upon an island of the Rhenus?—Name some of the northern tributaries to the Padus —Near what river did Hannibal obtain his first victory?—What is mentioned in regard to the Addua?—What event gave proverbial celebrity to the Rubicon?—Where was Hasdrubal defeated?—What was the principal river of Apulia?—Name some of the rivers on the south-eastern coast of Italy —Where did Pyrrhus obtain his first victory?—When?—What battle was fought on the banks of the Sagras?

C. On the *Western* coast:

(1.) The VULTURNUS, the largest river of Campania, often mentioned in Roman history during the Samnite wars.

(2.) LIRIS (*Garigliano*), one of the principal rivers of Central Italy.

(3.) TI'BERIS (*Tiber*), the most important river of Italy. It receives numerous tributaries; those which are of any historical importance are the trifling streams, the *Allia*, on its *left*, where the Romans were defeated by the Gauls under Brennus (390 B.C.), which led to the capture and destruction of Rome by the barbarians; and the *Cre'mera*, on the *right*, celebrated for the memorable defeat of the 300 Fabii (477 B.C.):

Haec fuit illa dies, in qua Veientibus arvis
Ter centum Fabii ter ceciděre duo.
Ovid. Fast. II. 195.

(4.) Other rivers: UMBRO, ARNUS, VARUS, MACRA.

§ **116. Climate.**—The climate of Italy was in ancient times somewhat colder than at present, and the winters seem to have been more severe. Horace speaks of Soracte as white with snow, and Juvenal even alludes to the Tiber being covered with ice. The temperature of its climate was in general excellent, free from extremes of heat and cold, and well adapted to all kinds of plants and animals.

Productions.—Its varied climate rendered it suitable to the productions of the higher as well as of the lower latitudes of Europe. It produced grain, olives, wines, timber, sheep, goats, horses, and cattle. The mountains contained mines rich in various metals.

Inhabitants.—The inhabitants of Italy Proper may be grouped

QUESTIONS.—Name some of the rivers on the western coast of Italy. —What is the most considerable river of Campania?—What is the principal river of Central Italy?—What is the most celebrated river of Italy? —What are its tributaries?—Who defeated the Romans at the Allia?—What tragic event happened at the Cremera?——§ 116. What is said of the climate of Italy?—What of the productions?—How many different nations inhabited Italy?

under five heads: the Pelasgi, the Osci, the Sabelli, the Umbri, and the Etrusci:

(1.) The PELASGIC race, which inhabited the South-Eastern peninsula of Europe and the Western peninsula of Asia, appears to have very early attained importance in historical times, and in its purest and most original form, in the Southern part of the peninsula alone.

(2.) The OSCANS, called also in earlier times, *O'pici* and *Opsci*, inhabited a considerable portion of Central Italy, called *Opicia*, or *O'pica*. They constituted an important element of the Latin nation.

(3.) The SABELLIANS had their original abodes in the lofty ranges of the central Apennines and the upland valleys about Amiternum. They extended themselves gradually over the Western mountain slopes toward the Tyrrhene Sea, expelling the Oscans from the valley about Rea'te. At the same time they also sent bodies of emigrants to the East and South of their original abodes. Of these the most powerful and celebrated were the Samni'tes, the most persistent enemies of the Romans.

(4.) UMBRIANS. They were considered in antiquity as the most ancient of all the races of the peninsula, and their domain extended at one time from the Adriatic to the Tyrrhene Sea, and from the mouths of the Padus to those of the Tiber.

The three last-named nations were closely allied, being merely different branches of the same race.

(5.) ETRUSCANS, or Rase'na, were wholly distinct from the other races of Central Italy.

QUESTIONS.—What part of the world was inhabited by the Pelasgians?—What part of Italy did they inhabit?—What part of Italy was inhabited by the Oscans?—What name did they give to it?—Where were the original abodes of the Sabellians?—What parts of Italy did they overspread?—Which was the most powerful of their tribes?—Which was the most ancient of the Italian races?—What part of Italy was inhabited by them?—With whom of the Italian races were the Umbrians allied by race?—What was the fifth of the Italian races?

§ 117. Divisions of Italy.

I. NORTHERN ITALY, or GALLIA CISALPI'NA.

Subdivided into six parts: ISTRIA, CARNIA, VENETIA, GALLIA TRANSPADA'NA, GALLIA CISPADA'NA, LIGURIA.

II. CENTRAL ITALY, or ITALIA PROPRIA.

Subdivided into six parts: ETRURIA, UMBRIA, PICE'NUM, SABINIUM, LATIUM, and CAMPANIA.

III. SOUTHERN ITALY, or MAGNA GRÆCIA.

Subdivided into four parts: APULIA, CALABRIA, LUCANIA, and BRUTTII.

I. GALLIA CISALPI'NA.

Name.—The name, *Cisalpi'na*, denoted *Gallia on the Roman side South of the Alps*, as opposed to *Transalpi'na*, or *Gallia beyond the Alps*. It was also called *Gallia Toga'ta*, to indicate the numerical superiority of the *Toga'ti*, or Romans, over the Gallic population. The oldest name of Northern Italy among the Romans was simply *Gallia;* after the Romans became acquainted with Gallia *beyond the Alps*, they added the term *Cisalpi'na* or *Citerior* (Hither).

Boundaries.—North, ALPES; East, the ARSIA; South, RU'BICON and MACRA; West, VARUS.

Inhabitants.—It was inhabited by Galli, who, under the reign of Tarquinius Priscus, emigrated from Gaul into Italy. After

QUESTIONS.—§ 117 Into what three parts was Italia divided?—What name was given to Northern Italy?—What name to Central Italy?—What name to Southern Italy?—How was Gallia Cisalpina subdivided?—How Italia Proper?—How Magna Græcia?—What does the name, Cisalpina, denote?—Why is it called Gallia Togata?—What was its oldest name?—What other name were they accustomed to apply to it?—How was it bounded?—Who inhabited Gallia Cisalpina?—Under whose reign did the Gauls immigrate into Italy?

the Gallic conquest on the Allia (390 B.C.), the Romans became aware of the fact that in the Gauls they had an enemy whom they must destroy, or themselves suffer national extinction. The Romans in their long conflicts with the Gauls were fighting for their own existence, not for national glory. After many struggles, the Romans, under Publius Cornelius Scipio Nasi'ca, defeated the Boii, the greatest of the Gallic nations. Their country was made a Roman province (191 B.C.). In the subjugation a terrible butchery ensued: in the general massacre none but women, children, and old men were spared. The country was rapidly filled up with Romans, and became one of the most valuable of the Roman possessions.

Divisions.—ISTRIA, CARNIA, VENETIA, GALLIA *Transpada'na*, GALLIA *Cispada'na*, and LIGURIA.

§ 118. ISTRIA.

Boundaries.—North-West, the TIMA'VUS; North, CARNIA; East, PANNONIA, the ÆSIS, and the SINUS FLANA'TICUS; South-West, the ADRIATIC SEA; West, the SINUS TERGESTI'NUS.

It was subdued (177 B.C.) by the Romans, and until the time of Augustus it formed a part of the Roman province, Illy'ricum.

Inhabitants.—The Istrians were a tribe of the Illyrian race.

Towns.—TERGESTE (*Trieste*), the capital; POLA, a very ancient city, which, in the time of Augustus, became a Roman colony under the name of *Pi'etas Julia.*

QUESTIONS.—When were the Romans conquered by the Gauls?—What was the character of the Gallic wars?—Which was the principal of the Gallic tribes?—By whom were they conquered?—When?—Give the subdivisions of Gallia Cisalpina.——§ 118. Give the boundaries of Istria.—When was it subdued by the Romans?—To what province did it belong originally?—When was it considered a part of Italy?—What is said about the inhabitants?—Name some of its towns.

CARNIA.

Boundaries.—North, NOR'ICUM; East, PANNONIA; South, VENETIA and ISTRIA; West, RHÆTIA.

Mountains.—ALPES CA'RNICÆ, subsequently called ALPES JULIÆ, a mountain range that sweeps in a kind of semicircle round the present plain of *Frioul.*

Inhabitants.—The Carni were an Alpine tribe, belonging to the Celtic race. They were conquered by the Romans about 115 B. C.

Towns.—We know of two Roman towns, JULIUM CA'RNICUM, the capital, and FORUM JULII.

VENETIA.

Boundaries.—North, ALPES CA'RNICÆ; East, the TIMA'VUS; South, the ADRIATIC SEA; West, the A'THESIS.

Inhabitants.—The Ve'neti were a tribe of the wide-spread Slavonian race. They were a commercial people, who carried on a trade in amber, which was brought overland from the shores of the Baltic, and exchanged for other articles of commerce with Phœnician and Greek merchants. They were subdued (183 B.C.) by the Romans.

Venetia under the Roman empire became a very rich and flourishing province.

Towns.—(1.) PATAVIUM (*Padua*), situated thirty miles from the mouth of the river Medoa'cus (*Brenta*), and according to Virgil and other authors, founded by the Trojan Ante'nor:

> *Hic tamen ille urbem Patavi sedesque locavit*
> *Teucrorum, et genti nomen dedit, armaque fixit*
> *Troïa.* Æn. I. 247 seqq.

QUESTIONS.—How was Carnia bounded?—By what mountains was it traversed?—To what race did its inhabitants belong?—When were they conquered by the Romans?—What towns did Carnia contain?—What are the boundaries of Venetia?—To what race did the Veneti belong?—What is known about their trade?—When was Venetia subdued by the Romans?—Name some of the towns.—Where was Patavium situated?

It was at an early period an opulent and powerful city, and continued to flourish until quite a late period of the empire. This prosperity was brought abruptly to a close by A'ttila, who utterly destroyed it (A.D. 452). It was the birthplace of the historian Livy:

(2.) ADRIA, originally a seaport of great celebrity. It is now distant more than fourteen miles from that sea to which it gave the name of *Adriatic.* It was an Etruscan colony:

(3.) ALTI'NUM, situated on the border of the lagoons, whose shores furnished favorite sites for the residence of the wealthy Romans. In the course of time these shores were lined with villas rivalling those of Baiæ:

> *Æmula Baianis Altini litora villis—*
> *Vos eritis nostræ portus, requiesque senectæ,*
> *Si juris fuerint otia nostra sui.* Martial, IV. 25.

Its destruction by A'ttila (A. D. 452) gave occasion for the founding of the city of Venice:

(4.) AQUILEIA, situated sixty miles from the head of the Adriatic Sea, between the rivers Also and Natiso. It was a Roman colony, founded 181 B. C, and became afterward the capital of the country of Venetia. The neighboring Alps contained valuable gold mines, whose product, together with the profits derived from trade with the Pannonians and Illyrians, were considerable sources of wealth, and rendered it one of the most important and flourishing cities of Italy. It was besieged by A'ttila (A. D. 452), and finally taken, plundered, and burnt to the ground.

QUESTIONS.—What historian was born at Patavium?—Who destroyed the city?—What town gave its name to the Adriatic Sea?—Where is Altinum situated?—Describe the situation of Aquileia.—What is said of this town?

§ 119. GALLIA TRANSPADA'NA.

In connection with Gallia Cispada'na, it formed GALLIA CISALPI'NA PROPRIA, which was a Roman province subsequent to 222 B. C.

Boundaries.—North, RHÆTIA and NOR'ICUM; East, VENETIA; South, PADUS; West, GALLIA NARBONENSIS.

Nations and Towns.—(1.) The *Tauri'ni*, with the capital, AUGUSTA TAURINO'RUM (*Torino, Turin*), a Roman colony sent out by Augustus, situated on the river Padus, at its junction with the Duria Minor. The Padus here was navigable.

(2.) The *Salassi*, with the town AUGUSTA PRÆTORIA (*Aosta*), was situated at the foot of the Alps. This also was a Roman colony founded by Augustus, who, after the complete subjugation of the Salassians by Terentius Varro, established here a body of three thousand veterans. It was the most North-Westerly town of Italy.

(3.) The *Li'bici*, with their chief town VERCELLÆ, were situated on the Western bank of the Se'ssites. This town was distinguished for its worship of Apollo. Hence Martial (X. 12, 1) uses the expression, *Apollineas Vercellas.*

(4.) The *Lævi*, with the capital TICI'NUM (*Pavia*), were situated on the river Tici'nus, about five miles above its junction with the Padus. The city was destroyed by A'ttila (A. D. 452), and restored by Theodoric, the Goth, whose successors made it their chief stronghold in the North of Italy. After the Lombard invasion, it became the residence of the Lombard kings.

QUESTIONS.—§ 119. What was Gallia Cisalpina Propria?—At what period did it become a Roman province?—What were its boundaries?—Name some of the nations.—What was the capital of the Taurini?—What was the most north-westerly town of Italy?—Of what nation was it the capital?—What deity was particularly worshipped at Vercellæ?—Describe the situation of Ticinum.—Who destroyed the city?—Who restored it?

(5.) The *I'nsubres*, with—

a. The capital MEDIOLA'NUM (*Milano, Milan*), were situated in a broad and fertile plain about midway between the rivers Tici'nus and Addua, which situation adapted it to be the capital of that region. It was for a long period the metropolis of Cisalpine Gaul itself. After the battle of Clastidium, it was attacked and taken by the Roman consuls, Claudius Marcellus and Cn. Scipio (222 B.C.), and finally subdued (190 B.C.). Under the Roman empire, it became the principal city of Northern Italy. Literature flourished here, and young men from the neighboring towns were sent hither for their education. After A.D. 303, it became the imperial residence, till this was transferred to Ravenna (A.D. 404). After the fall of the Western empire (A.D. 476), Mediola'num became the royal residence of the Gothic kings, Odoa'cer and Theodoric.

b. NOVUM COMUM, also a city of the I'nsubres, was situated at the Southern extremity of the Lacus Larius, at the very foot of the Alps. It was the birthplace of both the elder and younger Pliny, the latter of whom had several villas on the banks of the lake, one of which is still known as the *Plinia'na.*

(6.) The *Cenoma'ni*, with the following cities:

a. BRIXIA (*Brescia*) was on the small river Mela. Under the Roman empire, it was a flourishing and wealthy town.

b. CREMO'NA was on the left bank of the Padus, about six miles below the confluence of the Addua. During the civil wars, it espoused the cause of Brutus, in consequence of which its territory was confiscated by Octavian. It is to this event that Virgil alludes, in the well-known line,

Mantua væ miseræ nimium vicina Cremonæ,
Ecl. IX. 28,

QUESTIONS.—What was the capital of the Insubres?—Where was it situated?—When was it taken by the Romans?—What was its condition under the empire?—When was it the imperial residence?—What city was the birthplace of Pliny?—Where was it situated?—Name the principal cities situated in the country of the Cenomani.—Where was Brixia situated?—Where was Cremona situated?—Who confiscated its territory?—Why?

VIRGIL.

a part of the territory of Mantua having shared the same fate with that of the neighboring city.

c. BEDRI'ACUM, between Vero'na and Cremo'na, was the scene of the decisive battle between Otho and Vitellius, which ended with the victory of the latter (A. D. 69).

d. MANTUA was on an island formed by the waters of the river Mincius. Its population, although much mixed, was for the greater part Etruscan:

> *Mantua, dives avis; sed non genus omnibus unum,*
> *Gens illi triplex, populi sub gente quaterni:*
> *Ipsa caput populis, Tusce de sanguine vires.*
>
> Virg. X 201 seqq.

Its chief celebrity was undoubtedly owing to its having been the birthplace of Virgil, who has, in consequence, celebrated it in

QUESTIONS.—What battle was fought near Bedriacum?—Where was Mantua situated?—What was the birthplace of Virgil?

several passages of his works. According to Dona'tus, however, the actual birthplace of the poet was Andes, a village in the territory of Mantua.

e. VERO'NA, situated on the river A'thesis, celebrated for the battle fought by Marius, in the Raudii Campi, in its neighborhood, against the Cimbri. It was the birthplace of Catullus:

Mantua Vergilio gaudet, Verona Catullo.
Ovid, Amor. III. 15, 7.

f. HOSTILIA, situated on the North bank of the Padus, was the birthplace of Cornelius Nepos.

§ 120. GALLIA CISPADA'NA.

Boundaries.—North, the PADUS; East, the ADRIATIC SEA; South, the RU'BICON and the APENNI'NI MONTES; West, LIGURIA.

Nations and Towns.—(1.) The *Ananes*, with the town CLASTIDIUM, situated on the borders of Liguria, celebrated on account of the victory gained by Marcellus over the I'nsubres (222 B.C.):

(2.) The *Anamares*, with the town PLACENTIA (*Placenza*), situated near the Southern bank of the Padus, near its junction with the Trebia. The city was plundered by the Gauls, 200 B. C. Under the empire, it was a populous and flourishing city:

(3.) The *Boïi*, with the towns:

a. PARMÆ, situated about fifteen miles South of the Padus. It was a *colonia civium*, its settlers retaining the privileges of Roman citizens:

QUESTIONS.—What was the birthplace of Catullus?—Where was it situated?—What was the birthplace of Cornelius Nepos?——§ 120. How is Gallia Cispadana bounded?—Name some of the towns.—Where is Clastidium situated?—What victory was gained there by Marcellus?—When?—Describe the situation of Placentia.—When was it plundered?—What towns were situated in the country of the Boii?—Where is Parma situated?—What is a colonia civium?

b. CRIXELLUM (*Bresello*), situated on the South bank of the Padus. The emperor Otho here committed suicide, A. D. 69:

c. MU'TINA (*Modena*), situated between Parma and Bononia. It was the scene of the Mutinensean war, *bellum Mutinense* (43 B. C.):

d. BONONIA (*Bologna*), an ancient Etruscan city, founded under the name of Felsina. It was situated on the river Rhenus, at the foot of the Apennines. In its neighborhood were arranged the terms of the second triumvirate between Antony, Le'pidus, and Octavian (43 B. C.):

e. FORUM CORNELII (*Imola*), situated on the Western bank of the river Vatre'nus. It was founded by the dictator, Cornelius Sylla, and is supposed to have derived its name from him:

(4.) The *Li'ngones*, with the following towns:

a. RAVENNA, situated a short distance from the sea-coast. Subsequent to the time of Augustus, it was the principal naval station in the Adriatic. From the beginning of the fifth century down to the decay of the Western Empire, Ravenna was the permanent imperial residence:

b. FORUM LIVII (*Forli*).

LIGURIA.

Boundaries.—North, the PADUS; East, GALLIA CISPADA'NA and the MACRA; South, SINUS LIGUS'TICUS; West, the VARUS and the ALPES MARI'TIMÆ.

In 14 B. C. it became subject to the Roman power.

Mountains.—ALPES MARI'TIMÆ (*Maritime Alps*), that portion of the Alpine range which extends to the Tyrrhene Sea. Their limit was at the Portus Monœci (*Monaco*), above which

---

QUESTIONS.—Who committed suicide at Brixellum?—When?—Where was the scene of the Bellum Mutinense?—Describe the situation of Bononia.—What happened there?—Who was the founder of Forum Cornelii?—What towns were situated in the territory of the Lingones?—Where was Ravenna situated?—When did it become the imperial residence?—What are the boundaries of Liguria?—Name the mountains.

rises a lofty headland, on which stood the trophy erected by Augustus to commemorate the subjugation of the Alpine tribes (*Tropæum Augusti*).

Liguria contained very few towns, the inhabitants living mostly in small villages.

Towns.—(1.) NICÆA (*Nizza*), situated on the coast of Liguria near the boundary of Gaul. It was a colony of Massilia:

(2.) GENUA, the chief maritime city of Liguria, and the principal emporium of trade for this part of the Mediterranean. It became most celebrated in the Second Punic War.

§ 121. II. ITALIA PROPRIA.

Boundaries.—North, RU'BICON and GALLIA CISALPI'NA; East, MARE SU'PERUM; South, SI'LARUS and FRENTO; West, LIGURIA, MACRA, and MARE I'NFERUM.

Divisions.—ETRURIA, UMBRIA, PICE'NUM, SABINIUM, LATIUM, and CAMPANIA.

ETRURIA, or TUSCIA.

Name.—The universal appellation by writers of the best period of Roman letters is *Etruria*. In the later times of the Roman empire, *Tuscia* was the official designation, which is still preserved in the modern appellation of *Toscana*, or Tuscany. The Greek name of the country was Tyrrhenia (*Τυρρηνία*).

Boundaries.—North-West, MACRA; North, APENNINES; East and South, TIBER; West, MARE TUSCUM.

Inhabitants.—The Roman authors applied to them the name of Etrusci, or Tusci. The Greeks called them Tyrrhènians, or Tyrsenians. They called themselves Rase'na, or Rasenna. The

---

QUESTIONS.—What was the Tropæum Augusti?—Where was it?—Did Liguria contain many towns?—Name some of the towns.—What is said of Nicæa?—Of Genua?——§ 121. What is remarked about the name Etruria?—What are its boundaries?—What name was given to its inhabitants by the Roman authors?—What name by the Greeks?—How did they call themselves?

population was mixed, containing Umbrians, Pelasgians, and Rase′na. The Umbrians were the original inhabitants, among whom a colony of the sea-faring Tyrrhene-Pelasgians settled at an early period. Both of these nations were afterward conquered by the Rase′na, who came from the Rhætian mountains. Before the period of the Roman dominion, the power of the Etruscans was widely extended both by sea and land. It was at its height from 600–500 B. C. There were two principal communities, one in Etruria, the other in the plains of the Padus, each of which was composed of twelve principal cities. A third Etruscan confederacy once flourished in Campania. The second and third of these confederacies were at an early period wrested from the Etruscans, the one by the Gauls, the other by the Samnites, 400 B.C. The main confederacy, in Etruria Proper, received the first fatal blow to its nationality at the fall of Veii (396 B.C.), and at the beginning of the First Punic War, the whole of Etruria acknowledged the supremacy of Rome (264 B.C.).

Language.—The Roman writers represent the Etruscan language as having been wholly unintelligible to the Latins. We now know it only by the specimens preserved in inscriptions, and it is supposed to have belonged to the Gothic group of the Indo-Teutonic tongues.

Civilization.—The Etruscans were by far the most cultivated and refined people of ancient Italy, and were especially devoted to the practice of the higher arts. In architecture, sculpture, and painting they were greatly distinguished

---

QUESTIONS.—What different nations formed the population of Etruria?—What were the original inhabitants?—Who settled among the Umbrians?—By whom were both of those nations conquered?—Whence did they come?—When was the Etruscan power at its height?—How many Etrurian unions were cemented at that time?—Describe their situation.—Who conquered the Etrurian confederacy in the plains of the Padus?—By whom was that in Campania subdued?—How many states constituted each of these confederacies?—Where was the chief confederacy situated?—When did it receive the first fatal blow to its power?—When did it acknowledge the supremacy of Rome?—What is known of their language and literature?—What is known about their civilization?—In what arts had they made great progress?

Religion.—The Etruscan religion was particularly characterized by the great number and peculiar strictness of its ritual observances. The Etruscans reduced the different modes of divination in vogue into a regular systematic form; and on this account, we find the Romans, throughout all periods of their history, consulting the Etruscan *haruspices.*

Political Constitution.—They formed a confederacy of twelve cities, each of which was a sovereign and independent state, possessing, not only the right of internal self-government, but also that of making war, or peace, on its own account. Regularly, once a year, they held a general meeting at the national sanctuary, the *Fanum Voltumnæ,* where they deliberated on the welfare of the nation, and elected their high-priest, who officiated in the name of the union. The internal government was aristocratic. The members of this body were called *Lucumo'nes,* and were at the head of the government of the towns.

§ **122. Cities.**—Nine of the twelve cities which composed the Etruscan league are known to us. These are as follows:

TARQUINII, VEII, VOLSINII, CLUSIUM, VOLATERRÆ, VETULONIA, PERUSIA, CORTO'NA, and ARRETIUM. CÆRE and FALERII also most probably belonged to their number. The twelfth, though unknown, was probably RUSELLÆ.

(1.) TARQUINII, the most ancient of the cities of Etruria, was situated near the Tyrrhene Sea. A nobleman of this city went to Rome, where he became king, under the name of Lucius Tarquinius (616–579 B.C.).

(2.) VEII, an ancient and purely Etruscan city, was situated about twelve miles North of Rome. It is chiefly celebrated on

---

QUESTIONS.—What is known about the religion of the Etruscans?—What influence did it exercise on Rome?—What is said of their political constitution?—What was the character of their government?—Where was their general congress held?—What topics were discussed at this meeting?—What was the form of the internal government?—What was a Lucumo?——§ 122. How many cities composed the Etruscan league?—How many of them are known to us?—What are their names?—What two cities probably belonged to their number?—What was the connection between Tarquinii and Rome?—What is said of Veii?

account of the wars it waged with the Romans. It was finally taken by Camillus (396 B.C.), after a siege of ten years.

(3.) VOLSINII was situated on the shore of a lake of the same name. The old city was destroyed (280 B.C.) by the Romans, who compelled the inhabitants to migrate to another spot The new city was the birthplace of Seja'nus, the chancellor of Tiberius. Juvenal (III. 191) says of it:

Positis nemorosa inter juga Volsiniis.

(4.) CLUSIUM (*Chiusi*), originally an Umbrian city, at an early period fell into the hands of the Rase'na. It was the residence of Po'rsena, the friend and ally of Tarquinius Priscus.

(5.) VOLATERRÆ was the largest and most powerful of all the Etruscan cities. It was the birthplace of the satirist, A. Persius (A.D. 34).

(6.) VETULONIA was the city whence the Romans received the insignia of magistracy.

(7.) PERUSIA was situated on the right bank of the Tiber, at one period one of the most powerful cities of Italy. The ancient city was destroyed by Octavia'nus.

(8.) CORTO'NA was situated in the neighborhood of Lacus Trasime'nus.

(9.) ARRETIUM (*Arezzo*), the most inland city of Etruria, was situated near the foot of the Apennines.

(10.) CÆRE, by the Greeks called Agylla (*Ἄγυλλα*), situated near the coast of the Tyrrhene Sea. It was an ancient Pelasgic city which, about 500 B.C., was taken by the Etruscans. When subsequently conquered by the Romans (353 B.C.), the inhabitants received the Roman franchise, but without the right of suffrage. Hence the proverbial expression for disfranchising a Roman citizen: *in tabulas Cæritium referre.*

QUESTIONS.—Where was Volsinii situated?—When and by whom was the old town destroyed?—Who was a native of the new town?—What was the residence of Porsena?—What was the native place of the poet A. Persius?—What did the Romans receive from Vetulonia?—Where was Perusia situated?—Who destroyed the ancient town?—Where was Cortona situated?—Where Arretium?—Where Cære?—What is said of it?—To what proverb did Cære give rise?

(11.) FALERII, situated West of the Tiber and North of Mount Soracte, was the scene of the well-known story of the schoolmaster and Camillus.

(12.) RUSELLÆ (*Rosello*) was not far from the river Umbro (*Ombrone*). The city was taken by the Romans 294 B.C.

Beside these twelve principal cities, there are the following:

a. North of the Arnus:

LUNA, LUCA, PISÆ, FLORENTIA, PISTORIA, and FÆ'SULÆ, the two last named both known from their connection with the conspiracy of Catiline:

b. Between the Arnus and the Umbro:

Beside Volaterræ and Rusellæ, already spoken of, SENA and POPULONIUM:

c. South of the Umbro:

COSA and VULCI may be added to those already mentioned as important cities. There were also many others, among which may be mentioned GRAVISCÆ, the birthplace of Seja'nus, and FESCENNIUM, which has given the name to the *Carmina Fescennina*, originally simple rustic dialogues, which, at a later period, degenerated into loose songs.

§ 123. UMBRIA.

Boundaries.—North, the RU'BICON; East, the ADRIATIC SEA; South, PICE'NUM and SABINIUM; West, the TIBER.

Productions.—The cattle of the valley of the Clitumnus were very celebrated. On its mountain slopes fed numerous flocks of sheep. The lower portions of the country abounded in fruit-trees, vines, and olives. Propertius (I. 22, 10) calls it, *terris fertilis uberibus.*

QUESTIONS.—Where is Falerii situated?—What happened there?—Where is Rusellæ situated?—What towns were situated north of the Arnus?—What towns between the Arnus and Umbro?—What towns south of the Umbro?—Who was born at Graviscæ?—What were the Carmina Fescennina?——§ 123. What are the boundaries of Umbria?—What is said of the productions?

Inhabitants.—The Umbrians were of Gallic origin, and one of the most ancient races established in Italy. At a very early period they appear to have been a great and powerful nation in the northern half of Central Italy, whose dominion extended from sea to sea, and comprised the fertile district on both sides of the Apennines. In 300 B. C. they were subdued by the Romans.

Towns.—The towns were numerous, though few were of special importance.

(1.) OCRIC'ULUM, the Southernmost town of Umbria. It was here that Fabius Maximus took the command of the army of Servilius, after the battle of the lake Trasime'nus (217 B. C.):

(2.) NARNIA, an ancient and important city, which before the Roman conquest (299 B. C.) bore the name of Nequi'num. It was the birthplace of the emperor Nerva:

(3.) AMERIA, the birthplace of Sextus Roscius the actor, who was defended in so masterly a speech by Cicero:

(4.) SPOLETIUM, the scene of the battle between the generals of Sylla and Carbo (82 B. C.):

(5.) MEVANIA, situated on the river Tinia, in a broad and fertile valley, which was celebrated for its breed of white oxen, the only ones thought worthy to be sacrificed on solemn occasions:

(6.) HISPELLUM, the birthplace of Propertius (52 B. C.):

(7.) TIFERNUM TIBERI'NUM, often mentioned in the epistles of the younger Pliny, who was a generous patron of the city, and built there, at his own cost, a temple to Ceres. His villa was in its neighborhood:

QUESTIONS.—What is said of the Umbrians?—When were they subdued by Rome?—Name some of the towns.—Where is Oriculum situated?—Which of the Roman emperors was a native of Narnia?—What made Ameria celebrated?—What battle took place at Spoletium?—Where was Mevania situated?—For what was it celebrated?—What place was the birthplace of Propertius?—Who was the patron of Tifernum Tiberinum?

(8.) ARI'MINUM, situated on the coast of the Adriatic, near the mouth of the river Ari'minus. It was justly considered as the key of Gallia Cisalpi'na, on the one side, and of the Eastern coast of Italia Propria on the other :

(9.) PISAURUM (*Pesaro*), an important, but unhealthful place, which suffered severely from an earthquake (31 B. C.) :

(10.) SENA GA'LLICA (*Sinigaglia*), on the coast of the Adriatic, where the two consuls, Livius and Nero, united their forces before the battle of the Metaurus (207 B. C.) :

(11.) SA'RSINA, situated in the Apennines, on the left bank of the river Sapis. It was the birthplace of the comic poet, Plautus (254 B. C.) :

(12.) Other cities: INTERAMNA (i. e. *inter-amnis*, as surrounded by the river Nar; comp. the Greek name *Mesopotamia*), the birthplace of the historian Ta'citus (A. D. 60); CAMERI'NUM.

§ 124. PICE'NUM, or AGER PICE'NUS.

Boundaries.—North, the ÆSIS; East, the ADRIATIC SEA; South, the MATRI'NUS; West, UMBRIA and the SABI'NI.

Rivers.—The whole country is traversed by numerous streams, which render it one of the pleasantest regions of Italy. These streams are the MATRI'NUS, VOMA'NUS, BATI'NUS, TRUENTUS, and others.

Productions.—Pice'num is a district of great fertility and beauty. Extending in a broad band of almost uniform width from the central ranges of the Apennines, it slopes gradually toward the sea. The greater portion is occupied by high hills whose summits are clothed with extensive forests, while the

---

QUESTIONS.—Where was Ariminum situated?—What is said of the importance of this situation?—What of Pisaurum?—What of Sena Gallica?—What was the birthplace of Plautus?—What is said of Interamna?——§ 124. How was Picenum bounded?—What is said of its streams?—Name some of them.—What was the character of the country?—Name some of its productions.

lower slopes produce abundance of fruit-trees and olives, and also excellent wine and corn :

Picenis cedunt pomis Tiburtia succo.
Hor. Sat. II. 4, 70.

Inhabitants.—The Picentes were of Sabine origin. The region they occupied was one of the most populous districts of Italy. After many years of alliance with Rome, they were subdued (268 B. C.). They afterward took a prominent part in the Social War (90 B. C.).

Towns.—The towns are numerous, but few have any historical celebrity :

(1.) ANCON or ANCO'NA, situated on a promontory, which forms a remarkable curve, or *elbow*, ἀγκών, whence its name. It was the only Greek colony on this part of the coast of Italy. It was founded by Syracusan exiles (380 B. C.). The triumphal arch erected in honor of Trajan still remains. Its once celebrated temple of Venus has entirely disappeared :

(2.) AS'CULUM, the ancient capital, a strongly fortified place, situated on the river Truentus. Here occurred the first open outbreak of the Social War (90 B. C.) :

(3.) ADRIA, or HADRIA, a colony of the celebrated Etruscan city of that name. The family of the emperor Hadrian was originally from this place.

§ 125. SABINI.

Boundaries.—North, the ÆSIS and PICE'NUM; East, the ADRIATIC SEA; South, the FRENTO, APULIA, and LUCANIA; West, CAMPANIA, LATIUM, and ETRURIA.

QUESTIONS.—What is said of the inhabitants of Picenum?—When were they subdued by the Romans?—In what war did they take a prominent part?—Name some of the towns.—Where is Ancon situated?—What is said of it?—Where was the first outbreak of the Social War?—Where was it situated?—What is said of Adria?——§ 125. What are the boundaries of Sabinium?

Mountains.—MONTES GURGURES, a portion of the central and highest ranges of the Apennines. *Taburnus Mons* is often mentioned by Virgil:

Juvat Ismara Baccho
Conserere, atque olea magnum vestire Taburnum.
Georg. II. 37.

Inhabitants.—The Sabi'ni were one of the most ancient races of Italy, and constituted one of the elements of the Roman people, whilst, at the same time, they were the original progenitors of the Picentes, Peligni, and Samni'tes, and most probably of the Marsi, Marruci'ni, and Vesti'ni. They were brave, hardy, and frugal mountaineers, dwelling principally in villages, or in unwalled towns. Subsequent to 268 B. C. they enjoyed the full rights of Roman citizens, and, therefore, in the Social War, took sides with Rome.

Divisions.—It was divided into two large parts; the most Northern part was called SABI'NA, and the most Southern, SAMNIUM.

SABI'NA, or *the Country of the Sabelli.*

It was for the most part of a rugged and mountainous character.

Nations and Towns.—(1.) The *Sabi'ni*, with—

a. The capital, CURES, the birthplace of Numa Pompilius.

b. REA'TE, one of the first places occupied by the Sabines, when they descended from the neighborhood of Amiternum, their original abode.

c. AMITERNUM, the birthplace of the historian, Sallustius (85 B C.).

QUESTIONS.—Name some of the mountain peaks of Sabinium.—Of what nation were the original Sabini?—What was the general character of the people?—What is said of their towns?—When did they enjoy the rights of Roman citizens?—What part did they take in the Social War?—Into how many parts was the country divided?—What was the name of the northern part?—Name some of its nations and towns.—What was the capital of the Sabini?—What was one of the first places they occupied after leaving Amiternum?—What was their original abode?

(2.) The *Vesti'ni*, with the capital, PINNA.

(3.) The *Marsi*, with the capital, MARRUBIUM, situated on the Eastern shore of the lake Fuci'nus.

(4.) The *Peligni*, with—

a. The capital, CORFINIUM (*Pelino*), situated in the valley of the Aternus. At the opening of the Social War, it was selected by the confederates as their common capital and the seat of government (90 B. C.).

b. SULMO, the birthplace of the poet Ovidius (43 B. C.).

(5.) The *Marruci'ni*, with the capital, TEA'TE, the birthplace of Asinius Pollio, the celebrated statesman and orator.

(6.) The *Frenta'ni*, with the towns HISTONIUM and LARI'-NUM.

SAMNIUM.

It was originally inhabited by Oscans, who at an early period were subdued by four Sabine tribes: the Pentri, Hirpi'ni, Carace'ni, and Caudi'ni, who soon broke off all political connection with the parent nation, and together formed the nation of the Samni'tes, so famous for their struggle with Rome, which eventually decided whether the supremacy of Italy was to rest with the Romans or the Samnites. The wars commenced in 343 B. C., and ended in 272 B. C. with the entire submission of Samnium. They again revolted in the Social War (90 B. C.), and once more became the terror of Rome under Pontius Telesi'nus, after whose death (82 B. C.) their whole country was devastated by Sulla.

Towns.—(1.) ÆSERNIA, a city of the Pentri, which, after the fall of Corfinium and Bovia'num, became the headquarters of the Italian allies (90 B. C.):

QUESTIONS.—What was the capital of the Vestini?—What of the Marsi?—What of the Peligni?—Where was Corfinium situated?—What place did it occupy during the Social War?—What was the birthplace of Ovidius?—Of Asinius Pollio?—What was the origin of the nation of the Samnites?—What made them famous?—During what period did those wars happen?—What was their result?—Who was their last successful general?—When did he perish?—Name some of the towns.—When did Æsernia become the headquarters of the Italian allies?

(2.) Bovia'num, a very wealthy and powerful city, the capital of the Pentri, which was entirely devastated by Sulla (89 B. C.):

(3.) Beneventum (*Benevento*), formerly called Maleventum. The vicinity was the scene of the famous battle in which Pyrrhus was defeated by M. Curius (275 B.C.):

(4.) Caudium, the capital of the Caudi'ni. In its neighborhood was the famous pass, called the Fu'rculæ Caudi'næ, the scene of one of the greatest disasters sustained by the Romans in the whole course of their history (321 B. C.).

§ 126. LATIUM.

Name.—The etymology of Latium is unknown. By the ancients it was derived sometimes from *latere*, because here Saturn *was concealed* from Jupiter; sometimes from the name of King *Latinus*.

Boundaries.—North, the Tiber; East, the Marsi and Samnium; South-West, the Tyrrhene Sea. The Liris separated it from Campania.

Divisions.—Latium Anti'quum and Latium Adjectum.

Latium Anti'quum.

This was the smaller portion of the Latian territory. Whenever Latium is spoken of in the earliest Roman history, this portion alone must be understood. It extended from the mouth of the Tiber to the Circeian promontory. The coast line comprises only about two hundred miles, and its greatest breadth is not much more.

Cities.—A. *In the country of the Lati'ni:*

Roma (see § 128):

Questions.—What battle took place near Beneventum?—What happened in the neighborhood of Caudium?——§ 126. What is said of the origin of the term Latium?—How was the country bounded?—What were its divisions?—Where was Latium Antiquum situated?—Name some of its nations and towns.

(1.) TIBUR (*Tivoli*), to the North-East of Rome, on the Anio, which there formed the celebrated cascade. The neighborhood was famous for its fruit-trees and orchards (*pomosi Tiburis arva*), and also for its grapes and figs. Its salubrity made it a favorite place of luxurious retirement for the wealthy Romans. Its reputed founder was Catillus or Ca'tilus, hence it is often mentioned under the name of *Mœnia Ca'tili:*

(2.) OSTIA(-AE), which derived its name from its position at the mouth of the Tiber. Originally founded by Ancus Martius, it formed the harbor of Rome:

(3.) TU'SCULUM (*Frascati*), one of the favorite resorts of the wealthy Romans. Here were the country residences of Cicero, Cato, Lucullus, and other distinguished citizens:

(4.) PRÆNESTE (*Palestrina*), situated East of Rome, opposite the Alban Hills. It was the stronghold of the party of Marius till 82 B. C., when it was taken and plundered by Sulla's general, Lucretius Ofella:

(5.) BOVILLÆ, situated on the Appian Way, and one of the thirty cities which in 493 B. C composed the Latin League. In its neighborhood Clodius was killed by Milo; hence, Cicero calls the affair, *pugna Bovillana:*

(6.) ALBA LONGA, the parent city of Rome and the ancient head of the Latin League, destroyed by Rome about 666 B. C. Some of the first Roman families originated from this city (the Julii, Tullii, Servilii). Its epithet, *longa*, was derived from its occupying a *long* and narrow ridge between the mountain and the lake.

B. *In the country of the Volsci:*

(1.) VELI'TRÆ (*Velletri*), on the Southern slope of the

QUESTIONS.—Where is Tibur situated?—Why is it so often mentioned as *mœnia Catili?*—Whence did Ostia derive its name?—What celebrated Romans possessed country seats near Tusculum?—Where was Præneste situated?—What part did it take in the civil wars between Marius and Sylla?—When and by whom was it plundered?—What is said of Bovillæ?—What was the ancient head of the Latin League?—When was it destroyed?—By whom?—Why was it called *longa?*—What towns were situated in the country of the Volsci?

Alban Hills, near the Pontine Marshes. It was the native place of the Octavian family, from which the emperor, Augustus, was descended:

(2.) LANUVIUM, the birthplace of the emperor, Antoni'nus Pius, who frequently made it his residence, as did also his successors, M. Aurelius and Co'mmodus:

(3.) NORBA, originally a Latin city, which afterward fell into the hands of the Volscians. It was the last city which remained faithful to the party of Marius:

(4.) SUESSA POMETIA, which bordered on the Pompti'nus Ager, or Pompti'næ Palu'des, *Pontine Marshes*, to which it is supposed to have given name:

(5.) CORI'OLI, celebrated from its connection with the legend of C. Marcius Coriola'nus (491 B.C.):

(6.) ANTIUM, situated on a promontory South of Rome. Here Augustus first received the title of *Pater Patriæ*, and it was the birthplace of Nero and Cali'gula. It possessed a very wealthy temple dedicated to the goddess *Fortu'na*.

C. *In the country of the Ru'tuli:*

A'RDEA, the chief city of the Pelasgian portion of the Latin nation, though in early times a very powerful place, finally declined in importance, until in Virgil's time its great name only remained:

Locus Ardea quondam
Dictus avis; et nunc magnum manet Ardea nomen.
Sed fortuna fuit. Æn. VII. 411 seqq.

§ 127. LATIUM ADJECTUM.

It comprised the country of the Æqui, He'rnici, Volsci, and Aurunci or Ausonii.

QUESTIONS.—What was the native place of the Octavian family?—What Roman emperors resided at Lanuvium?—What is said of Norba?—Where was Suessa Pometia situated?—What Roman legend is connected with the town of Corioli?—Where was Antium situated?—What was the chief town of the Pelasgians in Latium?——§ 127. Name some of the nations of Latium Adjectum?

Towns.—A. *In the country of the Æqui:*

(1.) CORBIO, situated North-East of the Alban Hills. It was destroyed by the Romans (456 B. C.):

(2.) BOLA, often mentioned in early Roman history. It was destroyed by the Romans (383 B. C.):

(3.) SUBLAQUEUM (*Subiaco*), *under the lakes* formed by the Anio. Here were the country residences of Claudius and Nero.

B. *In the country of the He'rnici:*

(1.) ANAGNIA, the chief city of the He'rnici. In its neighborhood was a country seat of Ci'cero. The territory belonging to the town was remarkably fertile.

(2.) FERENTI'NUM, often besieged and taken in the earlier times of the Republic, but at a later period, a quiet country town. Horace thus speaks of it:

> *Si te grata quies et primam somnus in horam*
> *Delectat, si te pulvis strepitusque rotarum,*
> *Si lædit caupona, Ferentinum ire jubebo.*
> Epist. I. 17, 6 seqq.

C. *In the country of the Volsci:*

(1.) ARPI'NUM, situated on a hill, rising above the valley of the Liris, near its junction with the Fibre'nus. It was the birthplace of two of the most famous characters in Roman history, Marius and Cicero:

(2.) FREGELLÆ, situated on the left bank of the Liris, often mentioned in the wars with the Samnites. It was razed to the ground by L. Opimius (125 B. C.):

(3.) AQUI'NUM, a populous and flourishing place during the latter period of the Roman republic. It was the birthplace of Juvenal (A. D. 42):

(4.) PRIVERNUM, situated in the Volscian mountains, and noted for the excellence of its wine:

QUESTIONS.—Name some towns of Latium Adjectum.—What towns belonged to the Æqui?—When was Corbio destroyed?—Bola?—What was the chief town of the Hernici?—Name some towns of the Volsci.—Where is Arpinum situated?—What celebrated men were natives of Arpinum?—What is said of Fregellæ?—Of Aquinum?—Of Privernum?

(5.) CIRCEII, situated at the foot of Mons Circeius, at a short distance from the sea, and often mentioned in the Great Latin War (340 B. C.), but afterward known chiefly as producing fine oysters:

(6.) TARRACI'NA, situated at the extremity of the Pontine Marshes. Its Volscian name was Anxur, which last name is generally used by the Roman poets; for instance, by Horace, where he speaks of its important position:

Impositum saxis late candentibus Anxur.
Sat. I. 5, 26:

(7.) LAU'TULÆ, a fortified mountain-pass, the scene of the mutiny of the Roman army, under Caius Marcius Rutilius (342 B. C.). At a later period, the Romans were defeated here by the Samni'tes (315 B. C.):

D. *In the country of the Aurunci:*

(1.) AMY'CLÆ, founded by Laconian exiles from the city of the same name on the Euro'tas:

(2.) FORMIÆ (*Mola di Gaeta*). Here was a celebrated villa of Ci'cero, from which many of his letters to A'tticus are dated. Near this villa he was captured and killed by his murderers (44 B. C.):

(3.) CAIE'TA (*Gaeta*), situated on the Tyrrhene coast, celebrated for its seaport. It afforded a place of retreat to Scipio Africa'nus and Lælius:

(4.) MINTURNÆ, on the right bank of the Liris, where C. Marius was imprisoned (88 B. C.). Under the empire, it was a very populous town:

(5.) SINUESSA, in whose neighborhood were the celebrated Warm Springs, called *Aquæ Sinuessæ*.

QUESTIONS.—In what war is Circeii often mentioned?—What was the Volscian name of Tarracina?—What happened at Lautulæ?—What towns belonged to the Aurunci?—Who possessed a villa near Formiæ?—What celebrated Romans retired to Caieta?—Where was Minturnæ situated?—What were the Aquæ Sinuessæ?

§ 128. ROMA. (ἡ Ῥώμη.)

Rome, said Pliny, *is the mistress of the world and the metropolis of the habitable earth, destined by the gods to unite, civilize, and govern the scattered races of men.*

It was said to have been founded by Ro'mulus on the Palatine Mt. on the left bank of the Tiber (753 B. C.). The walls erected by Servius Tullius included already seven hills (*urbs septicollis*), viz.: the Quirina'lis, Vimina'lis, Esquili'nus, Cælia'nus, Aventi'-nus, Capitoli'nus, and Palati'nus. He divided the city into four parts: *Esquili'na*, *Colli'na*, *Palati'na*, and *Suburba'na*. The city was twice almost entirely burnt down, first by the Gauls (339 B. C.), and the second time, under Nero (A. D. 64), who afterward caused the town to be rebuilt on a regular plan, with broad streets, open spaces, and less lofty houses. The third conflagration of the greater part of the city took place in the reign of Titus, and the city rose again to magnificence. Rome attained, however, its highest point of architectural splendor in the reign of Hadrian (A. D. 117–138). Aurelian fortified the city with a wall adorned with fourteen gates, but after his death (A. D. 275) the city declined rapidly, while the later emperors deserted the capital to fix their residence in the provinces. The transfer of the seat of empire to Byzantium by Constantine gave the last fatal blow to the civic greatness of Rome.

Population.—The population in the most flourishing epoch was about two millions, a greater part of whom were foreigners.

QUESTIONS.—§ 128. What does Pliny say of Rome?—Who founded Rome?—When?—Where?—How many hills were included between the walls of Servius Tullius?—Name those hills.—How was the city called after them?—Into how many parts did Servius divide the city?—Name those parts.—When was the city burnt down for the first time?—When again?—How was the city rebuilt after the second conflagration?—When did the third conflagration happen?—When did Rome attain its highest splendor?—When did the city begin to decline?—What were the causes?—What gave the last blow to the civic greatness of Rome?—How large was the population in the most flourishing epoch?

ROME.

§ 129. **Capitoline Mt.**—A. The *Capitolium*, in its restricted sense, denoted the temple of Jupiter Capitoli'nus, situated on the North-East summit of an elevation, *Mons Tarpeius*, the Tarpeian Rock, whose South-Western point was occupied by the *Arx Tarpeia*, the Citadel, which were separated from each other by the Intermontium: in a more extended sense, it designated the whole hill, including the temple and the citadel, hence called *Mons Capitoli'nus.* The original temple of Jupiter Capitoli'nus was planned by Tarquinius Priscus and built by Tarquinius Superbus. This building was burnt down 83 B.C. Sulla soon restored it, but before a century had passed, this structure also became a prey to the flames. Domitian again rebuilt it, and this edifice stood till a very late period of the Empire.

QUESTIONS.—§ 129. What was meant by the Capitolium?—Who planned the original temple of Jupiter Capitolinus?—Who built it?—When was it destroyed?—Who restored it?—Who again restored it?

Beside this temple of Jupiter Capitoli'nus, there were several other temples and *sacella* on the North-Eastern summit:

(1.) The small *temple* of *Jupiter Feretrius*, one of the oldest in Rome:

(2.) The *temple* of *Fides*, founded by King Numa, and often used for assemblies of the senate:

(3.) The *temples* of *Mens* and *Venus Eryci'na*, erected according to sacred vows made after the battle at lake Trasime'nus.

B. On the South-Western point, or *Arx*, stood the *temple* of *Juno Mone'ta*, erected in 345 B.C. by Camillus, after he had heard the voice of the goddess advising (*monens*) that expiation should be made. The Roman coinage was subsequently executed in this temple. Hence the supposed origin of the English words, *mint, money*. The only profane building on the summit of the Capitoline Mount was the *Tabularium*, or Office of Records, which was afterward used for a salt-warehouse.

Forum.—At the eastern foot of the Capitoline Mount, was a deep basin, called the *Forum*, which formed the great centre of Roman life and business. Its northern boundary was formed by the celebrated *Via Sacra*. From its southern limit issued the two most remarkable streets of Rome, the *Vicus Jugarius* and *Vicus Tuscus*, in the latter of which the shopping of the city was chiefly done. A slightly elevated piece of ground at the north side of the Forum was distinguished by being appropriated to the most honorable uses. This was the *Comitium*, or the place where the *comitia curia'ta* were held, and the people were addressed by their leaders. South of the *Comitium* was the *Rostra*, or platform for public speaking, adorned with the *beaks* (*rostra*) of the ships taken from the Antia'tes (in 337 B.C.). Tullus Hostilius built on the Forum the *Curia Hostilia*, the

---

QUESTIONS.—What other temples were at the north-eastern part of the Capitoline Mount?—What temple was on its south-western summit?—What connection may Juno Moneta have with our English words, mint, money?—What was the only building not devoted to sacred uses on the Capitoline Mount?—Where was the Forum situated?—What streets issued from its southern limits?—What was the Comitium?—What were held here?—What was the Rostra?

place where the senate usually met through the time of the Republic. This building was ruined by fire in the time of Sulla, and rebuilt by his son Faustus. Cæsar caused it to be pulled down, and his successor erected on its site the *Curia Julia.* Under the Empire, several new *fora* were constructed by different emperors (*Forum Cæ'saris, Augusti, Nervæ, Traja'ni*), to which the different courts of justice were transferred, while the political business continued to be confined to the ancient forum.

§ **130. Mount Palatine.**—After the Capitolium and the Forum, the Palatine is the most interesting point of Rome, as having been the cradle of *the Eternal City*, the seat of its matured power, and also the residence of the emperors, when those emperors ruled the world. On its declivity toward the Capitoline (called *Ge'rmalus* or *Ce'rmalus*) was the famous *Ficus Rumina'lis*, or *Sacred Fig-tree*, under which Ro'mulus and Remus were discovered suckled by the wolf. The mount itself, from its excel-

ROMULUS AND REMUS.

QUESTIONS.—What was the Curia Hostilia?—When was it built?—When destroyed?—What was the Curia Julia?—After whom was it named?—What fora were constructed under the emperors?——§ 130. What two circumstances make Mount Palatine particularly interesting?—Where was the *Ficus Ruminalis?*—What was it?

lent and convenient situation, early became a fashionable quarter. Here were to be found the residences of Ci'cero, Catili'na, Antonius, and many other celebrated Romans. Augustus also had his residence on the Palatine, and, in process of time, the buildings erected by successive *emperors* monopolized the hill and excluded all private possessions, and Palatium came to signify a royal residence in general, and has given us our word *palace.*

Mount Aventine.—The Aventine, although regarded as an ill-omened neighborhood, contained several famous places. Here was the *Temple of Dia'na,* built by Servius Tullius as the sanctuary of all the cities belonging to the Latin League. These cities, by building their common temple on one of the Roman hills, tacitly acknowledged Rome's supremacy. Here also was the *Temple of Juno Regi'na,* built by Camillus, after the conquest of Veii, to lodge the wooden statue of the goddess which was carried away from the last-named city.

Circus Ma'ximus.—Between the Palatine and Aventine was the *Circus Ma'ximus,* where the Roman population from the earliest times witnessed horse-races and chariot contests. It was founded by Tarquinius Priscus, but remained in a very rude and imperfect state till the time of Julius Cæsar. Here the fire broke out that destroyed the city in the reign of Nero. The Circus was soon restored, then again burnt up; and finally rebuilt on the most magnificent scale by the emperor Trajan, being so enlarged as to accommodate between three and four hundred thousand people.

Mount Esquiline.—North-East of the Circus Ma'ximus and North of Mons Cælius (the residence of Tullus Hostilius) is the Mons Esquili'nus, famous as the scene of the murder of Servius

---

QUESTIONS.—What residences were on Mount Palatine?—What was the common sanctuary of the Latin League?—Who built it?—Where was it situated?—What other temple was on this mount?—By whom built?—For what purpose?—Where was the Circus Maximus situated?—For what was it used?—Who was its founder?—How many times was it destroyed?—Who rebuilt it on the most magnificent scale?—What number of people could it accommodate?—Where was the residence of Tullus Hostilius?—Where was this mount situated?—Who was murdered there?

Tullius by his inhuman daughter. Here was erected the *Tigillum Sororium*, by passing under which Horatius expiated the murder of his sister. On this hill also was the princely town-residence of Mæce'nas.

Colosse'um.—In the valley between Mons Cælius, Esquili'nus, and the Velia, was the *Amphithea'trum Flavium*, probably designed by Augustus, but built chiefly by *Flavius* Vespasia'nus, and called from the seventh century onward *Colosse'um*, either from its size, or from the *Colossus* of Nero, a marble statue upward of one hundred feet in height, which stood near the Amphitheatre, and the basement of which is still to be seen. This building can be compared in magnitude only to the Pyramids of Egypt, and is perhaps the most striking monument at once of the material greatness and the moral degradation of Rome under the Empire. It became the spot where prince and people met together to witness those sanguinary exhibitions, the degrading effects of which on the Roman character can hardly be overestimated. It was a building of an elliptical form, founded on fourscore arches, and rising with four successive orders of architecture to the height of a hundred and fifty-seven feet. The outside of the edifice was incrusted with marble and decorated with statues. The slopes of the vast concave, which formed the inside, were filled and surrounded with sixty or eighty rows of seats, also of marble, covered with cushions, and capable of receiving with ease about eighty thousand spectators. It occupies nearly six acres of ground. Its ruins were (A. D. 1750) consecrated to the Christians who were martyred in it.

§ **131. The Three Northern Hills.**—The three northern hills of Rome were the Viminal, Quirinal, and Pincian Hills. They were called *Colles*, while the others were called *Montes*. After the Capitoli'nus and Palati'nus, the Quirina'lis was the most

---

QUESTIONS.—What was the Tigillum Sororium?—Where was the Amphitheatrum Flavium situated?—Why was it so called?—Why termed the Colosseum?—For what was it intended?—Describe it.—What area does it cover?—To what use are its ruins consecrated?——§ 131. Name the three northern hills.—Were they called *montes*, or *colles?*

ancient quarter of the city. As the seat of the Sabine part of the population of Rome, it acquired importance in the period of its early history, which, however, it did not retain when the two nations had become thoroughly amalgamated. All its interesting traditions belong to the reign of Numa.

Thermæ.—Afterward, the Quirina'lis was adorned with the magnificent *Baths of Diocletia'nus*, far surpassing in size and splendor those of Titus and Caracalla. They were called *Thermæ*, and were entirely different from the *balneæ*, or ordinary bathing houses. For, beside baths, the Thermæ contained also *gymnasia*, for exercise and sport; *e'xedræ*, where the rhetorician, the poet, and the philosopher might display their skill; and splendid libraries for the learned. The library of the Thermæ Diocletia'næ was the *Ulpia Bibliothe'ca*, founded by Trajan.

Pincian Hill.—North of the Quirina'lis was the *Collis hortorum*, or *Mons Pincius*, with the famous *Gardens of Lucullus*, the scene of Messali'na's infamous marriage with Silius, and also of her death by order of Claudius.

Campus Martius.—Along the Tiber, West of the Quirinal and Pincian hills, and the Capitoline, was a grassy plain called the *Campus Martius*, or, as was more common, simply the *Campus*, on which the principal part of modern Rome stands. After the expulsion of the Tarquins, the northern portion of this plain was assigned to public use, and, soon afterward, also the southern portion, or Campus Flaminius. Here was the place of assemblage for the Roman people at the *comitia centuria'ta*, in which they exercised their right of electing the higher magistrates, of making laws, and of deciding upon war, and subsequently, of concluding peace with foreign nations. The

---

QUESTIONS.—What hill was the seat of the Sabine portion of the population of Rome?—In what period of Rome did it enjoy the greatest importance?—What baths were afterward situated on this hill?—What other public baths adorned Rome?—Describe these public baths or Thermæ.—Where were the famous gardens of Lucullus situated?—On what part of ancient Rome is the modern city principally built?—Where is it situated?—When was it assigned to public use?—What meetings were held here?—What were the *comitia centuriata?*

Campus was from the beginning of the republic adorned with several temples and altars, but its most magnificent ornaments were added during the imperial era, and chiefly by Marcus Vipsanius Agrippa, son-in-law of Augustus. The most celebrated is the *Pantheon of Agrippa,* which is still in so good a state of preservation as to serve for a place of public worship. Augustus also erected a few monuments on the Campus. Among them was the *Solarium Augusti,* which served as a gigantic gnomon, and, on an immense marble flooring that surrounded it, exhibited not only the hours, but also the increase and decrease of the days. In the Northern part of the Campus, between the Via Flaminia and the Tiber, he constructed the superb *Mausolé'um,* the sepulchre of the Cæsars up to the time of Hadrian, when it became completely filled. This emperor built a new one on the opposite side of the river, and this edifice, though stripped of its ornaments, still forms the fortress of modern Rome (*Castello di S. Angelo*).

§ 132. **Transtiberine District.**—This part of Rome did not belong to the *Urbs,* or city proper. It consisted of three parts: Jani'culum, Mons Vatica'nus, and I'nsula Tiberi'na. The *island* contained a celebrated *Temple of Æsculapius.* The Jani'culum and Vatica'nus contained but few temples, or other public buildings. After the time of Aurelian, the city was surrounded on all sides by walls which were provided with fourteen gates leading into the highways of the empire.

Roads.—The most celebrated was the *Via Appia,* the great southern road commenced by Appius Claudius Cæcus when Cen-

---

QUESTIONS.—By whom was the Campus Martius chiefly adorned?—Which of the buildings he erected is still standing?—Describe the Solarium Augusti.—Where did Augustus build his Mausoleum?—What was the Mausoleum?—Who built a second Mausoleum?—Why?—Where?—Is it still in a state of preservation?—What is its present use?—What its present name?——§ 132. What part of the city did not belong to the *urbs* proper?—What were its three parts?—At what period was the entire city surrounded by a wall?—With how many gates was it provided?—How many highroads radiated from the city?—Which is the most celebrated?—By whom was it built?

sor (312 B.C.). It issued from the Porta Cape'na, and at first terminated at Capua, but was afterward extended to Beneventum, and finally thence to Brundisium. Another highway to Beneventum was the *Via Lati'na*. Next in importance is the *Via Flaminia*, the great northern road, begun in the censorship of C. Flaminius, and carried ultimately to Ari'minum.

Bridges.—Rome possessed eight or nine bridges, the most celebrated of which was the *Pons Sublicius*, built on *piles* (*sublicæ*), by Ancus Marcius, and which connected the Urbs with the Jani'culum. It was considered of such religious importance, that it was under the special care of the Ponti'fices, and was repaired from time to time even down to the reign of Antoni'nus Pius.

Aquæductus or **Aquæ.**—A great nuisance in Rome was the unwholesomeness of the water, both of the Tiber and of the wells sunk in the city. This led to the construction of aqueducts in order to supply the town with the pure water from the hills which surround the Campagna. The first was made 313 B.C., and the number was afterward increased to fourteen. These Aqueducts were artificial channels, supported on solid masonry and carried across valleys, rivers, and hills, on arches and embankments, or through tunnels and bridges. This method of conveying water was adopted by the Romans not because they were ignorant of the laws of hydrostatics, for they knew them, but because it was the best method where water was to be carried in large quantities, for a considerable distance, and over great inequalities of ground. This very plan has been preferred by

---

QUESTIONS.—When was the Via Appia built?—What direction did it take?—What was crossed by it?—Where was its original termination?—To what town was it afterward extended?—What other highway terminated at Beneventum?—What was the great northern road?—How many bridges did Rome possess?—Which was the most celebrated?—Who built it?—To whose care was it intrusted?—How long did it exist?—What great nuisance existed at Rome?—What was done to counteract it?—When was the first established?—What was the greatest number of aqueducts under the empire?—Describe a Roman aqueduct.—Why was it so built and what return to this method has recently been made?

modern science in the case of the Croton Aqueduct, built in 1837–42, to convey the water of the river Croton a distance of forty miles, for the supply of New York. The water, after being used, was discharged, together with the foul water of the city, through the Cloa'cæ into the Tiber.

Cloa'cæ.—The most celebrated of these drains was the *Cloa'ca Ma'xima*, which is said to have been the work of Tarquinius Priscus, and which was formed to carry off the waters brought down from the adjacent hills into the Vela'brum, a street on the Aventine, and the valley of the Forum. The mouth where it reaches the Tiber, nearly opposite one extremity of the *I'nsula Tiberi'na*, still remains in the state mentioned by Pliny (H. N. xxxvi. 15,25). It is about fourteen feet in diameter.

The Basi'licæ (for the name, comp. the Athenian *στοὰ βασίλειος*, the *tribunal* of the second archon, who was styled *ἄρχων βασιλεύς*), twenty-one in number, were buildings serving both as *courts of law* and also as exchanges, or places of meeting for merchants. The oldest and most celebrated was the Basi'lica Porcia, built in 184 B.C. by Marcus Porcius Cato.

Columnæ were columns erected to commemorate persons or events. The most important of these were the Columna Rostra'ta, erected in honor of Caius Duilius, the first Roman who conquered the Carthaginians on the sea (261 B.C.); and the column of Trajan, in the centre of the Forum Traja'num, one hundred and seventy feet in height, and the finest monument of the kind now existing in the world.

§ 133. CAMPANIA.

This region is one of the most beautiful and fertile in the world, and is unquestionably the fairest portion of Italy. Greek and Roman writers vie with each other in celebrating its natural

---

QUESTIONS.—What was the use of the Cloacæ?—Describe the Cloaca Maxima.—What were Basilicæ?—Which was the oldest?—What was the use of the Columnæ?—Name some of the most celebrated.—— § 133. Describe Campania.

advantages, the fertility of its soil, the beauty of its landscapes, the softness of its climate, and the excellence of its harbors.

Boundaries.—North and East, SAMNIUM; South-East, the SI'LARUS; South and West, TUSCUM MARE; North-West, LATIUM.

Towns.—(1.) LITERNUM, situated on the sea-coast between Cumæ and the mouth of the Vulturnus. Scipio Africa'nus here ended his life in voluntary exile (182 B. C.). He caused the following epitaph to be written on his tomb·

Ingrata patria, ne ossa quidem mea habes:

(2.) CUMÆ, situated on the sea-coast, North of Promontorium Mise'num or Mise'ni. It was one of the most ancient, as well as celebrated, of the Greek colonies in Italy. The period of its greatest prosperity was probably from 700 to 500 B. C., when it was the first city in Southern Italy, and had extended its dominion over the whole of Campania. After 338 B. C. it enjoyed the Roman franchise. It was the residence of the famous Sibyl (*Cumæa Sibylla*, Virg. Æn. VI. 98):

(3.) MISE'NUM, a town near Promontorium Mise'num. This was made by Augustus the permanent station of the fleet of the Tyrrhene Sea. Before this time, it had become already a favorite site for the villas of wealthy Romans:

(4.) BA'IÆ, celebrated for its warm baths. It was also a favorite resort of the Roman nobles. The emperor Hadrian died here (A. D. 138):

(5.) PUTE'OLI, formerly Dicæarchi'a (*Δικαιάρχεια*), a colony of Cumæ, on the sea-shore. Cicero had a villa in its neighborhood, called the Academia, or Puteola'num:

(6.) NEA'POLIS (*Νεαπόλις*, *Naples*), formerly Parthe'nope, a

---

QUESTIONS.—What are the boundaries of Campania?—Name some of its towns.—Where is Liternum situated?—Who died here in exile?—When?—Where was Cumæ situated?—When did it enjoy its greatest prosperity?—When did it receive the Roman franchise?—Where was the naval station in the Tyrrhene Sea?—For what was Baiæ celebrated?—Where was Cicero's Academia situated?

colony of Cumæ. It was, for a considerable period, the residence of Virgil, who finished his Georgics there. His remains were transferred thither from Brundisium where he died:

(7.) HERCULANEUM, at the base of Mount Vesuvius. In the reign of Titus it was buried by an eruption of Vesuvius (A. D. 79). Its exact site remained long unknown. But in 1738, the remains of the ancient theatre were accidentally discovered in sinking a well in the village of Resina:

(8.) POMPE'II, overwhelmed by the same eruption of Vesuvius. It was not till 1748 that an accidental discovery drew attention to the remains of Pompe'ii, and since 1755 it has been regularly excavated to a considerable extent:

(9.) SALERNUM (*Salerno*), situated on the northern shore of the Gulf of Pondonia, now called the Gulf of *Salerno*. Its celebrated School of Medicine (*Schola Salernitana*) belongs to the epoch of the Middle Ages:

(10.) CAPUA, the capital of Campania, situated about two miles from the river Vulturnus, whence its Tuscan name, *Vulturnum*. It was founded by the Etruscans (800 B. C.), and fell (423 B. C.) into the hands of the Samni'tes, who, eighty years later, were compelled to implore the help of Rome against their more hardy brethren, who had continued to inhabit their native mountain-fastnesses. They received the help asked for, but at the price of their liberty. After the battle of Cannæ (216 B. C.) the inhabitants of Capua opened their gates to Hannibal, who passed the following winter there. The luxurious quarters thus offered to the troops produced a highly injurious effect upon their discipline. Five years afterward, the faithless city was

---

QUESTIONS.—Who resided at Neapolis?—What did he finish there?—Where is Herculaneum situated?—When was it buried under the ashes of Vesuvius?—When was it brought to light again?—When was Pompeii discovered?—Where is Salernum situated?—Where Capua?—What is its Tuscan name?—When and by whom was it founded?—When did it fall into the hands of the Samnites?—How did it fall under the power of the Romans?—What part did it take in the Second Punic War?—What was the result of this sojourn upon Hannibal's army?—How were they punished by the Romans?

compelled to surrender to the Romans, who butchered its nobles and removed its citizens, and filled the city with strangers and Roman settlers, who were made subject to the jurisdiction of a Roman prefect. It afterward became a Roman colony. Capua was at an early period celebrated for its gladiatorial shows, and appears to have been a favorite training-place for those who took active part in them:

(11.) NOLA, situated in the interior, in the plain between the Vesuvius and the Apennines. In its neighborhood the Romans, under Marcellus, gained their first victory over Ha'nnibal. Augustus died there (A. D. 14). According to a well-known anecdote related by Aulus Gellius (VII. 20), it was originally mentioned with great praise by Virgil in the Georgics; but the people of Nola having given offence to the poet, he struck out the name of their city, and changed the verse so as to read:

> *Talem dives arat Capua et vicina Vesevo*
> Ora *jugo et vacuis Clanius non æquus Acerris.*—II. 224 seq.

instead of *Nola* jugo:

(12.) NUCERIA, situated on the banks of the river Sarnus. It was razed to the ground by Ha'nnibal (216 B. C.). It was afterward rebuilt, and, at the beginning of the Christian era, was one of the most flourishing towns of Campania.

§ 134. MAGNA GRÆCIA. (*Ἑλλὰς ἡ μεγάλη.*)

Name.—The name *Great Greece* (first found in Polybius c. 150 B. C.) was given to the assemblage of cities on the Southern shores of Italy, in consequence of the numerous and flourishing colonies which were founded by the Greeks in that part of the country. The name seems to have been bestowed at an early period, while the Greek colonies in Italy were at the height of

---

QUESTIONS.——Where was Nola situated?—Who died here?—What anecdote connects Nola and the poet Virgil?—Describe the situation of Nuceria.—What is said about it?——§ 134. Why did Southern Italy receive the name of Magna Græcia?—When?

their power and prosperity, and before Hellas had attained its fullest greatness.

Boundaries.—North and East, ADRIA'TICUM MARE; South, SINUS TARENTI'NUS; West, TUSCUM MARE and the SI'LARUS; North-West, CAMPANIA, HIRPI'NI, SAMNIUM, FRENTA'NI.

Divisions.—APULIA, CALABRIA, LUCANIA, BRUTTII.

APULIA. (nearly, Ἰαπυγία.)

Boundaries.—North and East, ADRIA'TICUM MARE; South, CALABRIA and LUCANIA; West, SAMNIUM.

Promontory.—GARGA'NUS (*Monte Gargano*), a projecting headland, extending not less than thirty-five miles from West to East, formed by a mountain elevated more than five thousand feet above the sea.

Rivers.—The TIFERNUS, the boundary toward the Frenta'ni; the FRENTO, and AU'FIDUS.

Productions.—The great plains of northern Apulia are exexceedingly fertile, and specially adapted to the rearing of sheep, which was one of the main sources of the country's wealth.

Population.—It contained three different nations:

(1.) *A'ppuli*, a branch of the great Oscan race.

(2.) *Daunii*, a branch of the Pelasgian race.

(3.) *Pencetii*, or *Pœdi'culi*, also a branch of the Pelasgian race.

The Daunii inhabited the country between the Frento and Au'fidus, and the Peucetii the country South of the Au'fidus.

Towns.—(1.) ARPI, situated in the centre of the great Apulian plain. It was one of the most important places in the history of the Second Punic War. It opened its gates to Ha'nnibal after the battle of Cannæ, but was reconquered by Fabius Ma'ximus (213 B. C.):

QUESTIONS.—Give the boundaries of Magna Græcia.—Its divisions.—How was Apulia bounded?—Describe the promontory of Garganus.—Name some of its rivers.—What is said about its fertility?—What nations did it contain?—Where did the Daunii live?—Where the Pencetii?—Name some of its towns.—Where is Arpi situated?

(2.) LUCERIA, situated West of Arpi, the residence of the prætor of Apulia. Its neighborhood was, and is yet, celebrated for the quantity as well as quality of its wool:

(3.) SALAPIA, situated on the coast of the Adriatic, burnt to the ground in the Social War:

(4.) CANUSIUM, situated near the right bank of the Au'fidus. C. Norba'nus was defeated there by Sulla (83 B. C.):

(5.) CANNÆ, a small town on the South bank of the Au'fidus, celebrated for the memorable defeat of the Romans by Ha'nnibal (216 B. C.):

(6.) AS'CULUM, situated in the interior; the scene of the great battle between Pyrrhus, king of Epi'rus, and the Romans (269 B. C.):

(7.) VENUSIA, situated on the Appian Way, South of the Au'fidus. It was the birthplace of Horace (65 B. C.).

§ 135. CALABRIA. (*ἡ Ἰαπυγία* or *Μεσσαπία.*)

It was also called Messapia, Iapygia, and Sallentia. It formed the South-Eastern peninsula of Italy.

Productions.—Olives, grapes, and honey; it was celebrated also for its sheep and horses.

Inhabitants.—Messapians and Sallentines, both Pelasgic races.

Towns.—(1.) BRUNDISIUM (*Βρεντέσιον, Brindisi*), situated on the Adriatic coast, the chief naval station of the Romans after 229 B. C. Virgil died here on his return from Greece (19 B. C.):

(2.) HYDRUNTUM (*Ἱδροῦς, Otranto*), a port on the coast of the Adriatic, which derived importance from being the point of Italy nearest to the coast of Greece:

QUESTIONS.—Where is Luceria situated?—For what was it celebrated?—Where is Salapia situated?—Where Canusium?—What battle took place here?—Where was Cannæ situated?—What battle took place there?—When?—Where was Asculum situated?—Where Venusia?——§ 135. What part of Italy formed Calabria?—What is said of its productions?—Inhabitants?—What was the chief naval station on the Adriatic coast?—Who died here?—What gave importance to Hydruntum?

(3.) TARENTUM (*Τάρας, Taranto*), situated on the Northern shore of the Sinus Tarenti'nus. It was a colony of Sparta, and owed its rapid rise to the excellence of its harbor, which was the only safe harbor of any extent on the Tarentine Gulf. It thus became the chief emporium for the commerce of all this part of Italy. In 272 B.C. it fell into the hands of the Romans. It was the birthplace of Livius Androni'cus, the earliest dramatic poet of the Romans (flourished 238 B.C.), and also of the Pythagore'an philosopher, Archy'tas:

(4.) MANDURIA, situated East of Tarentum, remarkable for the defeat and death of Archida'mus, king of Sparta (338 B.C.)., which occurred on the same day with the more celebrated battle of Chærone'a:

(5.) RUDIÆ, South of Brundisium, where Ennius, the father of epic poetry among the Romans, and indeed the parent of Roman literature, was born (239 B.C.).

§ 136. LUCANIA. (ἡ Λευκανία.)

Boundaries.—North, the SIL'ARUS; East, PENCETIA; South, SINUS TARENTI'NUS, the LAÜS, and BRUTTII; West, TUSCUM MARE.

Inhabitants.—The original inhabitants were Pelasgians, subsequently subdued by the Greek colonists who gradually encircled the whole of its sea-coast. They were conquered at length by a Sabellian race known as the Luca'ni, whose name does not occur in Italian history until 396 B.C.

Productions.—It was a very rough country, and large tracts were given up to pasture. Its herds of swine formed an important part of the supplies of Rome. Wild boars roamed on its

---

QUESTIONS.—Where was Tarentum situated?—Of what city was it a colony?—To what did it owe its rapid rise?—When did it fall into the hands of the Romans?—Name two famous persons born at Tarentum. ——§ 136. How is Lucania bounded?—What were its original inhabitants?—By whom were they surrounded?—Who at length conquered this country?—When does the name Lucani occur?—What is the character of the country?—What were its productions?

mountains, and also bears which were sent up to the imperial amphitheatres. Almost the only level region was the broad plain around the Gulf of Tarentum from the Bra'danus down to the Siris, which was, in ancient times, one of the most fertile spots of Italy, but now desolate and unhealthful. Lucania also produced wine (*vina Thuri'na*).

Towns.—(1.) METAPONTUM (*Μεταπόντιον*) was situated on the Gulf of Tarentum, between the rivers Bra'danus and Casuentus. The city was an Achæan colony, settled about 700 B.C. It was one of the chief seats of the philosophy of Pytha'goras, and his tomb was shown here in the time of Cicero:

(2.) HERACLE'A (*Ἡράκλεια*), situated on the Gulf of Tarentum, between the A'ciris and Siris, a colony of Tarentines and Thurians. The Congress (*πανήγυρις*) of the Italiot Greeks met here. In the neighborhood of this city, Pyrrhus defeated the Romans for the first time (280 B.C.). It is supposed to have been the birthplace of the celebrated painter Zeuxis:

(3.) SY'BARIS (*Σύβαρις*), situated on the Western shore of the Tarentine Gulf, between the rivers Crathis and Sy'baris. It was an Achæan colony founded about 720 B.C., and considered as the oldest of all the Greek colonies. In the sixth century B.C. it was the wealthiest and most powerful of the Hellenic settlements, and ruled over more than twenty-five cities. The city was destroyed by the Crotoniats, who turned the course of the river Crathis, so that it inundated the site of the city and buried the ruins under its deposits (510 B.C.). The descendants of those citizens who escaped the destruction founded, seventy years afterward, in combination with the Athenians:

QUESTIONS.—What is the difference between the ancient and present state of Lucania?—Name some of the towns of Lucania.—Where is Metapontum situated?—When was it founded?—By whom?—Whose tomb was pointed out here?—Where were the Romans for the first time defeated by Pyrrhus?—Where was this city situated?—What famous artist was perhaps born here?—Where was Sybaris situated?—When and by whom founded?—When did it enjoy its greatest prosperity?—When was it destroyed?—In what manner?—By whom?—When, and by whom, was Thurii founded?

(4.) THURII (Θούριον), within a short distance of the site of the old city. Among the earliest colonists were Hero'dotus, the historian; and Lysias, the orator. The new city reached its greatest prosperity about 400 B.C. The rise of the Bruttian race was the principal reason of the decay of the city. At length (204 B.C.) it was conquered by the Romans, and became afterward a Roman colony, under the name of Copiæ :

(5.) BUXENTUM, situated on the West coast, on the Gulf of Laüs. Its Hellenic name was Pyxus (Πυξοῦς). It was a colony from Rhegium, and the usual port of transit to Sicily :

(6.) ELEA, or VELIA (Ἐλέα), situated on the Tyrrhene Sea, between Posidonia and Pyxus, celebrated for its school of philosophy, generally known as the *Eleatic*, founded by Xeno'phanes of Co'lophon. It was the birthplace of his successors, Parme'nides and Zeno :

(7.) PÆSTUM (Παῖστον or Παιστός), or POSIDONIA (Ποσειδωνία), situated on the Tyrrhene Sea, a little south of the mouth of the Si'larus. It was a colony from Sy'baris. The city was celebrated for its roses, which possessed the peculiarity of flowering twice a year (*biferique rosaria Pœsti.* Virg Georg. IV. 119), and surpassed all others in fragrance; roses now grow wild among the ruins and are said to flower regularly both in May and November. The ruins are still known as *Pesto*, and are much visited. They consist principally of the walls of the city and three temples standing within them :

(8.) NUMISTRO, situated in the Northern part of the country, near the frontiers of Apulia. It was the scene of an undecisive battle between Ha'nnibal and Marcellus (210 B.C.) :

(9.) GRUMENTUM, situated in the interior of the province.

QUESTIONS.—Where was Thurii founded?—Who were among its earliest colonists?—When did it reach its greatest prosperity?—When was it conquered by the Romans?—Where was Bruxentum situated?—Where Elea?—What school of philosophy arose here?—Where was Pæstum situated?—For what was it celebrared?—What is said of the ruins of Pæstum?—What battle was fought near Numistro?—What battle near Grumentum?

The Carthaginian general, Hanno, was defeated under its walls by Tiberius Sempronius Longus (215 B. C.).

§ 137. BRUTTII. (Βρεττία.)

Boundaries.—North, the LAÜS and THURII; East, SINUS TARENTI'NUS; South, MARE SI'CULUM; West, TUSCUM MARE and FRETUM SI'CULUM.

The name *Italy* was originally confined to this peninsula.

Inhabitants.—The original inhabitants were the Pelasgic tribe of the Œnotrians, among whom the Greeks settled (700 B. C.). Three centuries after the first settlement of the Greeks, the Œnotrians were conquered by the Sabellian tribe of the Lucanians. A portion of them fled to the mountains and there united with Lucanian exiles and fugitives and destroyed the Lucanian dominion, which had lasted only fifty years. The Lucanians called them *Bruttii* (said to have signified *rebels*, in the Lucanian), which name was afterward adopted by themselves (356 B. C), and in the *classical* Latin writers it designates as well the country as the people. They became a powerful nation about 282 B. C. They joined Pyrrhus, Ha'nnibal, and in fact every adversary of Rome, till at length they were subdued by the Romans at the close of the Second Punic War.

Productions.—It was celebrated for its forests, which produced both timber and pitch, which were in great request for ship-building.

Towns. (1.) CROTO'NA (Κρότων, *Crotone*), situated on the East coast of the peninsula, at the mouth of the Æsa'rus. It was founded by a colony of Achæans, and became one of the

QUESTIONS.—§ 137. To what country was the name of Italy originally confined?—How is it bounded?—Name its oldest inhabitants.—Who settled among them?—When?—Who conquered the Œnotrians?—When?—How long did this foreign dominion last?—Who destroyed it?—What is said to be the origin and meaning of the name of Bruttii?—When were they at the height of their power?—When were they subdued by the Romans?—What were its productions?—Name some of its towns.—Describe the situation of Crotona.—By whom was it founded?

most celebrated Greek colonies in Southern Italy. It rose rapidly to great prosperity, and extended its dominion across the Bruttian peninsula. About the middle of the sixth century B.C. Pytha'goras established himself here, and he and his disciples soon exercised the greatest political influence, which lasted till the general expulsion of the Pythagore'ans from the cities of Southern Italy. During the time of this Pythagore'an influence, the Crotoniats, headed by the athlete Milo, destroyed Sy'baris:

(2.) LOCRI EPIZEPHYRII (*Λοκροί*), situated on the South-Eastern coast of the Bruttian peninsula, a Locrian colony, chiefly celebrated for the legislation of Zaleucus, who published the most ancient *written* code of laws conferred on any Greek city (666 B.C.). It was the inhabitants of this city that fought in the famous battle of the Sagras (see p. 222):

(3.) RHEGIUM (*Ῥήγιον*), situated near the Southern end of the peninsula, in the vicinity of a promontory of the same name, where Sicily was said by the ancients to have been *torn from* the mainland, Italy, *ἀπορραγῆναι*, Æsch. ap. Strab. VI., p. 258. So Virgil:

> *Haec loca vi quondam et vasta convulsa ruina—*
> *Tantum ævi longinqua valet mutare vetustas—*
> *Dissiluisse ferunt, cum protenus utraque tellus*
> *Una foret.* Æn. III. 414 seqq.

Thus, the name *Ῥήγιον* was connected with *ῥήγνυμι*, *to break, to burst.* Rhegium was a Chalcidian colony. The old city was destroyed by Dionysius and the inhabitants sold as slaves (387 B.C.). The site was soon reöccupied, and the place continued to exist as a considerable city throughout the period of the Roman empire. It was governed in accordance with the laws of Charondas until they were abolished by the tyrant Ana'xilas.

QUESTIONS.—How far did Crotona extend its dominion?—Who established himself here?—When?—When were his adherents expelled?—Describe the situation of Locri Epizephyrii.—For what was the colony chiefly celebrated?—Who were the conquerors in the battle of the Sagras?—Where was Rhegium situated?—Whence did it derive its name?—By whom was it founded?—Whose laws did they use?

Until a late period of the middle ages, the Greek language was spoken at Rhegium.

(4.) The other Greek colonies were:

a. *Scyllacium*, an Athenian colony.

b. *Caulonia* and *Teri'na*, colonies of Croto'na.

c. *Me'dema* and *Hipponium*, colonies of Locri.

(5.) Other towns: PETELIA, CONSENTIA, and PANDOSIA, which was the ancient residence of the Œnotrian princes.

§ 138. ISLANDS OF ITALY.

SICILIA, SARDINIA, CO'RSICA.

I. SICILIA. (ἡ Σικελία.)

Situation.—South-West of Italy and North of Africa.

Names.—This island seems to be designated *Thrinacie* (Θρινακίη) in Homer, and *Trinacria* (Τρινακρία) is said by Thucy'dides to have been its early name. These forms have commonly been thought to describe Sicilia as a *triangular* island, or island of *three promontories* (τρεῖς-ΑΚΗ, ἄκρον), just as the Romans used *tri'quetrus*, *three-cornered*, to signify *Sicilian*. It was afterward called *Sicania* after its *western* inhabitants, the *Sica'ni*, who were probably from Iberia; and finally *Sicilia*, after the *Si'culi* (Σικελοί), who are said to have immigrated from Central Italy.

Capes.—The three promontories which are supposed to have given the name of Trinacria to the island were PELO'RUS, or -*um*, North-East; PACHY'NUM or PACHY'NUS, to the South-East, and LILYBÆUM, on the West. Beside these, on the North-West was DRE'PANUM, and just West of Pelo'rus PHALACRIUM.

Rivers.—Most of the rivers are mere mountain torrents. The most important are:

QUESTIONS.—What language was used at Rhegium?—Name some other Greek colonies.—Some other towns.——§ 138. Where is Sicilia situated?—Give an account of its names.—Name the three capes.—What others are mentioned?

(1.) SYMÆTHUS, which flows around the base of Mount Ætna. It formed the boundary between Leonti'ni and Ca'tana:

(2.) HI'MERA: the name of two rivers both of which rise in the centre of the island, and which, by many ancient writers, were regarded as one and the same. The Southern river is the largest, and also the most remarkable. On its banks Aga'thocles completely defeated the Carthaginians (311 B.C.):

(3.) HA'LYCUS, the Eastern boundary of the Carthaginian dominions in Sicily:

(4.) HYPSAS, the name of two rivers, both in the Southern part of the island:

(5.) ANA'PUS, which flows into the great harbor of Syracu'sæ. Its marshy borders always proved fatal to those laying siege to the city:

(6.) ASSI'NARUS, a small stream South of Syracu'sæ, memorable as the scene of the final catastrophe of the Athenian armament in Sicily (Thuc. VII. 84):

(7.) CRIMISSUS, situated in the neighborhood of Segesta, celebrated for the conquest of Timoleon over the Carthaginians (339 B.C.).

Fountain.—ARETHU'SA, at the South-West extremity of Ortygia, a small island lying before Syracu'sæ, and forming its harbors. This fountain is still visible as described by Ci'cero, Verr. IV. 53: *In hac insula extrema est fons aquæ dulcis, cui nomen Arethusa est, incredibili magnitudine plenissimus piscium.* It is now a copious spring, but perhaps not so large as in ancient times. It was famous in mythology, and was said by the poets to communicate with the river Alphe'us in Elis, which last was said to flow under the surface of the sea to this island:

Extremum hunc, Arethusa, mihi concede laborem—
Sic tibi, cum fluctus subterlabere Sicanos,
Doris amara suam non intermisceat undam.
Virg. Ecl. X. 1–4, 5.

QUESTIONS.—Name some of the rivers of Sicilia.—What is remarked about the Himera?—What battle was fought on its banks?—What battle was fought near the Crimissus?—Give an account of the Arethusa.

Extent.—The ancients generally regarded it as the largest island known to them; a view which turns out to be correct, since its area, being 10,536 square miles (about equal to that of the state of Vermont), exceeds that of the island of Sardinia by about 1200 square miles.

Mountains.—The greater part of the island is mountainous. and the mountains seem to have been a continuation of the Apennines. The principal mountain range is formed by the NEBRO'DES MONS. The highest and most remarkable mountain peaks are:

(1.) ÆTNA, situated in the North-East part of the island, adjoining the sea-coast between Tauromenium on the North and Ca'tana on the South. Its volcanic phenomena early attracted the attention of the ancients. The following description from the pen of Virgil is considered one of the very best, and as such often imitated, not only by ancient, but by modern poets:

—sed horrificis juxta tonat Ætna ruinis,
Interdumque atram prorumpit ad æthera nubem,
Turbine fumantem piceo et candente favilla,
Attollitque globos flammarum, et sidera lambit:
Interdum scopulos avulsaque viscera montes
Erigit eructans, liquefactaque saxa sub auras
Cum gemitu glomerat, fundoque exæstuat imo.
Æn. III. 571 seqq:

(2.) ERYX or E'RYCUS (*S. Giulano*), situated on the Western side of Sicily, near the sea-coast. On its side was the town of Eryx, and on its summit stood the celebrated temple of Aphrodi'te (*Venus*), who thence derived the name of *Venus Eryci'na*, as she is often styled by Latin writers, and even in Rome a particular temple was dedicated to her.

Climate.—The climate is intermediate between that of Italy and Africa. In ancient times it was generally considered healthful, but it is now much subject to malaria.

QUESTIONS.—What is the principal mountain range of Sicilia?—Where is Mount Ætna situated?—What is said of its volcanic phenomena?—What goddess was worshipped at Eryx?—Describe the climate of Sicily.

Productions.—It was celebrated in antiquity for its exceeding productiveness and fertility. It was even said to be the native country of wheat (Diod. V. 2). It produced excellent honey; also, saffron, grapes, olives, and other fruits. Its cattle, sheep, and, above all, its horses, particularly those of Agrigentum, were very celebrated.

§ **139. Inhabitants.**—The oldest inhabitants were the Sica'ni, who, three centuries before the settlements of the Greeks, were driven to the North-Western part of the island by the Si'culi, who had passed from the Bruttian peninsula to the island, to which they afterward gave their own name. There were among them three Phœnician settlements, the remnant of the once numerous colonies of that people in Sicilia who were withdrawn on the arrival of the Greeks, a circumstance which opened a new era in the history of the island. The settlement of these Greek colonies began about the middle of the eighth century B. C., and was continued for above a century and a half. They rose to considerable power and importance, and enjoyed a high degree of wealth and prosperity, extending their dominion over a considerable part of the adjoining regions, and reducing to subjection a large population of native origin.

Cities.—The Greek colonies established directly by Greece were five in number, each of which sent forth other colonies:

(1.) NAXOS, which founded Leonti'ni, Ca'tana, Calli'polis, and Eubœa:

(2.) SYRACU'SÆ, which founded Acræ, Casme'næ, and Cama-ri'na:

(3.) ME'GARA HYBLÆA, which founded Seli'nus:

(4.) GELA, which founded Agrigentum:

(5.) ZANCLE (afterward Messa'na), which founded Hi'mera.

QUESTIONS.—Describe the productions of Sicilia. —— § 139. Who were its oldest inhabitants?—Who came afterward from Bruttii?—What third race was living in Sicily?—At what time did the Greeks begin to settle it?—What five colonies were sent out directly from Greece?—What colonies were founded by Naxos —What by Syracusæ?—What by Megara?—What by Gela?—What by Zancle?

A.——Along the East coast between Pelo'rus and Pachy'num were the following towns, enumerated in their order from North to South: Messa'na, Tauromenium, Naxos, Acium, Ca'tana, Tro'tilum, Me'gara Hyblæa, Syracu'sæ, Calli'polis, and Eubœa.

(1.) MESSA'NA (*Μεσσήνη* by Greek writers; *Μεσσάνα* by the inhabitants), situated at the North-Eastern extremity of the island, nearly opposite Rhegium, from which it was divided by the Fretum Si'culum, in which were the famous Scylla and Charybdis, two rocks, the former toward Italy, and the latter toward Sicily. This city was founded, under the name of Zancle, by Chalcidian settlers, about 735 B.C. Two centuries afterward, the inhabitants fell under the power of Ana'xilas, king of Rhegium, who changed the name from Zancle to that of Messa'na (493 B.C.) in remembrance of the land of his ancestors. A hundred years afterward the flourishing city was completely destroyed by the Carthaginians. It rose slowly again to prosperity, but only to undergo a yet more cruel fate. The mercenary troops of Aga'thocles, tyrant of Syracu'sæ, being compelled to leave the latter city, made themselves masters of the unhappy place by murdering its male inhabitants, who had received them with the utmost cordiality. They now assumed the name of Mamerti'ni (282 B.C.), and rapidly extended their power over the whole North-Eastern corner of Sicily. They came in collision with Syracu'sæ, were defeated by its king, Hi'ero (270 B.C.), and, when they were on the point of surrendering their city, they invoked the help of the Romans, which circumstance ultimately brought about the celebrated Punic Wars:

(2.) TAUROMENIUM (*Ταυρομένιον*). It was founded by the survivors of the Chalcidian colony of Naxos, after the destruction of Naxos by Dionysius:

(3.) CA'TANA, in inscriptions, CA'TINA (*Κατάνη*, *Catania*),

QUESTIONS.—What cities were situated between Pelorus and Pachynum?—Where was Messana situated?—By whom was it founded?—Under what name?—When was its name changed?—Why?—When was it destroyed?—By whom?—Who were the Mamertini?—When did they implore the help of the Romans?—What was the consequence of this?—Who founded Tauromenium?—Where was Catana situated?

situated almost at the foot of Mount Ætna, famous as the head-quarters of the Athenian armament in the great Sicilian expedition:

(4.) SYRACU'SÆ (see page 277).

§ **140.** B.——West of Pachy'num were: Camari'na, Gela, Agrigentum, Seli'nus, and Lilybæum.

(1.) GELA (*Γέλα*), founded (690 B.C.) by a joint colony of Cretans and Rhodians, on the banks of the river Gela. Æ'schylus, when driven from Athens, retired to this city, where he died and was buried (456 B.C.). The inhabitants of Gela paid great respect to his memory:

(2.) AGRIGENTUM (*Ἀκράγας*), founded by a colony from Gela (582 B.C.). About 570 B.C. it fell under the power of the tyrant Pha'laris, the supposed author of a series of Letters, whose spurious character was demonstrated by Bentley at the close of the seventeenth century in his *Dissertation upon the Epistles of Pha'laris* (1699), one of the most ingenious and learned works ever written. The city was taken and destroyed by the Carthaginians (405 B.C.), and never regained its former importance. It was celebrated for the beauty of its architecture, and the splendor and variety of its buildings, and was called by Pindar *the fairest of mortal cities:*

(3.) SELI'NUS (*Σελινοῦς*), the most westerly of the Greek colonies, was founded by Me'gara Hyblæa. It was destroyed by the Carthaginians (409 B.C.):

(4.) LILYBÆUM (*Λιλύβαιον*), situated on the promontory of the same name, was the most westerly point of the island, and the nearest to Africa, being immediately opposite the port of Carthage. This led the Carthaginians to spare no pains for its defence, and it twice became the last bulwark of their power in Sicily.

QUESTIONS.—§ 140. What cities were situated west of Cape Pachynum?—Who founded Gela?—When?—Who was buried here?—When was Agrigentum founded?—When destroyed?—For what was it celebrated?—Who founded Selinus?—Who destroyed it?—What was the bulwark of the Carthaginian power?—Where was it situated?

C.——Between Lilybæum and Pelo'rus were: Dre'panum, Eryx, Panormus, Thermæ, Hi'mera, and Mylæ.

(1.) DRE'PANUM (Δρέπανον), situated at the North-Western extremity of the island, a few miles from Mount Eryx. It was the scene of the funeral games, celebrated by Æne'as in honor of his father (Virg. Æn. V.):

(2.) PANORMUS (Πάνορμος, *Palermo*), one of the chief seats of the Phœnician power on the island, and the capital of the Carthaginian possessions. Under its walls Ha'sdrubal was defeated by Metellus (250 B C.). Its Greek name, which signifies *quite good for anchorage*, was probably given to it for the excellence of its spacious bay (*Bay of Palermo*):

(3.) HI'MERA (Ἱμέρα), a colony of Zancle. In its neighborhood, the Carthaginians were defeated by Gelo of Syracu'sæ, in a battle which was regarded by the Greeks of Sicily as worthy of comparison with the contemporary victory of Sa'lamis (480 B.C.) Seventy-two years afterward, the city was destroyed by the Carthaginians, and the citizens who survived this calamity settled at Thermæ (Θέρμαι):

(4.) MYLÆ (Μυλαί), celebrated for two important naval battles which were fought in its neighborhood:

a. The victory of Duilius over the Carthaginians, which was the first naval victory of the Romans (260 B.C.);

b. The victory of Agrippa, the naval commander of Octavian, over Sextus Pompeius (36 B.C.).

§ **141.** D.——The towns somewhat inland were: Segesta, Enna, Leonti'ni, Hybla.

(1.) SEGESTA, or EGESTA (Ἔγεστα), situated in the North-West part of the island, a few miles from the coast. The relief of this city from the oppression of Seli'nus and Syracu'sæ was the avowed object of the Athenian expedition to Sicily (416 B.C.),

---

QUESTIONS.—What cities were situated between Lilybæum and Pelorus?—Where was Drepanum situated?—What was the Carthaginian capital?—Who was here defeated?—What battle took place at the same time with the naval fight at Salamis?—When was Himera destroyed?—What naval battles were fought in the neighborhood of Mylæ?——§ 141. What towns were situated in the interior?—Where was Egesta situated?

which ended with the famous struggle between Syracu'sæ and Athe'næ, and the total defeat of the latter:

(2.) ENNA (Ἔννα), an ancient city, situated almost at *the centre of Sicily*, and hence called, *νήσου ὀμφαλός* (Callim.), *umbilicus Siciliæ* (Cic.). It contained a very celebrated temple of Ceres, which was much venerated by the Sicilians:

(3.) LEONTI'NI (*οἱ Λεοντῖνοι*), situated between Syracu'sæ and Ca'tana. It was a colony of Naxos, and chiefly remarkable for the great fertility of its territory. It was the birthplace of the celebrated orator or sophist, Gorgias, who was sent to the Athenians (427 B.C.) to implore their help, and who gave name to Plato's celebrated dialogue, *the Gorgias.*

SMALLER ISLANDS NEAR SICILIA.

I. ÆOLIÆ I'NSULÆ.

This is a group of volcanic islands, lying in the Tyrrhene Sea, between Sicilia and Lucania. They derived their name from some fancied connection with the fabulous island of Æ'olus, mentioned by Homer in the Odyssey, but were also called Vulcaniæ and Liparenses. They were seven in number; the largest and most important of them was Li'para, which alone was inhabited.

II. ÆGA'TES I'NSULÆ.

These are three small islands, situated almost opposite to Dre'panum and Lilybæum. Near these islands C. Lutatius Ca'tulus signally defeated the Carthaginian fleet, which action put an end to the First Punic War (241 B.C.).

QUESTIONS.—What was the professed object of the famous Sicilian expedition?—What was the result?—Where was Enna situated?—What was it called?—What temple was there?—Where was Leontini situated?—Who was born here?—Where are the Æoliæ Insulæ situated?—Whence their name?—What was their number?—How many were inhabited?—Where are the Ægates Insulæ situated?—Who were defeated here?—When?—By whom?

III. Me'lita (ἡ Μελίτη, *Malta*), with Gaulos (*Gozo.*)

Me'lita is situated in the channel between Sicilia and Africa. It was early colonized by Phœnicians, but subsequent to 218 B. C. it belonged to Rome. It was most probably the scene of the shipwreck of St. Paul on his voyage to Rome, A.D. 60 (*Acts* xxvii seq.); but some early writers transferred it to the Me'lita on the East coast of the Adriatic.

Gaulos, a small island near Me'lita, is by some identified with Homer's island of Calypso.

§ 142. SYRACU'SÆ. (αἱ Συράκουσαι.)

This most powerful and important of all the Greek cities in Sicily, was situated on a plateau on the Eastern coast of the island, about midway between Ca'tana and Pachy'num.

SYRACUSE.

Questions.—Where is Malta situated?—From what time did it belong to Rome?—For what is it chiefly celebrated?—Where is Gaulos situated?——§ 142. Where was Syracusæ situated?

In the time of its greatest prosperity, it was the largest city in Sicily, and one of the most important of the ancient world It was founded about 735 B.C. by Archias, a Corinthian, who settled in the island of Ortygia. The descendants of the first settlers exercised a kind of aristocratic power till their expulsion (492 B.C.), when a democratic government was established, which, however, was soon overthrown by Gelo, tyrant of Gela (485 B.C.). He was succeeded by Hi'ero, and then by Thrasybu'lus, his two brothers, the latter of whom was driven away by the people after a reign of one year (466 B.C.). But the people knew not how to use with any degree of moderation their newly attained liberty. Instead of securing the happiness of Sicily, Syracuse excited factious discontents, and gave occasion to foreign interference. At length deputies from Egesta and Leonti'ni, being pressed by the Syracusans in favor of Seli'nus, invited the Athenians to their aid. The Athenian expedition of a hundred and thirty-six triremes, with a considerable land force, under Nicias, Alcibi'ades, and La'machus, sailed (415 B.C.) for Sicily. Alcibi'ades, the most able of the three commanders, was recalled, and the supreme command remained with Nicias, who, although a man of sound understanding, had not the necessary ability and energy to subdue Syracuse, which he had now invested (414 B.C.), and whose resources seemed to increase with its dangers. La'machus died, and his successor, Demo'sthenes, was not equal to his position. Better plans were required, and the forces were deficient in numbers, although Athens had sent to Sicily 40,000 men. The result was that all either perished, or were taken prisoners; and the Athenians, thus defeated everywhere, lost at once, in a single catastrophe, their armies and their fleets (413 B.C.). This calamity, an important event in the

---

QUESTIONS.—What is said of the rank of Syracusæ?—By whom was it founded?—When?—What was the first form of government?—When was a democratic government established?—When overthrown?—By whom?—When was the democracy restored?—What was the origin of the war with Athens?—Who were at the head of the Athenian expedition?—Give an account of it.—What was the final result?—When?—Who has described it?

history of the art of war, has been ably described by Thucy'dides with minute and painful particularity (Hist. VI. seq.).

Ten years later Syracuse attained its greatest power and splendor under the government of Dionysius. He carried on long and successful wars with the Carthaginians, whom he at length entirely expelled from the island. They returned, however (396 B.C.), and laid siege to the city without being able to take it.

The city endured a third remarkable siege in 214 B.C.; two years later, it was obliged to surrender to the Roman general, Marcellus, who gave up the whole city to the indiscriminate pillage of his soldiers. Archime'des, one of the most famous of ancient mathematicians, who had contributed so much to the defence of the city, was accidentally slain in the confusion. From that time Syracuse was merely the capital of the Roman province of Sicilia; but, although its political significance was gone, it yet remained one of the most beautiful cities of the Roman Republic.

§ **143.** Cicero (Verr. IV. 52) speaks of it as *the greatest of Greek cities, and the most beautiful of all cities*, and enumerates four quarters of the city as being then inhabited. Originally it consisted of five quarters, or wards, adjoining each other, but separated by walls. Those five towns formed together the city, which was of a triangular form. Their names were Ortygia, Achradi'na, Epi'polæ, Tycha, Nea'polis.

(1.) ORTYGIA (*'Ορτυγία*), or *Insula, the Island* (νῆσος; Doric νᾶσος, hence often called *Nasus* in Latin authors), was connected with the mainland in the time of Thucy'dides, probably by a causeway, but afterward, as now, by bridges, and formed the citadel of the city. It contained two celebrated temples of

---

QUESTIONS.—When did Syracuse reach its highest point of power?—With whom did it continually carry on wars?—When was the city besieged a second time?—By whom?—When a third time?—By whom?—What was the result?—Who perished?——§ 143. In what terms does Cicero speak of Syracuse?—How many wards did the city contain at this time?—How many originally?—Name them.—Of what form was the city?—Describe Ortygia.—What temples did it contain?

Dia'na and Minerva, the latter of which was celebrated throughout the Hellenic world. Here was also the celebrated fountain of Arethu'sa (see p. 270):

(2.) Achradi'na (Ἀχραδίνη), or *the outer city*, as opposed to Ortygia, was the most important and extensive of the quarters of Syracuse. Here was the A'gora, or Forum, adorned with the temple of Jupiter Olympius, and the Prytane'um, with the celebrated statue of Sappho, which was carried away by Verres. Beneath the surface of this quarter is the extensive necropolis of the city:

(3.) Tycha (Τύχη), called after the ancient and celebrated temple of Fortune (Τύχη). It became in the times of the Empire the most populous part of the city:

(4.) Nea'polis (Νέα πόλις, *Newtown*) was a suburb which had originally grown up around the sanctuary of Apollo Temeni'tes, and hence was called Temeni'tis, and subsequently Nea'polis It was the most splendid portion of the city. Here was the theatre, which was the largest in Sicily. Near this theatre are extensive quarries (*αἱ λιθοτομίαι*), which form a part of the celebrated *Lautumiæ*, so often mentioned by ancient authors. Originally designed merely as quarries, they were afterward employed as prisons; and after the failure of the Athenian expedition, all the captives, more than seven thousand in number, were confined in them. They continued to be used for the same purpose under successive despots and tyrants. In the days of Ci'cero, they were used as a general prison for criminals from all parts of Sicily. The *Tullia'num*, or dungeon of the state-prison in Rome, was also called *Lautumiæ*:

(5.) Epi'polæ (Ἐπίπολαι) was the name originally given to the table-land on the summit of the neighboring hills. During the siege of Marcellus, the castle Eurya'lus (Εὐρύηλος) was here. This part of the city was the last settled. It was not, until the

---

Questions.—Describe Achradina.—Describe the Agora.—Where was the necropolis of the city situated?—Why was the third part called Tycha?—Describe Neapolis.—What was its former name?—Why was it called Temenitis?—Describe the Lautumiæ.—Describe Epipolæ.—When did it form a part of the city?

reign of the elder Dionysius, included between the city walls, which was then done merely to secure the heights against military occupation by an enemy. Subsequently it grew to be a considerable town.

These *five towns* together formed the celebrated city, the *Penta'polis* of Syracuse, which, with its two harbors, was one of the greatest mercantile emporiums of the ancient world.

§ 144. SARDINIA. (*Σαρδώ*, *Sardinia.*)

Situation.—In the Tyrrhene Sea, West of ITALIA, South of CO'RSICA, and East of HISPANIA.

Name.—It was known to the earlier Greeks by the name of Ichnu'sa (Ἰχνοῦσα), from the fancied resemblance of its outline to *a foot-print.*

Extent.—Its general form is that of an oblong parallelogram, above a hundred and forty geographical miles in its greatest length, and sixty in average breadth.

Mountains.—The island is traversed from North to South by the INSA'NI MONTES, which render the surface of the country rugged. The mountainous sections were the wildest and most uncivilized parts of the island.

Capes.—PROMONTORIUM URSI, the North-East point, and GORDITA'NUM, the North-West point.

Climate.—The climate was very unhealthful, and as such seems to have obtained among the Romans an almost proverbial notoriety. This was owing mainly to the extensive marshes and lagoons on the coast, formed at the mouths of the rivers. The mountainous tracts inland were more healthful, but, being the abode of savage tribes were not visited by the inhabitants of the plains.

Productions.—Although the greater part of the island is rugged and wild, it contains several plains of fertile land, rich in all kinds of produce, but especially in wheat.

QUESTIONS.—§ 144. Where was Sardinia situated?—Why was it called Ichnusa?—What is its extent?—Name its mountains.—Capes.—What is remarked about the climate?—What about the products?

Inhabitants.—The chief tribes of the island were: (1.) *Tolæ*, or *Thenses;* (2.) *Ba'lari;* (3.) *Sardi* or *Pelli'ti.* The island was conquered by the Carthaginians about 500 B. C., who retained possession till 238 B. C., when they were forced to surrender it to the Romans. After that time it furnished large supplies of wheat to the armies in Italy.

Towns.—They were not numerous, and but few of them attained to any importance.

CA'RALIS (*Cagliari*) was the most considerable city in the whole island, and is still the capital.

§ 145. CO'RSICA. (*ἡ Κύρνος, Corsica.*)

Situation.—North of Sardinia, from which it is divided by the narrow FRETUM TAPHROS (now *Strait of Bonifacio*).

Mountains.—A range of lofty and rugged mountains extends from North to South, called by the ancients, AUREUS MONS, a Western branch of which was MONS RHŒTIUS.

Capes.—SACRUM (*Capo Corso*), the Northern point; ATTIUM, the North-West point; MARI'NUM, the South-West point.

Productions.—The mountains are covered very generally with dense forests; their extent and the large growth and excellence of the timber which they produced, have been celebrated in all ages. The same forests produced resin and pitch, and abounded in wild bees, so that wax and honey were for a long period among the chief exports of the island. The country was also prolific in sheep, goats, and cattle, foxes and rabbits. Its mines were generally neglected in ancient times.

Inhabitants.—They were partly of Ligurian, partly of Iberian extraction. The island was early known to the Greeks, and the

---

QUESTIONS.—What were the chief tribes of Sardinia?—When did it fall into the power of the Carthaginians?—When into the power of the Romans?—What was its chief export?—Name some of its towns.—— § 145. How was Corsica called by the Greeks?—Where was it situated?—Name its mountains.—Capes.—What were the chief productions?—What were the chief exports of the island?—What is remarked about its mines?—Of what extraction were its inhabitants?

Phocæans settled themselves on its Eastern coast as early as 564 B.C. But about a quarter of a century later, they were driven away by the Etruscans. Their supremacy fell with the decline of their naval power, and Co'rsica appears to have been in a state of dependence on Carthage at the time of the First Punic War. On this account it was attacked (259 B.C.) by a Roman fleet under L. Scipio, who took the city of Aleria, and compelled the inhabitants to acknowledge the sovereignty of Rome.

The mountain tribes, however, remained unsubdued, and are described by Strabo as *wilder than beasts.* The Roman governors made, from time to time, an attack upon their fastnesses, and carried off a number of prisoners whom they sold as slaves. Little or no pains was taken to civilize them, and at length the island was selected as a place of banishment for political exiles, among whom was Se'neca, the philosopher.

Towns.—During the times of the Empire it contained thirty-three towns and two Roman colonies, Aleria and Maria'na.

§ 146. SMALLER ISLANDS NEAR ITALY.

A.——In Mare Adria'ticum.

(1.) I'nsulæ Diomede'æ (*Isole di Tremiti*), a group of three small islands off the coast of Apulia. One of them, Trimerus, was the place of exile of Julia, granddaughter of Augustus :

(2.) Pharos, near Brundisium, with a lighthouse, and hence its name (see Pharos, p. 125).

Questions.—At what time was Corsica colonized by Greeks?—By whom were they driven away?—In whose possession was the island during the First Punic War?—When did it fall under the power of the Romans?—Were the Romans masters of the whole island?—For what was the island afterward used?—How many towns did it contain?—How many Roman colonies?—Give their names.——§ 146. What islands were situated in Mare Adriaticum?—Who was banished to Trimerus?

B.——In Tuscum Mare.

(1.) Ilva (*Elba*), is an island off the coast of Etruria, opposite to the promontory and city of Populonium. Its Hellenic name was *Æthalia* (*Αἰθαλία*), which was regarded as derived from the *smoke* (*αἰθάλη*) of the numerous furnaces employed in smelting the iron, for which the island was celebrated in ancient, as it is also in modern times. The island has the advantage of several excellent ports, among which is Portus Argo'us.

(2.) Planasia (*Pianosa*), is a small island South-West of Ilva, where Po'stumus Agrippa, the grandson of Augustus, spent the last years of his life in exile.

(3.) Pontia was situated opposite the Circeian promontory. It is the most considerable of a group of three islands, the two others being Palmaria and Sinonia. Under the Roman Empire, they became a common place of confinement for state prisoners

(4.) Pandatoria, situated opposite the mouth of the Vulturnus, was also a place of confinement for state prisoners.

(5.) Capreæ (*Capri*) was an island off the coast of Campania, lying immediately opposite Minervæ Promontorium. It owes its chief celebrity to the fact that Tiberius there spent the last ten years of his life.

(6.) Sirenu'sæ I'nsulæ were situated opposite Minervæ Promontorium, off the coast of Campania, near Capreæ. Tradition has represented these rocks as the abode of the *Sirens* (*Sire'nes*).

Questions.—Where is Ilva situated?—What was its Hellenic name?—From what was this name derived?—What is the chief produce of the island?—What islands were situated in Mare Tuscum?—Where was Planasia situated?—What islands were situated opposite the Circeian promontory?—For what were those islands used?—Where is Pandatoria situated?—Where Capreæ?—Which of the Roman emperors resided here?—What was the traditionary abode of the Sirens?

§ 147. HISPANIA. (ἡ Ἰβηρία.)

Spain and Portugal.

When, in 236 B. C., Carthage had lost her two oldest provinces, Sardinia and Co'rsica, Hamilcar, aware that the weakness of Carthage consisted in her want of soldiers, turned his eyes to Hispania, which he desired to transform into a Carthaginian possession, from which large *national* armies might be obtained. His policy, therefore, was not only to subdue the Spaniards, but to win their sympathy. He succeeded in his plan, and acquired for Carthage a population of millions, which relieved her from the necessity of hiring faithless mercenaries, who had proved so fatal to the Carthaginian commonwealth. Thus Hispania became involved in the fate of the Roman world.

Names.—(1.) The name in general use among the Greeks, was *Iberia* (Ἰβηρία), which was understood to be derived from the river *Ibe'rus*.

(2.) *Hispania* was the Roman name, the origin of which is uncertain, but W. Von Humboldt maintains that *Hispania* is preserved almost unaltered in the modern native designation, *España*, which he derives from the Basque, *Ezpaña*, *a border*, as denoting that this country was the *border of Europe* toward the ocean.

(3.) *Hesperia*, *Land of the West* (see p. 89), was a poetical appellation. In contradistinction from Italy, it was also called *Hesperia U'ltima*.

(4.) *Ce'ltica* was a general name for the western parts of Europe, and more especially for Spain, as originally peopled by Kelts. The name was however usually confined to the Keltic parts of the peninsula.

(5.) The Southern part, especially beyond the Strait, is often called *Tartessis*.

Questions.—§ 147. In what way did Hispania become a Carthaginian province?—When?—By whose genius was this result attained?—What are the different names of Hispania?—Why was it called Iberia?—What is said of the derivation of the name Hispania?—What does it signify?—Why was it called Hesperia?—Why was it called Celtica?—What part was called Tartessis?

Boundaries.—It was a peninsula, bounded North-East by the MONTES PYRENÆI; East and South, by MARE INTERNUM; West, by OCE'ANUS.

Extent.—Its greatest length from North to South is about four hundred and sixty miles, and its greatest breadth from East to West about five hundred and seventy miles; its area, including that of the Balearic Isles, is about 171,300 square miles. The numbers given by the ancients are generally much larger, because they founded their estimates of distances almost entirely on the itinerary measurements.

Capes.—There are twelve large promontories on the coast, beside some others of less importance. We here enumerate only PROMONTORIUM TRILEUCUM (*Ortegal*), NERIUM, or A'RTABRUM (*Finisterre*), SACRUM (*St. Vincent*), CALPE (*Gibraltar*), DIANIUM (*St. Martin*).

Mountains.—The country is intersected throughout the greatest portion of its breadth by five great chains of mountains, separated by extensive valleys. These five mountain chains are to a certain extent united toward the east by another chain intersecting them all. A seventh chain, branching off from the Pyrenæi, runs along the entire north-east coast of the peninsula. These mountains do not rise from the plain, but from a high table-land, two thousand feet above the sea, like battlements on the summit of a huge tower. They did not all have distinct names in antiquity, but were called MONTES PYRENÆI, VA'SCONUM SALTUS (*Mountains of Asturias*), and HERMINIUS MONS (*Sierra de la Estrella*) which was of some importance in Cæsar's campaign in Lusitania.

Rivers.—The six mountain ranges give Spain five large valleys, through each of which flows a considerable river: DURIUS (*Douro*), TAGUS (*Tajo*), ANAS (*Guadiana*), BÆTIS (*Guadalquivir*), and, through the Eastern valley, the IBE'RUS (*Ebro*).

QUESTIONS.—Give the boundaries of Hispania.—Its extent.—How many capes did the peninsula contain?—Name some of them.—By how many mountain chains is Spain intersected?—What is said about the physical aspect of the country in general?—Into how many large valleys is Spain divided by those chains?—What rivers flow through them?

§ 148. **Climate.**—Some of the valleys of Bæ'tica which lie near the sea exhibit the vegetation of the tropics, while the interior consists of a bleak and arid table-land, very high, and piercingly cold and unhealthful. Lusitania enjoys, in general, a beautiful climate.

Productions.—Its fertility is generally celebrated by the ancients, who mention among its products, wheat, wine, oil, fruits, excellent grass for horses and mules, metals of all kinds, and precious stones. The mountains of the South contained rich silver mines, and yielded also in lesser quantities, gold, iron, quicksilver, cinnabar, rock-salt, and other valuable minerals.

Inhabitants.—The Southern part of Spain, Bæ'tica, is severed from the rest of Spain by the great chain of the Maria'nus Mons (*Sierra Morena*). This was the original home of the Iberians. The Kelts lived north of the mountains. The Iberians expelled this ancient Keltic population wherever the nature of the country did not prevent them. But the Kelts maintained themselves in the mountains between the Tagus and the Ibe'rus, and the Iberians only subdued them by settling among them, so that in course of time the two nations became amalgamated, and thus formed the *Celtiberians* (*Celtibe'ri*). The Kelts in Lusitania remained always pure and unmixed. In historical times, the great bulk of the population was Iberian. They were an ignorant, but cunning and mischievous race, addicted to robbery, of almost indomitable courage, fond of brigandage, though incapable of the higher combinations of regular war.

From the time of Augustus, the influence of Roman civilization which had long existed in Hispania yearly increased, so that

---

QUESTIONS.—§ 148. What is the climate of the valleys of Bætica?—What is the climate of the interior?—What the climate of Lusitania?—What are its chief productions?—What did the mountains of the south contain?—What was the original home of the Iberians?—What mountains separated them from the rest of the peninsula?—Where did the Kelts live?—Who were the Celtiberians?—In what part of the peninsula did the Kelts remain pure?—What formed the bulk of the population in historical times?—What kind of people were they?—When were they Romanized?—To what degree?

in the first century of the Roman Empire, the people about the Bætis had almost entirely adopted Roman manners, and spoke the purest Latin; and in course of time Hispania became more thoroughly Roman than any other province out of Italy, furnishing many names distinguished in the literature of Rome, as Se'neca, Lucan, Quintilian, Martial. Spain thus had the advantage of having for the basis of her language, a pure classic Latin, which probably neither France nor Italy possessed in like degree.

Divisions.—From the expulsion of the Carthaginians till the time of Augustus, Hispania formed two provinces, often called *Hispaniæ*, or *duæ Hispaniæ*:

I. The Eastern part, called HISPANIA CITERIOR, with the capital, *Ta'rraco*, and afterward *Cartha'go Nova*:

II. The Western part, called HISPANIA ULTERIOR, with the capital, *Cordu'ba*, and sometimes, *Gades*. .

Augustus divided Hispania Ulterior into two parts, the two provinces of Bæ'tica and Lusitania, and gave Hispania Citerior the name of Tarraconensis:

I. HISPANIA TARRACONENSIS, so called after its old capital, Ta'rraco:

II. LUSITANIA, the Westernmost part of the peninsula, the present PORTUGAL:

III. BÆ'TICA, the Southernmost part of the peninsula.

§ 149. I.——HISPANIA TARRACONENSIS.

This province was larger than the other two provinces combined.

Boundaries.—North, PYRENÆI and MARE CANTA'BRICUM; East, MARE INTERNUM; West, the DURIUS, OCE'ANUS, and LUSITANIA; South, LUSITANIA and BÆ'TICA.

QUESTIONS.—What is said of the Spanish language?—What was the division of Spain from the expulsion of the Carthaginians to the time of Augustus?—What was the division made by Augustus?——§ 149. Which was the largest of the three parts into which Augustus divided Spain?—What were its boundaries?

Nations.—Of these a large number is given by ancient authorities; we mention the following:

(1.) *Basteta'ni*, who inhabited the country East of Bæ'tica:

(2.) *Basti*, North-East of the Basteta'ni :

(3.) *Laleta'ni*, the inhabitants of Laletania, the capital of which was Ba'rcino:

(4.) *Ca'ntabri*, along the shores of Mare Canta'bricum :

(5.) *A'stures*, the Western neighbors of the Ca'ntabri:

(6.) *Gallæci*, a *Keltic* people in the North-Western part of the peninsula:

(7.) *Celtibe'ri*, between the boundaries of Lusitania and the Ibe'rus.

Towns.—This large and populous province contained in the times of the Roman Empire a hundred and seventy-nine large towns, and about two hundred and ninety-three villages. The seven principal cities and capitals were: Ta'rraco, Cartha'go Nova, Cæsar Augusta, Clunia, Astu'rica, Lucus Augusti, and Bra'cara Augusta:

(1.) CARTHA'GO NOVA (*Cartagena*), near the Southern extremity of the Eastern coast, was a colony of Carthage, and was built (242 B. C.) by Ha'sdrubal. The city, on the land side, was entirely surrounded by elevated mountain peaks, two of which were very rugged; on the eastern stood the temple of the chief deity, Æsculapius (*Esmun*), on the western, the palace of Ha'sdrubal. Thirty-two years after its foundation the city was taken by the Romans under Publius Scipio. During the Empire, it was the winter residence of the Lega'tus Cæ'saris, and was called Colonia Victrix Julia.

(2.) SAGUNTUM was situated on an eminence on the banks of the river Pallantias, between Sacro and Ta'rraco, not far from the

---

QUESTIONS.—Name some of the nations of Hispania Tarraconensis.—How many large towns did it contain?—How many villages?—What were the principal cities?—Describe the situation of Carthago Nova.—What temple adorned the eastern height?—What palace the western?—When was it founded?—When taken by the Romans?—Under whom?—Where was Saguntum situated?—How was it the cause of the Second Punic War?

sea. The fact of its being besieged by Ha'nnibal, when it was in alliance with the Romans (218 B.C.), was the immediate cause of the Second Punic War.

(3.) TA'RRACO (*Tarragona*), a colony of the Phœnicians, was converted into a fortress, for protection against the Carthaginians, by the brothers Publius and Cneius Scipio. Subsequently it became the capital of the province named after it.

(4.) CALAGURRIS (*Calahorra*), situated upon a rocky hill near the right bank of the Ibe'rus, obtained a horrible celebrity in the war with Sertorius, when its citizens slaughtered their wives and children, and after satisfying present hunger, salted the remainder of the flesh for future use! The capture of the city put an end to the Sertorian war (72 B.C.). It was the native place of the rhetorician, Quintilia'nus.

(5.) NUMANTIA, near the Durius, was famous for its siege and destruction by Scipio Africa'nus (134 B.C.).

(6.) SEGO'BRIGA was the chief city of the Celtibe'ri.

(7.) BI'LBILIS (*Belbili*) was the birthplace of the poet Martial.

(8.) ILERDA (*Lerida*), situated on the Western bank of the Si'coris, was the stronghold of the Pompeian party in Spain, but was taken by Cæsar (49 B.C.).

(9.) OSCA was the place where Sertorius was murdered (72 B.C.).

(10.) Other cities: VALENTIA, CÆSARE'A AUGUSTA (*Saragossa*), DERTO'SA (*Tortosa*), BA'RCINO (*Barcelona*), POMPE'LO (*Pampeluna*), LEGIO SE'PTIMA GE'MINA (*Leon*), ASTU'RICA AUGUSTA (*Astorga*), BRIGANTIUM, LUCUS AUGUSTI (*Lugo*), BRA'CARA AUGUSTA (*Braga*), CONTREBIA, TOLE'TUM (*Toledo*).

QUESTIONS.—What is said of Tarraco?—Describe the situation of Calagurris.—What happened there during the Sertorian war?—Who was born there?—Who destroyed Numantia?—What was the chief city of the Celtiberi?—What was the birthplace of Martial?—Where was Ilerda situated?—Where was Sertorius murdered?—When?

§ 150. II. LUSITANIA.

It was the Western part of the peninsula.

Boundaries.—West and South, OCE'ANUS; South-East, BÆ'-TICA (the ANAS here formed the line); East and North, HISPANIA TARRACONENSIS; the DURIUS being the boundary line on the North.

It contained therefore the modern kingdom of PORTUGAL, except the provinces *Entre Duero e Minho, Tras os Montes,* and the South-East part of *Alemtejo,* but including the Spanish provinces *Estremadura, Salamanca,* and the western part of *Toledo.*

Nations.—(1.) *Lusita'ni,* who inhabited the country between the Tagus and the Durius:

(2.) *Vetto'nes,* who inhabited the country East of the Lusita'ni:

(3.) *Ce'ltici,* who inhabited the country South of the Tagus.

Towns.—The province contained forty-six towns, among which were:

(1.) *South of the river Tagus:*

BALSA, MY'RTILIS, PAX JULIA (*Beja*), AUGUSTA EME'RITA (*Merida*), NORBA CÆSARE'A (*Alcantara*).

(2.) *North of the river Tagus:*

OLISIPPO (*Lisbon*), SCA'LABIS (*Santarem*), SALMA'NTICA (*Salamanca*).

III. BÆ'TICA.

The valley of the Bætis was, and still is, the most beautiful part of the peninsula.

Boundaries.—West and North, the ANAS, which separates it from Lusitania and Hispania Tarraconensis; East, HISPANIA TARRACONENSIS; South, MARE INTERNUM.

QUESTIONS.—§ 150. What part of the peninsula was called Lusitania?—Name the boundaries.—What part does it form of the modern kingdoms of Spain and Portugal?—Name the nations.—How many towns did it contain?—What towns were situated south of the Tagus?—What towns north?—How was Bætica bounded?

Nations.—(1.) *Turdeta'ni*, the most civilized people of the peninsula, inhabiting the banks of the Bætis:

(2.) *Tu'rduli*, East and South of the Turdeta'ni:

(3.) *Basteta'ni* and *Ba'stuli*, inhabiting the southern coasts of the peninsula.

Towns.—This thickly peopled province contained about two hundred towns, among which were:

(1.) GADES, built on islands (whence probably the plural form of its name) situated on the south-western coast, between the Strait and the mouth of the Bætis The original Phœnician name, *Gadir* (*Γάδειρα*), is preserved in the modern *Cadix*, or *Cadiz.* It was the chief Phœnician colony beyond the Pillars of He'rcules, having been established long before the beginning of classical history. It became at an early period the great western emporium of the known world, and in the time of Augustus the city was only second in point of population to Rome. It possessed a famous temple and oracle of He'rcules:

§ **151.** (2.) TARTESSUS, sometimes identified with Cadiz, lying to the West of the Pillars of He'rcules, and now believed by biblical critics to be the *Tarshish* of the Holy Scriptures, where it is spoken of as a region, rich in iron, tin, lead, silver, and other commodities. The Phœnicians are represented as sailing thither in large ships (*Ezek.* xxvii. 12; *Jer.* x. 9). Isaiah speaks of it as one of the finest Tyrian colonies, and describes the Tyrians as bringing its products to the market of Tyre (xxiii. 1, 6, 10). Classical authors use the name in a very loose and indefinite way. It has in fact the following various significations in different writers:

a. The whole of the peninsula:

b. The river Bætis, or a town situated near its mouth:

c. The country of the Tu'rduli.

It fell into decay before the Romans came into southern Spain.

QUESTIONS.—Name some of the nations of Bætica.—How many towns did it contain?—Where is Gades situated?—Whence is its modern name derived?—What is said of its origin?—Of its prosperity?—Of its inhabitants?—What was probably the Tarshish of the Holy Scriptures?—What is the signification of Tartessus in classical authors?—When did it fall into the hands of the Romans?

(3.) ILLITURGIS, situated at the North side of the Bætis, was destroyed by Publius Scipio (206 B. C.), but was soon afterward rebuilt.

(4.) BÆ'CULA was the scene of Scipio's victories over Ha's-drubal (209 B. C.), and also over Mago and Masinissa (206 B. C.).

(5.) MUNDÆ was the place where Cæsar conquered the sons of Pompey (45 B. C.).

(6.) ITA'LICA, situated on the right bank of the Bætis, opposite Hi'spalis (*Seville*), was the native place of Trajan, Hadrian, and Theodosius the Great.

(7.) CORDU'BA (*Cordoba*), on the right bank of the Bætis, was the birthplace of the poet Lucan, and of the philosophers Marcus and Lucius Annæus Se'neca :

Duosque Senecas unicumque Lucanum
Facunda loquitur Corduba.—Martial, I. 62.

(8.) MA'LACA (*Malaga*) has still a few remains of Roman architecture.

ISLANDS NEAR HISPANIA.

(1.) I'NSULÆ BALEA'RES were situated in the Mediterranean, off the East coast of Spain, not far from the mouth of the Ibe'rus. The ancient authors generally mention two:

A. BALEA'RIS MAJOR, or MAJO'RICA (*Mallorca*);

B. BALEA'RIS MINOR, or MINO'RICA (*Menorca*).

The inhabitants were chiefly celebrated for their skill as slingers, in which capacity they served, as mercenaries, first under the Carthaginians, and afterward under the Romans.

(2.) I'NSULÆ PITYU'SÆ were two islands on the South coast of Spain, included in the Balearic group, in the modern sense of the word. The larger island was called E'BUSUS (*Iviza*), and the smaller one OPHIU'SA (*Formentara*).

QUESTIONS.—Where is Illiturgis situated?—When was it destroyed?—By whom?—Who conquered at Bæcula?—Who at Mundæ?—Where is Italica situated?—Who were born there?—Who at Corduba?—What islands were situated near Hispania?—Where were the Insulæ Baleares situated?—How many are generally mentioned?—For what were their inhabitants celebrated?—Where are the Insulæ Pityusæ?—Name them.

§ 152. GALLIA TRANSALPI'NA.

Names.—The Greek name, *Ce'ltice* (ἡ Κελτική), was earlier in use than the Roman name, from the fact that the Greeks were settled on its southern coast long before the Romans knew anything of the country; and *Galatia* (ἡ Γαλατία) was employed by the Greeks from the time of the historian Timæus (300 B. C.). The Romans gave it the name of *Gallia*, calling it sometimes *Ulterior Gallia*, to distinguish it from the North part of Italy; sometimes, for the same reason, *Gallia Transalpi'na*. It was also called *Gallia Coma'ta*, with the exception of the southern part, because the inhabitants wore their *hair long*.

Boundaries.—It is subdivided into Western and North-Western, and into Eastern and South-Eastern parts by natural well defined lines: North, FRETUM GA'LLICUM; West, OCE'ANUS; South, MONTES PYRENÆI and MARE INTERNUM; East, the VARUS, ALPES, and the RHENUS.

Mountains.—PYRENÆI MONTES, CEBENNA (*Sevennes*), JURA with the MONS PERTU'SUS, a pass made by Cæsar, ARDUENNA SILVA (*Ardennes*).

Rivers.—(1.) RHO'DANUS (*Rhône*). This river was crossed by Ha'nnibal near the present situation of the village Beaucaire (218 B. C.). The principal branches of the Rho'danus are:

a. On the left bank:

I'SARA (*Isere*), on the banks of which Q. Fabius Ma'ximus Æmilia'nus conquered the Allo'broges (121 B. C.):

DRUENTIA (*Durance*) and SULGAS (*Sorgue*).

b. On the East bank:

ARAR, afterward called SAUCONNA (*Saone*), and VARDO (*Gardon*):

QUESTIONS.—§ 152. What was the Greek name of Gallia Transalpina?—Why was this name earlier in common use?—Why was it called Gallia Ulterior?—Why Gallia Transalpina?—Why Gallia Comata?—Name the boundaries.—Mountains.—Rivers.—Where was the Rhodanus crossed by Hannibal?—When?—What rivers are on its left bank?—What rivers on its right bank?

(2.) GARUMNA (*Garonne*), the most southern of the three large rivers of Gaul:

(3.) LIGER (*Loire*), SE'QUANA (*Seine*), MA'TRONA (*Marne*), SCALDIS (*Schelde*), MOSA (*Meuse*), RHENUS (*Rhine*), MOSELLA (*Moesel*).

Lake.—LACUS LEMANNUS (*Lake Leman*, or *Lake of Geneva*).

Productions.—It is for the greater part a level country, with a very large proportion of fertile soil, which produces corn, wine, and, in the South, olives. In the Roman times, it was rich in forests, which have now, however, almost disappeared.

Inhabitants.—The Galli of Cæsar's time were an ingenious people, and had made some progress in the working of metals and in other useful arts.

Divisions.—In the time of Augustus, it was divided into four parts: GALLIA NARBONENSIS, AQUITANIA, GALLIA LUGDUNENSIS, GALLIA BE'LGICA.

§ 153. I. GALLIA NARBONENSIS.

Name.—It was called after its capital Narbo (*Narbonne*). This part of Gaul was conquered by the Romans before Cæsar's time, and was called *Provincia Roma'na*, or simply *Provincia;* hence its present name, *Provence.* It was also called *Gallia Braca'ta*, as opposed to *Gallia Toga'ta* (see p. 225).

Boundaries.—East, GALLIA CISALPI'NA; South, MONTES PYRENÆI; West, AQUITANIA; North, GALLIA LUGDUNENSIS and BE'LGICA.

Nations and Towns.—(1.) *So'rdones*, who occupied the present territory of Roussillon, at the foot of the Pyrenees. Their

QUESTIONS.—What is the most southern of the large rivers of Gaul?—Name other rivers.—Name its lake.—What are its productions?—What kind of people were the Gauls?—Into how many parts was Gaul divided by Augustus?—Name those four parts.——§ 153. What part of Gaul was first conquered by the Romans?—What name did it receive from its conquerors?—What is derived from this name?—Why was it called Gallia Narbonensis?—Name the boundaries.—Name some of the nations.—Where was the territory of the Sordones?

principal towns were: ILLI'BERIS (*Elne*) and RUS'CINO (*Perpignan*).

(2.) The *Volcæ* inhabited all the province from the Rhone to its Western limits. They were divided into two tribes: Volcæ Areco'mici and Volcæ Tecto'sages:

a. TOLO'SA (*Toulouse*), the chief city of the Tecto'sages, situated on the right bank of the Garumna. It possessed a celebrated temple enriched by the offerings of Gallic superstition. It was plundered by Q. Servilius Cæpio (106 B. C.).

b. NARBO (*Narbonne*), a town of the Areco'mici on the river Atax (*Aude*). It was an important position during Cæsar's wars in Gaul.

c. NEMAUSUS (*Nîmes*), the chief city of the Areco'mici. No district in France is richer in Roman remains than the neighborhood of Nîmes. Three or four miles from the city is a Roman aqueduct (now called *Pont du Gard*), which is the noblest Roman monument in France The city itself still contains the remains of a large amphitheatre which could accommodate 17,000 persons.

(3.) The *Salyes* inhabited the country between the Druentia (*Durance*) and the Mediterranean. They were a mixed race of Galli and Li'gures. Although a very warlike people, they were the first of the transalpine nations who were subdued by the Romans:

a ARELA'TE (*Arles*), situated on the left bank of the Rho'danus, where the river divides into two branches. It contained the largest amphitheatre in Gaul, which could seat more than 20,000 persons.

b. AQUÆ SEXTIÆ (*Aix*). In its neighborhood C. Marius defeated with immense slaughter (102 B. C.) the Cimbri and Teu'tones, which latter consisted of Germans mixed with Kelts.

QUESTIONS.—Where was the territory of the Volcæ?—Into what tribes were they divided?—What was the chief town of the Tectosages?—Where was it situated?—What is said of it?—Where was Narbo situated?—Where Nemausus?—What remains of antiquity are in its neighborhood?—What territory was occupied by the Salyes?—What cities are situated in their territory?—Where was Arelate situated?—Where Aquæ Sextiæ?—What battle took place in its neighborhood?

c. MASSILIA (*Marseilles*), founded about 600 B. C. by the Phocæans. About fifty years later, the greater part of the Phocæans left their native land to avoid subjection to the Persians, and settled here. The worship of the Ephesian A'rtemis (*Dia'na*) was cherished with peculiar reverence, both in Massilia itself and in its colonies. After its political independence was overthrown by Cæsar, the inhabitants directed their attention to literature and philosophy. Their city became to the West of Europe what Athens was to the East. Even some of the most noble Romans went thither to complete their education. The studies pursued there were Latin, Greek, Rhetoric, and Medicine. Cicero calls this city *Athe'næ Ga'llicæ.*

(4.) The *Oxybii*, a Ligurian people on the South coast of Gallia Narbonensis, East of Forum Julii (*Frejus*), the birthplace of Agri'cola.

(5.) The *Ca'vares*, who inhabited the present district of Avignon. Their towns were AVENIO (*Avignon*), VI'NDALUM, ARAUSIO (*Orange*), the scene of a defeat of the Romans by the Cimbri and Teu'tones.

(6.) The *Decia'tæ*, East of the Oxybii, with the town ANTI'-POLIS (*Antibes*).

(7.) The *Catu'riges* inhabited the Alpine passes, and were among the Galli who entered Italy in the early period of Roman history; among their towns were EBURODU'NUM or EBRODU'NUM (*Embrun*) and BRIGANTIUM (*Briançon*).

(8.) The *Allo'broges*, who inhabited chiefly the country between the Rho'danus and the I'sara. They were conquered by Q. Fabius Ma'ximus (121 B. C.). It was the ambassadors of this

---

QUESTIONS.—Who founded Massilia?—When?—Why did they leave their native place?—What goddess was worshipped by them?—Who overthrew their political independence?—What became of Massilia after this?—What studies were pursued there?—What is it called by Cicero?—Where was the country of the Oxybii situated?—What country was inhabited by the Cavari?—What towns were situated in their territory?—What country was inhabited by the Caturiges?—What country by the Allobroges?—Who conquered them?—What had they to do with the conspiracy of Catiline?

people that betrayed the conspiracy of Catiline. Their capital was VIENNA ALLO'BROGUM.

ISLANDS BELONGING TO GALLIA NARBONENSIS.

I'NSULÆ STOE'CHADES, or I'NSULÆ MASSILIENSIUM (*Isles de Hières*), are five in number. They were occupied by the citizens of Massilia.

§ 154. II. AQUITANIA.

Boundaries.—East, GALLIA NARBONENSIS; North, GALLIA LUGDUNENSIS; West, OCE'ANUS; South, HISPANIA.

Inhabitants.—The inhabitants were an Iberian race, differing entirely from the Keltic population of Gaul, having settled in that part of the country at a much earlier period than the Kelts.

Nations and Towns.—(1.) The *Vasa'tes*, with BURDI'GALA (*Bourdeaux*), the birthplace of the poet Ausonius (A.D. 309):

(2.) The *Arverni*, who inhabited the valley of the E'laver (*Allier*), one of the most powerful of the Gallic nations, and the rival of the Ædui for the supremacy. Their capital was AUGUSTONE'METUM.

(3.) The *Cadurci*, a Keltic people who occupied the basin of the Oltis (*Lot*), a branch of the Garonne, with UXELLODU'NUM, conquered by Cæsar.

(4.) The *Lemovi'ces*, whose chief town was AUGUSTO'RITUM (*Limoges*).

(5.) The *Pic'tones*, who were living South of the Loire and on the ocean. Their chief city was LIMO'NUM (*Poitiers*).

QUESTIONS.—What islands belong to Gallia Narbonensis?——§ 154. What are the boundaries of Aquitania?—What is said of the inhabitants?—Name some of the nations.—Name some of the towns.—What was the birthplace of the poet Ausonius?—To what people did this town belong?—What country was inhabited by the Arverni?—What is said about them?—What country was occupied by the Cadurci?—Where did the Pictones live?

(6.) The *Bitu'riges Cubi*, who inhabited the basin of the Loire, were at one time the most powerful nation in Gaul (about 600 B. C). Their capital, AVA'RICUM (*Bourges*), one of the finest towns of Gaul, was plundered by Julius Cæsar.

III. GALLIA LUGDUNENSIS; previously, GALLIA CE'LTICA.

Boundaries.—North and West, OCE'ANUS; East and South, GALLIA NARBONENSIS; South, AQUITANIA.

Nations and Towns.—(1.) The *Segusia'ni* occupied the territory between the Rho'danus and the boundaries of Aquitania. The Roman settlement, LUGDU'NUM (*Lyons*), at the junction of the Arar (*Saône*) and Rho'danus, was in their territory. It was the most populous of the Gallic towns, after Narbonne, and was the centre of the Roman highways in Gaul. In the angle between the Arar and the Rho'danus was the Ara Augusti, dedicated to Augustus by all the Gallic states, sixty in number. It was the capital of Gallia Lugdunensis, the residence of the governors, and the native place of the emperor Claudius:

(2.) The *Ædui*, who inhabited the Western banks of the Arar (*Saône*), were one of the most powerful of the Celtic nations, but before Cæsar's proconsulship in Gallia, they had been brought under the dominion of the Se'quani, who had invited the Suevi from beyond the Rhine to assist them. Before this calamity happened, they had been styled friends by the Romans. For this reason Cæsar restored them to their former independence. Their chief town, in Cæsar's time, was BIBRACTE, on which site afterward was built AUGUSTODU'NUM (*Autun*):

QUESTIONS.—Where was the country of the Bituriges?—What was their capital?—How was Gallia Lugdunensis bounded?—Name some of the nations and towns.—What territory was occupied by the Segusiani?—Describe the situation of Lugdunum.—Describe the town.—What territory was inhabited by the Ædui?—By whom were they subjugated?—Who restored them to their former power?—What was their chief town?

(3.) The *Mandubii*, a small people, with the town ALESIA (*Alise*), which was besieged by Cæsar (52 B. C.):

(4.) The *Seno'nes* or *Se'nones*, one of the great Keltic nations who bordered on the Belgæ: their capital was AGE'NDICUM (*Sens*).

(5.) The *Parisii*, a Gallic people about the Se'quana, whose chief place was *Lutetia Parisi'orum* (Cæs. B. G. VI. 3), a small town on an island in the Se'quana, which was approached by means of two bridges. This town finally took the name of the people and was called *ci'vitas Parisio'rum* (whence the modern *Paris*). During the Roman period it seems not to have been a place of any importance, though in the year 360, Julian was proclaimed Emperor there:

(6.) The *Aulerci*, a generic name, which included several Keltic tribes, among which were the Cenomanni, Diablintes, and Eburovi'ces:

(7.) The *Carnu'tes*, who occupied the country between the Seine and Loire, and also a portion of the territory South of the Loire. Their principal town was GE'NABUM, afterward called URBS AURELIENSIUM (*Orleans*). It was destroyed by Cæsar:

(8.) The *Armo'rici*, probably, *the Dwellers near the Sea* (*ar*, near; *mor*, the sea). They inhabited the coast between the Se'quana and Liger. They formed different states, of which the Ve'neti were the most powerful. The Armo'rici were a maritime people, and commanded the seas and ports. In Cæsar's time they formed a kind of confederacy.

ISLANDS BELONGING TO GALLIA LUGDUNENSIS.

I'NSULÆ VENE'TICÆ: Numerous small islands near the coast, inhabited by the Ve'neti (the modern department of *Morbihan*).

QUESTIONS.—To what nation did Alesia belong?—To what nation Agendicum?—Where was the territory of the Parisii?—What is said of Lutetia?—What tribes were comprised in the Aulerci?—What country was occupied by the Carnuti?—What does the name Armorici signify?—Where did this people live?—What is said of it?—What islands belong to Gallia Lugdunensis?

§ 155. IV. GALLIA BE'LGICA.

Name.—This was the largest of the four provinces into which Gaul was divided, and was the country of the BELGÆ (a term preserved in the modern *Belgium*), who gave name to the whole, but occupied only a portion of it.

Boundaries.—North, FRETUM GA'LLICUM and MARE GERMA'NICUM; East, GERMANIA, VINDELICIA, and RHÆTIA; South, GALLIA NARBONENSIS; West, GALLIA LUGDUNENSIS.

Nations and Towns.—(1.) The *Helvetii*, a Keltic people, who, in Cæsar's time, occupied the country between the Rhenus, Rho'danus and Mount Jura. Their country was divided into four *pagi* (in French, *pays*), which contained twelve towns and four hundred villages. Their chief city was AVE'NTICUM (*Avenches*), which is, however, not mentioned by Cæsar. It was originally the capital of the Tiguri'ni, one of the four Helvetic *pagi*:

(2.) The *Rau'raci* inhabited the territory of the present bishopric of *Bâle*. Their chief town was AUGUSTA RAURACO'RUM (*Augst*):

(3.) The *Se'quani*, a Keltic nation in the upper valley of the Arar (*Saône*). Their territory contained some of the best land in Gaul. Their chief town was VESONTIO (*Besançon*).

(4.) The *Remi* inhabited the shores of the Se'quana (*Seine*). Their capital was DUROCORTO'RUM (*Reims*), which was the occasional residence of the Roman governors. They were a shrewd people, and contrived to be in great favor with the Romans:

(5.) The *Tre'viri* inhabited the country between the Mosa and Rhenus. They are often mentioned by Cæsar on account of

---

QUESTIONS.—§ 155. Was the whole of Gallia Belgica inhabited by the Belgæ?—How was it bounded?—Name some of the nations.—Some of the towns.—Where was the country of the Helvetii situated?—Into how many *pagi* was it divided?—How many towns did they contain?—How many villages?—What was their chief city?—Describe the country of the Rauraci?—Of the Sequani?—Of the Remi?—What was their capital?—What country was inhabited by the Treviri?

their causing him much trouble. Their chief city, AUGUSTA TREVIRO'RUM (*Trêves*), was often the imperial residence, under the later Emperors:

(6.) The *Ubii*, a German people, who in Cæsar's time inhabited the Eastern banks of the Rhine, opposite the Tre'viri. In the time of Augustus, they crossed the Rhine, and received from the Romans a territory on the Western banks of the river. In this new territory was situated the rich city, COLONIA AGRIPPI'NA (*Cologne*). It was originally called O'PPIDUM UBIO'RUM. Agrippi'na, the wife of the Emperor Claudius, prevailed on her husband to send a colony of veteran soldiers there, and from that time the place bore her name.

(7.) The *Bata'vi* or *Ba'tavi* inhabited first the I'nsula Batavo'rum (*Betuwe*), an island situated between the Rhenus, Vaha'lis (*Waal*), and Mosa, and subsequently went further South. Their chief towns were LUGDU'NUM BATAVO'RUM (*Leyden*) and TRAJECTUM (*Utrecht*):

(8.) The *Suessio'nes* occupied an extensive and fertile country North of the Remi. Their chief town was NOVIODU'NUM, afterward AUGUSTA SUESSIO'NUM (*Soissons*):

(9.) The *Nervii*, a mighty and warlike people, who inhabited the country near the river Sabis (*Sambre*). They were almost entirely exterminated by Cæsar:

(10.) Other nations were the *Medioma'trici*, with DIVODU'RUM (*Metz*) as their chief town; the *Tribocci*, with ARGENTORA'TUS (*Strasbourg*); the *Ne'metes*, with NOVIO'MAGUS (*Spiers*); the *Gugerni*, with CASTRA VE'TERA (*Xanten*); the *Menapii*, with CASTELLUM MENAPIO'RUM (*Kassel*); the *Veromandui*, with AUGUSTA VEROMANDUO'RUM (*St. Quentin*); the *Toscandri*, *Adua'tici*, and *Sungri*.

QUESTIONS.—What was the capital of the Treviri?—What portion of the country was inhabited by the Ubii?—What city was situated in their territory?—How did it derive its name?—Describe the country of the Batavi.—Of the Suessiones.—Of the Nervii.

§ 156. GERMANIA.

Name.—The origin of the names *Germania, Germa'ni*, is unknown, but they were not employed by the Germans themselves, who seem to have had no common name for this region, or for its different tribes. These appellations were probably first employed by the Kelts in Gaul and from them adopted by the Romans. Some of the ancients regarded *Germa'ni* as the Latin appellation given to the Germans as *brothers* of the Galli or Celtæ, and this view has been adopted by eminent German scholars. Some modern inquirers derive the name from the Persian, referring to the Persian tribe called *Germanii* (*Γερμάνιοι*, Hdt. I. 125) and the Persian district *Carmania* (*Kerman*). Since the ninth century the Germans have called themselves *Deutsche* (whence, *Dutch*), and their country, *Deutsch-land*. This designation is supposed to have been derived from *Diot* or *Diut*, signifying *people*, and as a general epithet to have denoted what was *popular, national*, as opposed to what was *Roman, foreign*.

The country was called Germania Magna to distinguish it from the district on the West of the Rhine occupied by German tribes. The territories occupied by the latter received the name of Germania Inferior, or Secunda, in the North, and Germania Superior, or Prima, in the South.

Boundaries.—North, MARE SUE'VICUM and MARE GERMA'NICUM; East, SARMATIA; South, VINDELICIA, NO'RICUM, and PANNONIA; West, GALLIA.

Mountains.—The North of Germany is flat and marshy; mountains exist only in the South; they were all thickly wooded, and therefore called *Silvæ*. The principal ones were:

(1.) HERCYNIA SILVA (whence perhaps the modern name *Harz*-Mountain), a general designation for almost all the moun-

---

QUESTIONS.—§ 156. What is said of the origin of the terms Germania and Germani?—What are the modern designations and what is said of their origin?—Why was Germania called Germania Magna?—How was it bounded?—What is the character of its northern part?—Its southern?—Why were the mountains called Silvæ?—What was the Hercynia Silva?

tains of Southern and Central Germany. In later times, different ridges bore different names, as A'bnoba, Alpii Montes, Meli'bocus Mons and others:

(2.) GABRE'TA SILVA (*Böhmerwald, Woody Mountain*), in the North of the present kingdom of Bavaria:

(3.) SALTUS TEUTOBURGIENSIS, a mountain forest in Western Germany, where, in A. D. 9, the Roman legions under Varus, suffered a memorable defeat, and where, six years later, their unburied remains were found by Drusus.

Rivers.—(1.) RHENUS, the great barrier of the Romans against the German tribes; in the time of Tiberius eight legions were stationed on it. It was supposed to have had originally two arms. A third branch was made by Drusus (*Fossa Drusia'na*), which was dug to avoid the navigation around the sea-coast of Holland, and thus to facilitate the passage of the legions which were sent to the North of Germany:

(2.) DANUBIUS (Germ. *Donau*), the largest river in South-Eastern Europe, and bounding Germania on the South. The Romans learned the name *Danubius* from the natives on the upper part of the river, and the Greeks called the lower part *Istros* (Ἴστρος), Latin, *Ister*, *Hister*, which seems to have been its genuine name below the Savus. The Roman poets designated the whole river *Ister* and sometimes *Danubius*. Its principal tributaries were: the Dravus, Savus, Pathissus, and Margus:

(3.) VI'STULA (*Weichsel*), the stream which separated Germania from Sarmatia:

(4.) Other rivers: NICER (*Neckar*); MŒNUS (*Main*); LUPPIA (*Lippe*); AMISIA (*Ems*); VISURGIS (*Weser*); ALBIS (*Elbe*); VI'ADRUS or VI'ADER (*Oder*); CHALU'SUS or DRAVENNA (*Trave*).

QUESTIONS.—Where was the Gabreta Silva situated?—Where was the Saltus Teutoburgiensis situated?—Who were defeated there?—When?—Name some of the rivers of Germany.—What was the great barrier of the Romans against the German tribes?—By how many legions was it guarded?—What was the Fossa Drusiana?—What was the greatest river in south-eastern Europe?—What is said of its names?—What were its principal tributaries?—What river separated Germania from Sarmatia?

Lake.—FLEVO LACUS, a part of the present Zuyder See, in the kingdom of the Netherlands.

Climate.—The Romans describe Germany as a wild and inhospitable country, covered with forests and marshes. Cold winds are said to have prevailed constantly, and the barren soil was said to be covered during the greater part of the year with snow and ice.

Productions.—It produced little wheat, but luxuriant grass; there were no fruit-trees, at least no cultivated ones. The immense forests were the abodes of a great variety of wild beasts, some of which appear to have since become extinct.

Inhabitants.—The Germa'ni first became known to the civilized nations in the time of Cæsar, who invaded the country 55 B. C., and again 53 B. C. That they, as well as all the other nations of Europe, came originally from Asia, is a fact revealed in the language of the people, which bears the strongest organic resemblance to the languages of India and Persia. They belonged to the same great stock of nations as the Greeks, Romans, and Kelts, to the last of which they are said to have had a marked likeness in stature, character, and manners. They are described by the classic authors as very tall and handsome men, of clear complexion, with blue eyes, and fair or red hair, on which they bestowed great attention, and the color of which they made still brighter by the use of a peculiar kind of soap. The red hair of the Germans was an article of commerce with the Romans during the period of the Empire, for it was a fashion among the Roman ladies to wear peruques or curls of red hair. Their chief dependence for the means of subsistence was on war, the chase, and the rearing of cattle. The women were occupied with spinning, weaving, and tilling the ground, but were nowhere so much honored as among the Germanic nations. The country, with

---

QUESTIONS.—What lake was in north-western Germany?—How is Germany described by the Romans?—What are its productions?—What is said of the origin of the inhabitants?—How are they described by the classic authors?—What is said about their hair?—How were the women treated?

the exception of the mountainous regions, was for the most part thickly peopled. The numerous nations are divided by Ta'citus into three groups: the *Ingæ'vones*, on the sea-coast; the *Her-mi'ones*, in the interior; and the *Istæ'vones*, in the East and South of Germany.

§ **157. Nations and Towns.**—The principal nations were:

(1.) The *Frisii*, who belonged to the Ingæ'vones. They inhabited the country about Lake Flevo, between the rivers Rhenus and Amisia. During the fourth and fifth centuries, they were allied with the Saxons, with whom they sailed across to Britain, and shared in their conquests:

(2.) The *Chauci*, who inhabited the country between the Amisia and the Albis. They were distinguished navigators, but engaged also in piratical forays, sailing as far South as the coast of Gaul:

(3.) The *Sa'xones*, one of the most important nations of the middle ages, not mentioned in ancient history previous to A.D. 287, when they infested the coasts of Armo'rica. They inhabited, at that time, the narrow neck of the Chersone'sus Ci'mbrica (*Jutland*) between the Albis and Chalu'sus.

(4.) The *Angli*, also North of the Albis, in the district still called *Angeln*, in Schleswig. They joined the Sa'xones in their invasion of Britannia, which was hence called *England*, or *Land of the Angli*:

(5.) The *Cimbri* inhabited the Chersone'sus *Ci'mbrica.* In connection with the Teu'tones and others they invaded the South of Europe, and successively defeated six Roman armies, until in the end they were conquered by C. Marius in the Campi Raudii, near Vercellæ (101 B.C.):

(6.) The *Teu'toni* or *Teu'tones*, who were almost entirely destroyed by Marius near Aquæ Sextiæ (102 B.C.):

(7.) The *Suevi*, a generic name for a very large portion of the

---

QUESTIONS.—§ 157. Name some of the nations.—Some of the towns. —What is said of the Frisii?—Chauci?—Saxones?—Angli?—Cimbri? —When, where, and by whom, were the Cimbri conquered?—When, where, and by whom, the Teutones?—What is said about the Suevi?

inhabitants of Germania from which the modern appellations *Suabia* and *Suabian* are derived. The most illustrious among the Suevi were the *Se'nones* or *Se'mnones*, who inhabited the territory between the Albis and Vi'adrus. This territory contained an ancient forest (*Se'nonum Silva*), hallowed by superstition and sacrificial rites. In this forest the general meeting of the different Suevic nations was held:

(8.) The *Langobardi* or *Longobardi*, who originally dwelt in Scandinavia, and afterward inhabited the banks of the lower Elbe, whence they are thought to have derived their name, as denoting inhabitants of the *long bord* or *plain* of the river. They were not a numerous tribe, but their want of numbers was made up by their bravery. They were constantly emigrating toward the South, sometimes meeting with defeat, but often conquerors themselves, till, in the last half of the seventh century, they occupied the fertile plains of the country called from them *Lombardy*, which still preserves the ancient name:

(9.) The *Va'ndali*, who comprised the *Burgundio'nes or Burgundi*, the *Gotho'nes* or *Gothi*, and others. In the year 409 they crossed Gaul and passed into Spain, where they founded a powerful kingdom, and where their name is still preserved in that of the province of *Andalusia* (for *Vandalusia*). The Burgundio'nes in the fifth century obtained a portion of Gaul where they founded the kingdom of *Burgundy*. The Gotho'nes dwelt originally on the coast of the Baltic, but in the third century appear on the coast of the Euxine, where they were often at war with the Romans until Aurelian gave up Dacia to them (A.D. 272). They were soon afterward divided into *Ostrogoths* (*East-Goths*) and *Visigoths* (*West-Goths*). In the year 410, the Visigoths invaded Italy and the South-West of Gaul, and settled in Spain where they established a powerful kingdom, which was finally overthrown by the Moors. The Ostrogoths after harassing

---

QUESTIONS.—What is said of the Langobardi?—In what direction were they constantly emigrating?—Where did they settle at length?—What is said of the Vandali?—Of the Burgundiones?—Of the Gothones?—What is the meaning of the appellations Ostrogoths and Visigoths?

the Eastern Empire obtained permission from the court of Constantinople to invade Italy, which they completely conquered under their king, Theodoric the Great, A. D. 489, and where their dominion was maintained until it was overthrown by the Langobardi who invaded Italy A. D. 668 :

(10.) The *Cherusci*, the most celebrated of all the German tribes. They occupied the country between the Weser and Elbe. They were at the head of the confederation of the different tribes who, having been provoked by the tyranny of Varus, finally, under the leadership of Arminius, better known under the more familiar name of *Hermann*, destroyed the Roman legions stationed in Germania (9 B. C.) :

(11.) The *Alemanni* (probably *Alle Männer*, *All-Men*) as their name indicates, formed a confederation of several tribes on the upper Rhine and Danube. In the third century, they came in contact with the Romans, fought against them in Gaul and Southern Germany, and even invaded Italy. They finally established themselves in eastern Gaul and in Switzerland. From the *Alemanni*, Germany has been called by the French *Allemagne;* and by the Italians, *Alemagna.*

(12.) *Marcomanni* (*Bordermen*) was a name applicable to any nation or nations who inhabited and defended a *border* country. Marcomanni are first mentioned in history as driven back from Gaul across the Rhenus by Cæsar (58 B. C.). The most powerful who bore this name were those who had founded a mighty kingdom on the Eastern frontier of Germany, in Bohemia. It was a mixed union of different nations, united by the strong hands of the conqueror Marobu'dus. The object of this confederacy was to defend the German nations against the Romans in Pannonia. Among the towns of this confederacy were MAROBU'DUM (*Budweiss*) and USBIUM :

(13.) Other nations were the *Rugii; Bru'cteri*, with the town

---

QUESTIONS.—What is said of the Cherusci?—Under whom did they destroy the Roman legions?—When?—Give an account of the Alemanni.—What does the name Marcomanni signify?—What was the mightiest empire founded by these Marcomanni?

MEDIOLANIUM (*Metelen*); *Usi'petes; Tenchthe'ri*, with DIVITIA (*Deutz*); *Sygambri; Matti'aci*, with AQUÆ MATTI'ACÆ (*Wiesbaden*) and MATTI'ACUM (*Marburg*); *Chatti*, with MATTIUM; *Quadi*, with EBURODU'NUM; *Tubantes;* and the *Marsi.*

ISLANDS OF GERMANIA.

I'NSULÆ SCANDIÆ.

SCANDINAVIA (*Sweden* and *Norway*) was always regarded by the ancients as an island, thickly peopled, and its native inhabitants believed it to be a distinct continent.

Ptolemy speaks of four islands East of the Chersone'sus Ci'mbrica, which he calls *αἱ Σκανδίαι νῆσοι*. Their names are Scandia (probably, *Sweden*), Ne'rigos, Bergi, and Dumna.

§ 158. THE DANUBIAN PROVINCES.

I. RHÆTIA and VINDELICIA, or RHÆTIA PRIMA and SECUNDA.

These two countries were separated in the time of Augustus, but after the close of the first century they were united. Later, however, they were distinguished by the names of *Prima* and *Secunda.* Vindelicia, or Rhætia Secunda, was the North-Western part.

Boundaries.—North, GERMANIA; East, NO'RICUM and VENETIA; South, GALLIA TRANSPADA'NA; West, GALLIA.

Mountains.—ALPES RHÆ'TICÆ.

Rivers.—I'SARUS (*Isar*), ÆNUS (*Inn*), A'THESIS (*Adige*).

Lake.—LACUS BRIGANTI'NUS (*Lake of Constanz*).

Towns.—BRIGANTIUM (*Bregentz*), AUGUSTA VINDELICO'RUM (*Augsburg*), REGI'NUM (*Regensburg*), CASTRA BA'TAVA (*Passau*), TRIDENTUM (*Trient*).

QUESTIONS.—What name was given to Sweden and Norway?—How was it always regarded by the ancients?—Name the four Insulæ Scandiæ of Ptolemy?——§ 158. What is said of Rhætia and Vindelicia?—When were they separated?—When united?—How is it bounded?—What mountains are in it?—What rivers?—What lake?—What towns?

II. No'ricum.

The name was derived from Nore'ia, the capital of the country.

Boundaries.—North, Germania; East, Pannonia; South, Pannonia and Gallia Cisalpi'na; West, Rhætia and Vindelicia.

Mountains.—Alpes No'ricæ, Alpes Ca'rnicæ, Mons Cetius.

Rivers.—Dravus (*Drave*), Murus (*Muhr*).

Productions.—The mines of No'ricum were celebrated for their iron, which supplied the renowned factories of arms in Pannonia, Mœsia, and Northern Italy.

Inhabitants.—The No'rici, formerly called Taurisci, were a Keltic race. After a short, but severe struggle, they were conquered by Tiberius (13 B. C.).

Towns.—Nore'ia, famous as the scene of the destruction of a Roman army (113 B. C.), Boiodu'rum (*Innstadt*), Lauri'acum (*Lorch*), Juvavia (*Salzburg*).

III. Pannonia.

This was one of the most important provinces of the Roman Empire, its inhabitants always forming a considerable portion of the Roman legions.

Boundaries.—North, Germania; East, Dacia; South, I'llyris Roma'na; West, No'ricum and Gallia Cisalpi'na.

Mountains.—The vast plain of Pannonia is enclosed on the West and South by the Alpes Panno'nicæ.

Rivers.—Danubius, Dravus, Savus (*Save*).

Lake.—Lacus Pelso (*Platten See*).

Productions.—It was celebrated for its timber, which was imported into Italy in large quantities.

Questions.—Whence is the name Noricum derived?—How is it bounded?—Name its mountains.—Rivers.—Productions.—Inhabitants.—When were they conquered by the Romans?—Name some of the towns.—In what did the importance of Pannonia consist?—Name the boundaries.—Mountains.—Rivers.—Lake.—Productions.

Inhabitants.—The Pannonians were probably an Illyrian race; they are described as a brave and warlike people who, when the Romans first became acquainted with them, were notorious for their cruelty and love of bloodshed, as well as for their faithlessness and cunning.

Divisions.—During the first century it formed one province; in the second century it was divided into three parts: PANNONIA PRIMA, PANNONIA SECUNDA, VALERIA.

Towns.—VINDOBO'NA (*Vienna*), where the emperor M. Aurelius Antoni'nus died; ÆMO'NA, afterward JULIA AUGUSTA (*Laibach*), SISCIA or SEGESTA (*Sisseck*), TAURU'NUM (*Semlin*).

IV. MŒSIA.

The Greeks called it Mysia in Europe (*Μυσία ἡ ἐν Εὐρώπῃ*), to distinguish it from Mysia in Asia.

Boundaries.—North, DACIA; East, PONTUS EUXI'NUS; South, THRACIA; West, ILL'YRICUM and PANNONIA.

Mountains.—HÆMUS (*Balkan Mountains*), SCARDUS.

Rivers.—DRINUS (*Drino*), SAVUS, MARGUS (*Morana*).

Inhabitants.—It was inhabited by Thracian tribes, a portion of whom afterward went to the North-West part of Asia Minor.

Divisions.—In the reign of Trajan, it was divided into two parts; the Western half being called Mœsia Superior, and the Eastern half, Mœsia Inferior.

Towns.—As one of the frontier provinces of the Roman Empire, it was strengthened by a line of fortresses along the South bank of the Danube. The principal of these were VIMINACIUM, RATIARIA, NICO'POLIS, DUROSTO'RUM or DURO'STOLUM (*Silistria*), the birthplace of the general Aëtius, who with his rival Bonifacius was styled by the historian Procopius, *the last of the Romans*. On the Pontus Euxi'nus was TOMI or TOMIS, whither

QUESTIONS.—What is said of the inhabitants of Pannonia?—Into how many parts was it divided in the second century?—Name some of the towns.—What was Mœsia called by the Greeks?—Why?—Name the boundaries.—Mountains.—Rivers.—Inhabitants.—How was it divided?—What is said of its fortresses?—Name some of the towns.

Ovid was banished (A. D. 8). In the interior of the North-West part were NAÏSSUS, the native place of Constantine the Great, and TAURESIUM, the birthplace of Justinian.

§ 159. DACIA, or, The Land of the DACI or GETÆ, ἡ τῶν Γετῶν γῆ.

Dacia was the last of the Roman conquests in Europe, and received certain definite limits by its incorporation with the Empire under Trajan, an event immortalized by the column which still stands in Rome, bearing that Emperor's name. Though the dominion of the Romans lasted only for about a hundred and seventy years, yet in no country have they left a more lasting impression of their power, especially in the language. The present inhabitants, the Wallacks, style themselves *Romani*, and their tongue—the Wallachian—*Romania;* which, like the Italian, is soft, abounding in vowels, and deriving most of its words from the Latin, mixed up with many forms of Slavonic origin.

Boundaries.—North, CA'RPATES MONTES; East, SARMATIA EUROPÆA; South, MŒSIA; West, PANNONIA.

River.—The TISIA'NUS or TYSIA (*Theiss*) flowed into the Danube.

Inhabitants.—The Getæ, who at an unknown period changed their name into Daci, belonged probably to the Thracian group of nations. Being conquered by the Gauls, a great number of them were sold as slaves to the Athenians about 300 B. C., which appears from the names of slaves, *Davus* (i. e. *Dacus*) and *Geta* in the writers of the New Greek Comedy and their Roman imitator, Terence; with which usage may be compared our own

QUESTIONS.—§ 159. What was the last of the Roman conquests in Europe?—How long did this conquest last?—What boundaries were given to it after the Roman conquest?—What rivers were in Dacia?—What was the original name of the inhabitants?—What name did they afterward adopt?—To what group of nations did they belong?—By whom were they conquered?—How were they treated by their conquerors?—When?—What is an evidence of this?—Illustrate it.

designation of a bondman, *slave*, Germ. *Sklave*, that is, a *Slavonian* in bondage.

Town.—SARMIZEGETHU'SA, the capital, set on fire by its inhabitants in order that it might not fall into the hands of, Trajan.

Trajan built a bridge over the Danube, which seventeen years afterward (120 B.C.) was destroyed by Hadrian to prevent the barbarians crossing over into the Thracian provinces. Remains of this work are still to be seen. Beside this bridge, Trajan constructed three roads, which were connected with the Via Traja'na, which ran along the South side of the Danube, partly cut in the rock and partly supported on wooden beams.

SARMATIA EUROPÆA. (*ἡ Σαρματία.*)

This name was applied to the North-Eastern part of Europe.

Boundaries.—North, SUE'VICUM MARE and a tract of unknown country; East, the TANAIS and CHERSONE'SUS TAU'RICA (*Crimea*); South, DACIA; West, the VI'STULA.

Mountains.—CA'RPATES MONTES, SARMA'TICI MONTES, MONTES HYPERBOREI.

Rivers.—The TANAIS, BORY'STHENES, DANUBIUS, VI'STULA.

Productions.—It served only for pasturage.

Towns.—OLBIA (*'Ολβία*), a Greek colony, on the right bank of the Hy'panis, founded about 666 B.C. by settlers from the Ionic Mile'tus. At an early period, it became a point of the highest importance for the inland trade, which, issuing thence, was carried on in an easterly and northerly direction as far as Central Asia. It was visited by Hero'dotus, who obtained his valuable information about Scythia from the Greek traders of Olbia. The city was destroyed by the Goths (A.D. 250).

QUESTIONS.—What is the capital of Dacia?—What name was applied to the north-eastern part of Europe?—Name the boundaries.—Mountains.—Rivers.—Productions.—Towns.—When was Olbia founded?—Where?—By whom?—When destroyed?—What is said about its trade?

§ 160. TAU'RICA CHERSONE'SUS.

(*The Crimea* or *Tau'rica.*)

This is a peninsula stretching into the Pontus Euxi'nus from Sarmatia, with which it is connected by the Isthmus of Taphros or Taphræ (*Perekop*).

Name.—It received the appellation *Tau'rica* from its inhabitants, the *Tauri*, and that of *Scy'thica* from the *Scythæ* who dispossessed the Tauri. Its modern name, The *Crimea*, is probably derived from Eski-*Krim* (Old *Crim*), which Forbiger identifies with the ancient town *Cimmerium*. Since its incorporation with the Russian Empire, it has again been called *Tau'rica*.

Extent.—It contains an area of about 10,000 square miles, three-fourths of which consists of flat plains, little elevated above the sea; the remainder toward the South is mountainous.

Mountains.—TAU'RICI MONTES, the highest tops of which are Trapezus and Cimmerium.

Capes.—CRIUMETO'PON (*Κριοῦ μέτωπον*, *Ram's Head*; prob. *Cape Aithodor*), on the Southern side of the peninsula; PROMONTORIUM PARTHENIUM (*Cape Khersonese*), the westernmost point, famous for a temple of A'rtemis.

Productions.—Between the mountains are many deep and warm valleys open to the South, and sheltered from the North wind, where the olive and vine flourish, and the apricot and almond ripen to perfection. The present character of the country does not correspond with the description of the ancients. The very spots praised by ancient authors for their fertility, are now desolate and monotonous steppes.

Inhabitants.—The original inhabitants were the savage Tauri,

QUESTIONS.—§ 160. Describe the situation of Taurica Chersonesus.—What is said of its names?—How many square miles does it contain?—Describe its physical appearance.—Name some of its mountains.—Capes.—What is said of its productions?—What difference exists between the former and present state of the peninsula?—What were the native inhabitants?—Who settled among them?

who dwelt in the interior, which was but little known in antiquity. The interest connected with the history of the peninsula is derived chiefly from the maritime settlements of the Greeks. The coast was early visited by the Milesians, who planted some flourishing colonies upon it. Beside this, there was a Dorian colony near the site of the present *Sebastopol*, and the Athenians are said to have possessed the town of Nymphæon on the Cimmerian Bo'sporus.

Towns.—(1.) CHERSONE'SUS (*Χερσόνησος*), a colony from the Dorian city Heraclei'a in Pontus, situated at the Westernmost point of the peninsula, and conjectured to have been founded about the middle of the fifth century B.C. The ancient city of Chersone'sus, of which considerable remains were to be seen as late as the end of the last century, had fallen into decay before the time of Strabo (born probably about 54 B.C.); but the new town was flourishing, which seems to have been situated on the West side of the present Quarantine Harbor of Sebastopol, and was one of the principal commercial cities of antiquity; under the name of *Cherson*, or *Chorson*, it flourished till a late period of the middle ages. East of Chersone'sus was SY'MBOLÔN PORTUS (*Gulf of Balaklava*), a harbor with a narrow entrance, which was anciently the chief station for the pirates of the Tauric peninsula:

(2.) THEODOSIA (*Θεοδόσια*, *Caffa*), situated in the South-Eastern part of the peninsula, a flourishing colony of the Milesians, which had an extensive commerce, particularly in grain:

(3.) PANTICAPÆUM (*Παντικάπαιον*) was situated on the Western side of the Cimmerian Bo'sporus, and not far from the entrance to the Lacus Mæo'tis (*ἡ Μαιῶτις*). It is now called *Kertch*, and in the tumuli around this place many valuable works of ancient

---

QUESTIONS.—Name some of the towns of Taurica Chersonesus.—Who founded the earlier Chersonesus?—When?—Where?—What is said of the later town?—What is said of Symbolôn Portus?—Where was Theodosia situated?—By whom was it founded?—Where was Panticapæum situated?—What is it now called?

art have been discovered. Panticapæum was the capital of Bo′s-porus, a Greek kingdom which existed till near the end of the fourth century, and whose territory in its palmiest days extended as far North as the Tanais, while to the Westward it was bounded on the land side by the mountains of Theodosia. This fertile but narrow region was the granary of Greece, especially of Athens, which drew annually from it a supply of four hundred thousand *medimni* (about 600,000 bushels) of corn. Beside this territory, the kings of Bo′sporus possessed a tract of land on the Asiatic side of the strait.

QUESTIONS.—Of what kingdom was Panticapæum the capital?—What was the extent of this kingdom?—What is said of its fertility?

§ 161. ISLANDS OF NORTHERN EUROPE.

I'NSULÆ BRITA'NNICÆ. (*Νῆσοι Βρεττανικαί.*)

They comprised BRITANNIA (*Great Britain*), HIBERNIA (*Ireland*), and some smaller islands.

I. BRITANNIA.

Name.—The name I'nsulæ Brita'nnicæ is older than Britannia. The distinction between *Britannia* as Great Britain and *Ierne* begins with Cæsar, and that between *Britannia* as South Britain and *Caledonia* as North Britain, is later still. The origin of the designations *Britannia* and *Britanni* is uncertain, but there is no evidence that any part of the population of the British Isles called themselves *Britons*. They were called so by the Gauls and the Gallic name was adopted by the Romans, the term being probably Iberic and Gallic as well. The name *Albion* (in Ptolemy, *Ἀλουΐων*) is first found in Pliny (H. N. IV. 16). Some derive it from the Keltic *alb* or *alp, high* (compare *Alpes, the Alps*) with reference to *the lofty coasts* of the island as it faces Gallia; others connect it with the Latin *albus, white*, supposing the name to have been given to Britain on account of its *chalky* cliffs.

Mountains.—MONS GRAMPIUS (*the Grampian Hills;* in the Gaelic, *Grantz-bain*), rendered memorable by the victory over Ga'lgacus by Agri'cola in the last year of his government (A. D. 84), which entirely broke the spirit of the Britons.

Capes.—CANTIUM (*North Foreland*), BOLERIUM (*Land's End*), DAMNONIUM or OCRINUM (*Lizard Point*).

QUESTIONS.—§ 161. What islands did the Insulæ Britannicæ comprise?—What is said of the names of Britannia?—Derive Albion.—What mountains of Britannia are mentioned by the ancients?—Name some of the capes.

Rivers and Inlets.—BODERIA ÆSTUARIUM (*Frith of Forth*), TINA (the *Tine*), ABUS (the *Humber*), ME'TARIS ÆSTUARIUM (the *Wash*), TA'MESIS or TA'MESA (the *Thames*), SABRI'NA (the *Severn*), ITU'NA ÆSTUARIUM (*Solway Frith*), GLOTA ÆSTUARIUM (*Frith of Clyde*).

Climate.—The island, almost always wrapped in fogs, was believed to have a mild climate, and to be covered with large forests and marshes.

Productions.—The articles of foreign commerce were tin and lead, chiefly the former. The most ancient Greek designation of the British Isles is *Cassite'rides* (*Tin Islands*), found in Hero'dotus (III. 115):—*islands, called Cassite'rides, from which tin* (*κασσίτερος*) *comes to us.* The historian learned this from the Phœnicians, and indeed this name of tin is of Oriental origin, being in Sanskrit, *kastîra*, and in Arabic, *kasdîr*. The Phœnicians carried on the traffic in tin with the Britons probably as early as 1000 B.C.; the Britons taking in exchange salt, furs, and bronze vessels. Other productions were lumber, wheat, and also iron, silver, and gold.

Inhabitants.—The population of South Britain was British (aboriginal), Britanno-Roman, with a Gaelic element, and Germanic, the latter destined to replace all the rest. The inhabitants of North Britain were British and Gaelic with Pict elements and only a slight Roman admixture. The occasion is taken to add here the various designations showing how wide-spread the Keltic element was in Western Europe: *Κελτοί*, later, *Κέλται*, *Γαλάται*, *Celtæ*, *Galli*, *Gauls*, *Gael*, *Welsh* (French, *Gallois*), *Celtibe'ri*.

The civil history of Britain begins with the invasion by the

QUESTIONS.—Name some of the rivers and inlets of Britannia.—Describe its climate.—What were its productions?—What were the British Isles called by the early Greeks?—Give an account of this designation.—What other productions are mentioned?—What is said of the inhabitants?—Which of the intrusive elements has shown itself the most powerful?—Repeat the designations of the Kelts in western Europe.—When does the civil history of Britain begin?

Romans. During one of Cæsar's campaigns in Gallia, the Ve'neti (in the vicinity of the present town of *Vannes*) obtained assistance against Cæsar from the Britons. To chastise them for the succor they were accustomed to send to the enemies of the Romans, Cæsar made his first descent (in the Summer of 55 B.C.). He is opposed on his landing, but overcomes the Britons and retires to Gallia. In the spring of the next year he makes a second invasion, is resisted by Cassivelaunus and withdraws his whole army. His operations in the first instance were confined to the south-west corner of the island; in the second, he pushed on as far westward as the modern county of Herts, a distance of about eighty miles. In the reign of Claudius the Romans returned to Britain under Plautius (A.D. 43). The Britons led on by Cara'ctacus and Togodumnus make a brave resistance but are overpowered. Plautius' successor, Osterius, defeats and captures Cara'ctacus (c. A.D. 51). The Britons afterward (A.D. 62) rise in revolt to the number of 230,000 under the great and brave Boadice'a, Queen of the Ice'ni, and give battle to the Roman general, Suetonius, but are conquered with a loss of 80,000 dead on the field. Several generals are then successively sent to the command of Britain, but the Romans make little progress till the time of Vespasian (A.D. 70–78), when the Brigantes and the Silu'res are subdued. The glory of completing the conquest of Britain was reserved for Cnæus Julius Agri'cola whose exploits there achieved (A.D. 78–84) are recorded in the *Agri'cola* by his son-in-law, the historian Ta'citus. To check the incursions of the barbarians from the north, Agri'cola (A.D. 79) built a wall from Solway Frith to the mouth of the Tine; and (A.D. 81) constructed another far north of the first, from the Frith of Clyde to the Frith of Forth. These proving insufficient, Hadrian (A.D. 120) planned and executed a much stronger work where Agri'cola's first wall had been drawn.

QUESTIONS.—Describe the two descents of Cæsar.—What further movement was made in the reign of Claudius?—What did Plautius' successor achieve?—What is said of Boadicea?—Who accomplished the conquest of Britain?—Give an account of the Walls of Agricola.—Of that of Hadrian.

Twenty years afterward the second wall of Agri'cola was restored under Antoni'nus and called *Vallum Antoni'ni* (still traced, and called *Grimes Dyke*). But the greatest work of all was that constructed by the Emperor Seve'rus (A. D. 209–10) a few yards north of Hadrian's Wall. It was seventy-four miles long, twelve feet in height, and eight in thickness, built of stone laid in the most durable mortar. This stupendous work was garrisoned by 10,000 men. The Roman power gradually decaying in Britain and the distresses of the Empire rendering the withdrawal of the troops necessary, near the middle of the fifth century, or according to some, about the year 420, nearly five hundred years after their first invasion under Julius Cæsar, the Romans finally abandoned the island.

Divisions.—I. BRITANNIA; also called, BRITANNIA ROMA'NA, or PROVINCIA INFERIOR.

II. CALEDONIA; also called, BRITANNIA BA'RBARA, or PROVINCIA SUPERIOR.

The boundary of Britannia Roma'na in the time of Claudius (A. D. 41–54) was the Abus on the north, and the Sabri'na on the west, but Agri'cola conquered the island as far north as the Frith of Clyde and the Frith of Forth. During the reign of Hadrian, this acquisition was abandoned, and the boundary line between Britannia Roma'na and Britannia Ba'rbara was fixed by the wall erected between Solway Frith and the Tyne.

Nations and Towns.—A. In *Britannia Roma'na* were eight important tribes:

(1.) Those who inhabited Cantium (now *Kent* and a part of *Surrey*). They carried on the chief traffic with Gaul, and were the most civilized people of the island. In their territory was

---

QUESTIONS.—Describe the Wall of Antonine.—That of Severus.—When did the Romans abandon the island?—Why?—Name the divisions of Britain.—How was Britannia Romana bounded when formed into a province?—How far north did Agricola push his conquests?—Where was the northern limit fixed under Hadrian?—How many important tribes were in Britannia Romana?—What is said of the people of Cantium?

Cantium Promontorium. Among their towns the most celebrated were:

a. LONDINIUM (*London*), called also in the fourth century *Augusta*, the capital of Britannia Roma'na, originally situated on the south bank of the Ta'mesis, but soon extended over the northern bank of the river. Londinium is first mentioned by Ta'citus (c. A. D. 60) who calls it a much frequented commercial town. It was the central point from which the military roads of the country started, for which reason it had the *milliarium* or *mile*-stone, by which the length of roads was measured:

b. Other places: DUBRÆ or DUBRIS PORTUS (*Dover*), DUROVERNUM (*Canterbury*), DUROBRI'VÆ (*Rochester*), RUTUPIÆ (*Richborough*), about which Cæsar probably fixed his camp in his second descent on Britannia:

(2.) The *Trinobantes*, a warlike tribe, who inhabited the country North of the Ta'mesis. Their chief town was CAMALODU'NUM (*Colchester*), the oldest Roman colony on the island:

(3.) The *Ice'ni*, who inhabited the country North of the Trinobantes (*Norfolk* and *Suffolk*, i. e. *North-people* and *South-people*):

(4.) The *Belgæ*, South-West of the Ta'mesis. Here were Aquæ Solis or Aquæ Ca'lidæ, *Ὕδατα θερμά*, in Ptolemy (*Bath*, specially celebrated for its Roman remains), the waters of which were highly valued and often used by the Romans; VENTA BELGA'RUM (*Winchester*, where Roman remains are still found); and MAGNUS PORTUS (*Portsmouth*):

(5.) The *Dumnonii* or *Damnonii* occupied the south-west part of the island and gave their name to *Damnonium* Promontorium. They were the inhabitants of Devon, Cornwall, and the western part of Somerset. Their name *Dumn* probably still subsists in the modern *Devon*. The Damnonians traded in tin, for which they received salt, skins, and bronze vessels:

(6.) The *Cornavii* were settled along the banks of the Sabri'na.

QUESTIONS.—Give an account of Londinium.—Name other places —What is said of the Trinobantes?—Of the Iceni?—Of the Belgæ—Of the Damnonii?—Of the Cornavii?

Among their towns were UROCONIUM (*Shrewsbury*), and DEVA (*Chester*), at the mouth of the DEVA (*Dee*):

(7.) The *Corita'ni* on the east coast, south of the Abus, with the towns of LINDUM (*Lincoln*), and RATÆ (*Leicester*):

(8.) The country above the Abus to the wall of Hadrian was occupied by the *Brigantes.* Their chief town was EBORA'CUM (*York*), next to Londinium, the most important place on the island, and the seat of government under the Roman dominion. Here two Roman emperors, Seve'rus and Constantius resided till their death. Other towns among the Brigantes were LUGUVALLUM (*Carlisle*), LUTUDA'RUM (probably, *Leeds*), MANCUNIUM (*Manchester*, i. e. *Man-castra*).

The only British tribes mentioned by Cæsar are the people of *Cantium*, the *Trinobantes*, the *Cenimagni*, the *Segonti'aci*, the *Anca'lites*, the *Bi'broci*, and the *Cassi*, all which probably dwelt in the south-eastern part.

The northern part of Britain was termed CALEDONIA, a name which first occurs in Pliny (c. A. D. 50), and which is variously derived. The native critics regard it as a Romanized form of the Welsh *celeddon*, the plural of *celyd*, *a retreat*, *a woody shelter* (compare the Latin *celo*). The Scots of the present day call their division of Britain, *Gael-doch* from *Gael*, *Gallic or Keltic*, and *doch*, *a district*, and from this designation other authorities suppose the Romans to have formed the word *Caledonia*.

The Caledonii are mentioned in the fourth century as the PICTI (perhaps so called as being *picti*, *painted* on going into battle) and the SCOTI (compare the word *Scythæ*). They were defeated by the Romans, but were never incorporated into the Empire.

QUESTIONS.—What is said of the Coritani?—Of the Brigantes?—What British tribes are mentioned by Cæsar?—What was the northern part of Britain called?—What is said of the origin of the name?—What is said of the Picti and Scoti?

§ 162. II. Hibernia.

This island is called Ierne (ἡ Ἰέρνη) by Aristotle; by Mela, Iverna, and by Cæsar and Pliny, Hibernia, which are probably mere variations of *Ierne*, which seems closely akin to the present Gaelic name *Eri* or *Erin*, supposed to be of Phœnician origin, and for which, on account of its resemblance, the Greeks employed their word Ἱέρα to designate the island, and hence the Roman *Sacra* (Insula). In Keltic *Iar* or *Eir* means *western*, and may have been applied to the island to designate its position relative to Europe. From *Eri* we have *Irish* and *Ire*-land. Toward the end of the third century the name *Scotia* was applied to Hibernia, from which time till the beginning of the eleventh century it denoted that island exclusively; so on the other hand, the Gaelic, or ancient language of the Scots, is also called *Erse* (*Irish*), both facts indicating the close relation of Scotland and Ireland in past times. Little was known of Hibernia by the ancients, and that chiefly by the Iberians, the Phœnicians, and the Greeks, but monuments and relics attest the presence of a people considerably advanced in civilization in Ireland before the fifth century, such as Cyclopian buildings, sepulchral mounds containing stone chambers, mines, and bronze instruments and weapons of classic form and elegant workmanship. Agri'cola gathered some scanty information respecting the island from the Britons who traded with its inhabitants, but the Romans never attempted to conquer or invade it.

Questions.—§ 162. What is said of the ancient names of Ireland?—What is said of the ancient use of the term Scotia?—What is the Gaelic also called?—What may be inferred from these two facts?—To whom was Hibernia known?—What is said of its antiquities?—How did Agricola learn something of the island?

III. Smaller Islands.

(1.) Cassite'rides; by this designation must have been specially meant the *tin*-county of Cornwall, with which the *Scilly Isles* were more or less confounded:

(2.) Vectis or Vecta (*Isle of Wight*), first known to Massilian merchants who went thither for tin, which was brought over to the island from Cornwall by Britons. It was conquered by Vespasian:

(3.) Mona (*Anglesey*), off the coast of the Ordovi'ces. This densely populated island was the chief strong-hold of the Druids and Bards:

(4.) Monari'na, or Monaœda (*Isle of Man*), situated half-way between Britannia and Hibernia:

(5.) Ebu'dæ, or Hebu'dæ (*the Hebrides*), North-West of Britannia:

(6.) O'rcades (*Orkneys*), North of Britannia:

(7.) Thule or Thyle, a celebrated island discovered and described by the Greek navigator Pytheas of Massilia (prob. 300 B.C.). From the time of its discovery it was regarded as the most northerly point of the known world (*ultima Thule*, Virg. Georg. I. 30), though no further knowledge was obtained respecting it. According to some it is the modern *Mainland*, the largest of the Shetland Islands; according to others *Iceland;* some believe it to be the part of Norway now called *Thile* or *Thile*mark; some, the extreme point of Jutland now known as *Thy* or *Thy*land; and some, the whole Scandinavian peninsula. With its name compare the Gothic *Tiel* or *Tiule* (τέλος, end, *goal*) which denoted *the remotest land.*

Questions.—What did the Cassiterides specially denote?—What is said of Vectis?—Who conquered it?—What is the modern name of Vectis?—What of Mona?—What is said of Mona?—What was the ancient name of the modern Isle of Man?—What two island groups were situated to the north-west?—What is said of Thule?—What are the various opinions in respect to its application?

ATLANTIS. (ἡ Ἀτλαντὶς νῆσος.)

Plato, in his Timæus (c. VI.), relates a conversation between Solon and an Ægyptian priest, in which this priest says:

That sea (i. e. the Atlantic) *was then navigable, and had an island fronting that mouth which you in your tongue call the Pillars of Hercules; this island was larger than Libya and Asia put together; and there was a passage hence for travellers of that day to the rest of the islands, as well as from those islands to the whole opposite continent that surrounds the real sea. For as to what is within the mouth now mentioned* (i. e. the Mediterranean), *it appears to be a bay with a narrow entrance; and that sea is a true sea, and the land that entirely surrounds it may most correctly be called a continent.——Subsequently by violent earthquakes and floods, which brought desolation in a single day and night—the Atlantic Island was plunged beneath the sea and entirely disappeared; whence even now that sea is unnavigable by reason of the shoals of mud created by the subsiding island.*

Whether this opinion was founded on the vague records of some actual discovery in early times, or on mythical or poetical representations, it is impossible now to determine. But the following lines of Se′neca are said to have made a powerful impression on the mind of Columbus, and may thus have really contributed to the discovery of the Western Continent:

Venient annis sæcula seris,
Quibus Oceanus vincula rerum
Laxet, et ingens pateat tellus,
Tethysque novos detegat orbes;
Nec sit terris ultima Thule.
Medea, Act II. 375–379.

QUESTIONS.—What Greek philosopher speaks of Atlantis?—What does he say of it?—Has this statement any real foundation?—In which of the Latin poets do we find an anticipation, as it were, of the discovery of our continent?

INDEX.

THE END.

MEARS & DUSENBERY, ELECTROTYPERS. C. SHERMAN & SON, PRINTERS.

CATALOGUE

OF

Approved School and College Text-Books.

PUBLISHED BY E. H. BUTLER & CO.,

137 South Fourth St., Philadelphia.

Goodrich's Pictorial History of the United States. A Pictorial History of the United States, with notices of other portions of America. By S. G. Goodrich, author of "Peter Parley's Tales." For the use of Schools. Revised and improved edition, brought down to the present time (1860). Re-written and newly illustrated. 1 vol. 12mo., embossed backs. Upwards of 450 pages. Price $1.13

Goodrich's American Child's Pictorial History of the United States. An introduction to the author's "Pictorial History of the United States." Will be published in July, 1860.

Goodrich's Pictorial History of England. A Pictorial History of England. By S. G. Goodrich, author of "Pictorial History of the United States," etc. Price $0.94

Goodrich's Pictorial History of Rome. A Pictorial History of Ancient Rome, with sketches of the History of Modern Italy. By S. G. Goodrich, author of "Pictorial History of the United States." For the use of Schools. Revised and improved edition. . Price $0.94

Goodrich's Pictorial History of Greece. A Pictorial History of Greece; Ancient and Modern. By S. G. Goodrich, author of "Pictorial History of the United States." For the use of Schools. Revised edition. . Price $0.94

Goodrich's Pictorial History of France. A Pictorial History of France. For the use of Schools. By S. G. Goodrich, author of "Pictorial History of the United States." Revised and improved edition, brought down to the present time. . . . . . . Price $0.94

Goodrich's Parley's Common School History of the World. A Pictorial History of the World; Ancient and Modern. For the use of Schools. By S. G. Goodrich, author of "Pictorial History of the United States," etc. Illustrated by engravings. . Price $1.13

Goodrich's First History. The First History. An Introduction to Parley's Common School History. Designed for beginners at Home and School. Illustrated by Maps and Engravings. By S. G. Goodrich, author of the Pictorial Series of Histories, etc. . . . Price $0.38

Hows' Ladies' Reader. The Ladies' Reader. Designed for the use of Ladies' Schools and Family Reading Circles; comprising choice selections from standard authors, in Prose and Poetry, with the essential Rules of Elocution, simplified and arranged for strictly practical use. By JOHN W. S. HOWS, Professor of Elocution. . . Price $1.13

Coppee's Elements of Logic. Elements of Logic. Designed as a Manual of Instruction. By HENRY COPPEE, A. M., Professor of English Literature in the University of Pennsylvania; and late Principal Assistant Professor of Ethics and English Studies in the United States Military Academy at West Point. . . . . Price $0.75

Coppee's Elements of Rhetoric. Elements of Rhetoric. Designed as a Manual of Instruction. By HENRY COPPEE, A. M., author of "Elements of Logic," etc. New edition, revised. . . . . . Price $1.00

Tenney's Geology. Geology; for Teachers, Classes, and Private Students. By SANBORN TENNEY, A. M., Lecturer on Physical Geography and Natural History in the Massachusetts Teachers' Institutes. Illustrated with Two Hundred Wood Engravings. . . . Price $1.13

Stockhardt's Chemistry. The Principles of Chemistry, illustrated by Simple Experiments. By Dr. JULIUS ADOLPH STÖCKHARDT, Professor in the Royal Academy of Agriculture at Tharand, and Royal Inspector of Medicine in Saxony. Translated by C. H. PEIRCE, M. D. Fifteenth Thousand. . . . . Price $1.96

Reid's Essays on the Intellectual Powers of

Man. Essays on the Intellectual Powers of Man. By THOMAS REID, D. D., F.R.S.E. Abridged, with notes and illustrations from Sir WILLIAM HAMILTON and others. Edited by JAMES WALKER, D. D., President of Harvard College. Price $1.31

Stewart's Philosophy of the Active and

Moral Powers of Man. The Philosophy of the Active and Moral Powers of Man. By DUGALD STEWART, F.R.SS. Lond. and Ed. Revised, with omissions and additions, by JAMES WALKER, D. D., President of Harvard College. Price $1.31

Mitchell's First Lessons in Geography.

First Lessons in Geography; for young children. Designed as an Introduction to the author's Primary Geography. By S. AUGUSTUS MITCHELL, author of a Series of Geographical Works. Illustrated with maps and numerous engravings. Price $0.38

Mitchell's Primary Geography. An Easy

Introduction to the study of Geography. Designed for the instruction of children in Schools and Families. Illustrated by nearly one hundred engravings and sixteen colored maps. By S. AUGUSTUS MITCHELL. . . . Price $0.42

Mitchell's New Intermediate Geography.

An entirely new work. The maps are all engraved on copper, in the best manner, and brought down to the present date. It is profusely illustrated with beautiful engravings, and is the most complete quarto Geography ever issued in the world. . . . . Price $1.12½

Mitchell's School Geography and Atlas.

New Revised Edition. A System of Modern Geography, comprising a description of the present state of the World, and its five great divisions, America, Europe, Asia, Africa, and Oceanica, with their several Empires, Kingdoms, States, Territories, etc. Embellished by numerous engravings. Adapted to the capacity of youth. Accompanied by an Atlas containing thirty-two maps, drawn and engraved expressly for this work. By S. AUGUSTUS MITCHELL. . Price $1.20

Mitchell's Ancient Geography and Atlas.

First Edition. Designed for Academies, Schools, and Families. A System of Classical and Sacred Geography, embellished with engravings of remarkable events, views of ancient cities, and various interesting antique remains. Together with an Ancient Atlas, containing maps illustrating the work. By S. AUGUSTUS MITCHELL. . . . . Price $1.25

Mitchell's New Ancient Geography. An

entirely new work, elegantly illustrated. . Price $1.13

Mitchell's Intermediate Geography. First

Edition. Intermediate or Secondary Geography. A System of Modern Geography, comprising a description of the present state of the World, and its great divisions, illustrated by more than forty colored maps, and numerous wood-cut engravings. By S. AUGUSTUS MITCHELL. . Price $0.84

Mitchell's Geographical Question Book, comprising Geographical Definitions, and containing questions on all the maps of Mitchell's School Atlas; to which is added an Appendix, embracing valuable Tables in Mathematical and Physical Geography. . . Price $0.25

Mitchell's Biblical Geography. Sabbath School Geography, designed for instruction in Sabbath School and Bible Classes, illustrated with colored maps and wood-cut engravings. By S. AUGUSTUS MITCHELL. Price $0.75

Smith's English Grammar. English Grammar on the Productive System: a method of instruction recently adopted in Germany and Switzerland. Designed for Schools and Academies. By ROSWELL C. SMITH. Price $0.25

Comstock's Elocution. A System of Elocution, with special reference to Gesture, to the treatment of Stammering and Defective Articulation; comprising numerous diagrams and engraved figures illustrative of the subject. By ANDREW COMSTOCK, M.D., Principal of the Vocal and Polyglott Gymnasium. Twentieth edition, enlarged. . . . . Price $1.00

Flanders's Constitution of the United States. An Exposition of the Constitution of the United States. Designed as a Manual of Instruction. By HENRY FLANDERS, author of "The Lives and Times of the Chief Justices," etc. . . . . Price $0.84

Hart's Constitution of the United States.

A Brief Exposition of the Constitution of the United States, for the use of Common Schools. By JOHN S. HART, LL. D., Principal of the Philadelphia High School, and Professor of Moral, Mental, and Political Science in the same. Price $0.30

Hart's English Grammar. English Grammar, or An Exposition of the Principles and Usages of the English Language. By JOHN S. HART, A. M., Principal of the Philadelphia High School, and Member of the American Philosophical Society. . . . . Price $0.34

Hart's Class Book of Poetry. Class Book of Poetry, consisting of Selections from Distinguished English and American Poets, from Chaucer to the present day. The whole arranged in chronological order, with Biographical and Critical Remarks. By JOHN S. HART, LL. D., Principal of the Philadelphia High School. . Price $0.84

Hart's Class Book of Prose. Class Book of Prose, consisting of Selections from Distinguished English and American Authors, from Chaucer to the present day. The whole arranged in Chronological order, with Biographical and Critical Remarks. By JOHN S. HART, LL. D., Principal of the Philadelphia High School. . Price $0.84

Coleman's Historical Geography of the Bible. An Historical Geography of the Bible. By Rev. LYMAN COLEMAN. Illustrated by maps, from the latest and most authentic sources, of various countries mentioned in the Scriptures. New edition, with additions. . Price $1.25

Angell's Reader, No. 1. The Child's First Book: containing Easy Lessons in Spelling and Reading. Being the first of a series, complete in six numbers. By Oliver Angell, A.M., Principal of the Franklin High School, Providence. New Edition. . . Price $0.08

Angell's Reader, No. 2. The Child's Second Book: containing Easy Lessons in Spelling and Reading. Being the second of a series, complete in six numbers. By Oliver Angell, A.M., Principal of the Franklin High School, Providence. New Edition. . . Price $0.14

Angell's Reader, No. 3. The Child's Third Book: containing Easy Lessons in Spelling and Reading. Being the third of a series, complete in six numbers. By Oliver Angell, A.M., Principal of the Franklin High School, Providence. New Edition. . . Price $0.17

Angell's Reader, No. 4. The Child's Fourth Book: containing Easy Lessons in Spelling and Reading. Being the fourth of a series, complete in six numbers. By Oliver Angell, A.M., Principal of the Franklin High School, Providence. New Edition. . . Price $0.30

Angell's Reader, No. 5. Angell's Fifth Reader: containing Lessons in Reading and Spelling. Being the fifth of a series, complete in six numbers. By Oliver Angell, A.M., Principal of the Franklin High School, Providence. New Edition. . . . . Price $0.50

Angell's Reader, No. 6. The Select Reader:

designed for the higher classes in Academies and Schools. Being the sixth and last of the series. By OLIVER ANGELL, A.M., Principal of the Franklin High School, Providence. New Edition. . . . . Price $0.75

Kendall's Uranography. Uranography; or

a Description of the Heavens, designed for the use of Schools and Academies; accompanied by an Atlas of the Heavens, showing the Places of the Principal Stars, Clusters, and Nebulæ. By E. OTIS KENDALL, Professor of Mathematics and Astronomy in the University of Pennsylvania, and Member of the American Philosophical Society. The Uranography contains 365 pages, 12mo., with 9 fine engravings. The Atlas is in 4to., and contains 18 large maps. Price $1.50

Fleming and Tibbins' Pronouncing French

and English, and English and French Dictionary, abridged. A New and Complete French and English, and English and French Dictionary, on the basis of the Royal Dictionary, English and French, and French and English. By Professor FLEMING, formerly Professor of English in the College Louis le Grand, and Professor TIBBINS, Professor, and author of several lexicographical works. With Complete Tables of the Verbs, on an entirely new plan, to which the verbs throughout the work are referred. By P. W. GENGEMBRE, Professor of Foreign Languages in the Girard College. The whole prepared by J. DOBSON, Member of the American Philosophical Society, of the Academy of Natural Sciences of Philadelphia, etc., etc. . . . . . Price $1.13

Fleming and Tibbins' French and English,

and English and French Dictionary. 8vo. fine sheep. A New and Complete French and English, and English and French Dictionary, on the basis of the Royal Dictionary, English and French, and French and English. By Professor FLEMING, formerly Professor of English in the College of Louis le Grand, and Professor TIBBINS, author of several lexicographical works. With Complete Tables of the Verbs, on an entirely new plan, to which the verbs throughout the work are referred. By P. W. GENGEMBRE, Professor of Foreign Languages in Girard College. The whole prepared, with the addition, in their respective places, of a very great number of Terms in the Natural Sciences, Chemistry, Medicine, etc., etc., which are not to be found in any other French and English Dictionary, by J. DOBSON, Member of the American Philosophical Society, of the Academy of Natural Sciences, etc., etc. New edition, revised and corrected. 1 vol. 8vo. . . . . Price $3.00

Nugent's French and English Dictionary.

A New Pocket Dictionary of the French and English Languages, in two parts: 1. French and English; 2. English and French. Containing all the words in general use, and authorized by the best writers. By THOMAS NUGENT, LL. D. Price $0.62

Porney's Syllabaire Français, or French

Spelling Book. Revised, corrected, and improved, with the addition of the most necessary verbs, adjectives, and idiomatical phrases alphabetically arranged. By J. MEIER, late Professor of French and German in Yale University. . Price $0.34

Geographie Elementaire a l'Usage des

Écoles et des Familles. Illustrée par 15 cartes et 30 Gravures. Par Peter Parley. . . . . Price $0.60

Histoire des Etats Unis d'Amerique, avec

Notices des autres parties du Nouveau Monde. Par Samuel G. Goodrich. . . . . Price $0.94

Petite Histoire Universelle a l'Usage des

Écoles et des Familles. Par S. G. Goodrich. Price $0.94

Philosophie Proverbiale. Par Martin F.

Tupper, Docteur en Droit, et Membre de la Société Royale. Traduite en Français d'après la Dixième Edition, par George Metivier. Revu et corrigé par F. A. Bregy, Professeur de Français à la Haute École Centrale de Philadelphie. . . . . Price $0.75

Donnegan's Greek and English Lexicon.

A New Greek and English Lexicon, on the plan of the Greek and German Lexicon of Schneider; the words alphabetically arranged—distinguishing such as are poetical, of dialectic variety, or peculiar to certain writers and classes of writers; with Examples, literally translated, selected from the classical writers. By James Donnegan, M. D., of London. Revised and enlarged by Robert B. Patton, Professor of Ancient Languages in the College of New Jersey; with the assistance of J. Addison Alexander, D. D., of the Theological Seminary at Princeton. 1 vol. 8vo. 1400 pp. . . Price $3.00

Becker's Book-Keeping. A Treatise on the Theory and Practice of Book-keeping by Double Entry. Designed to elucidate the Principles of the Science, and impart a knowledge of the forms observed by Practical Accountants, in the various departments of business. By GEORGE J. BECKER, Professor of Drawing, Writing, and Book-keeping in the Girard College. . . Price $1.00

Becker's Book-Keeping. Blanks. Second Series. . . . . Price $0.94
Third Series. 0.75
Fourth Series. 1.00

Becker's System of Book-Keeping. A Complete and Practical System of Double Entry Book-keeping, containing three sets of Books, illustrative of the forms, arrangements, and uses of all the principal and auxiliary books employed in the various kinds of mercantile, mechanical, and professional pursuits, designed as a Key to Becker's Treatise on the Theory and Practice of Book-keeping, and as a Guide for Teachers and Accountants; to which is added a complete set of Practical Business Forms, including the most important in use by Forwarding and Commission Houses, a number of miscellaneous forms adapted to various kinds of business, Abbreviated Journal Forms, Executors' and Administrators' Accounts, &c. By GEORGE J. BECKER. Price $1.50

Booth's Phonographic Instructor. Being an Introduction to the Compounding Style of Phonography. By JAMES C. BOOTH. A new edition. . . Price $0.37

Green's Gradations in Algebra. Gradations in Algebra, in which the first Principles of Analysis are inductively explained, illustrated by copious exercises, and made suitable for Primary Schools. By RICHARD W. GREEN, A. M., author of "Arithmetical Guide," "Little Reckoner," etc. . . . . Price $0.62

The Scholar's Companion. Containing Exercises in Orthography, Derivation, and Classification of English Words. Revised Edition, with an Introduction and Copious Index. By RUFUS W. BAILEY. . Price $0.60

Walker's Pronouncing Dictionary. A Critical Pronouncing Dictionary and Expositor of the English Language. To which is annexed a Key to the Classical Pronunciation of Greek, Latin, and Scripture Proper Names, &c. By JOHN WALKER. . . . . . . Price $1.12½

Mann & Chase's Primary Arithmetic, Part 1. The Primary School Arithmetic; designed for Beginners. Containing copious Mental Exercises, together with a large number of Examples for the Slate. By HORACE MANN, LL.D., and PLINY E. CHASE, A.M., authors of "Arithmetic Practically Applied." . . . . Price $0.25

Mann & Chase's Arithmetic, Part 2. The Grammar School Arithmetic; containing much valuable Commercial Information, together with a system of Integral, Decimal, and Practical Arithmetic, so arranged as to dispense with many of the ordinary rules. By HORACE MANN and PLINY E. CHASE, authors of "Primary Arithmetic." Price $0.62½

Mann & Chase's Arithmetic, Part 3.

Arithmetic Practically Applied, for Advanced Pupils, and for Private Reference, designed as a Sequel to any of the ordinary Text-Books on the subject. By HORACE MANN, LL.D., the First Secretary of the Massachusetts Board of Education, and PLINY E. CHASE, A.M. . . . . Price $1.00

Historia Sacra. Epitome Historiæ Sacræ;

with a Dictionary containing all the Words found in the Work. . . . . Price $0.38

Viri Romæ. Viri Illustres Urbis Romæ;

to which is added a Dictionary of all the Words which occur in the Book. . . . . Price $0.40

Coates's School Physiology. First Lines

of Physiology; being an Introduction to the Science of Life, written in popular language, designed for the use of Common Schools, Academies, and General Readers. By REYNELL COATES, M.D., author of "First Lines of Natural Philosophy." Sixth edition, revised, with an Appendix. . Price $1.00

Parke's Arithmetic. Parke's Farmers' and

Mechanics' Practical Arithmetic. Revised and improved edition. By URIAH PARKE. . . . . Price $0.34

Parke's Key to Parke's Farmers', Mer-

chants', and Mechanics' Practical Arithmetic. Price $0.45

Hurd's Grammatical Corrector. A Grammatical Corrector, or Vocabulary of the Common Errors of Speech: being a collection of nearly two thousand barbarisms, cant phrases, colloquialisms, quaint expressions, provincialisms, false pronunciations, perversions, misapplication of terms, and other kindred errors of the English Language, peculiar to the different States of the Union. The whole explained, corrected, and conveniently arranged, for the use of Schools and Private Individuals. By SETH T. HURD. . . . . Price $0.34

Young's Algebra. An Elementary Treatise on Algebra, Theoretical and Practical; with attempts to simplify some of the more difficult parts of the Science, particularly the Demonstration of the Binomial Theorem in its most general form; the Summation of Infinite Series; the Solution of Equations of the Higher Order, &c., for the use of Students. By J. R. YOUNG, Professor of Mathematics in the Royal College, Belfast. . . . . Price $1.25

Young's Geometry. Elements of Geometry, with Notes. By J. R. YOUNG, author of "An Elementary Treatise on Algebra." Revised and corrected, with Additions, by M. FLOY, Jr., A.B. . . . . . Price $1.25

Young's Analytical Geometry. The Elements of Analytical Geometry; comprehending the Doctrine of Conic Sections, and the General Theory of Curves and Surfaces of the second order, intended for the use of Mathematical Students in Schools and Universities. By J. R. YOUNG. Revised and corrected by JOHN D. WILLIAMS. Price $1.25

Young's Plane and Spherical Trigonometry.

Elements of Plane and Spherical Trigonometry, with its application to the Principles of Navigation and Nautical Astronomy; with the Logarithmic and Trigonometrical Tables. By J. R. Young. To which are added some Original Researches in Spherical Geometry, by T. S. Davies, F.R.S.E., F.R.A.S., &c. Revised and corrected by John D. Williams. . . . . Price $1.25

Young's Mechanics. The Elements of

Mechanics; comprehending Statics and Dynamics, with a Copious Collection of Mechanical Problems, intended for the use of Mathematical Students in Schools and Universities. With Numerous Plates. By J. R. Young. Revised and corrected by John D. Williams. . . . Price $1.25

Rand's Copy-Books.

By an arrangement with Mr. B. H. Rand, we shall hereafter publish his Series of Copy-books and Penmanship. The following is a list of the same, with the prices.

Rand's Copy-Books. Nos. 1 to 8, per dozen, ...	$1.50
Rand's Appendix to Copy-Books. Nos. 1 to 5, per dozen,	1.50
Rand's American Penman, each, ...	2.25
Rand's Penmanship, per dozen, ...	6.00
Rand's Penmanship Abridged, per dozen, ...	3.00
Rand's Practical Small Hand Copies, per dozen, . . .	3.00
Rand's Piece Book, per dozen, ...	3.00
Rand's Ornamental Copies, per dozen, ...	3.00
Rand's Small Alphabetical Copies (Xylograph), per dozen,	3.00
Rand's Small Alphabetical Copies (Steel Plates), per dozen,	3.00

www.ingramcontent.com/pod-product-compliance
Lightning Source LLC
LaVergne TN
LVHW010145110826
845151LV00002B/432

* 9 7 8 1 4 2 5 5 3 7 7 8 4 *